THEATRE ON THE AMERICAN FRONTIER

THEATRE

ON THE

AMERICAN
FRONTIER

THOMAS A. BOGAR

LOUISIANA STATE UNIVERSITY PRESS
BATON ROUGE

Published by Louisiana State University Press
lsupress.org

DESIGNER: Michelle A. Neustrom
TYPEFACE: FreightText Pro

Cover image courtesy of the Library of Congress.

LIBRARY OF CONGRESS CATALOGING-IN-PUBLICATION DATA

Names: Bogar, Thomas A., 1948– author.
Title: Theatre on the American frontier / Thomas A. Bogar.
Description: Baton Rouge : Louisiana State University Press, [2023] |
    Includes bibliographical references and index.
Identifiers: LCCN 2022062126 (print) | LCCN 2022062127 (ebook) | ISBN
    978-0-8071-7978-9 (cloth) | ISBN 978-0-8071-8052-5 (pdf) | ISBN
    978-0-8071-8051-8 (epub)
Subjects: LCSH: Theater—United States—History—19th century. | Frontier
    and pioneer life—United States. | Actors—United States—Biography |
    Theatrical producers and directors—United States—Biography.
Classification: LCC PN2245 .B64 2023 (print) | LCC PN2245 (ebook) | DDC
    792.0973/09034—dc23/eng/20230622
LC record available at https://lccn.loc.gov/2022062126
LC ebook record available at https://lccn.loc.gov/2022062127

CONTENTS

Illustrations follow page 98.

ACKNOWLEDGMENTS

NEARLY A HALF CENTURY AGO, LSU Professors Gresdna Doty and the late Bill Harbin instilled in me a love for, and curiosity about, the marvelous actor-managers of early American theatre. This book is a direct offspring of their inspiration. In researching it, I accrued an ever-extending debt of gratitude to the tireless staff of the Newspapers and Periodicals Room of the Library of Congress, the Harvard Theatre Collection, the Folger Shakespeare Library, the Missouri Historical Society, and the Filson Historical Society in Louisville, Kentucky. In publishing it, I developed a respect for the professionalism of Rand Dotson, Neal Novak, Sunny Rosen, and Michelle Neustrom of LSU Press, and freelance editor Stan Ivester, which I greatly appreciate. I also appreciate the feedback along the way from historian Terry Alford, and the loving support of my wife, Gail Carr, who doubtless learned more about frontier theatre than she ever wanted to know.

THEATRE ON THE AMERICAN FRONTIER

INTRODUCTION

"YOU MUSTN'T BELLOW OUT *Romeo!* that way, like a bull—you must say it soft, and sick, and languishy, so—R-o-o-meo! that is the idea; for Juliet's a dear sweet mere child of a girl, you know, and she don't bray like a jackass." So commands the vagabond "Duke" to the bewhiskered, geriatric "King" as they prepare to stage Shakespeare for town yokels in Mark Twain's *Adventures of Huckleberry Finn*. The "King's" objection to his suitability to play the virginal Juliet, and their contorting of Hamlet's "To be or not to be" soliloquy, are rationalized by the "Duke" with the words, "Don't you worry—these country jakes won't ever think of that."[1]

And they may well not have. There were documented cases of "kings" and "dukes" fleecing frontier audiences of that era with their version of Twain's "Royal Nonesuch." Twain knew of what he wrote and created his "rapscallions" from experience, albeit exaggerated for humorous effect. As a schoolboy in Hannibal, he had watched a couple of raw Englishmen enact the climactic swordfight of *Richard III* with "maniac energy and prodigious powwow," backed by "all the mysterious paraphernalia of the theatre." By age twenty he had seen at least four performances by the bombastic, uber-masculine Edwin Forrest and watched melodramatic, "blood and thunder" Bowery Theatre actor George W. Jamieson enact *Ingomar the Barbarian* and *Merchant of Venice*. Twain knew well the language of Shakespeare, having listened by the hour to readings of the Bard by the riverboat pilot to whom he was apprenticed, and he recognized when it was being mangled.[2]

The acting troupes that reached the "country jakes" of the American frontier in the early decades of the nineteenth century would for the most part have fallen short of the standards of Broadway impresarios, but the locals ate it up. It didn't matter if soliloquys were mangled a bit, if the painted backdrops were a little cracked and faded from overuse, if the costumes didn't quite match the era of the script, or if the actors themselves did not quite fit their roles. It was live theatre, and it was, more often than might be thought, Shakespeare.[3]

By 1790, as George Washington was settling into the nation's first presidency, the perception of "frontier" to those living in established cities along the East Coast—the thirteen original colonies—meant anywhere beyond the Appalachians. There, facing unknown challenges, settlement was beginning on what historian Frederick Jackson Turner famously termed a "perennial rebirth" along a "continually advancing frontier line" which eventually reached the Pacific. (Others would call this movement Manifest Destiny.)[4]

The first pioneers along that line flowed into Kentucky by raft and by keelboat down the Ohio River from Pittsburgh, or trudged with their families alongside teams of oxen pulling heavily laden wagons through the Cumberland Gap (facilitated particularly by the widening of the Wilderness Road by 1796). Postwar Tories fleeing the confiscation of their homes during the Revolution merged with victorious Continental Army veterans and recent immigrants from Europe. All fixed their hopes on open land and a new life in "the West." They came in waves—first the isolated hunter, then the small homesteader-farmer, then larger landowners who were in turn displaced further westward by urbanization.[5]

So too did theatre arrive on the frontier in waves. Small bands of amateurs strutted and fretted their hour, then yielded the stage to itinerant actors and small troupes, who were in turn supplanted by better-capitalized managers building theaters and founding limited touring circuits, with a secure base of operations that include a salaried stock company. Such conditions were already established in New York, Philadelphia, Baltimore, and London, from which they emanated.[6]

Most accounts of life on the frontier justifiably focus on pioneers' efforts to keep their families safe, provide for their sustenance, and carve a homestead out of primeval forest. It would seem that one of the last things on their minds was entertainment. But soon, their need for amusement to ease the hardship of their lives asserted itself, and the first wave of amateur actors, along with barn-dance fiddlers, roving banjo-playing troubadours, and "rope dancers" (tightrope walkers), stepped up to provide modest entertainment.

For professional actors, either alone or in small troupes, forging into the frontier was a foolhardy, risky venture. An occasional strolling player or banjo-toting troubadour was one thing. But an entire troupe of actors, with scenery and props and costumes, traveling by rude, horse-drawn farm-wagons or crude flatboats? "Actors of the Eastern cities, with few exceptions, had no idea at that time what the West really was," observed early actor-manager Noah Ludlow. "The population of that region were supposed by many to be semi-barbarians; and to go to Kentucky or Tennessee was banishing yourself from civilization. When actors were asked to go to those new States or Territories, they would shake their heads and say, 'No, I've no desire to be devoured by savages.'" The frontier was variously perceived as a "landscape of fear," a "place of desolation and danger," and a "realm of cultural darkness."[7]

Those intrepid souls who did venture west, to try in part to illuminate that darkness, sought a success which had escaped them in the East. Their intentions were partly to bring entertainment to struggling settlers in virgin territory, but a larger piece of it was a need to earn a living the best way they knew.

It seemed as if every other ship from England brought new competitors, pushing actors already in America further afield. Trying to earn a living as an actor outside of established eastern theatrical centers was extraordinarily difficult. Trying to support a family was next to impossible. Touring in the East was hard enough; in the West, it meant arduous wagon journeys over primitive trails and alternately tedious and dangerous river travel, with virtually no protection from the harshest, unpredictable elements, wild animals, or attacks by natives resentful of white encroachment. (This lessened significantly, at least in the Northwest Territory, after the 1795 Treaty of Greenville following General Anthony Wayne's victory at the Battle of Fallen Timbers, achieved in part through the efforts of about fifteen hundred Kentucky volunteers.)

Arrival on the frontier meant wretched inns (or camping in the wild) and subsistence meals (or outright hunger), with no promise of an audience sizable enough, or open-minded enough, to understand and enjoy their dramatic offerings. Upon arriving in any new town, actors had to obtain a suitable—or at last adequate—venue for performing, often a local inn, warehouse, or courtroom, then widely post their bills to attract an audience, and hope for the best. This was a far cry from the stereotypical cinematic portrayal of a colorful troupe of actors careening into a frontier town by stagecoach, with luggage piled high atop it. Nor was this the frontier of the movies, with a main street of dry goods store, livery stable, and a saloon or two. This was the frontier primeval, eventually denominated "the Midwest" and, later, the rustic conditions of Gold Rush California.

Fortunately for many of the first actors who ventured into the frontier, small troupes of amateurs laid an indispensable groundwork on which they could build. These amateurs allowed a handful of itinerant professionals to form a beachhead for small, then gradually larger, professional companies who followed them. "The purpose of these [amateur] organizations," asserted Nicholas Longworth, a founding member of the Cincinnati Thespian Society, "was the glorification and amusement of the members through the medium of the drama and the benefit of the public." That amusement was sorely needed, and the professionals who followed them made a practice of staging occasional benefits for local causes. Ultimately, while some of the amateurs were assimilated into the professional companies, more often than not their companies were superseded and dissolved.[8]

The early, bare-bones professional troupes on the frontier were not cohesive, well-rehearsed companies like their contemporaries in the East. Itinerant troupes or families traveling and acting together were in continual flux, pledging little loyalty to a given manager or paterfamilias for any length of time. The same names crop up in different troupes in successive seasons. Most of them absorbed any available professionals who could credibly act, in many cases regardless of their ability to perform within a given "line of business" ("leading lady," "old man," "low comedian," and so forth). Sometimes with ludicrous results, locals would be commandeered to fill small roles.

Frontier actors confronted audience expectations and behavior considerably at odds from those in the East. A frontier theatregoer, wrote one who knew, was a far cry from an eastern swell strolling up to a box office to buy a ticket to entertain his lady friend. "Many a man who watched the play at night" on the frontier "had done the roughest of pioneer work during the day." To buy his ticket, "perhaps he had toiled in the fields, irrigated an orchard, or dug on a water-ditch. Perhaps he had helped at building a saw-mill, or at blazing a trail up to the mountain pines. It may be that he had brought down a load of logs and stood, thereafter, for many hours in rain and shine, in the wood-yard opposite to the play-house, until he had sold that load of fire-wood, and the pay that he received for it might have partly been used for his theatre admission fee."[9]

Often unruly, frontier audiences reared on gaming, cockfighting, and other rowdy entertainment were a swirling mass of late arrivals and early departures. Their constant, noisy eating and drinking (predominantly alcohol, readily available in adjacent saloons), and smoking "segars," chewing and spitting tobacco, all competed with the action on the stage, and they freely shouted out their approbation or disapproval of a given actor or character or turn of plot. They perched on the ledges of boxes, stood on benches in the appropriately named pit, felt entitled to wander into the wings—or occasionally onto the stage itself—during performances. Many "paid not the slightest attention to the stage, but walked about, drank together, and argued as if nothing else were going on." A typical frontier crowd "heaves continually in wild and sullen tumult" with occasional interjections of "shuddering oaths and obscene songs." An understandable dearth of females led to any audience in which they did appear to be designated in the press as "fashionable."[10]

But not all frontiersmen were the brawling, buckskin-clad roughnecks portrayed in dime novels. Some were educated men—doctors and lawyers—who had brought with them eastern tastes and experiences as well as a knowledge of, and appreciation for, the arts and sciences. Their small libraries often included volumes of respected authors, especially Shakespeare, and a few favorite playscripts, which would spawn some of the first performances on the frontier. Refined pioneers heading west on the Ohio might even have stopped in at Blennerhassett Island, where Margaret Blennerhassett, amid her elegant surroundings in her Palladian mansion, was known to read aloud to her guests from Shakespeare.

Itinerant actors, though, were causes of immediate suspicion on the frontier, recognized as outsiders, understandable in an environment fraught with danger. As Elizabeth Perkins has noted, "Making accurate judgments about the character and intentions of strangers was important in small towns; . . . it could be, quite literally, a matter of life and death in sparsely settled border regions."[11]

Such actors also had to contend with a prevalent misperception of their profession as promoting loose morals. Religious opposition was rife. Lexington, Kentucky, correspondent "Gregory Grindstone" in 1812 asserted his opposition to "the vulgarity and indecency of most of the farces and many of the tragedies and comedies." These were "such as to efface all the good impressions that the exceptional pieces make, and leave a large balance in favor of vice." He attributed this dissolution to "(1) the general ignorance of the audience which unfits them for enjoying anything refined and sublime; (2) the opposition of strictly moral and religious people who think the pulpit ought to be the only theatre; (3) the common depravity of managers and players which results from the encouragement of the ignorant to licentiousness."[12]

The Selma, Alabama, *Free Press* in 1838 printed a typical frontier diatribe against the dangers of the theatre: "It is a profession that eminently tends to corrupt the morals, not only of those who engage in it, but of all who come within the reach of its atmosphere. . . . To patronize it is to patronize vice." How, the writer questioned, can a Christian "countenance and support a profession so universally condemned, so immoral in its nature, and so licentious and disorderly in its indecency? . . . A profession whose business it is to [arouse] all the baser passions of the heart, and to recommend vice and error under such bewitching form as to corrupt and ruin the purity and simplicity of our children and youth?" Its lessons, "if universally adopted and acted out, would lead to anarchy and misrule."[13]

Any actress appearing in a "breeches" role—that of a young man—which exposed her shapely limbs in tights, could trigger an outburst of cringing embarrassment on the part of females in the audience. Even slightly risqué farces elicited disgust. Watching one, a rural theatregoer was revolted by its "oaths and obscenity," which caused his female companion to lean into him and hide her face.[14]

Nearly all historiography of American theatre history focuses on the East Coast cities and visits predictable stations of the cross: the Hallam Douglass troupe, New York's John Street Theatre, the Chestnut Street Theatre and Walnut Street Theatre in Philadelphia, and the Charleston Theatre, but virtually nothing west of the Appalachians. A few chapters, notably Mary Henderson's laudable "Frontier Theatres and Stagecraft" in *The Cambridge History of American Theatre, vol. 1*, consider the challenges and accomplishments of frontier performers, but more often only perfunctory coverage is granted to a handful of pioneer managers, usually Noah Ludlow, Sol Smith, and the Drakes.

Ludlow's 1880 *Dramatic Life as I Found It* is probably the most relied upon, though not entirely reliable, memoir. Many later sources have automatically depended on Ludlow for accuracy, whereas contemporary accounts, especially newspapers, maps, and playbills, clarify the errors which the intervening decades of his memory created. Smith's 1868 *Theatrical Management in the West and South for Thirty Years*, while more accurate chronologically than Ludlow, devotes much of its space to lighthearted anecdotes. (The two men, partners for two decades, subsequently fell out, and their memoirs, Ludlow's more than Smith's, reflect that enmity.)

These men, though, were preceded by others who unfortunately for historians failed to pen memoirs. They include Noble Luke Usher, William and Sophia Turner, Joshua Collins and William Jones, names which have been lost to history. Their story, in most cases, is a litany of failure, exemplifying playwright Samuel Beckett's mantra, "Ever tried. Ever failed. No matter. Try Again. Fail again. Fail better."[15]

This book arose from a frustration while researching previous books on Thomas S. Hamblin, Maggie Mitchell, and presidential theatre attendance, as I realized how many accounts of frontier theatre depended solely and excessively on Ludlow, particularly where he erroneously credits himself with being the first to perform or manage in a given town, and minimizes or denigrates the efforts of others. My intent is to verify, clarify, or repudiate Ludlow where appropriate, and to create a definitive account of frontier theatre.

The endpoint for this book is 1890, when the superintendent of the U.S. Census pronounced the frontier closed, an assertion famously reinforced three years later by Turner. In the century preceding 1890, as the frontier closed in from east and west, various towns dropped out of consideration once they could boast regular, financially successful theatrical seasons in dedicated theater buildings, featuring routine visits by established eastern stars. Once these criteria had been achieved, most frontier towns could viably compete with eastern theaters, and hence I dropped each out of this narrative. I have also chosen to exclude minstrel shows, circuses, vocal or instrumental concerts, variety performers (rope walkers, for example), and Wild West shows, nor do I analyze the styles of acting on the frontier, as they generally attempted to replicate those brought from the East.[16] If not always conscientiously, they did the best they could for the "country jakes."

1
~~~~~~~

AVANT AMATEURS

(1790–1810)

THE EARLIEST THEATRE on the trans-Appalachian frontier took place in 1790 in western Pennsylvania and in Lexington, Kentucky (until 1792 part of Virginia). Tiny Washington, Pennsylvania, a day's travel southwest of Pittsburgh, briefly supported an amateur troupe, which in February 1790 performed James Thomson's 1745 romantic tragedy *Tancred and Sigismunda* to an appreciative audience that included many impressionable young ladies.

Two months later, and barely fifteen years after the first settlements began in Kentucky, at the new Presbyterian Transylvania Seminary (now University) in Lexington, two of its thirteen students offered as part of the school's first commencement exercises a tragedy and farce, their titles unrecorded. These earned "general applause" from "a very respectable audience," likely their families, fellow seminarians, and professors. It would be another decade in Lexington before a rudimentary theater would be converted from a community hall. In the meantime, the Transylvania students soldiered on, despite a Board of Trustees ban on any involvement in theatre. Among their efforts, in March 1799, were Susanna Centlivre's 1709 comedy *The Busy Body* and Charles Macklin's 1759 farce, *Love-à-la-Mode*, both a trifle risqué.[1]

During the 1790s the students were joined by troupes of amateurs—usually styling themselves the "Theatrical Society" or "Thespian Society"—in Lexington and in Washington (now part of Maysville), Kentucky. They performed in local courthouses—ubiquitous, convenient venues—and the upstairs great rooms of taverns, often the only sizable gathering place in frontier towns. One of the earliest such venues, which opened in Lexington on June 5, 1797, was an "exhibition room, adjoining Coleman's tavern," set up by George Saunders.[2]

Amateur theatre groups also emerged in the 1790s in the industrial town of Pittsburgh, its population barely 400 (by 1800 this would grow to 1,565). Some performed on the third floor of William Irwin's tavern, while soldiers performed in a blockhouse redoubt of Fort Pitt. Among their performances—the first publicized—was Joseph Addison's 1712 tragedy *Cato*, on April 20, 1790. The favorite play of revolutionary hero and new American president, George Washington, its hero, Roman statesman-general Cato championed the republican ideals for which the war of independence had been fought.[3]

The foremost early amateurs in Pittsburgh were members of the Pennsylvania Population Company—incorporated in 1792 for post-Revolutionary land speculation—some of whom had invested in Philadelphia's famed Chestnut Street Theatre. By 1795 they were performing plays in the "New Theatre over the Allegheny" on Pittsburgh's northern edge.

~~~~~~~~~~

The scripts these amateurs chose were for the most part inspirational tragedies or light-hearted comedies and farces. But tragedies, too, drew well. Especially popular on the frontier were the struggles of Young Norval, the protagonist of Reverend John Home's 1756 gothic melodrama *Douglas*. A hit on the East Coast, it would be performed dozens of times on the frontier over the next three decades. Its opening line, intoned by Lady Randolph, its leading female role, sets its tone: "A melancholy gloom . . . accords with my soul's sadness, and draws forth the voice of sorrow from my bursting heart!" Having lost both her husband and her son, she gains a measure of hope when the latter returns alive, but has it dashed when he is brutally killed defending her. In despair she leaps to her death over a cliff.[4]

In lighter fare, early settlers enjoyed Isaac Bickerstaffe's *The Padlock*, which portrayed an old man's attempts to keep his young wife confined, eventually thwarted by a bibulous, impudent servant. Other works performed in the closing decade of the century on the frontier by amateurs were equally frivolous: *Like Master Like Man*, *The Landlord Ousted*, *Who's the Dupe, High Life Below Stairs, He Would Be a Soldier, The Mock Doctor,* and (especially popular) Richard Cumberland's 1771 romp, *The West Indian.*

~~~~~~~~~

While not yet American territory, the frontier city of New Orleans also saw an emerging theatre during the eighteenth century. An isolated occurrence in 1753 was the first known theatrical performance there. *Le Père Indien,* the story of a Choctaw's sacrifice for his son, written and produced by LeBlanc Villeneuve, a former officer in the French Army who had worked among the Choctaw, was performed in the mansion of New Orleans governor Louis Billouart, Chevalier de Kerlérec.

October 4, 1792, witnessed the opening of the Crescent City's first theater, the "small, but quite pretty" St. Peter Street Theatre (Le Théâtre de la Rue St. Pierre) on the street's uptown side (today no. 732) between Royal and Bourbon streets, built by brothers Jean-Marie and Louis-Alexandre Henri, the latter also acting there. A Madame Durosier was hired as director in 1793, but it was not until late 1794 or 1795 that regular performances took place.[5]

The initial troupe of actors was less than commendable. "Two of the male actors [were] tolerable, the others bad; the actresses are fit only to be run off with a broom," reported one observer. Censorship and audience discipline were strict, prompted in part by a production which ridiculed then-governor Francisco Luis Héctor, Baron de Carondelet.

New, better actors appeared between 1795 and 1797, among them the celebrated Mme. Jeanne-Marie Marsan from Saint-Pierre, Martinique. These were likely among the casts of five documented productions in 1796: May 8, *L'Honnête Criminel,* a five-act verse drama by Fenouillot de Falbaire; May 22 (what may have been the first opera in New Orleans), J. Marmontel and Andre Grétry's comic one-act *Sylvain;* July 17, *Blaise et Babet* by Dezède and Monvel; and November 4, *Eugénie,* a five-act prose drama by Beaumarchais, and *Le Père de Famille,* a five-act prose drama by Diderot.[6]

The 1797–98 season, managed by impresario Barthélemy Lafon, added other actors for a performance on September 3, 1799, of a Dalayrac opera, *Renaud d'Ast,* which closed with a ballet performed by Jean-Baptiste Francisquy from Charleston.[7]

The theater, though, was perennially beset by financial difficulties. In April 1799, Joseph Antonio de Boniquet and Bernardo Coquet assumed its lease, and that fall integrated actors who had fled from Saint-Domingue (a center of Caribbean theatrical activity until threatened by slave revolts and the independence of Haiti). By 1800, already in disrepair, the theater closed over a capacity issue with authorities.

It was repaired, though, and reopened in 1804 by another Saint-Domingan, Jean-Baptiste Fournier, only days before the governor turned the Louisiana Territory over to American administrators. June 5, 1805, saw the first opera to be staged in American-administered New Orleans, a production of *Les Visitandines,* a scandalously irreverent comic opera about nuns.[8]

That same year a ruined French colonist turned actor-manager named Louis-Blaise Tabary, thirty-two, appeared in New Orleans, eventually hiring some of the Saint-Dominguen professionals for an acting troupe he planned to manage in a new theater on a different site on Orleans Street between Royal and Bourbon. But after purchasing the lot and beginning construction in October 1806, he was forced to abandon the effort due to a dearth of shareholders. Still, this was the embryo of the later, distinguished Théâtre d'Orléans.[9]

<hr />

The nineteenth century opened with amateur theatrical activity in several other cities. Sometime in spring 1801, a group of students (mostly of the law) at the all-male Pittsburgh Academy (later the University of Pittsburgh), enacted *Cato* and Edward Ravenscroft's 1697 farce, *The Anatomist,* in a tavern to raise money for maintenance of their graveyard.

Amateurs in Lexington performed in an unrecorded public room, possibly the "Hotel Theatre" on the corner of Water and Limestone streets. Their bill on May 21 was *The School for Arrogance,* a five-act moralistic comedy adapted from the French by Thomas Holcroft, and *The Farmer,* a two-act comic opera by John O'Keeffe. They followed this with O'Keeffe and William Shield's rustic romantic comedy *The Poor Soldier* in October, and on January 14, 1802, Edward Moore's five-act tragedy *The Gamester* and O'Keeffe's farce *The Dead Alive.*[10]

Cincinnati, its population barely above seven hundred since its founding in 1788 as Losantiville, gained its first theatrical activity on October 1, 1801. In the Cincinnati Theatre, a converted frame stable behind Yeatman's tavern on Front Street east of Ludlow Street, on the eastern edge of town beside the river, "between a ragged roof and sorry floor," an assortment of amateurs and soldiers from nearby Fort Washington performed *The Poor Soldier*. Their thirty-two-line dedicatory prologue proclaimed their intention to produce comedy: "The laughing muse here for the first time sate / And kindly deign to cheer our infant state." The production elicited the first recorded instance of dramatic criticism on the frontier. The unidentified critic for the *Western Spy* declared that the production's scenery was excellent and that "every character was so well filled that the whole met with general approbation."[11]

The Cincinnatians followed this up in December with *She Stoops to Conquer* and O'Keeffe's *Peeping Tom of Coventry*, and in February 1802 with *Agreeable Surprise* and *Mock Doctor*. By 1805, two years after Ohio statehood, these amateurs, their ranks swelled with some of the most respected local citizens, had moved to a spacious room above Vattier's stable at Second and Sycamore streets. For the season's first performance, *The Mountaineers* and *The Padlock* on October 26, Mayor David Ziegler, "replete in knee breeches, gold laced coat, cocked hat, and sword greeted the opening night audience." After this came George Colman the Younger's *Poor Gentleman* on November 15 and *Wild Oats* and *The Old Maid* on December 30. On September 30, 1806, they performed *Secrets Worth Knowing* and *Love-à-la-Mode*, and on December 7, reprises of *Mountaineers* and *Padlock*. Their activity continued in fits and starts until 1811, when a small professional troupe arrived, absorbing some of their more talented members.[12]

O'Keeffe's popularity on the frontier can be attributed to several factors. His universal plots consisted of misunderstandings, complications, and intrigues of amour. His characters tended to be unsophisticated rustics familiar to these audiences. And his themes focused on widely shared emotions, notably patriotism and love. *The Poor Soldier* is representative: rustic

Revolutionary War infantryman Patrick returns home to reunite with his true love, whom he must win away from an arrogant captain, succeeding only with the assistance of an earnest-yet-bumbling sidekick named Darby who provides ample low comedy. It became one of the most frequently performed comic operas on the frontier for thirty years.

Colman's comedies were equally popular, exhibiting equal measures of wit and sentimentality, with enough rustic characters to appeal to pioneers. His *Poor Gentleman*, performed on the frontier dozens of times in the next three decades, is representative. The centerpiece of its humor, the plum role played by a company's most accomplished low comedian, is meddling village apothecary Ollapod. He attempts to facilitate a lecherous nobleman's seduction of the beautiful daughter of the titular gentleman, who is beset on all sides by financial difficulties. The chivalrous young nephew of the local sheriff rescues her and, after nearly fighting a duel with the nobleman, wins her heart. His father in a *deus ex machina* ending cancels her father's debts. Additional low humor is provided by the girl's boastful maiden aunt.

～～～～～～～

In many frontier communities, religious opposition (often Presbyterian) to the theatre was strong from the outset. Several preachers echoed the sentiments of St. Augustine, who declared, "Stage-plays are the most petulant, the most impure, impudent, wicked, unclean, the most shameful and detestable atonements of filthy Devil-gods," and those of clergyman John Witherspoon, who professed that "the stage is not merely an unprofitable consumption of time, it is further improper as a recreation because it agitates the passions too violently." Citizens of Lexington were exhorted by their preacher to "aid in counteracting the strong infidel tendency" of the stage. Still, "members of the Presbyterian elite were among the most prominent theatre practitioners and consumers of the era."[13]

Civic leaders from time to time attempted to regulate theatrical performances. In 1805 and 1806 the Trustees of the City of Lexington unanimously adopted ordinances requiring written permission prior to performances. An 1806 edict by the mayor of New Orleans required his presence, or that of his representative, at all performances. But journalistic support for the theatre was generally robust on the frontier. Lexington audiences were encouraged to attend by the *Kentucky Gazette,* which routinely lauded the "splendid display of beauty and fashion [read: ladies] which graced the theatre."[14]

〰〰〰〰〰〰

Between 1803 and 1805 a few semiprofessional actors wandered into the West. The first, in Pittsburgh, were the duo of Bromley (variously Bromly) and Arnold, who merged their talent with that of the "Young Gentlemen of the Town" to perform on Tuesdays and Fridays in January and February 1803. Their venue was the Great Room of the county courthouse in Diamond (now Market) Square, using adjoining jury rooms as greenroom and dressing rooms. In performing popular comedies and occasional tragedies, these actors followed established, clearly defined, stereotypical lines of business (for example, genteel comedy, low comedy, Irishman, Yorkshire farmer). By necessity men played female roles as in Cincinnati, with varying degrees of success. As one visitor recorded, "The female characters being sustained by young men are deficient of that grace and modest vivacity which are natural to the fair sex, and which [they] vainly attempt to copy."[15]

After this initial effort, Bromley and Arnold abandoned the troupe, but it continued without them through 1808 with a repertoire expanded to include classical works such as *Romeo and Juliet, She Stoops to Conquer, The Merchant of Venice,* and *Pizarro.* These are arguably the first productions of each of these on the frontier, although they were likely abridged, a common practice at the time for shorthanded companies appealing to unsophisticated audiences. *Romeo and Juliet* was almost certainly the sentimentalized David Garrick version of 1748 which allowed the two young lovers to speak to each other before they die.[16]

Richard Brinsley Sheridan's *Pizarro* (1800) would become the most oft-produced script on the frontier over the next two decades, performed at least eighty times. Adapted from the German of August von Kotzebue, it is set in the sixteenth century amid the attack by the titular conquistador and his Spaniards on the Incan civilization. Pizarro seeks revenge against Alonzo, who has deserted him for the Incas and fathered a child with Cora. Pizarro's mistress, Elvira, turns on him to help the Incas. Alonzo's friend Rolla, who had also loved Cora, eloquently rouses the Incan army to fight, then sacrifices his own life to save those of Alonzo and the child. The script provides a meaty, grandiloquent role in Rolla, as well as captivating female roles in the fiery Elvira and the tender Cora. To have performed this work only eight years after its introduction in England and New York reinforces the idea that actors on the frontier, even amateurs, brought with them from the East promptbooks or library editions of plays.

~~~~~~~~~~

In April 1805, ventriloquist-magician-actor John Rannie, thirty-six, exiled from Scotland in 1801 for his involvement in anti-government protests, arrived in Kentucky via Boston and New York. This short, thickset, pugnacious performer and his convivial American wife, an actress with experience in Boston, New York, Philadelphia, and the Caribbean, performed in Limestone (also now a part of Maysville), Frankfort, and Lexington. Their repertoire consisted primarily of comedies and farces.[17]

By late January 1806 the Rannies had moved on, becoming the first recorded professional actors in Natchez, the capital since 1798 of the Mississippi Territory. A remote yet vital center of commerce on the Mississippi River, Natchez boasted "an opulent, suave and aristocratic community" of nearly twelve hundred, seemingly receptive to entertainment. The Rannies performed at City Tavern, comfortably above the disreputable half-mile-wide strip of land known as Natchez-Under-the-Hill. Their appearance may have been the catalyst for Natchez officials in February passing an ordinance regulating all types of public amusements in the city. They may also have inspired the formation in August 1808 of the amateur Natchez Theatrical Association, who performed intermittently during peacetime in a converted Spanish hospital (also comfortably "above-the-hill") until 1813, staging dozens of productions and building their own theater before yielding it to a professional company.[18]

In mid-March the Rannies opened in New Orleans, alternately appearing at Tessier's Long Room on St. Philip Street and Moore's Large Building on Chartres Street. The centerpiece of their repertoire was now a "theatrical entertainment in three acts" of unknown authorship (likely Rannie himself) called *The Counterfeit Lord; or, The Doctor's Courtship*. They closed in mid-May with a spectacle, *The Battle of the Nile*, which chronicled the 1798 naval engagement between Napoleon and Nelson. It adventurously featured "men sinking and swimming and crokadiles [*sic*] molesting them and whales, sharks, dolphins, swords and flying fish and mermaids." From New Orleans, the Rannies traveled east, never to return.[19]

~~~~~~~~~~

The first theatrical impresario to appear on the frontier was forty-six-year-old Luke Usher, a minor comedic actor for seven years in London who had emigrated from Birr, Ireland, with his wife and nephew, Noble Luke Usher. Soon after their arrival in Baltimore in 1795, Luke's wife died, and in 1799 he married the widowed Ann Adams. This "active, thrifty man," recalled Noah Ludlow, was "a fine English gentleman of the olden time. He was a man of large hospitality, and had a heart in proportion to his body, which latter was of the Falstaffian model, and his wife was no less remarkable for size and generosity" with "a broad, smiling, good-natured face."[20]

From 1800 to 1805 Usher unsuccessfully operated a Baltimore umbrella manufactory, assisted by Richard Marsh, his step-son-in-law and sometime actor. Both likely enjoyed performances at the nearby New (1794) Theatre on Holliday Street just above Fayette Street, where Noble Luke acted in the early years of the new century under manager William Warren.

After habitually losing both money and workers, Usher announced in October 1805 his intention to relocate to the West. He became part of a rush of craftsmen at the turn of the century to migrate from the East to the booming town of Lexington. Opportunities abounded, as one new resident from New Jersey observed: "Our little town that we observe every day is improving so fast that it is altered since we came to it that it is almost beyond exception and expression."[21]

There, in April 1806, Usher opened on High Street a new umbrella manufactory, combined with a dry goods store and pharmacy, next door to

Traveller's [*sic*] Hall Inn, where the Lexington Thespian Society had performed popular comedies and farces until 1802, resuming them in spring 1807. This was a fellowship of male students and clerks and deputies of the court, some of whom later became distinguished attorneys.

To further their cause, Usher the following September purchased at auction for $250 a 67-by-222-foot lot on South Hill, on the northwest corner of Spring Street (now South Broadway) and Water (now Vine) Street (today the site of Rupp Arena), soon widening it with the purchase of another property. To fund this, Usher first attempted to sell his house, then sold his less-than-successful umbrella business to Marsh.

On these lots he built a brewery and "Soda Water Fountain" (imported mineral waters), with a 30-by-80-foot theater above it seating 500 to 600 on backless benches in a pit, boxes, and gallery, adorned in a "very handsome style." In the rear of his brewery, below the stage, he installed dressing rooms. The theater opened on October 12, 1808, with the amateur thespians' production of Cumberland's *The Sailor's Daughter* and a Colman farce, *Ways and Means*.[22]

For two months, these thespians ran through a repertoire of scripts that included melodramas (Matthew Gregory "Monk" Lewis's *The Castle Spectre*), domestic dramas (Elizabeth Inchbald's 1798 adaptation from Kotzebue, *Lovers' Vows*), comedies (Thomas Morton's *Speed the Plough*), and a variety of farces.

Among their farces was one destined to be repeated often on the frontier: Colman's 1800 two-act slapstick musical farce *The Review; or, The Wags of Windsor*. A vehicle for low comedians portraying the roles of garrulous jack-of-all-trades Caleb Quotem, rustic Irishman Looney MacTwolter, and Yorkshireman John Lump, its banter loosely ties together songs and comic material that Colman had already acquired. The thespians' scenery was improbably painted by noted landscape painter George Beck and pronounced by "competent judges" to be "equal to what is seen to the eastward." During the 1808–9 season their ranks were augmented by itinerant (most recently from Canada) professional actor James Douglass.[23]

By 1810 these amateurs faced competition from three similar troupes, alternating in their rental of Usher's theater, with men again covering female roles. Among these troupes were the Lexington Military (Thespian) Society, the Roscian Society, and the indefatigable Transylvania students. These attempted to match the cachet of Douglass by adding a few professionals. The Military Society hired Marsh, who played Zanga in Edward Young's *Revenge* and an unknown role in *The Rivals*, and the Roscians hired another actor from Canada, John Henry Vos, who capably doubled as a scene painter.

For two years these companies attracted decent audiences with such fare as Royall Tyler's *The Contrast*, Inchbald's *Animal Magnetism*, Colman's *Sylvester Daggerwood*, William Macready's *The Irishman in London*, Centlivre's *The Busy Body*, and James Kenney's *Raising the Wind*. Vos provided the Roscians with a credible Rolla in *Pizarro* (for a remarkable four performances) and—arguably the first Shakespeare in Kentucky—*Macbeth* on October 11, 1810, repeated three times.

This *Macbeth*, performed dozens of times in subsequent decades on the frontier, was likely Garrick's 1744 adaptation of Sir William D'Avenant's 1674 version, which rendered Macbeth as a melodramatic "frightful figure of horror" and the Witches as a song-and-dance chorus played by male low comedians, performing to music by Matthew Locke. It deleted a few characters, including in some cases even Lady Macduff, and added a maudlin dying scene for Macbeth. It may also have included elements of J. P. Kemble's acting version of 1794.[24]

When the Lexington town trustees in June 1809 tried to close the theater, Usher mollified them by announcing a benefit for a public works project (a needed bridge), and followed it up in September with several nights of a patriotic spectacle, Morton's *Columbus*. Not to be outdone, the Transylvania students a month later staged a charity benefit of *Castle Spectre*.

During these years, amateurs continued to be active in other towns on the frontier. In Frankfort, Kentucky—since 1792 the state capital, with a population hovering around six hundred—audiences from 1807 to 1810 enjoyed such comedic fare as *The Padlock*, Thomas Sheridan's *The Brave Irishman*, Colman's *The Heir at Law*, and Morton's *The Way to Get Married*, along with the usual farces. A like-minded group in 1808 began performing in Louisville, which then consisted of only 120 houses and even lacked a formal church building. They performed in the City Theater, a three-story brick building on the north side of Jefferson Street between Third and Fourth streets (today the site of the Louisville Convention Center). This early theater, described as "little better than a barn" and "a miserable concern hardly fit to be attended," met with little success.[25]

Barely a decade after Tennessee statehood in 1796, theatre emerged in Nashville, its population not yet one thousand. Either unidentified itinerant actors or local amateurs performed *The Child of Nature* and *The Purse* there on December 4, 1807. The following November, Dublin-born William Duff, a versatile former associate of John Rannie, appeared in Nashville soon after his arrival in America. He and his wife delivered a comic dialogue called *The Oppressive Landlord*. They then spent two years circulating through small towns in the (then) Southwest, ending up by 1811 in New Orleans, and then headed east to seek their fortune.[26]

~~~~~~~~~~

New Orleans by 1808 had surpassed any other town on the frontier in terms of theatre. It had gained its second theater when Bernardo Coquet converted his ballroom on Rue St. Philippe, between Royal and Bourbon streets, into a theater, eventually rechristened Le Théâtre de la Rue St. Philippe (in English-language ads, the St. Philip Street Theatre). Costing $100,000, it seated seven hundred in a tiered parquet and boxes. Under Louis Tabary as its first director, its lavish opening on January 30, 1808, featured an 1802 opera comique by Étienne Nicolas Méhul, *Une Folie* (productions were given in French). A subsequent pantomime, *Le Sourd and L'Ecossias à la Louisiane,* utilized the first corps de ballet in the city.

Through various vicissitudes, Le Théâtre de la Rue St. Philippe from 1808 to 1832 rose to become the premier site of French opera in New Orleans. Various attempts, such as the September 1808 effort by amateurs under St. Domingan François de Saint Just in the briefly reopened Théâtre Saint Pierre and the November 1809 debut of the smaller Théâtre d'Orléans, using decidedly mediocre talent, provided little competition.[27]

The last gasp of the Théâtre Saint Pierre came on December 9, 1810. After a performance of *Pauvre Jacques*, a 1789 romance by Jeanne-Renée de

Bombelles, Marquise de Travanet, it closed, its entire contents auctioned off. The amateur company which had been using it moved four blocks to Coquet's Théâtre St. Philippe, recently remodeled and enlarged. With direction and lead roles taken by Fournier and a Miss Laurette, they performed into spring 1811 on Thursdays and Sundays a variety of French comedies and comic operas, with an occasional Kotzebue for cultural diversity. By now, all advertisements for theatrical productions in New Orleans were headed "By Permission of the Mayor," a necessary condition.[28]

Thus, through two decades of theatrical activity on the frontier, as statehood was granted to Kentucky, Tennessee, and Ohio, and America gained its fourth president, James Madison, amateur thespians held sway, augmented by occasional itinerant professionals. With another war with Great Britain on the horizon, it would seem inopportune for professional companies to venture west, but precisely that, they did.

2

ITINERANTS

(1810–1814)

IN SPRING 1809 JAMES DOUGLASS, entering his fifties, deemed Lexington receptive to his bringing in a professional company. Returning to Canada, he assembled one, pulling actors from a troupe that had performed in Montreal and Quebec under the serial management of Noble Luke Usher, William H. "Seth" Prigmore, and John Mills, each of whom had incurred considerable debt. Another member, John Bernard, had begged off from management, calling the troupe "as deficient in talent as in numbers."[1]

The company Douglass assembled, arguably the first professional theatre company to perform on the American frontier, comprised William and Sophia Turner and their two children, Frederick and Emma; John and Mary Cipriani and their daughter Mary; Mr. and Mrs. John Richard Jones; Joseph "Joey" Williams; and a Mr. Kennedy.

The Turners, born in London, came to America in 1807 in their early thirties at the behest of James A. Dickson for his Federal Street Theatre in Boston. Sophia parlayed her experience from Bath and Bristol into brief engagements in Boston, New York, and Philadelphia. Her primary assets, according to chronicler Charles Durang, were "an agreeable voice, a handsome face, a very interesting petite [persona] and a youthful aspect. . . . She possessed all the requisites of a well-educated lady, combined with an amiable disposition and very affable manners." Her husband, originally a bookbinder and printer, had acquired rudimentary acting skills in Philadelphia and Canada sufficient for juvenile roles.[2]

John Cipriani had been a clown and ballet master at Sadler's Wells and Manchester, England, and after arriving in Boston in 1806, dance master at the Federal Street Theatre. His wife enacted character roles, and their daughter danced. The Joneses could cover supporting roles, and he doubled as scenic artist. Williams could sing and play comic roles. Little is known of Kennedy (including his first name), but Douglass considered him talented enough to carry leads opposite Sophia Turner.

After a brief stop in York (now Toronto) in September 1810, where they performed *Douglas* and a William Macready's farce, *The Village Lawyer*, Douglass took the troupe in late October to Pittsburgh. There, the only acceptable venue for performance was the large room in Mr. Morrow's Tavern on the corner of Fourth and Wood streets. Their opening bill on November 2 was a comedy, *The Reconciliation; or, the Birth-Day*, translated from Kotzebue's German; recitations by Sophia and Douglass; a song by Kennedy, a dance by Cipriani; and *Village Lawyer*. Minimal competition came from the Pittsburgh Academy students in a small wooden building on Third Street, whose offerings included Thomas Otway's *Venice Preserved*.[3]

But Douglass sought a wider audience. During the next month he led his company down the Ohio River to Maysville, then by wagon to Lexington, where he added Richard Marsh, Luke Usher's step-son-in-law. Usher had repainted his theater's interior and added more boxes, and cheerfully announced the troupe's arrival: "It is with sincere pleasure we are at length enabled to congratulate the lovers of the drama and the fashionables of the town upon the arrival of Mr. Douglass with a company of theatrical performers from Montreal and Quebec. . . . The citizens of Lexington and Frankfort will be gratified during the present winter with their performances, which . . . will contribute much to dispel the gloom of the season."[4]

Their opening performance at Usher's Theater of Nicholas Rowe's tragedy *Jane Shore* on December 20 was well attended, as was Inchbald's drama *The Child of Nature* and O'Keeffe's comic opera *Sprigs of Laurel* two nights later. Planning to take his company to Frankfort for the impending legislative session, Douglass closed in Lexington on December 25 with *Reconciliation*, a dance by Cipriani, a recitation on jealousy by Sophia, a comic song by Williams, and John T. Allingham's farce *The Weathercock*.

What limited critical response existed in Lexington in 1810 was generally favorable, with some complaints. The *Kentucky Gazette* was disposed "to make every allowance and to grant many acknowledgements for the pleasure we are to derive from the arduous and romantic journey" the troupe had endured. While this critic did not "feel inclined to criticize the acting," he recommended Hamlet's advice to the Players regarding moderation. Jones in particular was called out for overacting, along with others' "buffoonery and baboon capers." This judgment earned an indignant defense from "A Lover of the Drama," perhaps Usher or Douglass himself, citing the concomitant rowdiness of a number of "little boys and men" in the audience. Sophia shone brightest, possessing "considerable talents and power, with grace, ease, and elegance combined, and a person beautiful and fascinating," but her husband did only "tolerably well."[5]

Frankfort, which had enjoyed only amateur performances since 1807, welcomed the company on January 12, 1811, at the Sign of the Buck Tavern at Ann and Montgomery streets in *Weathercock* and *Lovers' Vows*. On January 21 they performed *The Gamester* and a farcical ballad opera by Charles Dibdin, *The Waterman*. Then it was back over the same rutted wagon roads to Lexington and Usher's in time to open on January 30 with *Lovers' Vows* and *Love à-la-Mode*. These were the first of the company's nearly forty productions through May 4, which earned more frequent critical response.

Sophia Turner, with her "truly beautiful face and elegant figure," continued to carry the troupe in both comedy and tragedy. In breeches as *enfant terrible* Little Pickle in Bickerstaffe's 1792 farce *The Spoiled Child*, she provided "universal satisfaction." In *Jane Shore* she was "almost inimitable. . . . Words seemed to flow from the impulses of feeling rather than from memory. . . . Her pronunciation and delivery are just and clear, her cadence musical." Mrs. Cipriani, also praiseworthy, specialized in "old women, buxom country girls, and scheming, sprightly waiting maids." She may have lacked the "attractive graces of person which in part rendered Mrs. Turner the favorite," but she had "an equally pleasing and interesting countenance" and was more versatile. It was remarkable "for a woman of twenty to personate to the life an old woman of seventy, a prim old maid of forty, a sprightly chamber maid of eighteen, and a wood nymph of fifteen." Williams's specialty of eccentric comic characters was thought exemplary, if at times overdone ("too much the buffoon").[6]

A citizen who identified herself only as "Matilda" had "lately enjoyed very great satisfaction . . . at our infant theatre." She rebutted religious objections to attendance by asserting, "The most pleasing and instructive lessons of morality are to be obtained at a *well-regulated* Theatre, and the frailty and vices of mankind are there depicted in the strongest colours. . . . Instruction and amusement are so delightfully blended, as scarcely to fail producing a good effect." Riding the crest of such encomia, the troupe on February 23 essayed Shakespeare's *Romeo and Juliet*, with Kennedy and Sophia in the title roles, Douglass as Friar Laurence, Jones as Mercutio, and Mrs. Cipriani as the Nurse, and on March 13, *Othello*—likely the first time the latter had been professionally performed on the frontier.[7]

The *Othello* they performed was probably the least altered of Shakespeare's plays from its 1603 original. If London or New York promptbooks were used, the character of Bianca was cut, and several of the longest speeches trimmed, but otherwise, frontier audiences would have been as gripped by Iago's fiendish entrapment of the volatile Othello as those of Shakespeare's Globe. It is unclear which lead Kennedy played, but Sophia was undoubtedly Desdemona and Mrs. Cipriani, Emilia.

For her benefit on April 13, Sophia played for the first time on the frontier the modest, cautious Widow Cheerly, the titular character of Andrew Cherry's 1804 sentimental comedy *The Soldier's Daughter*. Won over by the kindness and philanthropy of the benevolent Frank Heartall, Cheerly provides another case for theatre serving as an agent for the improvement of morals—an important factor in the play's being performed dozens of times in the coming decades.

Midway through the spring, William Turner fell out with Usher, and the Turners and Ciprianis announced that they were cutting ties with Douglass, all for unknown reasons. The Turners agreed, however, to continue performing for Douglass until May, with Sophia still carrying leads, but determined to seek new territory, looking specifically across the river at Cincinnati. Maintaining good will, they publicly expressed their gratitude to the citizens of Lexington for their warm hospitality. John Cipriani had opened a school of dance there in February, but it may not have thrived, as he and his wife and daughter threw in their lot with the Turners, as did Williams.

Ohio beckoned as an embryonic theatrical market. Since statehood was granted in 1803, the provisional state capital, Chillicothe, had spawned an amateur thespian corps that performed a few times at Mr. Keys' Tavern. Cincinnati, however, was emerging as the premier commercial center, its population having burgeoned since statehood from 750 to over 2,500. These were primarily immigrants from Ireland, Wales, and Germany, along with New England families, some already familiar with professional theatre, all seeking new, fertile land. By 1811 it was, observed lawyer-journalist Henry Marie Brackenridge, "a beautiful little city in the midst of a highly cultivated country," although much of its economy derived from marketing hogs, numbers of which often ran loose outside reeking slaughterhouses. It boasted "schools, churches, breweries, brickyards, tanneries, sawmills, grist mills, two newspapers, three market houses, thirty mercantile stores, and a limestone courthouse." Despite some clerical opposition it was, one citizen noted in 1807, "customary for people of taste to frequent the theatre on play nights." Cincinnati's amateur thespians who had been performing in the room over Vattier's stable had been drawing well, and they welcomed a merger with professionals.[8]

The Turners, Ciprianis, and Williams selected the more capable of the amateurs, notably Dr. John Drake and eleven-year-old John H. James (for juvenile and female roles). They also enlisted two itinerant actors, Thomas Morgan and Thomas Jefferson (the uncle of future star Joseph Jefferson III). On May 15, 1811, they staged Cincinnati's first professional production, a benefit for Jefferson, its script unrecorded. Twice a week for the next six weeks they performed a predominance of comedies and farces. But attendance apparently waned, for the Turner-amateur coalition soon dissolved. The Ciprianis and Williams returned to Douglass in Lexington, and the Turners left for Pittsburgh to form a new company and shepherd the erection of a new theater. The Cincinnati amateurs carried on alone, performing sporadically.[9]

Douglass had in the meantime acquired a new leading actor, the previously itinerant John Vos. Augmented by a few amateurs, they produced occasional pieces in Lexington from June 4 through August 3, Vos's talent enabling them to expand their repertoire. This now included tragedy

(Shakespeare's *King Henry IV*, the first on the frontier, Vos as Hotspur), melodramatic spectacle (Theodore Hook's *Tekeli*), drama (Charles Kemble's *Point of Honor*), and farce (*Love-à-la-Mode* and Kenney's *Matrimony*).

By September, with Lexington's population nearly forty-five hundred, Douglass mounted a full fall season. To his male-heavy company he added the Turner defectors, an actress recorded only as Mrs. Jordy, a promising amateur named Miss Scotland Greer (soon to marry Vos), and an actor named Huntingdon (first name unknown) said to be "a very queer fellow and a great rogue" who had fared poorly on the stages of New York. Huntingdon and Vos would carry leads opposite Mrs. Cipriani, whose husband reopened his school of dance and (now) fencing. An English traveler who attended could not help pointing out, "The performers acted very well, but there was a deficiency of actresses, and one of the men had to play a female character, which did not suit my taste at all."[10]

Theater owner Luke Usher, though, seems to have grown dissatisfied with Douglass's company and management. He summoned nephew Noble Luke Usher and his experienced actress wife, Harriet, to Lexington. (According to Noble Luke and Harriet's granddaughter, uncle and nephew were quite close and readily helped each other whenever they could.) The first notice of this infusion of talent (perhaps even to Douglass) was Usher's announcement in late September that the couple was "expected in a short time from Philadelphia," the implication being that they brought East Coast theatrical experience, standards, and repertoire.[11]

Unimpressed, Douglass forged on, presenting at least sixteen plays, some considerably challenging even without Sophia Turner (for example, *Douglas, Venice Preserved*, Lewis's romantic melodrama *Adelmorn, the Outlaw*, and Rev. James Miller's biblical tragedy *Mahomet; or, The Impostor*), each of course with a leavening farce.

The younger Ushers arrived in mid-November 1811 amid news filtering down from the Indiana Territory of the Battle of Tippecanoe, the first of many in what became known as the War of 1812 against Great Britain. (Although Kentucky provided many regiments of volunteers, many of them lost at Ft. Meigs and River Raisin, battles remained on the East Coast and Upper Northwest Territory.)

The Ushers brought to Lexington a higher level of professionalism—a formidable array of talent and experience. Noble Luke, brought to America by his uncle in 1795 at age sixteen, was within four years acting supporting roles at the Federal Street Theatre in Boston. In 1800 he joined the influential troupe of Thomas Wignell in Washington, DC, and Philadelphia. His "lines" were "cruel uncles and heavy villains" and supporting character roles (such as Friar John in *Romeo and Juliet* and Lodovico in *Othello*). He remained with Wignell through 1804, with brief forays into Alexandria, Virginia, under Mrs. Thomas Wade West. Along the way he met John Durang (father of chronicler Charles), Elizabeth Arnold (later Poe), and the actress he would marry, Harriet Anna L'Estrange Snowden.[12]

Harriet, twenty at the time of their marriage in April 1804, was a widow and actress of soubrettes (pert, witty, chambermaids who often sang) and breeches roles. Born into the world of theatre (her parents were members of the Chestnut Street company, although her mother had died in 1799 and her father would succumb in 1806), she was tall, thin, and ladylike with delicate features and a dark complexion. Her granddaughter thought her "beautiful and bewitching to look at, with wonderful hair and a beautiful, aristocratic head [with] grace of carriage and charm of manner."[13]

In 1805 the newlywed Ushers moved to Boston to act at the Federal Street Theatre, where they were joined a year later by David and Eliza Poe, whom they befriended, and to whom they lent their surname for a later story by the Poes' soon-to-be-born son, Edgar Allan. (Noble Luke and Harriet's first child, a son in 1807 they named James Campbell Usher, may have inspired the character of Roderick Usher.) Both the Ushers and the Poes enacted better roles in Boston than they had in Philadelphia (for example, Noble Luke's Prospero to Eliza's Ariel in *The Tempest*).

The Ushers spent 1808–10 in Canada, performing leading roles in the upper rooms of inns and taverns of Montreal and Quebec, earning positive reviews. Noble Luke was "a very perfect tragedian" who "would be gratifying to the best critics of the English Stage." A British traveler astutely noted that Usher in Boston had been "reckoned only a second-rate actor, but in Canada he shone as a star of the first magnitude." A daughter was born in 1809 during an engagement in Quebec under Col. Alving Hampden Pye, who became her godfather, and they named her Agnes Pye Usher. (She may have inspired the Lady Madeline of "The Fall of the House of Usher.")[14]

Noble Luke Usher's time in Canada, including a brief, unsuccessful stint as manager, yielded more influential connections. These included James Douglass and, during a trip to Boston to seek actors, Samuel Drake Sr., who would become a giant of frontier theatre, supported by his acting family. When the summons came from Luke Sr. in summer 1811, Harriet waited to leave until she had delivered their third child, but once en route they only got as far as Philadelphia in mid-October when the child, a boy, died, age six weeks. Burying him, they pressed on overland to Pittsburgh and down the Ohio to Kentucky, although Harriet remained weak and ill.

Their first performance in Usher Sr.'s theater came on November 16, as Hamlet and Ophelia, arguably the first frontier performance of *Hamlet* of dozens that would appear over the next twenty years. Like *Othello*, *Hamlet* came to the frontier largely unaltered, except for the deletion of some minor characters, including Cornelius, Voltimand, Fortinbras, and Reynaldo, and the interpretation of Polonius as a buffoon, played by a company's low comedian (who would then double as First Gravedigger).

Noble Luke and Harriet were a noticeable improvement to the company, especially since Sophia Turner's departure. "There appeared so much of nature and feeling in his performance that he was identified with Hamlet himself." He was "exempt from stage rant," and his soliloquies "were delivered with proper contemplative deliberation." She was "a universal favorite" whose "powers as a tragic actress were acknowledged." She was "super-eminently qualified for genteel, chaste comedy."[15]

For two weeks they carried leads, including what may be the first performance on the frontier of Dunlap's 1798 adaptation of Kotzebue's sentimental, melodramatic *The Stranger*, another script performed dozens of times over the next twenty years. Frontier wives and husbands struggling to balance the desire for entertainment with clerical objections to theatre must have found solace and inspiration in its morally redemptive theme of sin and repentance. It is the story of a young wife, Mrs. Haller, who is seduced by a local lothario and elopes with him. In her absence, her legal husband retreats into misanthropic hermitage (the titular stranger). When she returns alone in shame and unfeigned repentance, they are reconciled, which inevitably generated copious tears. As had been the case in New York, it almost never failed to draw an audience.

From Lexington the Ushers went with the company to Frankfort. Richard Jones, however, angrily left, publicly condemning the elder Usher's unwillingness to adequately compensate the actors for their travel expenses. This, Jones declared, was "contemptible, . . . tyrannical and avaricious," a clear case of bullying, fraud, and dishonesty. He considered himself "deserted and left penniless after having worked like a slave for him and his theatre." (This penuriousness may have been a factor in the Turners leaving.) Usher defended himself in print, clarifying his finances and reminding Jones (and the public) that salaries and expenses were clearly stipulated in the actors' contracts. Moreover, Jones was indebted to him for nearly $150.[16]

In Frankfort, with Noble Luke Usher increasingly in charge, the company (Douglass, the Ushers, the Voses, the Ciprianis, Marsh, Kennedy, and Huntingdon) edged into classical works. Beginning on December 9, the Ushers carried leads, among them Hamlet and Ophelia, the Macbeths, Catharine and Petruchio in Garrick's 1754 broadly physical abridgement of *Taming of the Shrew*, Rolla and Cora in *Pizarro*, and Jaffier and Belvidera in *Venice Preserved*.

They remained in Frankfort through January 1812, performing twenty-eight plays in fourteen nights. During that time they were forced to suspend their performances for several weeks due to the citizenry's overriding unease about, and damages caused by, a series of horrific earthquakes centered 350 miles away in New Madrid, Missouri, with several thousand tremors continuing into April. Its effects were felt over an area of 1.5 million square miles, as far away as Canada, Mexico, and the East Coast of the United States. Naturalist John James Audubon, traveling near Frankfort, felt "the most imminent danger around, and expecting the ground at every moment to open and present to my eye such an abyss as might engulf myself and all around me." To make matters worse, word filtered in throughout January of the nightmarish Richmond, Virginia, theater fire the day after Christmas, that had resulted in the deaths of seventy-two people. No one in Frankfort was much inclined to attend the theater.[17]

Douglass returned to Lexington ahead of the other actors, performing with amateurs not in Usher's theater, but in a refurbished Traveller's Hall. Lacking the younger Ushers, it is difficult to imagine how they staged *Macbeth, Pizarro,* and Colman's *The Mountaineers,* but they did. The full strength of the company was not realized until the return in mid-February (just after the worst of the aftershocks) of the Frankfort actors, less John Cipriani, who abandoned acting entirely for another attempt at a dancing-fencing school. In the wake of the Richmond fire, in which most of the fatalities were caused by inadequate egress, Usher publicly assured patrons that "additional doors have been opened to admit the audiences, and such other arrangements have been made to facilitate their departure."[18]

Despite the tremors, despite the war, the company launched into full-scale productions of *Othello, Pizarro, Isabella, Soldier's Daughter, Village Lawyer,* Colman's historical play *The Battle of Hexham,* Joanna Baillie's Gothic tragedy *De Monfont,* and others, including nightly farces, until April 25. The Ushers again carried leads. For the first time, though, a guest "star" was introduced on the frontier, a Mr. Cross who had played only minor roles at the Chestnut Street Theatre in Philadelphia, as Iago on February 18, his only appearance. But it was not a financially rewarding season, and Noble Luke Usher sent word to Boston seeking additional professionals.

The pickings were slim, as few actors wished to undertake a rugged journey into an unknown and perilous environment in wartime. Until they arrived, Usher temporized with amateurs, including a benefit in May 1812 (a month before word reached Kentucky of the declaration of war with England) of Colman's chauvinistic *John Bull* for the members of the Lexington Light Infantry Company. Finally, in late July, two brave souls appeared: John Vaughan and a Mrs. Doige, both with experience in Boston and New York. For three nights in early August they performed *Point of Honor* and *Midnight Hour,* then left for Frankfort. The amateurs stayed behind and performed occasionally.

In Frankfort, Luke Sr. opened the town's first actual theater, a refashioned 58-by-42-foot second-floor room on the southeast corner of Broadway and St. Clair streets. This Frankfort Theatre seated only a few hundred, but was nevertheless divided into pit, box, and gallery. The short-handed company erected a makeshift stage and opened on August 10, closing nine days later with *She Stoops to Conquer* and a Robert Jephson farce *Two Strings to Your Bow; or, The Servant of Two Masters.*

When they returned to Lexington, they welcomed three additional professionals. The London-born George Bland, considered "a very silent, reserved and eccentric individual" who had immigrated to avenge a slight to his wife's honor, but who by now "had seen better days," could passably sing and act. Mr. and Mrs. Thornton, he an actor of minor parts at the Park Theatre in New York and she primarily a dancer, would offset the loss of the Voses, he to paint houses and carriages and she to make mantuas.[19]

The company, still utilizing amateurs, opened at Usher's theater in Lexington on October 1 with Cumberland's *The Jew* and a J. D. Cross musical farce, *The Purse.* Apparently disorganized, with leads swapped among numerous actors, for a month they performed such standard pieces as Nathaniel Lee's *The Rival Queens, Animal Magnetism, The Mountaineers,* Colman's five-act romance *Blue-Beard, The Poor Soldier,* and numerous farces. Attendance, due to the war, was scant.

They had not performed for three weeks when a strong-willed singer-actor (particularly of Irish characters) named Webster, who had spent the past year wandering through the West as "a celebrated actor from Europe," appeared. He had achieved transitory fame in London, Dublin, and Philadelphia, where managers praised his voice as "well-cultivated," deemed by "musical people" to "exceed in power as well as sweetness any tenor heard on our stage." Chestnut Street Theatre manager William Wood, however, had fired Webster over his quarrels with the audience and with Wood himself, who then had to settle a termination suit with Webster for $1,000. Another manager considered him "a disgrace both to himself and his profession." He was, however, an immediate hit in Lexington: "the wonderful display of his vocal powers . . . surpassed all we have heard or can conceive of harmony."[20]

Webster reanimated the Lexington troupe, taking leads and earning a star's benefit night. From November 25 through December 5, when Usher closed the season, they performed twice a week, then departed for Frankfort, where they played once a week through January 27, 1813. The night that the dire news reached Frankfort of the massacre on January 22 of Kentucky Volunteers at River Raisin in Michigan Territory, many townspeople were at the theater. Governor Isaac Shelby received the news in his box and immediately arose and departed. By the end of the third act, the entire audience had dispersed.[21]

Despite the war news, the company gave a few performances in Louisville in March 1813 and then returned to Lexington, opening on May 19 with Dimond's *Foundling of the Forest*, followed a week later by Kotzebue's *The Virgin of the Sun* (essentially the first part of *Pizarro*) and *The Padlock*. The company remained relatively unchanged, but on June 1 the Ushers (uncle and nephew), dealing with financial setbacks of their own, relinquished control over the company, converting its management to a commonwealth/sharing plan. Decisions would be made jointly with input from Douglass, Thornton, Kennedy, Vaughan, and Mrs. Doige. Through June they performed semiweekly.[22]

Harriet Usher, however, was suffering from the consumption that would prove fatal, and her name then drops from bills. For the first two weeks of July, Sophia Turner graciously returned, taking Harriet's roles in *Jane Shore, Spoiled Child*, and *Romeo and Juliet* (opposite Noble Luke). She was also recruiting. Following her farewell address on July 17, she returned to Pittsburgh, taking with her Kennedy, Webster, mother and daughter (both named Mary) Cipriani, and Mrs. Doige. The remainder of the Lexington company struggled on through September 9, including a special benefit for Harriet Usher on August 14.

~~~~~~~~~~

In New Orleans, amateurs had continued to perform and were organized in April 1811 by itinerant actor-dancer William Duff (with the help of Louis Tabary) into the American Company. They alternated with French players at the remodeled St. Philip Street Theatre (still owned by Coquet), performing two or three nights a week, including Sundays (rare in other cities), into the summer. At times the two nationalities combined, as in a joint

July 4 celebration that year, presenting a "heroic comedy," *A Trait of Washington; or, France and America*, with Tabary as Washington, repeated on September 12, 1811, and on August 16, 1812.[23]

Duff's efforts produced comedies, comic operas, "grand heroic" pantomimes (for example, *The Death of Captain Cook*) and pantomime-ballets (such as *The Two Hunters*, the principal parts by innkeeper-turned-actor Tessier and Mrs. Douvillier), with an occasional melodrama (for example, *Tekeli*), interspersed with such olio acts as Duff on a slack wire "imitating the drunken man." Duff's hybrid company also performed occasionally at Bienville Street Hall, including several nights in May 1812 of the musical farce *Two Blind Fiddlers*.[24]

During the war, though, these grew less frequent. A January 24, 1812, benefit performance of *John Bull*, shortly before Louisiana was admitted to the United States as the eighteenth state, raised $531 for Charity Hospital. The following year would see the emergence in New Orleans of the cooperatively managed "Thespian Charitable Society," which presented such standards as *Poor Gentleman* and *Weathercock* in the St. Philip Street Theatre on three nights in January and February 1813, one performance of which raised $426.50. Their November 13, 1813, production of Morton's *Cure for the Heartache* and a December 13 celebration of Franco-American alliance (in French), *Washington; ou, L'Amérique et la France Reunies*, brought the city's theatrical activity to a close until war's end.

~~~~~~~~~~

Early in 1813 the amateur Natchez Theatrical Association had erected their first real theater, on the edge of the bluff above the infamous Natchez-Under-the-Hill, performing such tried-and-true pieces as *Highland Reel* and *Spoiled Child*. In other frontier towns, including Cincinnati; Vincennes, the capital of the embryonic Indiana Territory; Nashville; Natchez; and St. Francisville, Louisiana, amateur thespians performed sporadically through 1814.

~~~~~~~~~~

Pittsburgh's first real theater arose early in the war. Until 1812, the city's amateurs had been performing in Masonic Hall on Wood Street. Perhaps inspired by the Douglass troupe's visit and the arrival of the Turners, they had mounted an adventurous repertoire, including *She Stoops to Conquer*, *Isabella*, *Romeo and Juliet, and Merchant of Venice.* In May 1812 William Turner announced the sale of shares in a new theater, payable in three installments, to be built by Charles Weidner on a forty-by-sixty-foot lot on the north side of Third Street near Smithfield Street. Turner would be its first lessee.

Still not an incorporated city (that would occur in 1816), Pittsburgh seemed an unlikely host for a theater. This sooty industrial town functioned as a stepping-off point for civilians and the military who were moving westward, and provided practical necessities for their migration: "glass, cannons, tin ware, keelboats, wagon wheels, whiskey, cabinets, shoes and Windsor chairs." Further, once the city was incorporated, its authorities would tightly regulate "any show, spectacle, or natural or artificial curiosity, where money may be demanded for admission."[25]

By summer 1813 the Pittsburgh Theatre was completed. Up to four hundred patrons could be entertained in its pit, dress circle, gallery, and a tier of boxes by the conjoined troupe of the Thespian Society and the professionals Turner had brought from Lexington. From their opening in late August, Kennedy and Sophia Turner carried leading roles along with Webster as visiting star. His benefit on September 11 was typical of the troupe's repertoire: Cumberland's *West Indian*, a transparency "representing the apotheosis of the Immortal Washington," a recitation by Sophia, and a farce, *The Faithful Irishman* with Webster as Teague (with songs).[26]

Through October the company persevered, presenting a variety of plays which would become perennial favorites on the frontier. These included *Merchant of Venice*, *Pizarro*, *Of Age Tomorrow*, *Romeo and Juliet*, *The Spoiled Child* (Sophia of course as Little Pickle), and *Honey Moon*. The younger Mary Cipriani provided "fancy dances," and Mrs. Doige and William Turner, still only a minimally talented actor, delivered an occasional recitation.[27]

The universality of *Honey Moon*, performed over sixty times on the frontier over the next two decades, would have appealed to Western audiences. Written by John Tobin in 1805 for Drury Lane, it had caught on in New York the same year and for much of the century was seldom off the boards.

Repurposing Shakespeare's *Taming of the Shrew*, it is set in seventeenth-century Spain and tasks Duke Aranza with taming "the proud and haughty spirit" of his new bride, Juliana, not by violence but by subterfuge (pretending to be poor and despotic), unerring persistence, and persuasive discourse. Her resistance and ripostes provide witty as well as earthy humor, but as could be expected, by play's end they have reached an affectionate détente. It is tempting to conjecture how many recalcitrant frontier wives identified with Juliana's character, yet allowed themselves to be persuaded to endure for love what was certainly a hardscrabble existence.[28]

By mid-November, however, Turner was in serious financial trouble and closed the short season with *Venice Preserved, Liberty or Death,* and *Matrimony*. Efforts to recoup some of his expenditures with additional sales of shares proved unavailing. It would be another fifteen months before he made another attempt at management in Pittsburgh, although the amateur Thespian Society carried on into spring 1814, its final performance on March 25 being *Isabella* with Sophia in the title role, and *Poor Soldier*.

3

USHERS & TURNERS

(1814–1816)

IN KENTUCKY, the Ushers persevered. It had been Luke Sr.'s plan for some time to establish a theatrical circuit in the state—arguably the first in the West—comprising Lexington, Frankfort, and Louisville. During 1813 and 1814, despite the war, he brought it to fruition.

On October 6, 1813, the "Kentucky Company," still operating as a co-operative venture, opened with a new Gothic drama, *Fontainville Forest*, by James Boaden from Ann Radcliffe's novel, *Romance of the Forest*, and a Colman farce, *The Blue Devils*. The company that fall consisted of Noble Luke Usher, James Douglass, John Vaughan, Mrs. Cipriani (back from Pittsburgh), Thornton, and three new actors: a Mr. Ferguson, a Mr. Little (both probably former amateurs) and a Mrs. Rivers (billed as being from New York, but whose name is not recorded in accounts of the New York stage). Harriet Usher was by now too ill to perform.

They closed November 13 with a benefit for Noble Luke (out of sympathy for his wife's illness) of a Colman comic opera, *The Spanish Barber*, and a pantomime, *Don Juan*. Luke Sr., however, fell afoul of the Lexington Trustees and was fined $170 for not having obtained prior approval for these performances. He appealed, the issue was protracted, and was finally settled in his favor. The usual stand in Frankfort followed, from November 23 into January 1814.

On February 16, expanding the circuit, they opened in Louisville in the "little better than a barn" City Theater with a well-hyped *Jane Shore*, with Noble Luke in the lead role opposite Mrs. Rivers. Performing only once a week (usually Wednesdays), they managed for little over a month as Harriet's consumption grew worse. She died late on March 23 in their Louisville boardinghouse, leaving Noble Luke with three small children. The troupe had performed that night in the first of a series of benefits, this one for Thornton, with *Fontainville Forest* and *Catharine and Petruchio*. Subsequent benefits, for Douglass, Mrs. Rivers, Vaughan, Little and Ferguson (shared) and Mrs. Cipriani brought them to a close on April 27 (postponed from April 25 when it failed to draw) with *Adelmorn* and *Highland Reel*. Of their twenty-two plays in eleven nights, the most artistically venturesome effort had been *Hamlet*, performed twice, presumably with Noble Luke and Mrs. Rivers in the leading roles.[1]

Then it was back to Lexington, where they opened on May 20, 1814, with *Richard III*, probably with Noble Luke in the title role, as it was one of his favorites, performed as often as he could, including on June 1. This *Richard III*, which appears to be the first performed on the frontier, would have been Colley Cibber's shortened, bloodier, melodramatic 1699 version, the highlight of which was the climactic sword fight between Richard and Richmond. Cibber only kept about 25 percent of Shakespeare's original, eliminating minor characters and allowing the title role to dominate as a starring vehicle, filling in with fragments of Shakespeare's *King Henry IV, V, and VI*. Cibber also included the appearance of the ghosts of the murdered King Henry, Lady Ann, and the two young princes, whose brutal murder is shown onstage. Close on the heels of *Hamlet* and *Othello*, *Richard III* would be the third most frequently performed Shakespeare on the frontier.

Perhaps due to the war, as well as an epidemic of spotted fever that spring causing eight to twelve deaths a day, attendance ebbed and the troupe abruptly ended its Lexington season on June 8 with *Stranger* and *Blue Devils*. A Louisville stand in July and August was similarly truncated after an August 29 performance of *Venice Preserved*. With the departure of Mrs. Rivers and the death of Harriet Usher, the company may simply have been unable to fully cast their productions.

To remedy that situation, leaving two of his children in his uncle's care, Noble Luke Usher left Louisville before the end of that short season and headed east with five-year-old Agnes, determined to secure competent actors. The trip would prove fortuitous for frontier theatre, but tragic for Usher himself.

He and Agnes arrived in New York by mid-September 1814. The city was agog with righteous patriotic fervor, the newspapers carrying details of the burning on August 24 of the U.S. capital by British soldiers. New York's premier theater, the Park, had little to offer Usher, but he secured a brief engagement—his debut in that city—at the failing, second-rate Anthony Street Theatre, a house primarily of melodrama under manager John Joseph Holland (primarily a scenic artist). Its company was competent, its strongest performers being members of the Placide family, notably newly-wed sixteen-year-old Caroline Placide (whose brother Henry and sister Jane would later achieve stardom of their own) and their mother Charlotte Wrighten Placide, who brought British experience. The company's low comedian, James Entwistle, would soon make a name for himself in Pittsburgh, perhaps encouraged to go west by Usher.

Usher debuted as Richard III on September 22 opposite the Lady Anne of Charlotte Placide. Two nights later he enacted Othello, with Caroline as Desdemona and a visiting Park Theatre actor named Doyle as Iago. Business must have suffered, for the Anthony Street Theatre closed within days. In fact, when Usher migrated to Albany, the Placides went with him.

At the Green Street Theatre in Albany, Usher stood a better chance of recruiting actors for Kentucky. He knew the manager there, John Bernard, from their time together in Canada and Boston. For the season opener there on October 3 of *Soldier's Daughter*, little Agnes was awarded the child's role of Julia. Four nights later her father again played Richard III, followed on October 10 by his Macbeth. Albany critics deemed him "respectable," with admirable pronunciation, but lacking "the figure of a hero" or "enough education to polish or refine his manners."[2]

The primary object of Usher's recruitment was the Green Street's stage manager, Samuel Drake Sr., whom Usher also knew from Boston and whose family *en masse* would make a providential addition to the Kentucky circuit. After several persuasive conversations, a plan was hatched. Drake would organize the "Kentucky Company of Comedians." When the Albany season was done in May, they would perform across New York State and southwest Pennsylvania, then follow the Ohio River into Kentucky. Usher, though, would depart immediately, to pave the way for their arrival. (Green Street actress Diana Lewis apparently agreed to care for Agnes in the meantime.) But Usher never made it back to Kentucky, dying en route at age thirty-five in a roadhouse in the Alleghenies near Chambersburg, Pennsylvania. Buried there, he was later disinterred at his uncle's direction and reinterred in Lexington next to Harriet.[3]

~~~~~~~~~~

In various frontier towns, amateur theatrical activity continued throughout the war. The Natchez Theatrical Association forged on, performing a few times a year, including among others *Othello, Poor Gentleman, Lovers' Vows, John Bull, The Rivals,* and *The Review.* In December 1814 a new Thespian Society emerged in Washington, Kentucky, performing mostly farces.[4]

The same month, the amateurs of Cincinnati determined that they deserved an actual theater. They began selling shares, but ran into concerted religious opposition led by Presbyterian minister Joshua Lacy Wilson. Two factions emerged, the "foes of the drama" versus the "friends of the drama." The latter won out, and by early 1815 a small wood-frame theater arose on the south side of Columbia (later Second) Street near Sycamore Street. This was known informally as the Shellbark Theatre for the hickory bark left on its exterior at construction.[5]

The first English-language theatrical activity west of the Mississippi River occurred on January 6, 1815. Amateurs in St. Louis, the unincorporated capital of the Missouri Territory, performed John Tobin's comedy *The School for Authors* and Kemble's farce *A Budget of Blunders.* Their venue was the largest interior space in town, a forty-by-eighty-foot one-story frame courthouse converted from a blacksmith's shop on the west side of Third Street below Spruce Street (today under the Gateway Arch). With fewer than two thousand people, surrounded for hundreds of miles by wilderness and war, St. Louis was still recovering from the effects of the 1811–12 earthquakes. Nevertheless, "a great many attended [and] all were pleased." As in other towns, they faced religious opposition, this time from Catholic Bishop Benedite Flaget, who had discouraged theatrical activity while St. Louis was French. These amateurs presented comedies and farces (for example, *Who Wants a Guinea? Heir at Law, Fortune's Frolic,* and *Poor Gentleman*) every three or four weeks through March.[6]

Amateurs were also active in New Orleans as soon as the war ended. Amid the exuberance over the victorious Battle of New Orleans in January 1815, the Thespian Benevolent Society, with many prominent citizens among its members, provided comedies and farces in the St. Philip Street Theatre. Their efforts, though, were hindered by inadequate rehearsal space, a harshly proscriptive edict by the City Council controlling theatrical activity, and attempts by Louis Tabary to revive the Théâtre d'Orléans. (When it burned in September 1816, the Benevolent Society provided a benefit on November 20 for sufferers.) They continued to stay on the good side of the council by staging other benefits, including three for the Female Orphan Society in early 1817, with Tabary among the casts. Their efforts were welcomed for being among "the few opportunities of rational amusement afforded to that portion of our fellow citizens who do not understand the French language." There appears to have been considerable cooperation, though, between the English- and French-speaking theatre companies using the St. Philip Street Theatre, as their bills during 1817 contain titles and actors' names in both languages.[7]

〰〰〰〰〰〰

Still trying to establish professional theatre in Pittsburgh, William Turner during the winter of 1814–15 organized the Pittsburgh Company of Comedians. The earliest indication of their existence is a benefit there for low comedian Joshua Collins on November 10 of Cumberland's *Wheel of Fortune.* Collins played Penruddock, "a deceived, disappointed, and melancholy recluse [whose] heart is brimful of benevolence, . . . a character well-suited to [his] talent." Destined for greater things, Collins was, according to Ludlow, "a small wedge-faced man, with a turned-up nose, face badly pock-pitted, [and] his body a skeleton." He had accrued experience in Scotland, Ireland, and England with his wife (first name unknown) before Charles S. Powell brought them to America in 1794 for his Federal Street Theatre in Boston. After briefly being imprisoned and subsequently expelled from

Massachusetts three years later for preparing to duel with a fellow actor, Collins with his wife had migrated to New York and Charleston, thence to Pittsburgh.[8]

Turner's troupe in general was formidable, reflecting his yearlong recruiting effort. In addition to himself and Sophia, there were Mr. and Mrs. Collins (he now improbably playing tragic leads), Mr. and Mrs. Milner, Mr. and Mrs. Thomas Morgan, Thomas Jefferson, Thomas Caulfield, Austin Cargill, Mr. Lucas, Mr. Beale, William Anderson, Robert Laidly/ley, Alexander Williams (in comic leads), Miss Emily Tempest, Miss Scotland Greer (still the stage name of Mrs. John Vos, playing soubrettes) and Mrs. Giles Lennard [sic] Barrett. Female leads would be covered by Sophia Turner and Mrs. Barrett, an experienced British actress who had been performing in Boston and New York since 1796. Neither young nor beautiful, she compensated with "a commanding figure, tall and striking," and an "intelligent countenance and impressive personal appearance." Several members of the company were accomplished vocalists and dancers. Turner, notes historian West T. Hill Jr., "had managed to organize the largest and most talented theatrical group ever witnessed by western audiences."[9]

From early February until mid-March they provided a viable array of productions in their new theater, including *Richard III* (Collins as Richard and Sophia as Lady Anne), Colman's popular comic opera *Inkle and Yarico*, *Speed the Plough*, Inchbald's *Wives as They Were and Maids as They Are*, Morton's *Town and Country*, and Holcroft's melodrama *The Lady of the Rock*. Their *King Lear* (with Collins as Lear and Sophia as Cordelia) on March 13, arguably the first *Lear* on the frontier, would have been the 1681 Nahum Tate version, abridged from Shakespeare, with a sentimentally happy ending: Lear back on the throne, Cordelia alive after attempting to aid her father in the storm and escaping a near-rape, and betrothed to Edgar, her true love interest unknown in Shakespeare's original. Tate also eliminated minor roles, including the Fool.[10]

Most nights were someone's benefit, including young Emma Turner's on March 6. Sophia's on February 13 was "the last she expects to receive in Pittsburgh," suggesting that the company had already determined to move farther west. Although Turner publicly expressed his gratitude for his efforts "to render the theatre as deserving of encouragement as he possibly could," his company never returned to Pittsburgh.[11]

By April 1 they were in Cincinnati, where Turner found its amateurs had performed in a small frame building in February, then in their completed Shellbark Theatre since March 15 (their scant resources necessitating their printing tickets on the back of playing cards). Turner arranged with the thespians to rent it, enlisting their members as needed to fill out casts. In doing so, they reignited Reverend Wilson's ire. Undaunted, Turner planned his season and also sent word to Lexington of his intent to bring his company there, leasing Usher's theater. (Amateurs in Lexington had continued to rent it, but they too were about to be superseded by professionals.) Thus, as historian James Rees notes, could Turner "claim rank with the earliest pioneers in the drama's cause beyond the Blue Ridge."[12]

Turner's Pittsburgh Company of Comedians opened in Cincinnati on April 3, 1815, with *The Stranger* and *Love Laughs at Locksmiths*. All amateur thespians received complimentary admission. Playing once, twice, or sometimes three times a week through May 29, they brought Cincinnatians such elevated fare as *Richard III*, *Romeo and Juliet*, *Macbeth*, *Othello*, *Hamlet*, *George Barnwell*, *Stranger*, *School for Scandal*, and *The Rivals*. Mr. and Mrs. Collins, Mrs. Barrett, and Sophia Turner still carried most leads. Benefit performances began in late April, including two nights for the Cincinnati amateur thespians, who continued on their own after Turner left, through fall 1815.[13]

Curiously, a benefit was announced in mid-May for new company member Noah Ludlow and actor/scene painter Lucas, of *Heir at Law*, *Sylvester Daggerwood*, and *Mayor of Garratt*. In *Dramatic Life as I Found It*, the chronology of which is often erroneous, Ludlow makes no mention of performing for Turner in Cincinnati and then Lexington, but he does relate going ahead of Drake to finalize venues for their performances. It is possible in that early age of steamboat travel that he could have performed for Turner in these places. He did rejoin the Drake troupe at some point in late summer in Pittsburgh.[14]

As it turned out, Reverend Wilson's "crusade was earnest, but futile, and only succeeded in generating antagonisms which long survived the dying out of the public debate." Settlers "from the cultivated centers of the east knew what acting really was," and Turner's company drew well. Still, "the hoodlum element sometimes broke loose inside the theater itself and created disturbances which were hard to quell." One night, a "riotous and abusive disturbance" was created "by a parcel of contemptible vagabonds during the dramatic performance."[15]

By April 25, Turner learned that his agreement with Usher in Lexington had been abrogated. From Albany, Drake had sent word of *his* intention to occupy Usher's theater and circuit, placing notices in Lexington, Louisville, and Frankfort newspapers stating his intention "of reforming the theatres there and putting the frontier drama on a firm foundation." Furthermore, he would "prevent invaders from any attack on those theatres, which I now consider mine, and which I shall open at a proper season." His "itinerant friends" Vaughan and Douglass would be joining him upon his arrival. Turner immediately filed suit against Usher for breach of contract and damages.[16]

Nevertheless, figuring that Drake would be committed in the East until the end of the 1814–15 season, and even then would not be able to arrive until fall, Turner took his company to Lexington. On the heels of a last gasp by amateurs in Usher's theater (the only house available), a charity benefit on April 26 of *Honey Moon* and *The Review,* Turner's company opened there on June 12 with *The Rivals.* They persevered, once or twice a week, with a repertoire that again included a fair share of Shakespeare, with Collins and Sophia Turner still carrying leads (for example, Lear and Cordelia, Hamlet and Ophelia, Othello and Desdemona). Other major roles were enacted by Mrs. Barrett and Cargill (such as Gertrude and Claudius) and Morgan (for example, Iago). Almost nightly, Emma Turner, nine, provided a dance, and Cargill, Lucas, and/or Morgan delivered songs between the main pieces. The bills for several Lexington productions between June 26 and September 5 list Ludlow among their casts, usually in a minor role (such as Rosencrantz in *Hamlet* on July 24), and he is the honoree of a benefit on August 21.

A valuable addition to Turner's company arrived on July 27. Mr. and Mrs. Francis "Frank" Blissett, he of theatre royalty going back several generations in England. They were contracted to Drake, whom they knew from

Boston, but in the meantime joined Turner's company. Arguably the most talented performers yet in the West, they brought extensive experience from Philadelphia and Baltimore, he as an eccentric comedian and she as soubrette.[17]

Turner proactively announced on July 31 that he was planning alterations to Usher's theater to make it more "commodious and agreeable." By August 7, new boxes and improved pit seating were in place. One wonders why he did so, knowing he was to lose the use of the venue, unless it was a ploy to ensure he might not. If so, he lost the calculated gamble when Drake arrived.[18]

August and September were taken up with semiweekly benefits, including three for the Turner family. Intending to close what had been a successful engagement on September 30, Turner prolonged it when another of Drake's actors arrived early. John Vaughan was treated as a visiting star, performing Hotspur in *Henry IV, Part I*. At the close of the season on October 9, Mrs. Barrett returned east, having found the company (according to Ludlow) "poor and inadequately supported."[19]

Having presented forty-five plays in twenty-four nights, Turner gratefully acknowledged "the liberal encouragement he has received from the Patrons of the Drama" in Lexington. He also laid before them his case against Usher, noting that he and his family had "abandoned every other prospect for the express purpose of residing with his family in Kentucky." Citing his suit against Usher, he "trusts that a jury will do him justice and prove by the verdict that contracts are not to be violated with IMPUNITY."[20]

But Turner lost the suit, compounding his and Sophia's previous ire against Usher. They never returned to Kentucky, turning instead toward Cincinnati. Still, as Durang notes, Turner could rightly claim "the second honor [after Usher] of planting the dramatic standard in the western world," Ludlow's later claims of Drake's primacy to the contrary. (Usher may have gotten a higher rent from Drake.)[21]

~~~~~~~~~~

Samuel Drake Sr., the man with whom Noble Luke Usher had forged an agreement in Albany to establish a new company for Kentucky, was a seasoned professional. Heavyset, bordering on obese, he projected a gravitas that led others to refer to him as the Old Man despite his being middle-aged. And despite Drake's well-earned reputation as an inveterate practical jokester, Durang considered him "a man of integrity, possessing good sense, dramatic business tact, besides being a musician."[22]

Born in 1768 in Barnstable, England, he had been apprenticed to a printer and may for a time have studied theology at Oxford before becoming an itinerant actor-manager in the provinces. Taken to Covent Garden by Colman to see *Hamlet,* he had fallen in love with its Ophelia, Martha Fisher, born in 1770 in Bath. After a suitable courtship they had married, and she bore him five children before they emigrated to America in 1810, joining the Federal Street Theatre company under John Bernard. There, Martha played supporting roles and Sam acted and stage managed. In 1813, with two more children, they followed Bernard to Albany.

But soon after Noble Luke Usher's fatal departure from Albany, Martha Drake had died, leaving Sam with seven children, two in their infancy. Now he had to organize a traveling theatre company, obligated to reach Kentucky by December. Of necessity, he enlisted his oldest five children: Martha, twenty-two; Sam Jr., eighteen; Alexander "Aleck," sixteen; Julia, fourteen; and James, thirteen. (His two youngest children, Georgia, two, and Charles, one, were left behind, their care and upbringing unknown.) Drake often billed his family members by their first names, as "Mr. Alexander, Mr. James," and so forth, resembling Dickens's Crummles in *Nicholas Nickleby.*[23]

Young Martha never showed the motivation and talent of her siblings, but tolerably filled in when needed, especially in tragedy. The handsome, ambitious, convivial Sam Jr. was both a talented violinist and a versatile actor who could play tragedy, light comedy, or melodrama. "A well-proportioned man, nearly six feet in height, with black hair and a healthy English face, rather a pleasant expression, more indicative of good nature than intelligence," he was "very agreeable in female society" and "fond of good eating and drinking." Aleck had debuted in Boston at age twelve as the Prince of Wales in *Richard III* and had grown into "a very cheerful, social and good-hearted" manhood, willing to help out everywhere from the paint room to the footlights, his specialty being rustic low comedy. Although he suffered from a congenital deafness, he worked assiduously to overcome it. Julia was already competent at juvenile tragedy (especially Juliet), genteel comedy, and hoydens in farces. Within a few years "in face and figure, [she] was a perfect specimen of the ancient Italian beauty—with dark hair and long, dark eyelashes; her eyes had a peculiarly happy, lively expression." Soon to become "a beautiful and dashing woman and a vivacious actress," her signature role would be Lady Teazle in *School for Scandal.* James, almost as handsome as his brothers, happily filled minor "utility" roles.[24]

Complementing Drake's company were Mr. and Mrs. Lewis (first names never cited, in bills or memoirs), who had acted for fifteen years in Virginia and Albany, he in minor roles and she "the heavy tragedy ladies," although lately grown "quite fleshy"; she would soon enact "first old women." Mr. Lewis, who provided a carriage for the journey along with Samuel Drake's farm wagon and two workhorses, would also function as stage carpenter. Others were scenic artist Joe Tracy, theatrical apprentice Noah Ludlow, and Fanny Denny, the stagestruck seventeen-year-old daughter of the widow whose boardinghouse had served as the Drakes' home for two seasons. (The widow had repeatedly refused to allow her daughter to join a company of traveling players, only relenting at the moment of departure. Little could she have imagined that that daughter would within a decade, as Mrs. Alexander Drake, become the first widely renowned western actress.) Drake hoped for additional actors in Pittsburgh and Kentucky.[25]

Ludlow, nineteen, had been stagestruck since seeing his first professional performance six years before at the Park Theatre in New York, but had to forego any aspirations in that direction until he was eighteen, being apprenticed to a mercantile house. At eighteen he had moved to Albany, where he approached Bernard, who took him on as an apprentice. Now, since he was not actually under contract to Bernard, Drake sent him ahead to scout towns and buildings which might provide audiences and performance spaces, affording the fledgling company both experience and a nominal income. (This advance work apparently included Ludlow's performing for the Turners in Cincinnati and Lexington.) Their first destination was to be Cherry Valley, New York, a town of slightly over three thousand some sixty miles west of Albany. Ludlow's account of the company's journey to Kentucky, replete with anecdotes—most relating rustic credulity and the perils of travel—form the early chapters of his memoir.

At season's end in Albany on May 19, Drake loaded his wagon, drawn by his two horses, with six all-purpose painted backdrops ("a wood, street, parlor, kitchen, palace, and garden"), painted wings, an adjustable painted proscenium/curtain, and a rolled-up green baize carpet—all of which could be set up in a few hours—along with the most essential costumes, properties, scripts, and sheet music. The actors would travel in Lewis's carriage or walk alongside, except for rare stretches when stage travel was feasible and affordable. (While the Turner company left no account of their methods of travel and equipment, they must have been similar.)[26]

Amid unusually heavy rains the Drake company set out, with Tracy deputized as wagon driver. From the start the going was difficult, despite some portions of the Cherry Valley Turnpike being completed. They wended their way "over uncut roads, passing through mountain gorges and crossing the great Alleghanies," performing anywhere that "a tavern, hall, barn or courtroom could be had." Durang recalled traveling a parallel route in 1811: for the first "forty or fifty miles not a house of any description could be seen, and . . . not a solitary village of ten houses was met until Pittsburgh. . . . All was one vast view of wooded valley and mountain."[27]

In Cherry Valley, on a stage of rough boards in the courthouse, the troupe performed for six nights, opening with *The Prize* and *The Purse*. On the second night, Fanny Denny made her acting debut in the lead role of Julia in Inchbald's comedy *The Midnight Hour*. Ludlow, too, was acquiring experience, with noticeably poorer results by his own account. Unfortunately, with no newspaper there yet, no reviews exist.[28]

They repeated their six-night repertoire fifteen miles away, in Cooperstown, with the addition of *Adelgitha*. This gave Denny her first opportunity to act tragedy, as Imma, a key supporting role as a grief-stricken Byzantine princess. Mrs. Lewis played the title role—in which Denny would later excel—Sam Drake Sr. the villain, and Ludlow the unfortunate hero beloved by Imma.

The pattern was repeated for fewer than six nights where populations were small, through June and July in other upstate New York towns: Herkimer, Utica, Oneida, Manlius, Onondaga, Skaneateles, Auburn, Geneva, and Canandaigua. In most places the courthouse provided the fittest venue. From Canandaigua they trekked southwest through a hundred miles of wilderness to Olean, seeking the headwaters of the Allegheny River, which would carry them to Pittsburgh. It was on this leg of their journey that their most harrowing incident occurred. Mrs. Lewis, grown restless from riding, decided to walk and fell behind the others, causing her when darkness fell to spend the night in a tree to escape a pack of wolves, before the next day's frantic search by the others recovered her.[29]

There was no point in performing in Olean, in 1815 a village of only a few scattered log cabins. There, Drake traded his wagon and horses for a twenty-five-by-fifteen-foot flat-bottomed broadhorn boat containing two small rooms. Ten days on the tortuous river took them by mid-August to soot-begrimed Pittsburgh, arriving sooner than anticipated, which Ludlow attributes to the upstate New York towns being dispensed with in four or five weeks.[30]

Since Drake did not wish to arrive in Frankfort before the Kentucky legislative session in December, he announced a three-month season in Pittsburgh. He leased the new theater last used by Turner's company and the amateurs, derided by Ludlow as "the poorest apology" for a theater he had seen. Several actors joined Drake's short-handed company in Pittsburgh: Mr. and Mrs. Alexander Williams, who had performed with Turner; George Bland, who had performed with Usher (but who soon absconded from the Drakes); Mrs. Mary Riddle; and two young male novices (likely from the local Thespian Society). Fortunately, Fanny Denny was showing such promise that she was soon playing romantic leads.[31]

Pittsburgh, on the verge of incorporation, struggled to provide audiences for its four-hundred-seat theater from its population of six thousand. Ludlow questionably paints a rosy portrait of full houses, but their audiences were predominantly male, including many foundrymen and keelboat men who could be rude and inattentive. The fledgling company opened on Saturday evening, August 15, with *The Honey Moon* (leads by Williams and Denny) and *No Song, No Supper* (an ensemble Prince Hoare musical afterpiece with Sam Sr., Sam Jr., Aleck and Martha Drake, Ludlow, and Mrs. Lewis). The next night featured *Adelgitha* and a Dibdin farce, *The Quaker*. Williams yearned to play the meaty role of Rolla in *Pizarro* and pressured Drake into staging it, with Denny as Cora. This required new scenery and considerable doubling of parts, which yielded the hilarious result of the theater's cleaning lady and property man being recruited for, and unintentionally exposed in, their roles as vestal virgins. Other performances included *Castle Spectre*, *Inkle and Yarico*, *Speed the Plough*, *The Way to Get Married*, and *The Prize*, with Denny and Ludlow gradually assuming greater responsibility.[32]

By mid-November, Drake decided it was time to move on. Purchasing another broadhorn, he embarked with his company and all its equipment on a week-long voyage down the Ohio River to Limestone (Maysville), Kentucky. There, he traded the boat for two wagons which carried them to Frankfort in time for the legislative session. Performing in Usher's 1812 theater, their ranks were filled out by Kentucky veteran James Douglass, John Vaughan (from the Usher circuit), and his younger brother Henry, Frank Blissett and Tom Jefferson (both from Turner).

Frankfort in 1815, despite being the state capital, had a population of fewer than fourteen hundred, making Drake's effort a questionable venture. But he had promised Usher, and saw a future in the Kentucky circuit. As he made clear to Kentuckians, he intended "establishing the drama on a permanent and regular plan." He boasted "a company of well-known talent and unblemished reputation" whose performances would demonstrate that a "moral tendency is inculcated and instruction is blended with innocent amusement."[33]

Drake's timing was fortuitous. A ready audience awaited. After the close of the War of 1812, settlers poured into Kentucky "like a mountain torrent, . . . faster than it was possible to provide corn for breadstuff," recalled one pioneer, and that torrent quickly became "an avalanche." Drake's company opened on December 4 with *Mountaineers* (with John Vaughan and Fanny Denny—still improving—in the leads) and *Midnight Hour*. Other scripts that winter in Frankfort included *Speed the Plough*, *Of Age Tomorrow*, *Merchant of Venice*, and *The Purse*.[34]

A two-day wagon trip took the troupe to Louisville, where Drake found its "dark, dingy and dirty" circa-1808 theater on Jefferson Street, with its ill-lit interior of "dismal colors" and its "badly painted" scenery, requiring immediate attention. For this, he hired actor-turned-housepainter John Vos, with his mantua-maker wife as costumer. Louisville's *Western Courier* hyped the impending opening, congratulating "the lovers of the drama upon the prospect of a well-governed rational amusement."[35]

On February 28, 1816, the company opened there with *Heir at Law* and *Midnight Hour*, the first of twenty-four plays in twelve evenings. Nearly all were lighthearted and morally circumspect, providing "innocent amusement and useful instruction." The *Western Courier* lauded the company's ability to fill seats and its superior talent, citing individual actors for specific skills: "The company has far exceeded our most flattering anticipations." Manager Drake's talents "do honor to himself and entitle him to the applause of a discerning public" (that is, the company does not mug for cheap laughs). He managed not only to "please the taste and gratify the judgment of his audience, but he absolutely created a high standard," the effects of which were felt for decades in Louisville.[36]

Drake took a stand, however, against the city's tax on theatre, on the grounds that its intent was to protect citizens from "imposters, charlatans, vagabonds," and "corrupters of the moral of the community," and he certainly was none of these. To ameliorate concerns, he instituted occasional charity benefits. It took nine years for Drake to be vindicated when such taxes were finally repealed statewide.[37]

In mid-May, a week after closing in Louisville, the Drake company—a year and a half after agreeing to Noble Luke Usher's proposal and a year since leaving Albany—arrived in Lexington. They found the town of nearly five thousand residents, many of the planter class from Virginia and North Carolina, amenable to culture and learning, a "high-minded people" exhibiting "an enthusiasm, a vivacity, . . . courage, frankness and generosity," striving to be the "Athens of the West." Drake found Usher, however, in dire financial straits, having been forced that January to put his house and theater up for auction, the latter without success. The brewery-turned-theater was, according to Ludlow, another venue in wretched condition, "the poorest specimen of a theatre" he had seen, the seats "simply covered with canvas and painted, without being stuffed or having any backs." The scenery "was very limited, and not very well painted." The dressing rooms below the stage barely met his approval, being "comfortable enough." But "after considerable sweeping and cleaning and painting," the place was ready.[38]

Drake's personnel in Lexington were slightly altered. Since Louisville, he had lost Mrs. Williams and Tom Jefferson, the former to rejoin the Turners and the latter returning to Philadelphia, dissatisfied with the roles Drake had awarded him. Drake in turn had gained a valuable new asset from Turner, heralded by the *Lexington Gazette*: "If anything could add to our gratification" at the arrival of Drake's company, it was the addition of "our friend [Joshua] Collins (who is now a resident of our neighborhood)," held in "high opinion."[39]

Drake opened in Usher's theater on May 21 with *Foundling of the Forest* and *Poor Soldier* and continued performances on Mondays, Wednesdays, and Saturdays through July 1. His stated reason for closing was the heat, but 1816 was infamous as the "year without a summer," with frost across much of the nation in May, in some parts into July and again by late September, with widespread crop failure, caused by the massive April 1815 eruption of Mount Tambora in the Dutch East Indies.

But Drake had every reason to feel a sense of accomplishment, having established his company in the Kentucky circuit while rehearsing and staging at least thirty-four different productions in thirty weeks. They had ranged from Shakespearean tragedy (for example, *Othello*—but only after Collins's arrival) to melodrama (such as *Tale of Mystery, Castle Spectre*), to comedy (for example, *She Stoops to Conquer, The Midnight Hour*) to musical farce (such as, *The Purse, The Review*).

Why did Drake succeed where others had failed? First, his company was larger and more experienced—not to mention more loyal to him, being family—than others, such as Turner's, with the bonus of a developing star among them in Fanny Denny. Second, Drake brought, and applied, management skills he had learned in Albany from Bernard, along with a broad repertoire of scripts. Third, he faced conflicts squarely, including taxation in Louisville and the competition with Turner over the use of Usher's Lexington theater.

He had planted his flag in Kentucky and had no intention of being dislodged, but was already eyeing cities beyond it, even if they were occupied by another troupe.

4

~~~~~~

TURNER v. DRAKE
(1816–1818)

DRIVEN OUT OF LEXINGTON by Drake, William Turner looked across the Ohio River to Cincinnati. He took the remnants of his company—his family, Mr. and Mrs. Milner, Thomas Morgan, Martin, and actor/scenic artist Lucas—there in early January 1816, joining its still-active amateur thespians. A performance on January 4, repeated five nights later, of *Point of Honor* and *How to Die for Love* went to benefit a local family victimized by fire. One attendee praised their altruism and their ability "to pay for their house, scenery and dresses [costumes], and give money to the poor." The Turners chose to remain with these thespians for the entirety of 1816, during which they performed intermittently, including such popular standards as *Raising the Wind, Cure for the Heartache, Love Laughs at Locksmiths,* and *Douglas.* They were forced to postpone a performance on December 6 of *Speed the Plough,* as their green act curtain had been stolen.[1]

Amateur thespian activity still predominated in other frontier towns. In the Michigan Territorial capital of Detroit, amateurs in 1816 converted the upper floor of a brick warehouse on Wayne Street with the help of soldiers, who acted in the plays and constructed scenery and whose wives painted it. In February 1816 the Natchez Theatrical Association staged two pantomimes, *Don Quixote* and *Harlequin Hunter,* and the following winter turned to comedy with *The Rivals, The Review,* and *Who Wants a Guinea?* The Roscian Society of St. Louis, who specialized in serious drama (for example, *Douglas*), entertained audiences in the immediate postwar years. In Pittsburgh, in the wake of the Turners and Drakes, amateurs in June 1816 presented a few, varied bills, including *Catharine and Petruchio; The Highland Reel;* a Lewis melodrama, *Timour the Tartar;* and Morton's *Columbus;*

or, the Discovery of North America. In Natchez, St. Louis, and Pittsburgh, the arrival of professionals in 1817 would curtail amateur activity.[2]

~~~~~~~~~~

Looking to glean a few dollars and possibly expand his circuit further, Drake in July 1816 sent most of his company—including sons Sam Jr., Aleck, and James, daughters Martha and Julia, Blissett, Douglass, both Vaughans, Ludlow, Denny and Mrs. Lewis—out to barnstorm neighboring small towns for a few nights to "amuse the admirers of the drama." They visited Harrodsburg, Danville, and Paris, Kentucky—a round-trip of 115 miles. Their reception remains unrecorded.[3]

That fall Drake solidified his presence in Kentucky by mounting a season with his reunited company. They opened in Lexington on September 30 with Dimond's *Adrian and Orilla* and Samuel Foote's *The Liar.* This was a formidable company, able to mount Shakespearean tragedy (for example, *Macbeth, Hamlet, Othello*) as well as hilarious farces, with most members of the company able to acceptably carry a tune. Joshua Collins carried most leads along with John Vaughan and Fanny Denny (such as Othello, Iago, and Desdemona, respectively) or opposite only Denny (for example, Hamlet and Ophelia, Shylock and Portia, Petruchio and Catharine). Drake expanded their repertoire with several new pieces, including O'Keeffe's *The Agreeable Surprise* and *The Miller and His Men,* and Kemble's *Plot Counterplot.*

By November 4, he was providing ample benefits, closing on November 26. Moral objections to Drake's efforts must have still simmered, however, because the Debating Society of Lexington on December 14 considered the issue "Ought the Theatre under any regulations to be encouraged?"[4]

Before departing for Frankfort, he strengthened his company with the addition of Aaron J. Phillips, a Philadelphian who despite being barely twenty brought two years of experience from New York's Park Theatre and showed sufficient promise to carry such juvenile leads as Young Norval in *Douglas.* Arriving in Frankfort a few weeks in advance of the new legislative session, Drake opened with his usual repertoire, but attracted insufficient interest until the legislators convened. Late February through late May 1817 saw the troupe in Louisville, where Collins defected back to the Turners. Drake successfully replaced him with Phillips in tragic Shake-spearean leads (such as Richard III, Othello, and Macbeth). Continuing to placate civic leaders, Drake staged benefits, including one on April 26 for town improvements.

~~~~~~~~~~

In Cincinnati, the hybrid Turner-Thespian company closed out 1816 with *Child of Nature* and *Animal Magnetism* on December 30. By mid-January 1817 their inadequacy was becoming increasingly evident, so they added a few capable professionals. John and Elizabeth Savage, in their mid-twenties, had been acting at the Federal Street Theatre in Boston but, dissatisfied with their roles, had headed in fall 1816 to Pittsburgh. There, with the city's Thespian Society, John received praise for his "correct and manly acting," and Elizabeth for her "chastened elegance," but they made only a minor impression in such reliable pieces as *The Stranger*. By November, the Thes-pian Society had "not been enabled to pay the contingent expenses of the House," and the Savages drifted down to Cincinnati. The Turners also added William Jones, thirty-seven, specializing in Falstaffian old men, and his wife, Julia, who played eccentric old women. William had originally aspired to tragedy, recalls Durang, "but soon found comedy more conge-nial to his natural gifts, and so gradually fell into the hearty and eccentric old men." At the end of February, Turner reacquired Joshua Collins from Drake. Things were ostensibly looking up.[5]

But problems persisted. In a performance of *Point of Honor* on Janu-ary 19, many of the actors "did not know their parts, and they were so deficient in general that the audience became apathetic." Jones "left the audience untouched," and Sophia Turner was just "respectable." Morgan was good in comedy but not in tragedy. Lucas "left much to be desired." To be regretted was "the undiscriminating applause. Sometimes mere ranting received more applause than good acting." More distracting was the "un-paralleled rudeness and profligacy of the mob of ragamuffins" who "pelted the outside of the theater with stones." Religious-minded citizens objected to "the indelicate language" in the scripts, which would "raise a blush on the cheek of modesty." Turner replied with reassurances that all future plays will be "replete with character, interest and delicacy, . . . calculated to gratify," and conclude "at a seasonable hour."[6]

Through mid-March they tried to make a go of it with a repertoire that should have appealed to all segments of Cincinnati society: Shakespeare (*Merchant of Venice, Othello,* both with Sophia and Collins in the leads), drama (*Pizarro, Timour the Tartar*), comedy (*Honey Moon, Magpie and Maid*), farce (*Laugh When You Can, Love Laughs at Locksmiths*) and even pantomime (*Harlequin in the Moon*). Lucas created vivid new scenery with recognizable details of local color. Financial help came via benefits for favorite actors, including the thespians' benefit for Sophia on January 31, she as Angela in *Castle Spectre.* Reviews improved, too, with Sophia praised for her "judgment, taste and feeling," and Morgan, Lucas, Martin, and Mrs. Milner recognized for their talents.[7]

Promising to "patch up the present apology for a Play House with new Boxes, Scenery and Dressing Rooms" and to return in fall with "as full and respectable a company as [could] be obtained," Turner in June 1817 took his company across the river to Maysville, Kentucky, for a short engagement. A British visitor caught their *Honey Moon* and *'Tis All a Farce* in a crude frame building: "The scenery and the performance were miserable, but the buffoonery of the farce, and an orchestra of negroes, who performed two tunes with two fiddles and two triangles, kept the audience in good humour. Segar smoking during the performance was practiced by most of the men."[8]

Turner returned to Cincinnati sooner than fall, as his reason for leaving in June had been abrogated. Drake had planned to build a new theatre there, but negotiations with city fathers over their intended theatrical tax had quickly reached an impasse. Drake, refusing to go forward if he had to pay the tax, withdrew, leaving Cincinnati clear for Turner.

To further bolster his company, Turner advertised for actors and by July acquired the stout yet "handsome" Mrs. Alexander Cummins, who brought minor New York experience, to play serious leading roles, and her husband, formerly a printer, who was now trying his hand at acting, with limited success. Turner himself rarely acted, but Sophia continued to carry leads, and they introduced their eldest child, Frederick, to the stage in minor roles. Through July the company performed twice a week, primarily offering melodramas, including *Barbarossa, Timour the Tartar, Forty Thieves* ("the original music" for which cost "upwards of three hundred dollars"), *The Voice of Nature* (translated from a French melodrama, *The Judgment of Solomon*), Colman the Younger's *Blue-Beard,* and *Battle of Bunker Hill* (with new scenery by Lucas), always with farce afterpieces.[9]

~~~~~~~~~~

Another acting couple now ventured into the frontier. At the close of the 1816–17 season at Philadelphia's Chestnut Street Theatre, newlyweds James and Mary Ann "Molly" Mason Entwistle, dissatisfied with their situation, headed like the Savages for Pittsburgh. James had acted in New York with Noble Luke Usher, who may have planted the notion of acting in the West. According to Durang, Entwistle "was a good actor in the line of country boys, and sang a comic song very well." "Poor Molly," playing both comic and tragic roles, "had a very fine figure" but "was not handsome in face, especially off the stage." However, once on stage, "attuned by her mind—lightning-quick—her countenance would responsively echo to every emotion. Her peculiar vivacity and arch playfulness in every simplicity caught the taste and enchanted all at once." Her performances were "distinguished by ease and elegance."[10]

In late May 1817, Entwistle announced his intention of bringing to Pittsburgh a company "composed of performers of the first-rate talents from the Theatres, New York—Philadelphia—Boston and Charleston," which would open the first week of August. Molly, heralded by the *Pittsburgh Gazette* as "by far the most superior actress that has ever graced the boards," would star. The others, gathered from a slew of eastern venues with unknown but likely unrealistic promises, were Mr. and Mrs. Monier, Mr. and Mrs. Legg, Mr. and Mrs. Jackson, Samuel Emberton, Joseph Hutton, and actors named Thomas and Carr. Entwistle also took on a management partner, a rude, slovenly actor named Henry Y. Lewis. The son of a celebrated British comedian, Lewis was only a "faint imitation of his father's manner" who "failed to conceal the want of genius, or the disadvantages of a person not gracefully made."[11]

Although the Pittsburgh Thespians had persevered with a reasonable repertoire, including *Venice Preserved, Day After the Wedding, Bertram,* and *Soldier's Daughter,* Entwistle upon arriving set himself up as their manager. But he lacked the personality for it, being overly convivial (drank to excess). He "was not the most prudent and energetic man in the world, . . . often in the Falstaff mood, delighted with his boon companions and merry jest." Using the "handsome sum of money" Molly had acquired before their marriage for this Pittsburgh venture, Entwistle thoroughly renovated the theater on Third Street in preparation for an August 6 opening. It featured her as Widow Cheerly in *Soldier's Daughter* and himself in *The Irishman in London.* Other well-known scripts would include *The Stranger, Honey Moon, Review, Heir at Law, Merchant of Venice, The Foundling of the Forest, As You Like It* (Molly as Rosalind), and *Hamlet.*[12]

In the company's favor was the fact that religious opposition had ebbed somewhat. As the *Gazette* acknowledged, "Society has been released from the chains of superstition," and the propriety of theatre was no longer "doubted by any man of liberal feelings and enlightened understanding. . . . The stage conveys a moral in colours more vivid than the awful and elevated station of the preacher permits him to use."[13]

Entwistle, however, seems to have aimed too high for his audiences. For example, they were unable to differentiate between *Hamlet* and "that irresistibly amusing burlesque, 'Hamlet Travestie.'" Throughout the latter, the audience remained "solemn, serious, and dull. The affecting entrance of the deranged Ophelia, who, instead of rosemary, rue, &c. had an ample supply of turnips and carrots, did not move a muscle of their intelligent faces—the ladies, indeed, excepted, who evinced by the frequent use of their pocket handkerchiefs, that their sympathies were engaged on the side of the love-sick maiden. Some who had seen the original *Hamlet* for the first time a few evenings before, gave vent to their criticisms when the curtain fell. They thought Mr. Entwistle did not look sufficiently grave; and that, as it was his benefit, he acted very dishonorably in shaving [cheating] them out of two acts."[14]

Through the fall, reviews and audiences—still overwhelmingly male— were generally favorable, especially for Molly's Mrs. Haller in *Stranger,* her Mrs. Oakly in *Jealous Wife,* and her Portia in *Merchant of Venice* (with her husband improbably as Shylock). She carried the company: "Never perhaps in the annals of the drama did any lady appear to greater advantage." Her "performance was certainly of the highest order. . . . She was eminently successful [and] did not look like acting; it seemed reality. . . . She is one of those rare beings that shed a lustre round the female character. . . . There is a dignity in this lady added to the correctness of her pronunciation," earning her the sobriquet "the Siddons of America." The rest of the company was "entirely respectable. . . . All acquitted themselves with great credit." While on some evenings "there was not a single deviation from the author," on others—particularly those on which the bill had been changed on short notice due to illness—obvious prompting was necessary.[15]

The company performed twice weekly through October, but revenue must not have remained sufficient for viability. Lewis in November defected to the Turners (playing the title role opposite Sophia in *Bertram* on November 21). Entwistle in early December ended the actors' contract by mutual agreement, although he "regret[ed] that occurrences inimical to his interests compel him" to do so. Amid Pittsburgh's griminess, Molly had not thrived. Her "youthful days had begun to fade. She possessed no beauty (so called) to lose, yet she continued to preserve her prime personal points intact." Within a year the company was dissolved and the Entwistles had divorced. Both left Pittsburgh, never to return. Another frontier effort had failed.[16]

〰〰〰〰〰〰

In early June 1817 Noah Ludlow, although only twenty-two and relatively inexperienced, with characteristic hubris decided to break off from Drake to form a new, separate commonwealth company. (It is unknown how Drake felt about such defections.) Ludlow's "Theatrical Company of Kentucky" comprised himself and his new fiancée, Nashville widow Mary Maury Squires (a complete novice, performing as "Miss Wallace"); John Vaughan and his new wife, a tall, pretty blonde from Frankfort (who had roomed with Mary Squires in Louisville); Henry Vaughan, Aaron Phillips (despite Ludlow's later calling Phillips "an actor of no particular excellence"); and a British musician named Bainbridge.[17]

"Having obtained a set of travelling scenes, a wagon and horses" (presumably from saved salaries), the little troupe set off toward Nashville, which had previously known only itinerants such as Rannie and occasional amateur performances. En route they stopped to briefly perform in three small towns, Elizabethtown, Russellville, and Hopkinsville, Kentucky. Their repertoire was predictable—for example, *Soldier's Daughter*, *Village Lawyer*, *Gamester*, *The Liar*. As the first professional company to appear in Nashville, a town of nearly three thousand settlers, they opened on July 10 in a converted salt house on the town square. Atypically, ladies attended as well as men, rosily recalled Ludlow, and "would sit out a long five-act comedy or tragedy on a narrow board not more than ten inches wide, without any support for their backs, and appear delighted with the performance."[18]

In August, Ludlow and Phillips decided to broaden their horizons. They scouted Cincinnati as a possible stop for their small company and as somewhere they might scour up some additional actors. They found Turner discouraged, and the ambitious Ludlow inferred the man was quitting management. Ludlow claims Turner had not paid his actors, "and consequently there was nothing but complaint and insubordination among them." Several of Turner's company did sign on with Ludlow and Phillips, including Lucas (playing old men), Mr. and Mrs. Thomas Morgan (he in low comedy, she as old women), Mr. Hanna (a Cincinnati actor—likely a former amateur—in juvenile roles), Mrs. Wilkins, and two or three male utility players. To show their good will, Ludlow and Phillips contributed their talents on Sophia Turner's benefit night, in *Honey Moon* (she as Juliana). But Ludlow ultimately passed on Cincinnati and retreated with his new actors to Nashville. The remnants of the Turner company struggled on in Cincinnati until November 25, when he (and the amateur thespians) threw in the towel, yielding another city to Drake (apparently having settled the tax issue). Turner turned further west, to try his luck in St. Louis.[19]

~~~~~~~~~

For a few weeks in August 1817, Drake had taken his remaining actors to Paris, Kentucky, then returned to Lexington to open his regular circuit. Bringing managerial touches from the East, he established coffee and refreshment rooms, announced the sale of season tickets, and pledged "that no effort on his part will be wanting to prove himself deserving of their patronage."[20]

From August 28 through November 15 they ran through their repertoire, now replete with Shakespeare (for example, *Macbeth, Merchant of Venice*), comedies (such as *Catharine and Petruchio,* Frederick Reynolds's *The Dramatist,* with John Savage back as visiting star), several new pieces (for example, Cibber and VanBrugh's *The Provoked Husband,* Sheridan and Colman's "grand operatical romance," *Forty Thieves,* and Isaac Pocock's "dramatic romance," *The Miller and His Men*), and a healthy share of diverting farces. Members of the Drake family, who with Savage received the lion's share of positive notices, were each assured a benefit night. The elder Drake received a glowing notice from the *Gazette* for having "proved, by his skill and ability, his qualifications [and who] by persevering industry and his own liberality has snatched our theatre from obscurity."[21]

Once again, though, Drake ran afoul of local authorities. On September 10, the Lexington Board of Trustees, citing an 1811 law, obtained an injunction against any further performances since Drake had not paid the five-dollar-per-day tax. He argued that he had merely leased the theater from Usher, whose responsibility the tax was. Further, Drake questioned the trustees' right to levy fines at all. In February 1818 the court decided it was indeed Usher's responsibility, and upheld the injunction. (Since performances continued, Usher apparently paid the tax.)[22]

Drake then proceeded into the next two legs of his Kentucky circuit, Frankfort in December and Louisville in spring 1818. In Louisville he bought and began renovating its weather-beaten theater, which was soon "fitted up with a degree of taste that does honor to its manager." This entailed adding a new row of boxes in front of the first tier, regilding the proscenium decorations, frescoing the interior walls, and installing new curtains, new scenery, and large new chandeliers with sperm-oil candles (which did not drip on the audience as did wax candles). Its expanded capacity was eight hundred, optimistic for a town of less than four thousand. Drake rechristened it "The Falls Theatre" (for the nearby falls of the Ohio River).[23]

In August 1817 Ludlow and his company had returned to Nashville, where he and Mary married on September 1. That very evening the company performed, appropriately, *The Day After the Wedding*, along with *Speed the Plough*. They settled in to perform four times a week, with only moderate results (a local newspaper correspondent called them "an erratic company of players.") Thinking ahead, Ludlow met with prominent Nashvillians, including General John H. Eaton and Sam Houston, about the possible erection of a theater there.[24]

He also corresponded with scenic artist Richard Jones (formerly of Douglass's company, whom Ludlow knew from Pittsburgh) about possibly renting a theater in New Orleans. Ludlow polled his company about relocating there, but several were loath to go, due to its prevalent yellow fever. Phillips begged off, returning to New York (but soon to travel the frontier as a visiting star). The rest resignedly departed in late October for New Orleans via the Cumberland, Ohio, and Mississippi rivers.

On his journey east that winter, Phillips escorted Fanny Denny, who had left the Drake company after Frankfort, hoping to achieve wider fame in the East. They would part ways in Pennsylvania, she continuing north to perform in Montreal, and then to debut in New York in April 1820 on her way to international stardom. (She would, however, loyally return to perform from time to time with the Drake company.) There were at that time "no comfortable and regular lines of stages," Durang recounts, and horseback (sidesaddle for her) allowed them to "journey at their leisure with less fatigue than in a jolting stage wagon." But upon reaching Bedford, Pennsylvania, Phillips paused for a nap, whereupon the determined Denny fed and watered the horses and rode on without him. Their journey took two and a half weeks. Denny, notes Durang, "had not only a strong physical development but she had equally a generous heart and mind."[25]

Ludlow had early on admired her determination, which he termed "spunk." On their 1815 journey west from Albany, the troupe at one point had been reduced to traveling in a rude oxcart, whose high sides made entry difficult. Denny announced, "'Well, I never saw the place yet I couldn't climb to, if I set myself about it.' So saying, she stepped out to the cart, saying to me, 'Ludlow, lend me a hand.' I did so, and before they could see how she did it, placed one foot on the hub, and with a bound landed inside the cart, to the great applause of the by-standers."[26]

On December 10, 1817, stopping in Natchez en route to New Orleans, Ludlow and his actors were persuaded to give a performance from the deck of their keelboat of *Catharine and Petruchio* for the denizens of Natchez-Under-the-Hill (who undoubtedly relished the crude, physical nature of the comedy). Five nights later the troupe opened in Natchez proper with *Honey Moon* and *Lying Valet* in the small theater amateur thespians had constructed atop the bluff, becoming the first professional troupe to appear there. For the next two weeks, still ragged and relying considerably on the prompter, they gained additional experience as a coherent troupe. Individual actors were improving, though Ludlow needed to have them polished in time for New Orleans. Attendance in Natchez was strong, with audience ranks swelled by state legislators currently in session (Mississippi having gained statehood the previous winter, with Natchez its first capital).

Leaving Natchez in early January 1818, the troupe rehearsed on board their (now) steamboat, the *Orleans*. Mary Ludlow was becoming more comfortable in soubrette roles, Mr. and Mrs. John Vaughan were now creditably handling comedic and tragic leads, Hanna (his salary raised to twenty-five dollars per week) shone in juvenile leads, and Ludlow regarded Lucas (who had taken on additional responsibilities as scenic artist), the Morgans (low comedy and old women), and Mrs. Wilkins as "very valuable." A few others joined, either in Nashville or upon arrival in New Orleans on January 7: Mr. and Mrs. Baldwin, Mr. and Mrs. Cummins (from the Turners), and a young Mr. Plummer (who had tried and failed with Drake in Lexington), and Richard Jones.[27]

Ludlow had surmised correctly that opportunities awaited in New Orleans, but his were not, of course, the first professionals in the Crescent City, as he often liked to proclaim. There had been the French troupes, the Rannies, and also Austin Cargill. Cargill, in the same independent managerial vein as Ludlow, had left the Turners to organize a company for the

St. Philip Street Theatre in March 1817. Joining him had been Jones and John Vos (formerly with Drake), and Arthur F. Keene.

They merged with the city's amateur thespians, whose leader named Robinson (sometimes Robertson) would play major supporting roles, to mount *Miller and His Men* (with Cargill as Lothair) and *Weathercock* (with Jones as Tristram Fickle) on May 23. They followed this up with *Othello* on June 2 for Cargill's benefit, with Jones in the title role to Cargill's Iago. The two men delivered dramatic speeches in English as part of a June 5 pantomimic production by the amateurs entitled *Bunker Hill; or, the Death of General Warren.* Four nights later the Olympic Circus (an equestrian theater) presented *The Battle of New Orleans* by an unnamed gentleman of New Orleans. The combined French-English amateurs continued on their own through December, with such offerings as Dominique Brevost's three-act tragedy *La Mort d'Abel* and Picard's *The Old Aunt*.

For the fall 1817 season, which opened on November 4 with Kotzebue's *How to Die for Love*, Cargill patriotically renamed the St. Philip Street Theatre the American Theatre. *Othello* must have gone down well, for he scheduled more Shakespeare for the months ahead, including *Henry IV* (taking the title role himself, with Vos as Hotspur and Jones as Falstaff) in early December, *Richard III* on December 31, and *Othello* again on January 5, 1818. They carried on successfully through Cargill's February 26 benefit of *Timour the Tartar*, with some of the amateurs performing at the Olympic Circus on St. Charles Street.

By that time Ludlow and his "American Theatrical Commonwealth Company" had been in New Orleans for seven weeks, during which time they shared with Cargill use of the St. Philip Street Theatre (back to its original name). By mutual agreement, Jones repainted the theater's interior and renovated it, creating two tiers and a parquet, to seat seven hundred. "Having obtained the mayor's permission" and met the appropriate fees, Ludlow opened on January 13 with *Honey Moon* and *Midnight Hour*.[28]

For the next two months, his actors forged on with such standard pieces as *She Stoops to Conquer, Douglas, Stranger, Merchant of Venice,* and *Romeo and Juliet.* Ludlow recalls full houses, but the *Louisiana State Gazette* reported on March 20 that the company "will not continue many weeks longer" due to "a want of support." Why? "Because they are destitute of merit," which has "done much injury." Still, while the troupe was admittedly inferior to those in London, New York, or Philadelphia, "yet they are respectable." Ludlow acknowledges only an initial lack of success, due to Anglophobia—sometimes threatening—among the French and Spanish populations there. His attempts to defuse this included a joint performance with the city's French troupe of *Don Juan* on April 23, directed by Monsieur Douvillier, who had acted professionally for seven seasons and now played the title role.[29]

During the winter Richard Jones had lost his wife to yellow fever and fallen seriously ill himself, recovering slowly and suffering "great pecuniary losses." By the end of February 1818, he, Cargill, and Vos had merged with Ludlow, with the understanding that each would receive a benefit and have a chance at leads. In April, interrupting season-ending benefits, the itinerant Savages appeared to take a star turn in *Venice Preserved*, *The Romp*, *Foundling of the Forest*, and *Day After the Wedding*. By the time Ludlow closed on May 1, his company's fortunes and (somewhat) their abilities had rebounded, although he was uncertain whether or not he would return to New Orleans. The *Gazette* reported the company dividing a profit of $3,000 (about $62,000 today) and asserted, "Their private deportment while among us has been so universally correct that not even the tongue of slander has dared to assail it." Their talent, "though criticized rather severely by the fastidious few, has been always respectable" (hardly a glowing testimonial).[30]

Ludlow took the actors, again on the *Orleans*, back to Natchez, where they opened above the bluff on May 14 with *Turn Out* and *Catharine and Petruchio* (Mrs. Cummins and John Vaughan). A week later, however, Ludlow fell dangerously ill (an inflamed throat which doctors were unsuccessful in treating). Fearing death, he left with his new wife for Nashville, turning control and his shares over to John Vaughan, with Bainbridge as treasurer. Within days a man identified by Ludlow only as "West India Jones" (to differentiate him from Richard Jones), who had acted with the troupe in New Orleans, in turn bought out Vaughan.[31]

Jones's debut production was *The Gamester* on May 22, in which he played Stukely, the Machiavellian villain. He showed promise, according to the *Mississippi Republican*, but Vaughan's Beverly, the lead, "was the favorite. Mrs. Cummins displayed much force and judgment, in Mrs. Beverly." A crowded house granted "timely applause" since "*The Gamester* is a favorite with those who believe in the efficacy of reforming this evil." The rest of the company was only mediocre. Jones maintained Ludlow's repertoire (for example, *Castle Spectre, Lovers' Vows, Jane Shore, Stranger, George Barnwell, Weathercock*), and provided the usual benefits, closing July 21. He was apparently a divisive figure, however, and several actors left at that time. Ludlow subsequently blamed Jones for the breakup of the company.[32]

Ludlow, healed by drinking purer spring water in Tennessee, remained there until fall. (Comedian Thomas Morgan was less fortunate, dying in Natchez on July 21, age thirty-two.) Renting a house in Nashville, Ludlow offered his services as stage manager for the Nashville Thespian Society. Its members included Eaton, its manager, and Houston, its secretary, both of whom would soon apply their acting skills in the field of politics. Their first bill was *Douglas*, with Mary Ludlow—one of only two actresses in the group—as Lady Randolph and Houston as the duplicitous Glenalvon. (Although Houston acquitted himself capably in serious drama, Ludlow minimizes Houston's talent and relates difficulties in getting him to perform farce.)[33]

~~~~~~~~~~

Through the spring of 1818 the undaunted Turners had been trying to make a go of it in St. Louis, by now a town of nearly three thousand. It, too, was profiting from that postwar "avalanche" of new settlers, but in a territory still two years short of statehood. Arriving by steamboat on January 3, they had connected with the amateurs who had been performing there for three years. An initial impediment was finding a suitable venue. They tried the old courthouse, then a church on the square, then a loft above a stable attached to the Green Tree Tavern. With Sophia as leading lady, the rest of the company was an inexperienced bunch: Emma Turner, now twelve, her brother Frederick, acting juvenile roles; Isaac Henry, William DeGrushe, men named King, Martin, Wallace, James, Blythe, Smith, Pelham, Peyton, Luckey, and Guthrie, and a "Master Maud"—mostly amateurs.[34]

They opened on February 17 with *Bertram* (Henry as Bertram, Sophia as Imogine) and Fielding's *Mock Doctor*. A reviewer applauded their effort as "rational and refined," and was pleased with the "order and decorum uniformly observed" by the "crowded and highly fashionable audience" and—rare for the frontier in 1818—their "silent and respectful attention." Henry and Sophia deserved praise, he for his vivid "expression of heart-rending agony and despair," and she for her "powers of a very high order, surpassed by very few actresses in any country." Her Imogine was "a lively picture of a chaste and honorable woman" whose sufferings were "sketched with a boldness of coloring and a felicity of execution which evinced Mrs. T's [*sic*] knowledge of the human heart."[35]

They performed intermittently though April, with a preponderance of tragedy (for example, *Isabella*, with Henry and Sophia again as leads). In May, Turner and fifteen prominent St. Louis citizens began planning for a real theater. They drew up a covenant, proposed the sale of shares, and purchased a lot on the south side of Chestnut Street for $1,500, but the deal fell through. A salient factor may have been the fact that until nearly 1840 the preponderance of St. Louis settlers were French and lacked the time, funds, and appreciation for English-language theatre.

In July the Turners resumed performances, beginning with *Tekeli* on July 4, enhanced by the addition of Mr. and Mrs. John Vos, fresh from Ludlow's troupe in New Orleans. Vos, for his wife's benefit on July 25, played Hotspur in *Henry IV*, with his wife as Dame Quickly, Sophia as Lady Percy, Emma Turner as Prince John, and Henry as Falstaff. For his own benefit, Vos enacted *Richard III*, after which the company disbanded, the Turners once again on the move. Vos, though, stayed to persevere in St. Louis.

Two decades in, such was the pervasive fluidity and transience among acting companies on the frontier, along with a continuing dependence on amateur thespian societies to fill out casts and secure performance venues. But frontier audiences and newspapers were supportive, and by the end of another decade some stability and permanence would materialize.

5

DRAKE ASCENDANT

(1819)

BY FALL 1818, SAMUEL DRAKE had established a fairly strong monopoly in Kentucky and stood poised to claim preeminence on the frontier. The core of his company remained his family, with Sam Jr., Aleck, and Julia acting often, along with the loyal James Douglass.

Drake readily replaced any defectors with talent of a higher order. Drury Lane's Alexander Palmer Fisher, forty-three, Drake's British brother-in-law, brought a letter of recommendation from the renowned Edmund Kean, and a new wife, Agnes Lamacraft Diamond Fisher, making her American stage debut. British-born Mrs. Belinda Poole Goldson Groshon, thirty, brought five seasons' experience in New York, notably at the Park Theatre, and specialized in tragic heroines, notably Lady Macbeth. William Jones, back from the Turners, brought his wife, Julia, now twenty-one, also a native New Yorker. Durang believed of her that "there were none more useful" in "low, vulgar, and antiquated characters." Henry Lewis (Entwistle's erstwhile partner) defected from the Turners. Aaron Phillips was back from New York. Mr. and Mrs. Victor F. Mongin, she making her stage debut in soubrette/chambermaid roles, rounded out the newcomers. These highly capable performers had been recruited by Aleck, to whom his father began transitioning management of the company, billing him as "Mr. Alexander."[1]

This augmented company opened in Lexington on September 4, 1818, with *Macbeth* (with Fisher and Groshon in the leads, and Sam Jr., as Macduff), and over the next eight weeks performed at least forty different scripts, nearly all familiar standards. A few, though, were new: Colman's *The Iron Chest*, Pocock's *The Magpie and the Maid*, Knight's *The Turnpike Gate*, Lewis's *Alfonso, King of Castile*, and Murphy's *The Old Maid*. With

Fisher and Groshon covering most leads, important supporting roles were carried by William Jones, Sam Jr., Aleck, and Julia Drake.

Drake Sr. provided generous benefit nights beginning with Fisher's on October 14, and others for the theater's box keeper and the Lexington Female Benevolent Society. Opposite Fisher or Jones, Belinda Groshon attracted the most positive critical notices, acclaimed "the best actress that ever appeared on the western stage" (apparently eclipsing Sophia Turner, at least in Kentucky). Her "spirit of discernment and discrimination" earned "genuine merit." Closing on November 21, the company headed for its annual engagement in Frankfort.[2]

As the Drakes ascended, the Turners' fortunes declined. Repeatedly unsuccessful elsewhere, they appeared in Natchez in late October and merged for a short time with West India Jones's depleted American Theatrical Commonwealth Company. Sophia Turner's first performance came on October 29, in a benefit for the widowed Mrs. Morgan, as Belvidera in *Venice Preserved*. The other Turners, plus Vaughan, Hanna, Cargill, Lucas, Bainbridge, William DeGrushe (whom the Turners brought from St. Louis), and a new young man named Stuart, struggled to fill all roles.

Rare this early on the frontier, an unusually thorough account of their November 11 *Romeo and Juliet* in the *Mississippi State Gazette* reviews their effort. Vaughan as Romeo "played extremely well . . . with much animation and judgment. His conception of the character is certainly a correct one," although he sometimes resorted to "ranting." Sophia's Juliet was pretty and graceful and "united with considerable effect the lovely bashfulness of Capulet's daughter to the enthusiastic passion of Romeo's wife." In the first act, however, "Her voice was rather loud, and her manner not quite bashful and retiring enough." Jones's Mercutio was powerful in his dying: "The gradual ebb of life, and the painful approach of death, could not have been exhibited with more accuracy." A few shortcomings could not be overlooked: Jones, Stuart, Lucas, and Mrs. Vaughn did not know their lines, and "Bainbridge's buffoonery, in the character of Peter the nurse's servant, would have done very well in a farce, but, as it was, appeared entirely out of place." Manager Jones was criticized for his shopworn scenery.[3]

A week later Jones badly misjudged the modesty of Natchez theatre-goers when he presented Centlivre's 1752 comedy, *The Wonder! Woman Keeps a Secret*. It met "with mingled feelings of contempt and indignation" over its "lewd immorality, . . . coarse and vulgar allusions, and indecent expressions." Only "the good nature of the audience," especially the ladies, prevented them from getting up and leaving. Worse, Jones had not, as his contract stipulated, submitted this script in advance for approval by the theater owners. It was hoped this would not happen again.[4]

Jones also apparently mismanaged his actors. He and John Vaughan clashed on a regular basis. Sophia Turner chafed at Jones's highhanded apportionment of roles. His "disposition to control the stage" caused "that excellent actress" to quit the stage, which the *Mississippi Republican* asserted the public would not tolerate. She and Jones reached a temporary détente, but the winter would bring further conflict. Then, in mid-December, Cargill, Lucas, and Hanna abruptly quit and left for Nashville, where Ludlow was assembling a new company.[5]

~~~~~~~~~~

In January 1819 the first significant financial crisis of the embryonic United States hit frontier theatre hard. The bottom fell out of the land boom at the same time that European markets opted to purchase cotton from India rather than from the American South, on top of an overexpansion of credit following the War of 1812. Now, credit was unobtainable. Frontier farmers and planters, like newly unemployed craftsmen and tradesmen in urban areas, had no discretionary funds for anything as frivolous as entertainment.

In Frankfort, Samuel Drake Sr., atypically unaware of his bad timing, that winter bought for renovation the theater at Broadway and St. Clair Street that Luke Usher had opened in 1812. Prior to opening his season in early December 1818, he expanded its gallery and pit and added easier entrance and egress, especially to the theater's bar. From there he took his troupe to Louisville in February 1819.

Having partially renovated that city's theater on the north side of Jefferson Street between Third and Fourth streets in 1816, Drake compounded his indebtedness by purchasing it and completing its renovation. It became "a handsome three-storied building of brick," divided into a pit (still with backless benches), two tiers of thirty-two boxes, and a gallery, capable of seating about 800. A "separate entrance for ladies who are not received in society" (that is, prostitutes), who congregated in the theater's infamous third tier, created a "monstrous iniquity," according to one actress. The house was lit by chandelier of sperm oil candles. A redecorated saloon with ample fireplace provided convivial warmth for patrons between acts. Altogether it was "fitted up with a degree of taste that does honor to its manager."[6]

Drake opened this newly renovated theater on March 1, 1819. Two nights later, *Macbeth* received positive notices and a hearty ovation. Palmer Fisher and Belinda Groshon (despite a severe cold) in the leads again reaped the most praise, as they would for weeks. As Othello and in other roles, Fisher displayed "an unusual degree of excellence," and "natural, chaste" acting." Mrs. Groshon, "the most finished actress who had ever trod our stage," both "pleased and amused. . . . We were in raptures." *Richard III* on March 27, though, fell short, with Fisher in the title role cited for straying from the text and Groshon for enacting a "frigid" Lady Anne. As for the others, Sam Jr. was "an actor of no ordinary merit"; Mrs. Lewis in farces was "a rich feast of wit"; Julia Drake, nineteen and increasingly featured, showed "correctness and elegance. . . . The hold she has on our hearts cannot be loosened"; William Jones's old men were noteworthy; and in comic roles Aleck Drake "unquestionably deserved a high and honorable stand."[7]

By this time Drake had built up enough financial capital and goodwill to push through the Panic of 1819 in Louisville, presenting forty productions in twenty-two nights, all lavishly staged. (One visitor was stunned to see real food served on stage, with "the popping of real corks and the gurgle of real wine audible through the house.") In Louisville, Drake added three more actors: James Otto Lewis, twenty, new to the West; Plummer, back from Ludlow; and an amateur named Heran, all of whom became utility players, granted only minor roles. The company's repertoire remained that of Lexington and Frankfort, with the usual benefits, closing on June 10.[8]

The company that Cargill, Lucas, and Hanna had left Natchez for was assembled in fall 1818 in Nashville by Noah Ludlow and Alexander Cummins, who paid twenty dollars for a license to perform there. About half were amateurs Ludlow pulled from the Eaton-Houston troupe he had worked with over the summer, but a few were professionals, to carry leads. Their performance in Nashville of *King Henry IV* on December 15 was cast with William Jones (from Drake's company) as Falstaff to the Hotspur of John Vos (down from St. Louis), Cargill as King Henry, Ludlow as Poins, Julia Jones as Mistress Quickly, and Mary Ludlow (in breeches) as Prince John. Minor roles in it and the afterpiece, *Sprigs of Laurel*, were covered by amateurs named Young, Addison, George W. Frethy (formerly a Pittsburgh tailor), John C. Finlay (a peg-leg war veteran and popular singer), Peter Flanagan (an Irishman who converted any role into an Irish character), George Willis, a fifteen-year-old orphan named Clark, and a Miss Macaffrey.[9]

Soon after forming this company, Ludlow and Cummins took it in early 1819 to Huntsville, Alabama Territory. Founded in 1805, Huntsville in 1811 had become the territory's first incorporated town, with over one thousand citizens. It would become the capital once statehood was granted in December. Ludlow and Cummins converted a room over a confectioner's shop into a makeshift theater. But the financial panic had hit Alabama cotton growers especially hard, and the company barely broke even, forcing them within ten weeks to retrace their steps to Nashville.

But by the time they opened there, any experienced players had left, leaving Ludlow and Cummins with only amateurs. Still, they persevered, opening in an old frame salt warehouse on Market Street on March 16, 1819, with Kenney's *Turn Out!* and *Day After the Wedding*, acting on a bare raised platform. In early May, though, they closed up shop until fall, and a disheartened Ludlow considered other careers.

Without Cargill, Hanna, or Lucas, West India Jones forged on in Natchez with his remaining actors. They opened on January 2, 1819, with *Pizarro* and

Day After the Wedding. To Jones's good fortune, two highly capable leading players arrived a week later. Aaron J. Phillips and Sophia Turner, both attempting to make a go of it as visiting stars, quickly established themselves, beginning as Young Norval and Lady Randolph in *Douglas* on January 19. Light comedian and scenic artist James Cornell came on in April.[10]

But the détente of last fall between Sophia and Jones almost immediately deteriorated. Although Jones granted Phillips a star's benefit—on February 6 in *Barbarossa* and *Love-à-la-Mode*—he denied one to Sophia, regarding her as just another member of the company. She took her case to the public via newspapers notices, decrying the injustice. Jones grudgingly provided a date and the theater for her benefit (February 25), but withheld the company's support, forcing her to deliver an evening of recitations. This severed all communication between her and Jones, and she and Phillips immediately left to try their luck in New Orleans. The Vaughan-Jones dispute continued to simmer as well, but Vaughan stayed and got his benefit, playing the title role in *Blue-beard* on the last night of the season, April 27.

The New Orleans to which Sophia and Phillips journeyed had not seen professional theatre for two years, since Ludlow's departure. The city's population by 1819 of nearly twenty-seven thousand, with both a growing English-speaking aristocracy and a somewhat lowbrow "American Quarter" above Canal Street, supported theatre despite the ongoing financial panic.

There, the indomitable William Turner set out to assemble a new company for the St. Philip Street Theatre. They were a barebones group: Hanna and Cargill from Ludlow, Adams from Jones, Douvillier from the city's amateur thespians and briefly, Ludlow, and a Mr. Melville and a Mrs. Fitzallen, both apparently amateurs. Sophia opened their first night, March 8, 1819, with a defense of theatre, followed by Arthur Murphy's *Three Weeks After Marriage* and a recitation entitled "Ode to Jackson's Victory in New Orleans." They were received with "infinite pleasure." Phillips—having apparently conquered his fear of the city's pestilence—tried performing solo, presenting an evening of recitations on March 10 in the brand-new Orléans Ballroom. But he soon joined the Turners, playing leads opposite Sophia at the St. Philip Street Theatre in such pieces as *The Revenge, Venice Preserved,* and *Adelgitha.*[11]

By the end of April, Turner and Phillips realized the troupe was insufficient for their scripts and made separate plans to recruit additional professionals. Phillips again left for New York, promising to return with or without new actors. Turner departed for Liverpool, "for the express purpose of procuring a full company." In their absence the company kept together until May 17, then folded. Turner must have been unsuccessful in his recruitment (if indeed he actually went), for—as in all of his other cities—he never returned to management in New Orleans. (He did appear briefly without Sophia in New Orleans in January 1820 and in Natchez in March with Phillips, then followed her east.)[12]

Since the St. Louis theater for which Vos and the Turners had laid the groundwork in May 1818 had not materialized, Vos now settled for the use of a small frame building the Thespian Society had erected. It stood on the west side of Main Street between Olive and Locust streets (like the earlier courthouse theater site under the Gateway Arch today). Seating six hundred, it provided class separation with boxes and a broad pit, with a thirty-foot stage. Vos opened it on February 1, 1819, with *She Stoops to Conquer* and *The Village Lawyer.* Subsequent productions included *The Revenge, The Mountaineers, Douglas,* and *Raising the Wind.*

Vos advertised aggressively in St. Louis and other cities for actors, but kept his day job of painting parlors, drawing rooms, and coaches. After June, though, no evidence remains of any productions there for the rest of the year, the dearth of which prompted Vos to offer his acting talent elsewhere. A benefit for Mrs. Vos (no longer acting under the name Scotland Greer) on February 5, 1820, announced as being "for the relief of a distressed family," was at first postponed due to inclement weather and insufficient ticket sales.[13]

In the meantime, West India Jones attempted to branch out from Natchez, taking his small company forty miles northeast to Port Gibson, Mississippi, on Bayou Pierre. It was an unlikely, unreceptive town, consisting of a handful of houses, stores, taverns, a courthouse, and a jail. One traveler in 1808 called it "perhaps the most dissolute as well as the most thriving port of the territory." Its sole newspaper warned Jones to "select such plays as will not offend the moral sense and wound the delicacy of his audience," and to avoid scripts that were "abominably obscene" or "cannot be introduced without a great deal of pruning [censoring]." Even Shakespeare's plays "we should be tempted to cast . . . from us with disgust."[14]

Jones's opening bill on May 15, 1819, was suitably innocuous: *John Bull* and *How to Die for Love.* He and Mrs. DeGrushe (the widow of Thomas Morgan) carried most leads, but their performances only occurred about once a month. These included the presumably acceptable *Stranger, Venice Preserved,* and *Honey Moon.* Jones enlarged his company in fall with the return of Hanna with a new wife—heavy, stout, and specializing in housewives—and teenaged stepdaughter, Miss Amelia Seymour. Also, John Vos came down from St. Louis for a few weeks in leading roles. And although active amateur theatricals would not appear in Port Gibson until 1823, a handful appeared in Jones's casts. He was apparently unsuccessful there, for he left for Natchez in December, never to return to Port Gibson.

~~~~~~~~~~

As if there weren't enough struggling, competing actor-managers on the frontier, the summer of 1819 saw the formation of yet another managerial partnership. Joshua Collins, after several years with the Turners, and William Jones, from Drake and Ludlow, reunited for the first time since their abortive management in Lexington in late 1812. Their plan, honed from watching the vicissitudes of those other managers, was to create a new circuit, to consist of Pittsburgh, Lexington, and Cincinnati.

Pittsburgh had seen only rare performances by amateurs—variously the Thespian Society and the Dramatic Benevolent Society—in the great room above the courthouse, since the departure of Entwistle and Lewis in 1817. Religious opposition still flared there, but the *Pittsburgh Gazette* encouraged theatre, which "has a tendency to mingle us harmoniously together, to soften manners, [and] to relax the brow of care." Indeed, "Nothing is better calculated for the purpose than a well-regulated stage."[15]

Lexington was less promising. In March 1818 Luke Usher had been forced to mortgage his theater, and a year later a fire had destroyed his tavern. Then, for four months he sought in vain—as far afield as Baltimore and New York—for a manager for the theater despite investing $2,000 in its improvements, upping its capacity to seven hundred. Even Drake shunned its management, knowing there would be scant audiences. As the *Kentucky Gazette* pointed out, "the community suffer from the pressure of the times. . . . Confidence is immeasurably destroyed and credit must soon be at an end." Factories lay idle, and "property is exceedingly depressed."[16]

Hence, putting Pittsburg and Lexington on hold, Collins and Jones focused first on Cincinnati. That bustling manufacturing city had swelled with postwar immigrants, many of whom built "elegant mansions, live in style, and diffuse an air of business, life and activity all around them." It boasted a Main Street comparable to that of "the best of many of the eastern cities." Still, it lacked a permanent theater and had been bereft of performances since the Turners left in late 1817. Aleck Drake, on behalf of his father, had tried in spring 1819, when he met with Cincinnati civic leaders. Seeking shareholders at $150 a share, he pledged to "maintain high standards of theatre production, provide for regular performances by his organized companies," and—a crucial proviso—to "abstemiously preserve the purity and morality of the stage." But he had failed to generate sufficient interest.[17]

Collins and Jones thought they had a better plan, although it was complex. Capitalizing on Drake's groundwork, they began selling twenty shares at $150 each, keeping half for themselves, for the construction of a new theater on the south side of Columbia (later Second) Street between Main and Sycamore streets (the site of the old Shellbark Theatre). If the shares sold were insufficient for its total cost of $5,000, mortgage holders Thomas D. and Sally Carneal agreed to cover the rest. They in turn would lease the theater and the ground under it to civic leaders and amateur thespians Nicholas Longworth and Peyton S. Symmes for ninety-nine years at $300 a year. Longworth and Symmes in turn would lease it to Collins and Jones at the same rate. Each shareholder received one box-seat season ticket, or (at his choice) $15 annually as interest on his investment.[18]

Any profits (a dubious consideration) would to go to Collins and Jones, who agreed to oversee the laying of its foundation in September and to provide a "company of comedians." They succeeded in recruiting a fairly experienced group. From Drake came Henry Lewis, Belinda Groshon, Mrs. Mongin, and Heran; from Ludlow came Austin Cargill (to play heavies); and from West India Jones came Lucas. Mr. Groshon would act as company treasurer. Collins and Jones themselves would carry leads opposite Julia Jones (especially in "genteel comedy") or Mrs. Groshon. The company added local amateurs as necessary, sometimes a dozen or more, with the most promising being young Fred Henderson (who oddly played old men, notably Peter Teazle in *School for Scandal*).[19]

Until the theater was finished (which would not be until March 1820), they rehearsed and performed nearby in the ballroom of the Cincinnati Hotel and the second story of a tobacco warehouse owned by fellow Masons (a probable key to their success) at the corner of Columbia and Walnut streets. Their opening bill on June 21, 1819, of *Douglas* and *Fortune's Frolic* was well received. Belinda Groshon as Lady Randolph gave a "chaste and impressive performance," showing "great dignity and feeling." Her chief assets were her "fine, commanding person," her "voice of unusual power and flexibility," and her "graceful deportment and an elegance of gesture." For five weeks, she and Collins enacted leads in a predictable repertoire, including *Isabella, Venice Preserved, Soldier's Daughter, She Stoops to Conquer, The Stranger,* and *The Spoiled Child,* the last two comprising their final bill on July 24. Critical reception was good, especially for Collins, William and Julia Jones, Belinda Groshon, and Mrs. Mongin.[20]

In August, Collins and Jones took the troupe across the river to Lexington, where they traded off with Drake the use (but not management) of Usher's theater, providing *Macbeth, Pizarro,* and *Stranger* among others. They would perform intermittently there through February 1820, with managerial forays to Cincinnati to check on the progress of their theater. (While the Collins-Jones company was in Lexington in August, an itinerant family of actors under patriarch William Blanchard set up shop in Cincinnati in Dawson's schoolroom on Water Street. This undistinguished troupe, consisting of Blanchard, C. Blanchard, Miss J. Blanchard, and B. Blanchard [age six], plus a Mr. Howard and a Mr. Frankland, performed comedies such as *The Purse* and *The Village Lawyer.*)

Drake, beginning in early September, sought to attract Lexington audiences by merging his troupe with circus impresario James West's "Equestrian Melodramatic Company," which had performed in New York, Pittsburgh, and Cincinnati 1817–18. Now, they staged West's signature piece, *Timour the Tartar,* with Fisher in the tyrannical title role, Mrs. West as the duplicitous Zorilda, and Julia Drake as the lovestruck Selima. All were deemed commendable, but the production's most celebrated feature for Kentuckians was the use of live horses onstage, which met with "universal satisfaction."[21]

In late September this combined company left Lexington to Collins and Jones and moved on to Louisville, where they switched to comedy. A prominent piece was Inchbald's *Wives as They Were and Maids as They Are,* a biting satire on the condition and treatment of women in Georgian society. A visiting Philadelphian caught one performance and regretted the thin audience, "owing to the pressure of the times." He thought Drake and Groshon "were fine," but "more than one of the actors was unfeeling, unmeaning, made of wood and more like a gate-post than an animated being."[22]

From then on, Drake dropped Lexington from his circuit except for short visits, and it quickly declined as a center of theatre, with Louisville ascendant. The coup de grâce for Usher, still seeking a manager for his theater, came in November when his new, relocated tavern also burned down. His era had ended, and he relinquished the state to Drake. Still, as Durang notes, Usher "may claim the honor of being the first regular pioneer in the [theatre of the] great valley of the west."[23]

~~~~~~~~~~

In Nashville, Noah Ludlow, newly a father, was pursuing the study of law, ultimately in vain. The actors he had abandoned combined with local amateurs for a short summer 1819 season, adding Cargill to their ranks. Their production on July 3 of *Bunker Hill* capitalized on resurgent patriotism in the wake of the recent visit to Nashville of Revolutionary War veteran and now-president James Monroe, as well as the next day's holiday. But the effort, presenting occasional dramas and comedies, only lasted a few weeks. Similar failure came to an amateur thespian society (possibly some of the Nashvillians among them) in Clarksville, nearly fifty miles northwest of Nashville.[24]

By November, Ludlow and Cummins were determined to give it another go in Nashville or New Orleans. They realized they would need additional actors, but "the Western country was so barren of professional performers that it was next to impossible to procure any." Eastern actors, Ludlow surmised, "were afraid of the West, and still more so of the South." Cargill and vocalist Finlay returned, but the managers otherwise only attracted a handful of performers already in the West: the peripatetic John Vos from Natchez, William Jones briefly down from Lexington (likely scouting possibilities in Nashville), bringing his wife, Julia, and Lucas.[25]

They opened in Nashville in mid-November with various members carrying leads in an attractive array of productions, including *Honey Moon, Gamester, She Stoops to Conquer, Bertram,* and *School for Scandal,* with the usual farces. Critical notice was mixed. Jones impressed with "his comic powers," Lucas acted "with feeling and correctness" one night, but "did not display the passionate feelings" required on the next. Ludlow displayed "his usual merit" but in farces was guilty of mugging for cheap laughs (considered "if not indecent, at least improper," only serving "as a commentary on the taste of . . . the audience"). Cummins, damned with faint praise, was "more correct than usual." His wife exerted too little effort ("walking though" her parts), but Vos noticeably tried too hard. Finlay "did sing, but we knew not what he sang of—we heard none of the words."[26]

The venture proved fruitless, though, and by December 10 Ludlow and Cummins announced the dissolution of their dramatic copartnership. In mid-January 1820 the Cumminses left with Jones for Lexington and Cincinnati, and Vos headed back to St. Louis to work with its amateur thespian society. Vos urged Ludlow to do likewise, and in February the Ludlows would board a keelboat for St. Louis, trying like the Turners to succeed in another new town.[27]

~~~~~~~~~~

By 1820 the Turner era, like Usher's, had closed. For all their peregrinations, for all their ultimately unsuccessful attempts at management, for all of Sophia's frontier stardom, they cannot be dismissed as easily as Ludlow does. They comprised the advance guard of theatrical activity on the trans-Appalachian frontier. Before the vaunted Drake and Ludlow, the Turners established a beachhead, bringing theatre to the largely unschooled, often unruly audiences there, introducing them to tragedy, melodrama, comedy, and farce. Building on the work of—and coordinating their efforts with—amateurs, visionaries like Usher, and such itinerant actors as James Douglass, John Rannie, John Vos, Thomas Morgan, Thomas Jefferson, and John Vaughan, the Turners were the first to secure a performance space and then assemble and manage a theatrical company in five cities: Cincinnati, Pittsburgh, Lexington, St. Louis, and New Orleans.

Without question, the linchpin of their efforts was Sophia's acting, a loss lamented after her departure for the East by a St. Louis critic: "We must not expect to find [another] Mrs. Turner. Mrs. T. had not her superior as an actress in the United States." (Sophia did maintain a successful career for another fifteen years in Albany, New York, and Philadelphia acting "old women" and "the high-bred dames of comedy" and "matrons of the serious drama.")[28] The curtain would now rise on the Caldwell-Ludlow era, with the Drakes still playing a major role.

6

ENTER CALDWELL

(1820)

BATTLING THE RESIDUAL EFFECTS of the Panic of 1819, frontier towns and their theatre troupes alike struggled through 1820. Managers aggressively swapped actors and venues in an effort to establish a permanent base for a frontier circuit. A new, energetic competitor made it tougher for those already performing there.

He was James H. Caldwell, twenty-seven, who brought to New Orleans at the close of 1819 an accomplished, experienced company he had assembled on the East Coast. Born in Manchester, England, he had early gained recognition for acting light comedy there and in Bristol, Bath, Dublin, and Liverpool. In Liverpool, he had acted with Samuel Drake, supporting the renowned Thomas Abthorpe Cooper, who would become the first international celebrity to perform on the American frontier, at Caldwell's behest.

Immigrating to the United States in 1816 under the aegis of Charleston manager Joseph George Holman, Caldwell quickly gained a following in the Carolinas and Virginia. He began his managerial career at age twenty-four in Washington, DC, and Alexandria, Virginia, comanaging with James Entwistle following Entwistle's unsuccessful Pittsburgh venture. Entering the larger market of Philadelphia, they merged with Victor Pépin's Equestrian Company, an ultimately unsuccessful undertaking. "Entwistle as a comedian was very clever," recalled Durang, "but confined in range. His forte being principally country boys, he was deficient in force, in variety, where all fell on his exertions [that is, in leads]. Messrs. Caldwell and Entwistle did not move in harmony, even before they joined Pépin in management."[1]

In November 1819 Caldwell married aristocratic young widow Maria Carter Hall Wormeley of Fredericksburg, Virginia, but within days left her behind (as he would consistently do) to embark with his American Company on the schooner *Betsey* for New Orleans. After a turbulent thirty-four-day journey, they arrived downriver from the Crescent City (due to the captain's fear of yellow fever) and had to slog miles to their hotel. The actors, too, were fearful—displaying "an almost universal expression of horror"—but Caldwell's threat of leaving them behind without a job persuaded them.[2]

They arrived in a theatrical vacuum in a burgeoning, cosmopolitan city of over twenty-seven thousand. The last performances in New Orleans had been *The Mayor of Garratt* and *Raising the Wind* by an amateur troupe in August in the St. Philip Street Theatre. Caldwell leased that rundown venue, which he renamed the American Theatre, St. Philip Street, for three years. He opened on January 7, 1820, with *Honey Moon* and *The Three and the Deuce,* carrying the lead in both, earning $700 from a capacity crowd. The next night, his production of *Laugh When You Can* and *Rosina* faced competition from the opening night of Aaron Phillips's meager company three blocks away.

Phillips had returned to New Orleans from New York in December 1819 with a handful of actors to perform in the Théâtre d'Orléans on Orleans Street between Royal and Bourbon streets. It had been lavishly rebuilt after the fire of 1816 and reopened on November 27, 1819. Managed by another Saint-Domingue émigré and erstwhile colleague of Louis Tabary, Frenchman John Davis, it was intended primarily as a venue for opera and for French theatre, with two tiers of boxes, an elaborate ballroom, and adjoining supper room. Phillips agreed to share it, with Davis's troupe performing on Tuesdays, Thursdays, and Sundays, and Phillips's the other four nights.

Phillips did all the right things. He took out ads reminding potential patrons that he was American-born, offering varied levels of subscriptions for forty productions depending on seat preference and frequency of attendance. Having added a few Pittsburgh actors, his company consisted of James Entwistle (Caldwell's erstwhile partner), Mr. and Mrs. Monier, Charles Carpender, William Turner, William H. Benton, W. C. Drummond, Hunter, Abercrombie, and Mrs. Smith. Otherwise, he had to rely on amateurs.[3]

He announced his opening for January 7, 1820, the same night as Caldwell's, with *Venice Preserved,* featuring Carpender as Pierre and a young actor named Bartow as Jaffier, but Carpender's illness forced its cancellation. Phillips thus opened on January 8 with *The Turnpike Gate* with Entwistle as Crack, followed within a week by *Douglas, The Review, Point of Honor,* and *Love-à-la-Mode.*[4]

But Caldwell held the upper hand, being able to perform six nights a week with a much stronger company. He promptly dished up an impressive array of productions, including *Bertram, Richard III, Belle's Stratagem, Village Lawyer, West Indian, She Stoops to Conquer, Mountaineers, Spoiled Child,* and *Catharine and Petruchio* (in which, the *Louisiana Gazette* asserted, "no man in America could have played Petruchio better than Mr. Caldwell").[5]

That paper neglected Phillips entirely while promoting Caldwell, whose comedies and farces "went off well," but his "chief excellence is in tragedy." Joseph Hutton (formerly with Entwistle in Pittsburgh) as Richard III displayed the correct look and walk, but his voice was weak, as was his ability "to display the master passions of the soul." Worse, he was somewhat incorrect in his line readings. The paper hoped Caldwell "will give us no more tragedies until all his corps are well prepared," but looked forward to the *Hamlet* in preparation with the manager himself in the title role.[6]

Unable to gain traction against Caldwell, Phillips admitted on January 14 that his company "have not met as he warmly anticipated with [audiences'] decided approbation." He was thus reducing prices of admission despite "having incurred a very heavy expense in collecting and transporting" them to New Orleans. He announced the following night's productions of *Point of Honor* and *Love-à-la-Mode.*[7]

But five days later, unable to compete against the Caldwell juggernaut, Phillips folded. Jettisoning his less-talented players, he merged the rest with Caldwell's troupe. Their sizable combined company, the strongest yet fielded on the frontier, could competently enact the demands of any script. It included several couples (which promoted stability): Mr. and Mrs. William Anderson, Mr. and Mrs. Jackson Gray (she née Trajatta), Mr. and Mrs. Richard Russell, Mr. and Mrs. Thomas Price, Mr. and Mrs. Joseph Hutton. The others were Entwistle, Bartow, Boyle, Petrie, Carr, Jackson, Samuel Emberton, Thomas Fielding, Samuel Jones, Richard Jones (also house adapter of French comedies), vocalist Arthur Keene, Eliza Tilden,

Mrs. H. A. Williams, Master William McCafferty, and dance master Goll, plus Caldwell and Phillips. Caldwell sent a few excess actors—including Mr. and Mrs. Monier and Hunter—to explore possibilities in Alabama.

Caldwell granted Phillips a benefit on January 21 to ease his losses from the Théâtre d'Orléans, of *Romeo and Juliet* (Phillips and Mrs. Williams, with Caldwell as Mercutio). On January 26 Caldwell yielded the role of Hamlet to young Bartow, who three nights later distinguished himself as Young Norval in *Douglas* before a disappointingly small audience.

Caldwell arranged with Bernardo Coquet, the owner of the Théâtre d'Orléans, to lease that venue for four nights a week; he would revert to the St. Philip on the other two nights when French players were using the Orleans. Several "public spirited individuals" came forward to indemnify Coquet against possible losses, but Caldwell reassured him by signing a three-year lease, guaranteeing Coquet $100 a night plus fees for lighting.

He opened there on February 14 with *Honey Moon* and *Three and the Deuce*. For the next two months, he produced an array of titles equal to anything in the East, including *Othello, School for Scandal, Macbeth, Belle's Stratagem, Pizarro* (he as Rolla), *The Stranger, The Rivals, The Apostate, Henry IV, As You Like It, The Gamester,* and *Hunter of the Alps,* which closed the season on April 19. Even after paying Coquet and himself each $100 a night and purchasing return passage to Virginia for all of his company, Caldwell netted $1,740 for the New Orleans season, which left him satisfied: "Fame made me richer whether I was or not, and [my] actors had increased confidence."[8]

The mini-company which Caldwell sent to Mobile, Alabama, set up operations in an old hospital on Dauphin Street, which they fitted out "in a very neat and commodious manner." This saltwater port of fewer than nine hundred residents was poised to grow rapidly (by 1822 its population would top twenty-eight hundred) on the strength of revitalized international cotton trade. Caldwell's actors opened on January 31, 1820, with *She Stoops to Conquer* and *The Review,* providing a "highly respectable audience" with the town's first professional theatre—despite Ludlow's later claim of having done so. For two months laughter and applause greeted the troupe's generally lighthearted fare. They were adjudged good, with Hunter a standout, but a few "would be much improved by a greater exertion of voice, accompanied with somewhat more gestures." Caldwell had sent funds for a few subpar local musicians to accompany the actors, and the theater itself was clearly deficient, but little doubt remained that "the present company will prove themselves worthy of patronage." However, Caldwell must have then forsaken them, for they did not return, and dispersed.[9]

In late winter 1820 Phillips, too, departed New Orleans, taking his actors that Caldwell could not accommodate. Their destination was Natchez, where West India Jones had been struggling since January 4 to establish some theatrical permanence in the midst of a severe yellow fever infestation, which had delayed his opening from fall 1819. He had revamped the theater, installing separate pit and boxes (to be offered at public auction), so that patrons would no longer be forced to share the same benches. He also boasted a twenty-foot "coffee room and bar," and new scenery by James Cornell.[10]

No longer a commonwealth, Jones's company consisted of stage manager John Vaughan (still feuding with Jones, however) and his wife, Cornell, Stuart, Baker, Mrs. Hanna and her daughter Amelia Seymour (Mr. Hanna being in St. Louis), Mrs. DeGrushe, and a few amateurs from the Natchez Theatrical Association, which still owned the theater. Additional actors were "hourly expected." Jones opened the season with an address alluding to the epidemic and the theater's renovation, followed by *Lovers' Vows* and *The Sleep Walker.* For two months he provided a repertoire heavy on tragedies, including *Adelgitha, Bertram, Douglas, George Barnwell,* and *Pizarro,* with two benefits for himself along the way.[11]

In *Pizarro,* Jones awarded the role of Cora to Mrs. DeGrushe after Mrs. Vaughan was unable to con the part on two days' notice and he repeatedly refused to grant her an extra day. Jones also failed to adequately reimburse Vaughan for his expenditures as stage manager for scenery and costumes. All of this further inflamed Vaughan's resentment, resulting in Vaughan's public notice referencing *Othello:* "one can smile and still be a villain." Still, the Vaughans remained.[12]

In early March, Phillips arrived with his reinforcements: Thomas and Eliza Price, Richard Jones (also as scenic artist and dramatist), Boyle, Carr (these two primarily as vocalists), William F. Norton (also a competent musician), Samuel Emberton, William Turner (his last stage appearance), and Mrs. Yates.

Phillips took on leading roles, including Richard III and Reuben Glenroy in *Town and Country*. Mrs. Price shone in comedic leads, including Rosalie Somers in *Town and Country*, in which she displayed "uncommon beauty of face" and "an easy, modest, winning manner," although her voice was sometimes inaudible. Her husband, despite a noticeable Irish brogue, effectively portrayed comic supporting roles. The multitalented Richard Jones excelled in comedic leads, including Tony Lumpkin in *She Stoops to Conquer* and Patrick in *Poor Soldier*. Emberton specialized in "testy, gouty or impatient old men."[13]

The company performed three times a week, with an adventurous repertoire of at least thirty-five different productions ranging from tragedy (for example, *Henry IV*, Payne's *Brutus*, a reprise of *Pizarro* with amateurs in the three leading roles) to epic drama (such as *Alexander the Great*, with William Anderson, on leave from Caldwell to tour as a guest star, in the title role), to lyrical romance (for example, *Lady of the Lake*), to pantomime (such as *Don Juan*), to comedy (for example, Garrick's *Country Girl*, Colman's *Poor Gentleman*), to farce (such as the ineluctable *Catharine and Petruchio*).[14]

Nearly all met with enthusiastic support from audience and newspaper correspondents, one of whom claimed to have attended the theater in Natchez "regularly for the past eight years" (only possible if one counts the irregular amateur performances that far back). A visitor expressed his delight that "a country, which but a few short years ago was only a forest, the haunt of beasts of prey, is now become the seat of learning and polite amusements," with over twenty-one hundred inhabitants. The only quibbling resulted from a few actors not being perfect in their lines—understandable in a repertoire this varied and so new to many of them.[15]

But the bane of so many nineteenth-century managers, fire, struck on April 19, destroying the Natchez Theatre. But only three nights later Jones resumed performances in a new, temporary (unidentified) venue, with *Gamester* and *Ella Rosenberg*. Benefits began with Vaughan's on April 27. The *Mississippi Free Trader* urged attendance for *Iron Chest* and *The Review* by this "respectable man, a virtuous and an honest man, and a good actor." Unfortunately, though, "the unparalleled pressure of the period" (and possibly the constraints of the substituted venue) caused attendance to dwindle, even for yet another benefit for Jones on May 11. The season closed on June 20 with a benefit for Mrs. DeGrushe of *Poor Gentleman* and *Poor Soldier* by the Natchez Thespians. To garner every cent, the company performed two nights of songs and recitations, June 30 and July 17, at Parker's Hotel. The season overall had been grossly unproductive, yet Jones vowed to return in fall.[16]

<hr />

When Mr. and Mrs. Ludlow boarded their keelboat for St. Louis in February 1820 after their failed venture in Nashville, they had received additional encouragement from John Vos. The St. Louis Thespians' six-hundred-seat frame theater on Main Street, Vos wrote, along with its scenery, "could be had for a mere nominal sum if successful, or nothing if otherwise." The only thing that gave Ludlow pause was the prevalence in that city of Canadian French residents who "could not appreciate the English drama."[17]

His journey upriver was fraught. Switching in frustration to a steamboat, the Ludlows arrived in St. Louis in the first week of March 1820, and thought their chances unpromising. Still, Ludlow agreed to partner with Vos, and they put word out seeking actors, with scant results. Ludlow already knew, and could count on, Austin Cargill, George Frethy, and Mr. Young. A few others, some of whom joined in St. Louis, were stagestruck amateurs hoping to achieve professional status: singer-actor King, men named Roberts and Tull and young Miss Macaffrey. St. Louis Thespians also provided proficient scene painter John H. Dauberman.[18]

Ludlow and Vos plunged into the usual problems of publicizing their venture and gaining civic approval. "A Friend of the Drama" reassured the citizenry that Ludlow "stands fair as a general performer and excels in genteel comedy and during the time he resided in Nashville he was generally beliked and sustained the character of a gentleman." The contributor was "not acquainted with the performers in the employ of Messrs. Vos & Ludlow, but have been informed that the young men are not addicted to habits of dissipation." Ludlow and Vos reminded readers that they had gone to considerable trouble and expense to inaugurate their season, which would feature a "judicious selection of pieces," not one of which "shall be in any way indelicate or improper."[19]

A major problem was that the theater could not be adequately heated, resulting in poor attendance. From their March 9 opening, Ludlow and Vos struggled with old-fashioned stoves, which "although kept red-hot nearly all the time," failed to radiate far enough. That night's bill was Centlivre's *Busy Body* with Mary Ludlow and Hanna in the leads and the Voses as the secondary lovers, and *The Poor Soldier* with Cargill as the titular Patrick and Ludlow as his comic sidekick Darby. "A Friend of the Drama" deemed the evening "an intellectual repast," bound to have "wonderful effects on society." For the most part, there was "nothing that can injure the delicacy of the female ear," prompting hope that soon "we shall see the boxes filled with them." Still, a few mildly suggestive moments caused it "to be wished that a few sentences had been erased," as there were "persons standing with their mouths open, ready to cry down the establishment." "Friend" reassured anyone who had kept away lest the audience be rowdy, that such had not occurred.[20]

But other ills beset Ludlow and Vos. Mary Ludlow fainted onstage during her performance as Angela in *Castle Spectre* on March 18 and fell ill for a week. The same week, Samuel Drake and his Kentucky Company of Comedians descended on St. Louis, providing keen competition. After a brief engagement in Frankfort in mid-February which had included a benefit for the victims of a recent fire in Savannah (which raised over $200), Drake was looking for new territory. Now, in St. Louis, he set up in the (warmer) ballroom of Bennett's City Hotel on the corner of Third and Vine streets. In addition to his family, he brought James Douglass, James O. Lewis, Henry Lewis, Mr. and Mrs. Alexander Palmer Fisher and their daughter Anna, Mrs. Lewis, Mrs. Mongin, and a young, inexperienced Miss McBride.[21]

Drake opened "for a few nights" on March 22 with Colman's *The Jealous Wife* and *The Adopted Child*. Ludlow and Vos immediately realized that St. Louis "could not afford support for two companies; one, therefore, must be crowded to the wall, and it did not take long to determine which it should be." Ludlow acknowledged Drake's superiority and the better heat in the ballroom. He and Vos approached Drake to discuss combining their troupes, and all came to an agreement by March 25. The merger was effected, the whole to be under Drake's management. To encourage attendance, the *St. Louis Enquirer* commended "the private character and personal deportment of the company." Notably, "The females attached to the corps all are young and respectable." Furthermore, it was questionable "whether there is a stage in the United States that can boast of a constellation of female beauty superior to that of St. Louis." Julia Drake, now twenty, contributed to this image, having become "a very clever actress, and very beautiful."[22]

By necessity, some members of Ludlow and Vos's company had to be jettisoned, including all of the amateurs. Drake agreed to accept only Vos, Cargill, Mr. and Mrs. Hanna, and Amelia Seymour (soon to wed Cargill). Vos fought for the inclusion of his wife, but Drake refused. Ludlow himself would replace Henry Lewis, who left for England, as low comedian. "Walking Gentleman" James O. Lewis, described by Ludlow as "a wild, rackety young man [21], good-looking and spirited," hedged his bets, advertising his services as engraver and printer "during his stay in St. Louis," a career that would bring him greater fame than acting. Someone, disgruntled, broke into Ludlow and Vos's theater on March 27 and slashed their scenery to shreds.[23]

For the first few weeks the new company meshed well, presenting such sure-fire comedies as *She Stoops to Conquer, School for Scandal,* and Morton's *Cure for the Heartache.* "Dramaticus" of the *Enquirer* pronounced himself "much amused." He compared the acting favorably to "the best theatres in Europe and America," excepting Fisher, who exhibited an "ungraceful stoop" among affected "British" mannerisms, and Aleck Drake, who changed some of his lines in *Rival Soldier* "when there is nothing indecorous" in them, and overdid the drunkenness of his character, "trying the patience of the audience." Local contributor "Melpomene" lavished praise on Ludlow, Sam Jr., Mrs. Fisher, James O. Lewis, and Julia Drake, who was "all we can wish for."[24]

As the weather warmed, the new company moved from the ballroom to the theater. At this point the company began to include melodrama and tragedy, including *Foundling of the Forest, Road to Ruin, Iron Chest, Othello,*

King Lear, and *Douglas.* Benefits began on April 17 with Julia Drake's, followed by Cargill's, he being hailed as "a comedian of no mean merit [who] deserves a better fate than has attended him lately." The *Enquirer* urged the awarding of larger roles to Cargill, rather than "some who are put over his head." Mary Ludlow's benefit on May 15 ended the season. On April 27 the civic leaders of St. Louis were inspired enough by what they had seen to initiate plans for a new theater. But this never came to pass, likely another casualty of the Panic of 1819, to which Ludlow attributes the falling off of revenue: "A more unfavorable time than the year 1819–20 for the commencement of any new business venture in St. Louis has not occurred" since the town's founding in 1764.[25]

Drake then took the company to Vincennes, Indiana, for a short summer season, leaving Ludlow and Vos at a critical juncture. Ludlow was irate over Drake's miscasting of his wife, and Vos was equally put out over Drake's refusal to include *his* wife in the company at all. Both couples remained in St. Louis to continue to try their luck, as did James O. Lewis, who like Ludlow had some unspecified "difficulty with Mr. Drake."[26]

~~~~~~~~

The Blanchard company, which had filled in for the Collins-Jones company in Cincinnati in August, appeared in mid-January 1820 in Chillicothe, the first capital of Ohio, then returned to Cincinnati the next month. In late May they performed briefly in Cleveland, where the only theatrical activity had been recitations in November 1818 by the Theatre Royal (unknown actors, likely amateurs) in the Shakespeare Gallery. Blanchard's troupe, the first professionals in Cleveland, performed nightly for a week in Mowrey's Tavern, including *The Purse* and *Mountaineers.* They then disappeared from the frontier, and no other professionals appeared in Cleveland for seven years.

~~~~~~~~

Collins and Jones, still in Lexington in January 1820, had acquired more actors: James M. Scott, twenty-one, a brawny six-foot-plus native of Connecticut who had walked to Pittsburgh in 1818 to act with amateurs there, later known as "Long Tom Coffin" for his memorable role in *The Pilot;* a

Mr. Garner (also an accomplished vocalist); Mr. and Mrs. Alexander Cummins (from Ludlow, he for farce, she for tragedy); and a Mr. Green and a Mrs. Hoffman, possibly amateurs.[27]

They opened on February 10, 1820, with *Poor Soldier* and *Blue Devils* and proceeded to act in Lexington on Tuesdays, Thursdays, and Saturdays through February 25 (a shared benefit for Jones and Belinda Groshon). Their repertoire was limited to standards, including *Isabella, Wives as They Were, Fortune's Frolic, The Review, Soldier's Daughter,* and (by now one of the most frequently performed comedies on the frontier) *Honey Moon,* in which the young, promising Scott enacted Duke Aranza, closing the engagement on February 25.

A week later they crossed back to Cincinnati, greeting their new theater. Hailed as "the best structure of the kind in the western country this side of New Orleans," the new brick Columbia Street Theatre would be a "structure of neatness and elegance." At forty feet wide and ninety-two feet deep, to be fronted by a twelve-foot Ionic portico (not yet completed), it seated (variously) five hundred to seven hundred in an ample pit, two tiers of boxes, and a gallery. It also housed comfortable lobbies and a punch room. Its forty-by-thirty-foot stage was lit by sperm-oil footlights, illuminating a green act curtain proclaiming the company's intent "To Hold, as 'Twere, the Mirror Up to Nature." It came in below its projected cost of $5,000, financed by the sale of its $150 shares among the city's ten thousand citizens. Collins and Jones set ticket prices at fifty cents for the gallery and one dollar for box seats.[28]

Their company was a strong one, indicative of the ever-improving quality of frontier companies. Collins, although primarily a comedian, was versatile enough to pay Hamlet, Stranger, and Rolla. Jones, Scott, and Mrs. Cummins by necessity were almost equally versatile. Belinda Groshon, "of great histrionic powers and high moral worth," soon won over "the refined portion of the community" in tragic leads. Cargill enacted "heavies" (villains), Lucas was general utility, and Henderson, still the youngest of his company, still played old men. (Using his flexible facial features, he would soon become "a universal favorite throughout the West. . . . His excellent private character and suavity of manner made him a prince of good fellows.") Amateurs were hired as needed, and Mrs. Collins rarely appeared on bills. The company inaugurated the new theater on March 8, 1820, with Collins's dedicatory prologue, which announced, "Reared by your liberal aid at last behold / Our drama's dome its magic scenes unfold / And we upon this mimic world of ours / Appear with humble zeal to try our powers." Collins and Groshon then carried the leads in *Wives as They Were*, as they would for most scripts.[29]

For four months they struggled, sticking to a traditional repertoire, including *Douglas, Devil's Bridge, Apostate, Guy Mannering, Pizarro, Richard III*, and *Macbeth*. For Mrs. Groshon's benefit on May 15, she as Elvira in *Pizarro*, Lucas created gorgeous new scenery. Its Temple of the Sun featured a "richly ornamented altar, surmounted by a brilliant sun. . . . While hymns and invocations were chanted during the sacrificial ceremony on the eve of battle, a ball of fire descended to illuminate the altar."[30]

Collins and Jones elicited local support by giving an occasional lead (for example, Young Norval, opposite the Lady Randolph of Belinda Groshon) and a benefit to a Cincinnati amateur named Cooke. The only production to draw a full house was *Merchant of Venice*, with Groshon as Portia. A production of *The Battle of New Orleans* on Henderson's benefit night, May 17, promised exciting, climactic broadsword combat between Andrew Jackson (Scott) and Sir Edward Packham, but drew only moderately. Benefits for the town of Cincinnati and for the Cincinnati Female Benevolent Society failed to cover the costs of staging them. Newspapers urged patronage, but revenue was worse than it had been in Lexington, despite Collins and Jones' promise to return any profits "to the various classes from which they [had been] drained." On July 4, close to bankruptcy, with at least one shareholder offering his share at half price for cash, they closed their new theater, promising a strengthened company for the next season, and headed for Nashville (where Jones may have seen possibilities when there with Ludlow in fall 1819).[31]

~~~~~~~~~~

The poor economy forced actors and managers to pursue other options in the summer of 1820. Ludlow barnstormed neighboring villages with singer-actor King, but otherwise remained in St. Louis, trying the craft of decorative framing. Vos returned to painting and gilding. But the two men could not resist another attempt at management, and roused amateur thespians to present six nights of comedy and melodrama in the "old courthouse" in late June, and again in September and October. Among their bills were *Douglas*, *The Robbers*, *Raising the Wind*, and *Heir at Law*.

The rag ends of Aaron Phillips's troupe, augmented by amateurs, clung on in New Orleans for a few nights in mid-June in the St. Philip Street Theatre. West India Jones and the remnants of his company resorted to giving recitations and songs in towns like Port Gibson, Mississippi. Drake found no luck in Vincennes, with the additional sad result of James Douglass drowning while bathing in the Wabash River. The only positive aspect to that engagement was reconnecting with young Sol Smith, whom Drake knew from his days as a "super" in Albany.

Smith, nineteen, had in the meantime rambled through Pittsburgh, Cincinnati, and Louisville, finding work in early 1820 in Vincennes as a typesetter for the *Western Sun*. Its editor had formed an amateur thespian society, and Smith—far from the impresario he would become—joined, playing small roles. He later came to scorn their values: "I never knew any good to come from Thespian Societies; and have known them to be productive of much harm." A small measure of success with local audiences, he wrote, "begets in the performer a desire for an enlarged sphere of action," and he inevitably "applies to a [professional] manager," whereupon he "fails— takes to drink, and is ruined." Smith abhorred amateurs' ignorance of dramatic technique, coupled with the "consummate impudence with which they strut before the public." Their friends, he complained, pack the house and applaud them whether they deserve it or not.[32]

Smith had joined Drake's troupe in Vincennes, performing for six dollars a week for eight weeks, on a minuscule (eight-by-ten-foot) stage. In epics such as *Pizarro*, he found himself required to play as many as six different roles in a given script, which he found confusing, exhausting, and comical. It was all too much, and at the end of the summer he left to try his luck in Cincinnati and to dabble in the study of law.[33]

Sometime that summer Drake took his company back to Louisville, where the only extant evidence of their engagement is a production on August 19, 1820, of *Devil's Bridge* with Garner in the lead role of Count Bellino, in which "the scenery was rather elegant, and the performers generally met with the applause of a most respectable and numerous audience."[34]

〰〰〰〰〰〰

Still determined to expand their circuit, Collins and Jones, with the professional core of their company plus Dauberman for scenery, crossed back over from Cincinnati to Lexington, en route to Nashville. Since their last engagement there, Luke Usher had spent considerable effort and funds to attract visitors. In April he had added a "refreshment and recreation" garden beside his new, relocated tavern-cum-theater, advertising it and his house and stable for rent.[35]

Collins and Jones took the bait, and for a week in mid-July offered tried-and-true pieces, including *Othello*, *Apostate*, and *Stranger*, but failed to draw. As the *Lexington Public Advertiser* acknowledged, "the times are hard, a fact which has strongly impressed itself by the patronage extended to the present company. . . . The proceeds could not have covered the current expense." The company departed for Nashville, promising to return to Lexington in fall.[36]

They passed through the territory of amateur thespians in Danville, Kentucky, who were attempting a few performances (*Poor Gentleman* and *Mock Doctor*) in late July, then appropriated the audiences of amateur counterparts in Nashville (the remnants of the Houston/Eaton players) who had performed occasionally since spring and summer, as recently as August 5, primarily with comedies and farces.

Despite Ludlow's efforts to establish a theater in 1817—the converted salt house on Market Street—the town of Nashville sorely needed a permanent, dedicated building. Collins and Jones set out to rectify this, as they had in Cincinnati, when they arrived in the first week of August. By the middle of the month, they had converted a rudimentary theater built the year before by a Frenchman on the west side of Cherry Street. Seating about eight hundred in a pit and two tiers of boxes, it was sufficient for their small company. The *National Banner and Nashville Whig* supported their efforts, defending them against religious censure, since "most of the plays and farces . . . contain an excellent moral," and asserting that their acting ability "would not lose in a comparison with those of any theatre in the Union." With Collins and Belinda Groshon still carrying leads, they mounted a judicious mixture of tragedy (*Hamlet, Venice Preserved*), comedy (*School for Scandal*) and farce (*Catharine and Petruchio, Irishman in London*). Nevertheless, they drew only thin houses, a fact rued by the newspaper, which praised them all, especially the leads (although Green was chided for ranting and overacting).[37]

Their lack of patronage may have scared off Aaron Phillips and Alexander Cummins, who announced in September 1820 their intention of opening a "Minor Theatre" in Nashville on Spring Street, between Market and Water streets. They promised its thirty-four hundred residents that "the theatre, though small, will be fitted up and embellished in a superior style, and every attention will be paid to the comfortable accommodation of their audiences." But nothing ever came of it, and the two men sought a new location.[38]

They decided to try Huntsville, Alabama, where Cummins had tried and failed with Ludlow two years before. Since then, a small theater had been erected on the southwest corner of Lincoln and East Clinton streets by two men named Sammoner and Weekly, providing a venue for a few productions. Among them now were *Gamester*, with Phillips as Beverly and Mrs. Cummins as Mrs. Beverly, and *Blue Devils*, the bill for November 4, 1820. After this effort, both Phillips and the Cumminses retreated from the frontier, the former to manage small theaters in the East, and the latter to obscurity.[39]

Collins and Jones had remained in Nashville, joined that fall by Mr. and Mrs. Ludlow, he having given up his framing work in St. Louis and his disappointing efforts with Vos and James O. Lewis. In Ludlow's telling, the way was paved for his joining Collins and Jones's company by none other than Sam Houston, but his talent would likely have spoken for itself. Mary Ludlow's name, however, appears in no bills, and she may have been occupied with motherhood.

They began with benefits, with Mrs. Groshon's *Jane Shore* on November 1, with other company members receiving theirs in subsequent weeks.

The bill for Henderson's benefit on November 11 was a patriotic 1819 play by Mordecai M. Noah, *She Would Be a Soldier; or, the Plains of Chippewa* (sometimes titled in reverse order). Based on events of the recent war, it was one of earliest "noble savage" plays which reached their apex with John Augustus Stone's *Metamora* in 1829. One wonders, however, how such nobility was received by frontier settlers. By November 18, Jones's benefit night of *The Dramatist* and *The Lying Valet*, with their fortunes declining, Collins decided to take their company to St. Louis (encouraged to do so by Ludlow, according to Ludlow).

~~~~~~~~~

West India Jones, too, was struggling to remain solvent that fall, unable to afford even rudimentary notices in Natchez newspapers of his performances. His reduced company consisted only of John and Eliza Vaughan (he as stage manager, still feuding with Jones), Thomas and Eliza Price, Benjamin Carr, the eccentric Andrew Jackson Allen, and a Mr. Fosdick. Opening on November 11 with *Apostate* and *Lady of the Lake* (Thomas Price carrying leads in both), Jones soon resorted to gimmicks, including the use of a live elephant (its origin unknown, perhaps from a local traveling circus) on stage in *Blueb-beard*, which ran for several nights.[40]

With scenery constructed on a bare-bones budget, Mrs. Vaughan one night refused to step onto a shaky platform, thus averting a repeat of an injury she had suffered two years before. Her husband, chastised by the *Mississippi Republican* for being grossly negligent in fulfilling his responsibilities as stage manager, defended himself in print: "Formerly it was the duty of the stage manager to cast all plays, etc. but the stage manager is [now] of so little importance that those things are done by general consultation."[41]

By January 1821 Jones was increasingly relying on amateurs. He had married, and awarded his new wife most leads, such as Volante in *Honey Moon*. The troupe's repertoire remained predictable, including *Road to Ruin*, *Stranger*, *Wheel of Fortune*, *The Liar*, and *Forty Thieves*. But by mid-April, Jones threw in the towel and dispersed the company. He would continue for a short time to perform solo using actors from other companies in places like Port Gibson and Baton Rouge. His wife's fate is unknown.

~~~~~~~~~~

Amid the straitened circumstances of the winter of 1820–21, only Joshua Collins and William Jones, Noah Ludlow, and the Drakes would remain to vie for what little remuneration could be found on the frontier, while Caldwell hovered to pick up the pieces. The seven cities on the frontier where theatre had been established—Cincinnati, Lexington, Louisville, Nashville, New Orleans, Pittsburgh, and St. Louis—boasted by 1821 dedicated (rather than converted) theaters. These awaited managers who could, and would, ride the financial recovery to success.

Noah Ludlow, ca. 1848.
By Thomas M. Easterly, courtesy of Missouri Historical Society.

Fanny Denny Drake.
From Coad and Mims, *The American Stage,* 128.

James H. Caldwell.
Courtesy of Billy Rose Theatre Collection, New York Public Library.

New Orleans's Théâtre St. Philippe.
From Coad and Mims, *The American Stage*, 131.

Thomas Abthorpe Cooper, the first eastern star to perform on the frontier.
Portrait by John Wesley Jarvis, courtesy of Cleveland Museum of Art.

First Theater in St. Louis. From a painting by Emile Herzinger,
courtesy of Missouri Historical Society, St. Louis.

James H. Caldwell's American Theatre in Camp Street, New Orleans.
Public Domain Collections, picryl.com.

Sol Smith. From an engraving by W. G. Jackman for Odell,
Annals of the New York Stage 4: 52.

An early, confident Edwin Forrest.
Courtesy of Billy Rose Theatre Collection, New York Public Library.

Thomas D. "Jim Crow" Rice. Library of Congress.

Sarah Kirby Stark. From MacMinn, *The Theater of the Golden Age in California*, facing p. 72, courtesy of Caxton Press, Caldwell, ID.

James Stark as Hamlet. From MacMinn, *The Theater of the Golden Age in California*, facing p. 106, courtesy of Caxton Press, Caldwell, ID.

William B. "Uncle Billy" Chapman. From MacMinn, *The Theater of the Golden Age in California*, facing p. 147, courtesy of Caxton Press, Caldwell, ID.

Caroline Chapman. From MacMinn, *The Theater of the Golden Age in California*, facing p. 146, courtesy of Caxton Press, Caldwell, ID.

William Chapman's Floating Theatre, the first showboat, 1831.
Sketch by Dr. Judd, reproduced in Hornblow,
A History of the Theatre in America 1: 334.

Third Jenny Lind Theatre in San Francisco.
Library of Congress.

Junius Brutus Booth Jr. Portrait by Gurney, courtesy of Billy Rose
Theatre Collection, New York Public Library.

Junius Brutus Booth Sr. and Edwin Booth, courtesy of Billy Rose
Theatre Collection, New York Public Library.

7

THE FIRST FRONTIER STARS

(1821–1822)

AS THE FRONTIER DREW greater attention from the East in the 1820s, promoted by such statesmen as Henry Clay, Andrew Jackson, William Henry Harrison, and Thomas Hart Benton, so too did frontier towns and cities draw increased immigration and commerce, and consequently a greater need for entertainment.

Among the fastest growing towns, with a population topping four thousand, was St. Louis. Flourishing from its site on the Mississippi River, with Missouri poised for statehood but caught up in the congressional wrangling that would spawn the Missouri Compromise, it became the next focus of Joshua Collins and William Jones. A tedious journey involving eight days aboard a cordelling keelboat brought their company there from Nashville in December 1820. Collins himself continued on to Cincinnati, part of their plan to develop a circuit of Cincinnati, Nashville, and St. Louis.

Their experienced, competent St. Louis company consisted of Jones, the Ludlows, the Voses, the Groshons (he primarily as treasurer), the Hannas, their daughters Rosina Hanna and Amelia Seymour, James O. Lewis, Cargill, Frethy, Henderson, Pilley, and Dauberman (primarily as scenic artist). On December 13 they opened in the theater on Main Street last used by Drake, with *The Apostate* and *The Old Maid,* and continued for seventeen weeks on Mondays, Wednesdays, and Saturdays with an extensive repertoire. This included such mainstays as *Pizarro* (the first time in St. Louis, on February 24), *Gamester, She Stoops to Conquer, Venice Preserved, School for Scandal, Richard III* (Vos), *Catharine and Petruchio, Macbeth* (Mrs. Hanna as Lady Macbeth), and *Jane Shore,* plus an array of farces.

St. Louis newspapers were supportive, especially of Ludlow, Jones, and Vos, who "would do honor to any stage in the union," and the "celebrated" Belinda Groshon, who was "certainly superior to any actress we have ever seen on these boards." Her "intelligent countenance gave meaning to every action." Dauberman's scenery drew extravagant praise. The company was cautioned, however, not to overdo it with "oaths." Benefits, starting in mid-March 1821, drew moderate crowds.[1]

The performance on March 24 honored Missouri's imminent admission to the United States (finalized in August) with *Plains of Chippewa /She Would Be a Soldier* and *Fortune of Love*. Lewis carried the lead in the melodramatic opera *The Devil's Bridge* before departing for Michigan Territory. (Having achieved artistic recognition in October with an engraving of Daniel Boone, he would go on to earn fame for painting native chiefs and warriors, notably Tecumseh's brother Tenskwatawa, known as the Prophet.)

Jones, in increasingly poor health, closed the season with his own benefit on April 14 (*John Bull* and *Broken Sword*), then took part of the company to Cincinnati, where Collins waited. The Ludlows boarded a steamboat for New Orleans, where Noah hoped to act for James Caldwell. The actors left behind (the Voses, Belinda Groshon, Mrs. Hanna, Amelia Seymour, Frethy and Finlay) acted occasionally that spring with the St. Louis amateur thespians in their former courthouse venue. Their most noteworthy production, arguably the first play written by an American performed west of the Mississippi River, was Alphonso Wetmore's three-act farce *The Pedlar* [sic]. They then departed for Nashville, to bolster the planned Collins-Jones circuit.

In Cincinnati, which by 1820 had superseded Lexington in population, Collins had opportunistically merged with the Drakes, up from Louisville, at the Columbia Street Theatre. They opened in late January 1821 with Cumberland's *The Jew* and Dimond's melodrama *The Hunter of the Alps*, with Sam Sr. making his first appearance in Cincinnati in the latter.

He acted "with judgment and feeling," being "a sound and chaste performer" who is "easy in his manner, and does not 'overstep the modesty of nature.'" Collins, who "has seldom appeared to greater advantage," carried leads opposite the increasingly accomplished Julia Drake, who "fascinates by her beauty, rendered still more fascinating by her bewitching naiveté" and delightful olio songs. Aleck Drake earned "reiterated plaudits from every quarter. . . . Applause gave way to loud laughter and the spontaneous cries of bravo! bravo!" Sam Jr., Green, and Mrs. Mongin came in for their share of praise, along with Mrs. Fisher, who excelled in "antiquated women and the intriguing chambermaid," an unusual but necessary combination.[2]

Their repertoire was challenging, including *Othello*, *King Lear*, *Stranger* (on March 28, a benefit for the city, with Julia as Mrs. Haller and Collins in the title role) and *Forty Thieves* (with new scenery by Aleck Drake "expected to surpass in elegance any scenic spectacle ever exhibited in the western world"). It took in $500. "Superior" music was provided by Mr. Ratel's orchestra. However, the venture proved unremunerative. Despite the season having been conducted with "considerable ability and great propriety [always a priority in Cincinnati], it would seem from the vacant benches that the zest of our citizens has abated." Amid the indifferent patronage, even a benefit for Palmer Fisher designed to appeal to Masons, in which he extolled their virtues, drew few of them. Discouraged, the company closed on April 23, and the Drakes returned to Louisville, stopping briefly in Vincennes.[3]

~~~~~~~~~~

Having spent most of 1820 performing with his company on the East Coast, Caldwell brought them by sea from Charleston to New Orleans in January 1821, intending to establish his preeminence there. This second season would prove problematic for him, but would introduce the first major international star to frontier audiences.

Although a few of Caldwell's actors did not return with him to New Orleans, the company was experienced, cohesive, and accomplished, notable among them Caldwell, Hanna (from St. Louis), Thomas Jefferson (who had acted in the West since 1811), Thomas Burke and his wife Cornelia Frances Thomas Burke (who after Burke's death would marry Joseph Jefferson II and give birth in 1829 to the most famous American comedian of the century), Mr. and Mrs. Richard Russell, Molly Entwistle, Emanuel Judah, Mrs. Legg, and Miss Eliza Placide. While Caldwell himself would perform nearly all male leads, he would rotate fairly evenly the actresses in leads opposite him.

They opened on January 31 at the Théâtre d'Orléans with *Soldier's Daughter* and *The Liar*. For fifteen weeks they performed on Mondays, Wednesdays, Fridays and Saturdays in a repertoire that had succeeded in the East, but ran into some roadblocks in New Orleans. Caldwell began with such anodyne scripts as *Honey Moon, Devil's Bridge, Much Ado About Nothing, School for Scandal,* and *Mountaineers*. In *Mountaineers*, however, he encountered criticism for taking "unpardonable liberties" with the text and smiling with "approbation . . . when reading his own applause." He was "misplaced in parts which call forth the deep and tender feelings of the heart." While adept at comedy of manners, he "strains and distorts his voice in tragedy, . . . something extremely grating to the nerves."[4]

By late February, Caldwell's repertoire had grown stale. He was admonished not to think "he would derive large sums of money from the constant repetition of pieces we have already seen." Hence, he readied two adventurous new productions, New Orleans's first *Virginius* and *King Lear*, performed on February 26 and March 2, respectively. Caldwell of course took the title role of each, with *Lear* being his first (mid-season) benefit. It was not well received. One reviewer could not "conceive of anything more absurd, more monstrous, or more ridiculous, or of a more complete abortion." It was regretted that this company "mistake their own talents so much. . . . When they approach tragedy, it really appears to be all a farce of absolute caricature." That Caldwell had chosen to follow *Lear* with a slack-wire performer actually drew hisses.[5]

Virginius, though, would become one of the most oft-performed tragedies on the frontier, as it was in the East. Written in early 1820 by Sheridan Knowles for Edmund Kean, it had premiered in New York that fall, a production Caldwell likely saw or heard reports of. In ancient Rome, noble Virginius rushes back from battle to try to save his beautiful, innocent, betrothed daughter from being sold as a slave to a lustful decemvir. He fails, then kills her to prevent her ruin, goes mad, and kills the villainous decemvir.

Caldwell attempted to placate critics and audiences alike by announcing the imminent engagement of the first truly international star to appear anywhere on the frontier. London-born Thomas Abthorpe Cooper, forty-five, was the preeminent classical tragedian on the American stage. His stately, authoritative stage presence and magnificent voice combined to turn any role, particularly anything by Shakespeare, into an emotional powerhouse. Caldwell had developed his acquaintance while in the East and offered Cooper the then-remarkable sum of $3,333.33 (nearly $80,000 today) for sixteen nights. To cover his costs, Caldwell raised ticket prices from $1.00 to $1.50 and sold box seats at auction. This predictably produced a public outcry, but tickets still sold rapidly. The *Gazette* supported the increase, as doing so would "prevent the greasy Kentuckians and the rabble from leaning over the backs of the boxes to the great annoyance of the Ladies." (Since Caldwell eschewed acting secondary roles to Cooper, one wag decreed that the higher prices were worth it to avoid seeing him onstage.)[6]

After traveling overland in a covered wagon, Cooper opened in New Orleans on March 23 as Macbeth, with Molly Entwistle as Lady Macbeth. Although a considerable portion of the audience "were ripe for revolt" over the increased prices, their respect for Cooper quelled their outrage. Cooper followed this with *Rule a Wife and Have a Wife, Venice Preserved, Hamlet* (with Cornelia Burke as Ophelia), *Virginius, Bertram, Julius Caesar* (its first production in New Orleans, Cooper as Marc Antony), *Gamester,* and *The Robbers.*[7]

Caldwell happily extended Cooper's engagement for another eight nights, generating a profit for himself which averaged $700 a night, an accomplishment he gloated would take a generation to obliterate. "From that day," he knew he "wielded the tinsel sceptre, and commanded to the South and West every distinguished member of the profession." Now, "the national drama was firmly rooted" in New Orleans, and he "began to consider seriously of building a theatre for it."[8]

Toward the end of April, Noah Ludlow arrived in New Orleans, having stopped off in Natchez in mid-March to perform the lead in *Stranger* for a fellow actor's benefit. Caldwell offered Ludlow, now twenty-five, a permanent place in his company, and he debuted on April 27 as Young Wilding in *The Liar.* Two weeks of benefits began May 2 with Mrs. Entwistle's, a performance of Cibber's *The Provoked Husband* (an ironic title given her abusive husband's suicide in New Orleans in early June). Caldwell ended the season on May 12 with *Laugh When You Can* and *Lady of the Lake*, adapted from Scott's poem, with Cornelia Burke as Blanche of Devon. He then sent his company under Richard Russell by schooner back to Virginia without adequate provisions for their storm-plagued forty-two-day voyage. Many nearly perished for lack of water, a deprivation felt particularly keenly by Mary Ludlow, who on May 20 had given birth to their second child, a daughter they named Cornelia for the kindness shown them on board by Cornelia Burke.

Caldwell himself chose to travel overland, stopping first in Louisville. He may have intended to evaluate that town and Cincinnati for expansion of his circuit, either in competition or cooperation with the Drakes or with Collins and Jones. The Drakes supported Caldwell during June and July as he took on such roles as Belcour in *The West Indian*, Hamlet, Aranza in *Honey Moon*, Octavian in *Mountaineers*, and Rolla in *Pizarro*, with Julia Drake as Elvira. Her benefit on July 7, in *The Miller and His Men* and *Ways and Means*, ended the Louisville summer season. (A brief fall season there ended on October 13.) Before heading east to rejoin his actors, Caldwell offered positions in his company to Julia and Aleck Drake, but their loyalty to family and frontier led them to refuse.

By the time Caldwell reached Richmond, Russell had engaged on his behalf a dynamic new star, Junius Brutus Booth, just turned twenty-five, who had arrived from England on June 30, to perform in New Orleans. After witnessing Booth's powerhouse performances in Richmond, especially his Richard III, Russell shrewdly figured that he would prove as successful as Cooper had been in New Orleans, and booked Booth for the following January. (Booth's phenomenal success in New York in the interim confirmed Russell's judgment.)

〰〰〰〰〰〰〰

In Nashville, the reassembled Jones company opened on May 10, 1821, with *The Man of Fortitude* and *Blue Devils*. (Collins had remained in Cincinnati to oversee the final details of their new theater.) Their repertoire remained that of St. Louis and Cincinnati. Vos and Groshon carried the leads in *Macbeth* on June 27, and the company's shorthandedness—typical of frontier troupes—was apparent in Fred Henderson's enacting King Duncan and Murderer and Doctor and a Witch. Reviews were mixed, the most curious asserting that *Macbeth* was too gloomy: "a few lively comedies would enliven the town." Jones, Cargill, Henderson, and Mr. Groshon were respectable; Vos was "a man of fine genius" but inconsistent, often utilizing unnatural actions; Rosina Hanna was "promising"; and Belinda Groshon was "brilliant, . . . the best Lady Macbeth on the American Stage."[9]

But standards began to slip, perhaps a factor of Collins's absence. A performance of *Tekeli* and *Lying Valet* on June 30 prompted jaundiced reviewer "Asmodeus" to portray a listless lot of actors. Jones should limit himself to comedy and "not to attempt tragedy." Vos exhibited "eccentricities." His wife should "infuse more spirit into her performances." Cargill "appears to have lost much of his relish for the Drama" and needed to correct a speech impediment. Belinda Groshon similarly "appears to have lost a great deal portion of her zeal and fire," likely due to "thin houses which are well calculated to dampen the spirits." Her husband's harsh laugh grated on the ears. Mrs. Hanna was merely tolerable. An actor named De Grove seemed (justifiably) amateurish and needs to "control his violent disposition for buffoonery [and] monkey capers." Overall, the reviewer regretted "the absurdity of presenting such pieces [as *Tekeli*] in preference to plain genteel comedy." But there was potential. Henderson, "a man of the most amiable and unassuming manners," with work might advance to eminence. Samuel P. Jones may "become a good performer. He has a fine voice and not a bad person." Julia Jones "exceeded our warmest hope" but still has not yet reached her full potential. Misses Seymour and Hanna were "promising."[10]

For a July 4 performance of *She Would Be a Soldier*, John Vos declined to perform, reportedly due to "the thinness of the house," eliciting castigation from the *Gazette*. But Belinda Groshon again shone, and Cargill demonstrated "brilliant flashes of genius." Henderson's comic songs "contributed largely to the amusement of the evening." Having lost money on this Nashville season, Jones soon closed and took his actors to Lexington, where Collins was to rejoin them.[11]

When Ludlow had joined Caldwell's company in New Orleans, his original destination had been Pensacola, Florida, but its paucity of potential theatregoers—its most recent census revealed a mere 181 households—may have given him pause. Now, in July 1821, newly purchased by the United States from Spain as part of the Florida Territory, Pensacola offered a fledgling manager a chance to make his mark there. The population had swelled to 4,000, many of them land speculators.

At least one other potential manager had scoped out Pensacola: Andrew Jackson Allen, formerly with West India Jones in Natchez and briefly with Caldwell. On the very date Andrew Jackson invested Pensacola—May 24, 1818—Allen had assembled a few itinerant actors and taken the role of General Jackson, "the Victor at New Orleans" in "a dramatic piece called *Columbia and Her Heroes*." Now, he was ready to try again. With no venue expressly for theatrical performances, he leased the circular (forty-five-foot-diameter) Tivoli Ballroom owned by Juan Baptiste Cazenave at the corner of Zarragosa and Barracks streets on Public Square in the ancient Spanish town. Probably to curry favor with Jackson, now U.S. commissioner for Florida and a man Allen idolized, he changed its name to the Jacksonian Commonwealth Theatre, equipping it with benches and circumferential boxes to seat about 250.[12]

He had assembled a somewhat more professional troupe than previously, among them James M. Scott; Mr. Hanna, left behind by Caldwell; and John and Eliza Vaughan, who had chafed under West India Jones, Henry Vaughan (John's brother), Mrs. Legg, Mrs. Price, and an assortment of amateurs. On the evening of July 17, 1821, the day that territorial flags were exchanged, Allen commenced a season of fourteen weeks, with performances three evenings a week. Within days, the City Council of Pensacola passed an ordinance requiring a five-dollar-per-month tax to operate a theater, plus ten dollars per show. Within weeks the Tivoli's owner sequestered Allen's stage properties for unpaid rent. Nevertheless, he soldiered on, with Hanna and Scott carrying leads in such pieces as *Stranger, Catharine and Petruchio, Castle Spectre, Spoiled Child,* and *Fortune's Frolic.*

By October 8, however, Allen announced that he was closing up shop as of October 22 and leaving for New Orleans to reopen the St. Philip St. Theatre. His "company of comedians" announced their opening there in November. Their numbers were diminished, though, due to the deaths of Mrs. Price and Mrs. Vaughan. However, Allen failed to obtain approval from Bernardo Coquet, still proprietor of the St. Philip, who planned to convert it to a circus arena, so the venture collapsed and Allen headed with his actors up the Mississippi River toward Louisville.[13]

He stopped in Baton Rouge November 12–26, his Jacksonian Commonwealth Company drawing a favorable review from the *Gazette* despite an opening night that was "thinly attended." Then Allen, professing a "scarcity of money," abandoned his company "in want of provisions" and when he reached Louisville in January 1822, it was solely as a journeyman actor under Drake, and later under Collins and Jones in Cincinnati.[14]

~~~~~~~~~~

As much as theatre in Lexington was in full decline in fall 1821, it received a shot in the arm from a familiar figure. Fanny Denny reappeared there, doubtless to the relief of Collins and Jones. Over the past three years she had established herself as a talented, versatile actress who could transcend soubrette roles to perform serious drama, first in Montreal, then in the crucible of New York City, followed by Boston. No role, be it Kate Hardcastle in *She Stoops to Conquer*, Elvira in *Pizarro*, or Volumnia in *Coriolanus*, seemed beyond her ability. She held her own opposite such stars as Cooper and Kean, and was said to be "rarely equaled on the American stage." Now, in Lexington, she opened with Collins and Jones's company on October 11 as Violante in *The Wonder!* and Lady Elizabeth in *Day After the Wedding*. She was warmly received alongside Belinda Groshon, the two women "never fail[ing] to interest and sometimes to charm."[15]

Denny traveled with the company in November when they returned to Cincinnati. With her as their keystone, committed through early 1822 and billed as their star in large uppercase letters, Collins and Jones strove to establish a loyal following. The completion of their new theater's front portico had been repeatedly delayed, during which time they had advertised one year's free use of the theater as a prize for the best prologue when the season opened. The winner, penned by a young law student and delivered by Collins on opening night, November 19, promised "To deck fair Virtue in her loveliest charms and goad the monster Vice with Satire's arms," a clear allusion to the moral imperatives (and constrictions) of the stage. The theater was finished "in a style superior, we believe, to any thing of the kind in the Western Country. New and splendid scenery has been added."[16]

The company had remained largely intact: Collins, William and Julia Jones, Fred and Jane Henderson (her first mention), Austin Cargill, Hays, Bruce, Fanny Denny, Belinda Groshon, Mrs. Hanna, Miss Amelia Seymour, plus a new addition: young prompter and utility actor Sol Smith, who had given up studying the law.

Denny's appearance was highly anticipated, certain to provide "variety and strength to the company." She was touted as "a young lady of amiable character, and as an actress of very considerable merit." She appeared on opening night as Donna Violante and two nights later as Portia opposite the Shylock of Jones and the Antonio of Collins. Not only could she handle comedic and dramatic leads, she remained fetching in breeches roles, such as Young Norval on December 19 (with Belinda Groshon as Lady Randolph). At twenty-four she had become "a large and fine-figured woman" with a "vividly expressive" face. "Her form and powers were Amazonian and full of fire and energy." Her acting was "impulsive, . . . imbued with a measured energy." She demonstrated "the native impulsiveness of the American feeling and conception," which doubtless contributed to her popularity on the rough-hewn frontier.[17]

Until late December she remained the top attraction in Cincinnati, carrying such leads as Juliet (opposite Collins's Romeo, with Cargill as Mercutio), Kate Hardcastle, Catharine (opposite Collins's Petruchio), Florinda in *The Apostate*, Young Norval, and Lucy Rackett in *Three Weeks After Marriage*.

Aleck Drake, leaving his siblings behind in Louisville, joined the Collins-Jones troupe in Cincinnati, appearing (as "Mr. Alexander") on December 29 in *The Birthday; or, Reconciliation*, and *The Three and the Deuce*, both opposite Denny. He also delivered a popular song entitled "Love and Sausages" (anyone attempting to court a lady who is frying sausages might "feel the weight of a frying pan upon the pate").[18]

It soon became clear what drew Denny back to the frontier and Aleck back to Cincinnati: she and he, twenty-four and twenty-three respectively, were married in Cincinnati on December 30. Her first billing as "Mrs. Alexander Drake" came on January 2, 1822, when she enacted Maria in *George Barnwell*. Together, they performed the rest of that month, primarily in comedies and farces (his métier). The company celebrated another marriage on January 20 when Smith (a week after his benefit) wed Martha Therese Mathews, a soprano from Brunswick, New Jersey, who for now eschewed performing.[19]

A grievous loss soon followed, when the popular Belinda Groshon, thirty-three, collapsed onstage and died within hours on January 31, less than a week after her benefit night. Collins and Jones closed the theater for three days of mourning. Upon reopening, Henderson delivered from the stage an emotional eulogy, which he was barely able to complete for tears. Her burial in an Episcopal graveyard attested to the purity of her life.[20]

The season's benefits had been nearly completed by February, but Fanny Drake was inexplicably denied one. Collins and Jones offered no public justification, but her performances of late had reportedly been unimpressive (often "too ill to justify the effort," possibly due to a difficult pregnancy). Miffed, she issued a public statement decrying the slight and announced that she would hold her own "farewell" benefit in the ballroom of the Cincinnati Hotel on February 13. Newspapers took up her cause, informing the public that she had performed for weeks at a discounted wage and on some nights, no pay at all, while sending home "a good portion" of her earnings to support her aged, widowed mother. Hence, she "has a claim upon the patronage of the good people of Cincinnati which neither Taste, Feeling, nor Generosity will suffer them to forget." The evening, unsubtly titled *Ways and Means; or, An Actress' Appeal to Her Friends*, consisted of recitations and songs by Fanny and her new husband, supported by the "full band." It was apparently a modest success, and she and Aleck departed on a honeymoon through March.[21]

James Caldwell, determined to succeed in New Orleans, had brought his company back there in late November 1821 for their third season. They opened December 10 at the Théâtre d'Orléans with *Honey Moon* and *Three and the Deuce*. He absorbed Vaughan and Scott from Allen's failed venture, adding them to Mr. and Mrs. Richard Russell, Mr. and Mrs. Hughes, Noah Ludlow, Jackson Gray, Thomas Jefferson, Emanuel Judah, James Scholes, W. H. Benton, William McCafferty, Boyle, Mrs. Anderson, Miss Eliza Placide, and Miss Eliza Tilden.

Keeping in mind the furor triggered by his raised prices of last season, Caldwell emphasized his intention now to establish a permanent theater in New Orleans that would adhere to high standards and be "a school of moral ethics." Simultaneously, he eyed Natchez as potentially worthy of expansion of his circuit. Its theater had burned down on October 13, and he now solicited the support of its citizens with a public notice, asserting his willingness "to bring to Natchez the best Dramatic Talent of America" for two months each year, and to provide a "prospectus for the erection of a permanent Theatre."[22]

He evidenced his acquisition of the "best dramatic talent of America" in January 1822 by bringing to New Orleans—at $90 per night (about $2,000 today)—the brightest rising star in the theatrical firmament, Junius Brutus Booth (Cooper beginning a slow descent). Booth had already overcome dubious critics and audiences in New York at the Park Theatre in October with his inspired, bordering-on-madness performances of Hamlet, Lear, Richard III, and Octavian in *Mountaineers*. Following a twenty-two-day voyage from Charleston, Booth arrived in New Orleans in time to open on January 11 with his strongest piece, *Richard III*. He followed this with Giles Overreach in *A New Way to Pay Old Debts*, Payne's Brutus, Lear, Shylock, Romeo, and Mortimer in *Iron Chest*, drawing French- as well as English-speaking theatregoers, the former appreciating his Orestes in *The Distrest* [sic] *Mother*, Ambrose Philips's translation of Racine's *Andromache*, on January 25, some equating him with the great French actor Talma.

As Othello, "his features were wonderfully mobile and expressive. The eyes were the most brilliant I have ever seen. The feeling that was about to express itself in words leaped forth and announced itself in their piercing gaze." His resonant voice (when he chose to articulate) could "create a scene with the sound." One critic, however, was less than enthralled with Booth's Richard, assailing his mumbling delivery, omission of some lines, lack of grace, and erratic gesticulating, while still admiring his superior "fire" in the well-known "tent scene" (act 5, scene 3). The supporting company fared little better and "more resembled the soldiers of Falstaff than the warriors of Richard." Jefferson and Vaughan performed "like some school teachers and country preachers," accentuating words improperly. "Let us have actors who can speak well in prose and in verse, or else we do without them." The critic chided Caldwell for declining to act secondary roles to Booth or Cooper, and for managing a theater seemingly "run by charlatans."[23]

In an unsuccessful attempt to eclipse Booth, Caldwell's next star, the returning Cooper, chose *Richard III* for his opening on February 6, but following Booth, it was poorly received. For a week Cooper enacted tragic roles—for example, Othello (this time opposite Caldwell's Iago, with Seymour as Desdemona and Ludlow as Cassio), Virginius (opposite Eliza Tilden's Virginia), and Damon in John Banim's new *Damon and Pythias,* which had only debuted in New York the previous September. Cooper then went to Baton Rouge to deliver a series of dramatic recitations, drawing sizable audiences. In his absence, Caldwell engaged his friend Victor Pépin, whose equestrian troupe performed several nights of *Timour the Tartar.* Cooper returned by March 23 to enact *Alexander the Great,* followed four nights later as Orosmane in Voltaire's *Zaïre.*

Various efforts to build a new theater in the roughneck American Sector (the Faubourg St. Mary) of New Orleans had come to naught. Now, however, Caldwell leveraged his profits from his three successful seasons there to purchase—apparently at Pépin's suggestion—two adjacent lots on the west side of Camp Street between Gravier and Poydras streets, for $18,000, payable over twenty years with an annual ground rent of $1,140. On May 29, 1822, having closed his season at the Théâtre d'Orléans, he laid the cornerstone for the "New American Theatre" for which he would become best known. Before taking his company back to Virginia, he succeeded in raising via stockholder shares $14,000 of the anticipated $70,000 cost of erecting the building, and personally saw the completion of the first ten feet of wall.[24]

~~~~~~~~~~~

Seeming to sense Caldwell gaining on him, Samuel Drake had not been behindhand that winter of 1821–22. He had extensively renovated his Louisville theater "in a fanciful and elegant manner." With another tier of boxes, better lighting (including a chandelier of non-dripping sperm oil candles) and more stoves, it promised greater audience comfort. His company, with several new members from the East recruited by Aleck, was capable but inconsistent. Palmer and Agnes Fisher would carry leads until Aleck and Fanny returned from their honeymoon, as would Alexander M. Wilson (a former sea captain, merchant, and land speculator who had successfully debuted in New York in January 1817) and Julia Drake. Supporting players included Sam Jr., the peripatetic Andrew Jackson Allen, Mrs. Mongin, Samuel Emberton (prone to dizzy spells, perhaps from an occasional wee drop), Mr. King, and Mr. Frankland.[25]

They opened on January 7 with *Honey Moon* and *Adopted Child* and drew "a numerous and fashionable audience." Fisher's Duke Aranza "gave universal satisfaction" and "completely understood the character he represented." Julia Drake ("recently returned from a tour to the eastward [where] she made her debut at Philadelphia in this character") as Juliana also "gave universal satisfaction. . . . Her improvement since she left this place has been very considerable, and far surpassed our most sanguine expectations."[26]

Then followed predictable bills: *Pizarro* (Wilson as Rolla, Julia as Elvira, and Mrs. Mongin as Cora), *Mountaineers, Poor Gentleman, Othello* (Wilson), and for his farewell benefit on January 28, Wilson as *Bertram*. February brought *Lovers' Vows, The West Indian, John Bull, The Wags of Windsor,* and *Rosina,* the last three starring the visiting Mr. Hayes of the Dublin Theatre.

A poised, polished Julia consistently drew the choicest accolades: "The more we see this lady, the more we have reason to admire the scope and versatility of her talents." Her "superior style of acting . . . delights and rivets the attention of the beholder. . . . We have never seen better acting on the Louisville boards." Other actors were markedly deficient, persistently mispronouncing words. A visiting Cincinnati businessman and amateur actor decried their butchery of language ("sacrificed to suit the convenience or the idleness of the actor") and the erratic tempo due to missed or undelivered cues. This was a constant problem, sometimes yielding long moments without lines, and in at least one case, the omission of an entire scene.[27]

In early March, after Hayes departed, Drake announced his intention of moving on to Nashville in late March (postponed to early May as patronage improved in Louisville). Benefits continued throughout March, with Drake making sure everyone got one, including performances of *Soldier's Daughter*, *Ella Rosenberg*, *The Plains of Chippewa*, and *Miss in Her Teens*. King's benefit on April 1 was enhanced by the return of Aleck and Fanny Drake, she as the fashionable Mrs. Glenroy in *Town and Country* (apparently being already too mature for the role of Rosalie Somers). She further distinguished herself two nights later as Elvira (more of a tour de force than the sympathetic Cora), opposite Palmer Fisher's Rolla in *Pizarro*.

Her reviews eclipsed Julia's. Since her last time in Louisville, "it had never entered into our imagination that such an entire change in her manner and style of acting could have taken place. Her person is somewhat larger [her pregnancy disguised] than when we before saw her, her enunciation [is] clear and distinct," and her voice "clear and melodious. . . . Whenever she was on the stage, our recollection of every other performer was lost in admiration of her superior talents."[28]

Attendance improved markedly in mid-April when Cooper debuted in Louisville for six nights, including *Othello*, *Hamlet*, and *Virginius*. For Sam Sr. this was a reunion, as he, along with Caldwell, had supported Cooper's *Richard III* in Liverpool shortly before the Drakes emigrated to America. This Louisville engagement netted Cooper $1,200, much of which he converted to durable produce rather than trust dubious paper currency.

Cooper, who had been the earliest guest star on the frontier, then moved on to Lexington to play four nights for Collins and Jones, who had opened their spring season on April 4 with a special benefit for the children of widower Groshon, extolled for his "gentlemanly deportment and exemplary moral character." Cooper brought Fanny along to costar, and they opened on April 26 with *Othello*, followed by *Hamlet, Gamester*, and *Bertram*. (Either she and Collins and Jones had buried the hatchet over the withheld February benefit, or she performed according to contract and/or out of respect for Cooper.) Demand for tickets was so high that Collins and Jones limited the number available to each patron.[29]

One Lexington reviewer found himself "in raptures over Cooper's acting because he used no stage tricks nor claptrap to astonish and extort applause, but relied on his genius and power to excite the feelings and sympathies of his audience." Fanny, too, "well deserved the applause she received. She must ere long be classed with the first-rate actresses of the American Stage."[30]

Stopping back in Louisville for one night of *Richard III* on May 6, she and Cooper then headed for Cincinnati, again for Collins and Jones. Those managers had opened on May 1 inexplicably not at their Columbia Street Theatre but at the Pavilion Theater on the southeast corner of Main and Sixth streets, part of the Vauxhall Gardens operated by two French actor-necromancers, Dumilieu and Charles. The company consisted of Collins, Mr. and Mrs. Jones, Cargill, Scott, Davis, Eberle, Henderson, Mrs. Mary Riddle (specializing in "heavies") and her ten-year-old daughter Eliza (later a leading actress in her own right), Miss Amelia Seymour, and Miss Louisa Fenton, a seventeen-year-old New Jersey native.[31]

Fanny and Cooper opened there on May 11, 1822, again as Desdemona and Othello. The evening produced a moment of inadvertent hilarity. "A country lass of sixteen" unfamiliar with the inside of a playhouse arrived late and, unable to find a seat, wandered near the stage. "Casting her eyes upon the stage, she observed several chairs unoccupied" and moved to take one, just as Cooper's Othello, relating his history with Desdemona in act i, scene 3, announces, "Here comes the lady." "The [onstage Venetian] senators half rose, expecting to see the 'gentle Desdemona,' when lo! the maiden from the country stepped . . . onto the stage and advanced toward the unsuspecting Moor!" Audience and actors alike (including Cooper) collapsed in laughter until the bewildered, blushing lass was redirected to a proper seat out in the house.[32]

Subsequent nights brought *Macbeth, Hamlet,* and *Richard III* (Fanny's last performances before giving birth to her second son, Richard, on July 4, 1822). The *Liberty Hall and Cincinnati Gazette* pronounced Fanny "a favorite" and acknowledged that any criticism of Cooper was unnecessary, as he even surpassed Kean. To hear Cooper orate was to hear Shakespeare speak: "His countenance expressed the very feelings in ourselves." Unfortunately, Cincinnati did not embrace Cooper as had Louisville and Lexington. One reviewer expressed gratification that someone of Cooper's dramatic stature would perform in the West, but bemoaned that "an idle whim or the unfavorable weather" had kept many away and raises the possibility that Cooper will not wish to return.[33]

Would-be star A. J. Allen followed Cooper, providing comedic lead roles opposite Esther Hughes through July 4 in such pieces as *The Review,* he as Caleb Quotem and she as Grace Gaylove. For her benefit on May 30, though, she chose Payne's tragic *Thérèse, the Orphan of Geneva,* and was exemplary, both "for correct understanding of the true nature of the character" and for her "proper, graceful and energetic [line] delivery." As the benefits continued that summer, Collins and Jones disappeared from the bills, on their way to Philadelphia and New York to recruit more actors, a sign of their determination to provide high-quality entertainment to the citizens of Cincinnati.[34]

Cargill, hailed as "a man of irreproachable character in private life" and "a very respectable performer," must have hoped for a good crowd for his benefit on July 26 in *Spectre Bridegroom* and *The Prize; or, 2, 5, 3, 8,* as must Amelia Seymour have hoped for hers on August 2 in *20 Years Ago* and *Spoiled Child,* for they were planning to wed. The nuptials took place on August 11, and she was billed as Mrs. Cargill the following week. By the end of August, everyone got a benefit, including Dumilieu.[35]

Without waiting for the return of Collins and Jones (but using their actors), Dumilieu and Charles opened a short fall season on September 6. Collins and Jones returned in time to produce a timely script, *Each for Himself; or, Rival Candidates,* on election night, October 8, when future president William Henry Harrison lost his race for Congress to James W. Gazlay. The actors they had recruited would soon make their mark.

When Caldwell had left New Orleans for Virginia with his actors in late May, Noah Ludlow had remained, and that summer joined Drake's company in Nashville in the Cherry Street Theatre, built by Collins and Jones two years before. There, by Ludlow's own account, his popularity grew, especially for his delivery of the song "The Hunters of Kentucky." He describes then taking part of Drake's company (minus Fanny, due to pregnancy), south by wagon to Huntsville, Alabama, where they performed for four or five weeks in the Huntsville Inn, as the town's only theater had burned on August 5, 1821, reportedly the work of an arsonist. They then migrated to Fayetteville, Alabama, then back to Nashville, their effort not remunerative. In early November the Drake actors returned to Kentucky and Ludlow headed for New Orleans, planning to rejoin Caldwell.[36]

That summer another makeshift company had tried to establish theatre in Pensacola in the wake of A. J. Allen's failed venture. An assortment of second-tier actors from all over the Southwest opened on June 22, 1822, at the newly renamed Pensacola Theatre, still owned by Cazenave. Under the management of John Vaughan, they included Eliza Vaughan (in her last performances), Mr. and Mrs. John Vos, George Frethy, James Scholes, comedian-vocalist Benjamin Carr, Wells, Mrs. DeGrushe, and Mr. Twible and his thirteen-year-old son. For two months they presented occasional pieces such as *Douglas* and *Miss in Her Teens*, but were hampered by a severe yellow fever outbreak, which took Carr. Pensacola would enjoy no theatre for nearly six years.[37]

During the past few months, efforts had begun to introduce theatre into other areas of the South. Amateur thespian societies had cropped up in St. Stephens, Alabama, sixty-three miles north of Mobile, in summer 1820, and in Alexandria, Louisiana, in December 1821. The latter continued to perform intermittently for several years.

Following the trail blazed by the Caldwell spinoffs in early 1820, Emanuel Judah, a former Caldwell actor from Virginia, gathered a small group of players in Mobile in early June 1822 in the converted hospital on Dauphin Street. But he was unsuccessful, as would be a company under a Mr. Scott (possibly James M. Scott). However, that December, a number of Mobile residents, out of a population now of twenty-eight hundred, met to solicit subscribers for a new theater, to be built on Royal Street. After Mobile, Judah moved on to Montgomery, Alabama, a town incorporated only three years before, applying his talents to guide an amateur thespian society performing at the Montgomery Hotel in such adventurous tragedies as *Julius Caesar*. Nashville's amateurs continued performing, too, including *Heir at Law* in November 1822.[38] But these were already anachronistic sideshows, eclipsed by established frontier managers.

8

COLLINS & JONES

(1822–1823)

OCTOBER 1822 YIELDED the first fruit of Collins and Jones's recruiting effort in the East, reinforcing their discernment for talent which had recognized Fanny Denny Drake. They found the most promising actor in Philadelphia. Seventeen-year-old Edwin Forrest, on the cusp of the stardom that would make him the most celebrated American-born actor of the century, applied to them for work. They hired him at eight dollars a week "to play, without question, whatever parts he was cast in, no matter how high or how low," a standard clause in contracts for utility players. Durang credits Jones with igniting Forrest's career: "With his sagacious eye he saw the embryo genius in the boy and thought the soil worthy of careful cultivation. . . . Forrest appreciated this hand of care and culture and never forgot his almost foster father."[1]

Before embarking on the lengthy, bone-jarring stagecoach journey across the Alleghanies, Forrest sought the advice of Cooper, who advised him to "serve his apprenticeship in the West, where the field was less crowded." Accompanying Forrest west was an acting couple whom Collins and Jones also considered a valuable addition to their western circuit. American-born William and Rosalie French Pelby, twenty-nine and twenty-four, had proven themselves on the stages of New York, Boston, and Philadelphia, she far more than her husband, primarily in tragic roles.[2]

They appeared first in Pittsburgh on October 14, with Forrest as Young Norval in *Douglas*, under less-than-optimal circumstances. Forrest considered Pittsburgh "a sort of London in miniature, very black and smoky," and the long-neglected theater was so dilapidated that on rainy nights the audience needed umbrellas. After a week of poor houses, they boarded a flatboat down the Ohio River to Maysville for a week of "excellent success, greatly delighting the rude Kentuckians," and thence to Lexington.[3]

There, Collins and Jones toiled at another neglected theater: Usher's. By mid-December they had it in presentable shape and gathered their newly augmented Cincinnati company, now comprised of Collins, William and Julia Jones, Lucas (also scenic artist), Forrest, the Pelbys, Fred Groshon, Fred Henderson (now also stage manager), William Davis, James M. Scott, Mr. and Mrs. Charles Eberle and Miss Eberle, Mary Riddle and her accomplished daughters Sarah and Eliza (fourteen and ten), and Miss Louisa Fenton (seventeen).

From their opening on December 16, they generally kept their repertoire light (for example, *She Stoops to Conquer; No Song, No Supper; The Way to Get Married*), with occasional tragedies (such as *Hamlet, King Lear* with Forrest as Edmund) and melodramas (for example, *Broken Sword*). Other than a brief appearance in late December by middle-aged Irish comedian John H. "Handsome Jack" Dwyer, so obese and out of shape that he no longer fit his moniker, Collins and Jones relied on their company for all roles, including leads.[4]

As Forrest's experience grew, he played increasingly important supporting roles, including Pythias in *Damon and Pythias* (opposite Pelby), Frederic in *School for Reform,* and Bassanio in *Merchant of Venice.* Although he lacked a full understanding of Shakespeare's text, he so impressed Horace Holley, president of Transylvania University, that Holley urged him to eschew superficial comedic roles and concentrate on tragedy. Collins and Jones encouraged and promoted Forrest, providing the opportunity on February 1, 1823, for him to enact Richard III for the first time on the frontier (he had first played it in April 1821 at the remarkable age of sixteen, in Philadelphia). He would keep the role in his repertoire for nearly fifty years.[5]

The *Kentucky Gazette* that winter admired Collins and Jones's troupe, especially Forrest's "noble sentiment" and "manly virtue." He "could not fail to be interesting" and showed "great promise." The Pelbys, too, earned praise. Considered mediocre in the East, William proved popular on the frontier, compensating for an inadequate, husky voice with energetic stage combat and over-the-top emoting. This was most evident in his Virginius, with "his reeling reason, his mad laugh, his wild earnestness in the pursuit of revenge of his daughter after her death." Rosalie earned praise for her "fine person, an excellent face, [and] animated features." The acting of the "dignified and impressive" Collins "as usual occupies a place in the first rank."[6]

After a battle which had dragged on for over a decade, the Trustees of the City of Lexington on February 6, 1823, began to tax theaters. Originally five dollars a day, it would be reduced within the year to just two. Apparently unruffled by the tax, Collins and Jones continued performances, scheduling benefits for nearly all company members. Miss Eberle's on February 17 featured a rare American script. Mordecai M. Noah's 1821 Revolutionary War thriller, *Marion; or, the Hero of Lake George*, was "filled with highly dramatic dialogue, tense situations, pistol shots, hairbreadth escapes, persecuted females, villainous redcoats and happy reunions." Watching it, a Revolutionary veteran might reminisce while he "dries the tear of sympathy shed for his fellow sufferers in the great cause of liberty." On February 22 the managers closed the season, taking the company back to Cincinnati.[7]

There, they opened on March 6 at the Columbia Street Theatre with their new, "first class" actors recruited in the East. Forrest, his salary raised to twelve dollars a week, continued to distinguish himself. Seeing him enact Young Malfort in *Soldier's Daughter*, Cincinnati newspaperman and future actor/manager Sol Smith became an early advocate, predicting "his future greatness" based on his Richard III.[8]

Smith was not alone. In Forrest's first scene with Lady Anne in *Richard III*, he drew spontaneous applause as he changed "from stateliness to wheedling hypocrisy" and back to "the haughty strut of towering ambition." Displaying "horror, despair, rage, disappointment, guilt," the role was better than "any heretofore this side of the mountains." His pinnacle of emotion came in the "tent scene": "Departing from the usual stage business of rising in the dread dream within the tent, Forrest sprang in terror from his couch and rushed forward to the footlights, which were at that moment turned up with a flood of light. There he fell exhausted in a kneeling position, his whole frame trembling, his face blanched with awful fear, one hand grasping the hilt of his sword, the sword's point driven into the floor—the sword itself shaking and clanking so loudly that it could be heard from pit to gallery." (Forrest had had it specially made to produce that effect.) A reviewer who came in with high expectations of a "juvenile attempt," thinking it impossible that "a lad under eighteen years of age could have a proper conception of a part so difficult," was astonished by Forrest's mastery. Significantly, another noted Forrest's avoidance of a common pitfall: "We never caught his eye wandering towards the audience, a fault too prevalent with actors, who are inclined to be either counting the house or seeking for an approving glance."[9]

Throughout March, Forrest continued to expand his repertoire, adding tragedy (Virginia's true love Icilius to the Virginius of visiting Charleston actor Charles R. Pemberton, and Titus to Pemberton's *Brutus*), melodrama (Blaize in *The Forest of Bondy*), and comedy (Corinthian Tom in *Tom and Jerry*), even dancing in a ballet of *Little Red Riding Hood*. Encouraged by the response to his Richard III, Forrest repeated it for his benefit on March 31. March also brought Cincinnatians a short visit from the latest British operatic sensation from New York, twenty-one-year-old Thomas Phillips, whose technique and range, including a remarkable falsetto, were widely acclaimed, especially by his legion of female fans—another coup for Collins and Jones.

On April 12, Collins and Jones closed what had nevertheless been a losing season. Collins took the company to Louisville, to merge with the remnants of the Drake company, still performing at the dingy little theater on Jefferson Street. Julia Jones went along, but the lack of her husband's name on bills in Louisville suggests he remained in Cincinnati or traveled afield to scout new markets. Defying a savage yellow fever outbreak, they performed every Wednesday night, with Pelby and Pemberton carrying leads. On April 23, Pemberton took the title role in his benefit of Charles Robert Maturin's 1817 five-act tragedy *Manuel*, with Forrest as Torrismond and Rosalie Pelby as Victoria. For Collins's benefit on May 14, Pemberton enacted Macbeth, with Forrest as Macduff, Sam Sr. as Duncan, and Pelby as Lady Macbeth.

Leaving Pemberton, Mrs. Eberle, the Pelbys, and Misses Riddle and Fenton in Louisville, Collins took the others back to Cincinnati. There, they would perform three nights a week, again in the Pavilion Theatre, now known as the Globe Theatre–Vauxhall. They opened on May 19 with *How to Die for Love* and *The Hypochondriac,* with Amelia Seymour Cargill as leading lady. New scenery by Lucas depicted "a view of Cincinnati from the Kentucky side of the Ohio River." James M. Scott, up from Louisville, contributed a four-night engagement. Due to unseasonably warm weather, though, theater attendance was disappointing. Another factor was the Globe's location, in the less-than-fashionable "uptown" area, whereas the Columbia Street Theatre was located "downtown," below Third Street, bounded by the river. Hence, the Globe "soon dwindled into a place for mountebank and other exhibitions and then died out."[10]

Those who remained in Louisville contributed to Drake's benefit on May 21 to raise funds for draining a pond to combat contagion. Notoriously remiss in meeting his tax burden, Drake chose this method to remain in the Louisville trustees' good graces. His numerous benefits aided such causes as Greek Independence, the Louisville marine hospital, and various churches. As one cynic noted, "Drake generally gave the benefits when the season was dull, and was probably a gainer instead of a loser by them." An indication of his inability to otherwise fulfill his tax obligation was the sale at auction of his "lot, with theatre," in Frankfort the previous November. On May 31 he closed up shop with a benefit for Fenton of *Devil's Bridge* and sent Collins's remaining actors back to Cincinnati.[11]

There, the reunited company—the strongest that Collins and Jones had yet fielded—was ready to open at the Columbia Street Theatre by June 2. Pemberton left to pursue an unattainable stardom in the East, freeing up leads for Forrest, now billed as a star. These included Durimel in *Point of Honor,* in which "our favorite" was "perfect. . . . He bids fair to be an ornament to the stage." He also carried the title role in *George Barnwell,* Octavian in *Mountaineers* (compared favorably to Cooper's), and Florian in *Foundling of the Forest.* His ability to portray evil, developed in *Richard III,* reemerged as Rashleigh Obaldstone in the frontier's first *Rob Roy.* Throughout the summer he carried other leads or major supporting roles in *Venice Preserved, Iron Chest, Mountaineers, Virginius, Castle Spectre,* and *Brutus.* At some point he essayed his first Othello, with Cargill as Iago and Mary Riddle as Desdemona. He later recalled being so unprepared that he lacked sufficient footwear or costume, and to simulate Othello's Moorish robe, "got a bed blanket from a neighboring store and wound himself up in it."[12]

Male leads not taken by Forrest were covered by Scott, generally deemed excellent, although at times "too slow, formal and deliberate." Riddle, also groomed for greater things, played female leads in farce, such as Little Pickle in *Spoiled Child,* and in tragedy, for example, Lady Randolph and Millwood to Forrest's Barnwell. In the former she was "highly respectable. . . . We have seldom witnessed the maternal affections more forcibly or affectingly portrayed." Nearly every night, "Miss Riddle"—which may have been Sarah or Eliza, or both—entertained with songs, dances, and roles in farces.[13]

In mid-June either Collins or Jones (it remains unclear which) left for Lexington to make arrangements for a suitable venue there, leaving the other to manage in Cincinnati. Reviews remained positive: "There was nothing that approximated to vulgarity, nothing coarse, nothing forced"; all was "refined, polished, yet natural." Despite summer weather, the theater was "agreeably cool." Yet attendance lagged.[14]

Inching into a managerial role, Sol Smith rented the Globe Theatre for one night, July 17, and paid the actors two dollars to perform in "a mammoth dramatic program." This consisted of a comedy written by his brother Martin entitled *Dandyism; or, Modern Fashions,* in which Forrest played Tom Tipple; a farce, also by Martin Smith, called *The Tailor in Distress,* in which Forrest assumed blackface to portray Cuffee (in the process supposedly Shanghaiing his African American washerwoman to play a small role); and a pantomimic *Don Quixote* with Forrest as Sancho Panza to Scott's Quixote.[15]

By July 27, the evening of Forrest's benefit in *Richard III,* the Cincinnati actors were literally starving, beset by poor attendance and renewed religious objection, and so disbanded. (Smith, incensed at moralists' attacks, unleashed a counterattack on preachers who rake in "a tolerable fat salary for such services.") Left to fend for themselves, Forrest, the Riddles, and a few others hired an old horse and wagon and headed off to barnstorm nearby towns: Hamilton, Lebanon, Franklin, and Dayton in Ohio, and Newport, Kentucky. The crowded house on their first night in Hamilton, July 31, in the candlelit second story of an old barn, may have resulted from the participation of its local thespian society. The evening, featuring Forrest's *Richard III*, netted them about fifty dollars, but business dwindled as the week went on. In the other towns it was practically nonexistent. Forrest was "compelled to pawn his trunks of stage costumes in Lebanon for money to send the ladies to Newport." They survived on purloined, roasted ears of corn. In Newport, in an old army barracks, they performed *Douglas* (Forrest as Young Norval) and *Miss in Her Teens* "to a house of seven dollars." They would need to rejoin Collins and Jones.[16]

~~~~~~~~~~~

The early months of 1823 had not dealt kindly with James Caldwell, either. He returned to New Orleans with his company on January 2 for four months—his last season at the Théâtre d'Orléans, which he pointedly rechristened the American Theatre. They opened two nights later with *Road to Ruin*. But the American was only part of his grand, four-pronged strategy. He intended to offer a larger, more accomplished company; to provide occasional novelties, including operas; to introduce intriguing new stars; and to expand his circuit to other frontier towns. The company was considerably larger than previously and included a number of married couples, providing continued stability and harmony. Caldwell carried leads opposite H. A. Williams, Mrs. Baker, Rosina Seymour, and his newest discovery, the beautiful eighteen-year-old Jane Placide, whom he had acquired in Richmond late in 1821.[17]

Having performed professionally since her early teens, she possessed "a fine person, an expressive stage face and [a] strong native power." She immediately struck critics as superbly talented (she "surpassed expectation"), if a little unrefined ("the rolling motion which sets off a chambermaid does not become a queen"). Further study of "the proper attitudes . . . of the tragic muse" was recommended. She would soon become romantically involved with the married Caldwell.[18]

A new melodrama on January 13, *The Exiles of Siberia*, provided exciting special effects, including a snowstorm. Two nights later a new Isaac Pocock comic opera, *John of Paris*, featured Placide. She was also a decided hit in

Wandering Boys, which ran five nights in late January. For his own early benefit on February 17, Caldwell starred in a melodramatic 1815 Pocock opera called *For Freedom Ho!* He also offered more traditional pieces, such as *She Stoops to Conquer, School for Scandal,* and *Hamlet* (Caldwell, with Placide as Ophelia).[19]

A series of stars commenced in mid-February, when Fanny and Aleck Drake debuted, she as Portia to Caldwell's Shylock and he in *Foundling of the Forest.* Far anticipating the 1850s heyday of precocious child stars, Caldwell introduced on February 26 "the American Roscius," twelve-year-old Master George Frederick Smith and his even-younger sister. This duo took on such classic scripts as *Romeo and Juliet, Mountaineers, Richard III, Hamlet,* and *Pizarro,* with a game Fanny Drake and Caldwell toiling in supporting roles and farcical afterpieces. But these novelties produced "very thin" audiences, especially a "beggarly account of empty boxes," with their concomitant higher ticket prices. (The *Gazette* advised the two children to "study hard, exercise much, and play seldom.") Moreover, the theater was inadequately heated, the supporting acting not always up to par, and the prompter's voice heard too often.[20]

The timely return of Cooper for twelve nights provided some relief. He opened on March 21 with *Macbeth,* opposite Fanny's Lady Macbeth and Caldwell's Macduff, with the three witches of Aleck, Ludlow, and Williams. Supported by these and by Placide, Cooper followed up with *Virginius, Venice Preserved, Julius Caesar, Damon and Pythias, King John, Bertram,* and *Othello,* nearly all opposite Caldwell. Awarding himself another benefit, Caldwell shared the stage with Cooper in *The Fair Penitent* on April 11. Master Smith volunteered his services, as did the new Mrs. Rowe, née Rosina Seymour, who in March had married Caldwell's treasurer, James S. Rowe.

Cooper then departed for Natchez, and Caldwell brought in Thomas Phillips, fresh from performing for Collins and Jones, for a week in mid-April, before season-ending benefits. Caldwell's last production in the Théâtre d'Orléans came on May 9, a benefit for Jackson Gray—one of Caldwell's most faithful actors—of *The Way to Get Married* and *Turn Out.* From that point on, the theater was used only by French actors until its abandonment in 1859.[21]

When Cooper departed for Natchez, he took with him several of Cald-well's troupe. This was to be Caldwell's fourth strategic prong: expansion of his circuit. Following the serial failures and departures of Turner and Jones, exacerbated by the second burning of its theater in September 1822, Nat-chez was far from a promising site. No longer the capital of Mississippi Ter-ritory (changed to Jackson in December 1822), its population barely topped two thousand, including the notorious denizens of Natchez-Under-the-Hill. Cultured residents had waited nearly a year and a half for the fulfillment of Caldwell's announced intent to bring theatre. Until he could build a permanent theater there, he rented and outfitted a seventy-by-thirty-two-foot ballroom which seated three hundred, in the largest hotel in Natchez, William Parker's Traveller's [sic] Hall, on First South (now State) Street near Second (now Wall) Street. This would be the first of eleven theatrical seasons in Natchez, each averaging about eight weeks, four nights a week.[22]

Caldwell sent to Natchez those actors he deemed capable of supporting a star of Cooper's caliber, among them his brother Edwin "Ned" Caldwell, William H. Benton (also as stage manager), Mr. and Mrs. Ludlow, Mary Bloxton, H. A. Williams, Fanny Drake, Mrs. Baker, and Master Smith. They opened on April 19 with *Damon and Pythias* (Cooper and Ludlow, respec-tively), followed by *Bertram, Gamester* (Cooper as Beverly, with Fanny as his wife), *Virginius* (Cooper, to her Virginia and Ned Caldwell's Icilius), *Honey Moon* (Cooper as Duke Aranza to Fanny's Juliana) and Cooper's *Othello*, ending with a reprise of *Virginius* on April 30.

The over-the-hill Dwyer followed Cooper with comedic leads, improb-ably interspersed with Master Smith's Richard III, Young Norval, and Rolla (opposite the consummate professionals Mrs. Baker as Cora and Fanny Drake as Elvira). The next visiting star, beginning May 21, was William Pelby, who enacted leads opposite Ludlow and Fanny in *Stranger, Damon and Pythias, Pizarro, Macbeth,* and *Catharine and Petruchio*.[23]

The box office during Cooper's run grossed an average of $340 nightly, but after he left, the drop-off was pronounced, perhaps triggered by Cald-well's decision to continue charging $2. Newspaper correspondents iden-tified only as "A Citizen" and "Amicus" lamented the inadequacy of Cald-well's company, accusing him of being interested only in filling his purse by sending mediocre performers who paled by comparison even to those of the unfortunate Jones. Only Cooper and Fanny were worthy of attendance, "but the appearance for a few nights of performers of celebrity cannot give character to a company. Indeed, such performers tend more to expose its defects [and] cannot compensate for the absence of talent."[24]

When word of this assessment reached Caldwell in New Orleans, he determined to send the rest of his company up to Natchez as soon as feasible. In the meantime, he was fending off other difficulties. In February his doorkeeper had been murdered by an angry interloper, and the New Orleans City Council had refused him a loan of $6,000 to finish his new theater, citing previous losses on similar loans. His plans to light this theater with gas—the first building of its kind in the city—were also complicated. Its ultimate cost would rise to $120,000 (over $3,000,000 today).[25]

To demonstrate his determination, he announced that performances by his remaining New Orleans actors would commence on May 14 in his new, unfinished American Theatre on Camp Street between Poydras and Gravier streets, amid the mud and warehouses in the remote American Sector, away from the fashionable French Quarter (the Faubourg Marigny). He did so, he said, to ascertain acoustical defects "which have been found to exist in many Theatres." This would save time and trouble and expense "which would arise in the event of any such defect being discovered in the *finished* state of the house."[26]

Despite its unfinished state and unpaved street, the American that night showcased *The Dramatist,* with Caldwell as Vapid and Placide as Louisa Courtney, and *The Romp,* featuring Placide. "For the benefit of the theatre," the avaricious Caldwell charged "prices unlimited." For two more weeks, still playing leads opposite Placide, he continued this experiment with such standard productions as *Honey Moon, Iron Chest, Mountaineers,* and *Rule a Wife and Have a Wife,* before closing on May 28 with *Lovers' Vows,* a benefit for the ubiquitous Master Smith, supported by his sister and Placide.[27]

Remaining in New Orleans to oversee work on his theater, Caldwell sent the rest of his company up to Natchez, bringing the company up to its full strength of twenty-five. By June 4 they were ready to offer a full-scale production of *Soldier's Daughter,* with Ludlow (given increasingly larger roles) as Frank Heartall and Mrs. Russell as Widow Cheerly, and *Rosina*, with the new Mrs. Rowe fittingly in the title role.[28]

Other scripts requiring a full company followed, including *The Wonder!* (with Ludlow and Placide in the leads), the melodramatic *Warlock of the Glen, Guy Mannering* (with Placide as Meg Merrilies) and *Forty Thieves.* Caldwell arrived in time to play Charles Surface in *School for Scandal* opposite the Lady Teazle of Mrs. Russell and the Joseph Surface of Benton. He closed out this Natchez season on July 5 with a benefit for himself, playing Reuben Glenroy in *Town and Country.* The Natchez effort, however, was ultimately unprofitable.

Caldwell then sent his troupe under Richard Russell's direction to Nashville, while he headed back to New Orleans, and from there to Virginia to fulfill acting commitments. In Nashville, Russell's company opened on July 13 with *Soldier's Daughter* in the theater on Cherry Street erected in 1820 by Collins and Jones which Caldwell had disparaged as being little better than a barn. A few company members, including Benton, defected en route, but Russell easily replaced them in Nashville.

Nashville newspaper correspondents "A Lover of the Drama" and "Shakespeare" encouraged attendance, emphasizing that the actors were "very respectable." This "superior" company was expending "extraordinary exertions . . . to render themselves agreeable to the public." Ludlow and Russell (possibly among the correspondents) were acclaimed as "sometimes excellent," and Placide was "irresistible," with "abilities of a high order." It was feared that, if Caldwell lost money, his company would not return to Nashville. By October 27 he rejoined his company to enact *Hamlet,* and ended the venture by performing the title roles in *Henry IV* (with Gray as Falstaff) on November 26, and in *Bertram* two nights later.[29]

A factor which had contributed to their lack of success in Natchez and driven them north to Nashville was the worst yellow fever outbreak ever seen in the former city. By December an early frost had quelled the outbreak, allowing them to return. They opened in the same Natchez ballroom on December 10 with Ludlow and Placide playing the leads in *Stranger* and *Rendezvous.* Caldwell left part of the company, notably including the Ludlows and Placide, there and took the rest to Baton Rouge. After the Natchez group ended their engagement in late December, that town remained bereft of any professional theatre for four years. By Christmas, Caldwell had his reunited company back in New Orleans. But he would have to rethink the expansion of his circuit.

~~~~~~~~~~

When Collins and Jones had left Cincinnati in mid-June to solidify Lexington as part of *their* expanded circuit, they had widely disseminated notice of their intent to bring a strong company of actors there. This was received "with considerable pleasure" by "Garrick" in the *Kentucky Gazette*. Practicing the same strategy as Caldwell of splitting a company to cover two cities, by early July they had brought half of their actors over from Cincinnati, including the itinerant Mrs. Pelby. "Garrick" was certain that her every entrance would be greeted with rapture. Collins and Jones, too, were guaranteed to perform "truly great" tragedy as well as keep the house "in a roar of laughter." The *Lexington Reporter* concurred: their previous efforts had been "conducted with talent and judgment and won for itself the countenance and support of an intelligent community."[30]

By August the company was back to full strength, the others having arrived from Cincinnati, a necessity for adequately supporting their first visiting stars of the season. These were Fanny and Aleck Drake, he having detoured to perform a few nights in Louisville at the end of July in an ephemeral venue called the Dramatic Lounge. They opened in Lexington on August 27 in *Stranger*, followed by *Romeo and Juliet*, *Othello*, and Inchbald's *Every One Has His Fault*, with Aleck occasionally applying his artistic skills to the creation of new scenery.

When Aleck and Fanny left, Forrest and the Riddles arrived, ready for steady work after their barnstorming. From September 22 through November 6 Forrest played leads and key supporting roles. On November 4 he performed a more polished Othello—a role he would play at least 350 times in his career, to the Iago of Collins. On the night he played Myrtillo in Allingham's *'Tis All a Farce*, he was joined on stage by the Numpo of Sol Smith, now all of twenty-two, who had quit the newspaper business for good.

Smith tells of being informed by Jones that he and Collins were about to retire from management, leading Smith to contemplate forming a company of his own. According to Smith, Forrest sought to sign on, but Smith reminded him of his obligation to Caldwell. The Collins and Jones company, Forrest later recalled, "came to grief in Lexington and I cast about to see what I could do." Collins and Jones released him from his contract, and he departed, temporarily joining Pépin and Blanchard's traveling circus on his way to New Orleans.[31]

On the cusp of retirement, Collins and Jones limped along in Lexington through December, distributing leads among Henderson, the Pelbys, and the visiting A. M. Wilson. Julia Jones, too, had become a local favorite. Her personal demeanor was especially praiseworthy: "In almost every character . . . she has displayed justness of conception, decency and propriety of action, and has never overstepped the modesty of nature." Perhaps more importantly in that era, "In her domestic circle and private life, her conduct is exemplary, her moral character without a stain." But the season overall was a failure, "arduous and unprofitable," sending the company in bitter cold weather back to Cincinnati for another try.[32]

They opened there on January 10, 1824, with a standard, *The Poor Soldier*, in the City Theater (formerly the Globe, in a revolving door of appellations), revamped for warmth and comfort. They promised that "great care will be taken to select plays of sterling merit" and they would ensure "order and decorum in the house," the lack of which had been "a serious objection to patronizing the establishment; proper officers will be in readiness to take into custody all persons who shall make any disturbance." New additions to the regular company were touted. For three weeks, augmented by the comedy of the ineluctable "Handsome Jack" Dwyer, the company struggled to attract an audience with repetitions of *Poor Soldier* and similar fare (for example, *Castle Spectre, Hunter of the Alps, 'Tis All a Farce*).[33]

But failure loomed. In early February, with Collins in poor health, he and Jones offered the lease of their Columbia Street Theatre to Sol Smith, who then commenced an equally unprofitable management with the same actors, augmented by Cincinnati amateurs. A benefit for Greek Independence raised more than three hundred dollars, and another sought funds to finally complete the theater's portico. But by March, Smith had fallen over a thousand dollars in debt. He also battled with the amateur thespians, one of whom struck him on the head with a rusty prop sword in the greenroom one night just before an entrance. The two groups parted ways after the March 19 performance of *Daniel Boone, 1777,* with Dwyer in the title role, Fenton as Boone's wife, and the ailing Collins as George Rogers Clark. (One of the combined troupe's last performances had been a benefit for Collins.)[34]

Smith took Mr. and Mrs. Jones, James M. Scott, Henderson, and the newly married Louisa Fenton and George Rowe east, to Wheeling, Virginia, Steubenville, Ohio, and then Pittsburgh and various towns in central Pennsylvania and western Maryland, but they met with only "indifferent success." A brief return to Cincinnati in late August 1824, which Smith omits in his memoirs, appears to have been equally undistinguished.[35]

Collins and Jones then parted ways. Collins's health continued to decline—Ludlow termed him at that time "a living skeleton." Unwilling to totally abandon his art, he crossed the river to join the Drake company, but "broke down from the effects of his misfortunes," dying at Versailles, Kentucky, on March 16, 1825, and was buried there, "leaving his wife and daughter penniless."[36]

William and Julia Jones headed east, where he played minor roles in New York, then took over the management of the Arch Street Theatre in Philadelphia. But his health, too, rapidly declined, and he died on November 30, 1842, at age sixty-three, cared for in his final days in the home of Edwin Forrest, reciprocating the kindness Jones had extended to him at the start of his career. Julia Jones continued to act nearly until her death five years later.

Amateur thespians held on to the Columbia Street Theatre in Cincinnati until March 1824, when it was closed by the city. In spring 1825 it was sold at auction for arrears to long-time Cincinnati amateur thespians Nicholas Longworth and Peyton S. Symmes for $534 plus retiring the balance of its mortgage still held by Thomas D. Carneal ($1,200), a far cry from its original cost of $5,000.

Collins and Jones's legacy, like William Turner's, cannot be overlooked. Before the rise and preeminence of the Drakes, Caldwell, Ludlow, and

Smith, these men faced, and surmounted, considerable odds to bring professional theatre to the frontier. Building on the groundwork laid by amateur thespian societies, Usher and the Turners, they applied a shrewd eye for talent, for a potential market, and for the right material to overcome religious objection, to take that theatre to a higher level. Unfortunately, having never recorded their memoirs like the later Ludlow and Smith, they have been relegated to historical obscurity. But as Caldwell himself observed, Collins and Jones "were men of talent and would have succeeded," but "the death of Collins put an end to that attempt" until Drake and Caldwell moved in.[37] A generation, and a significant phase of frontier theatre, thus closed.

9

THE CALDWELL ERA

(1824–1826)

WHEN ALECK AND FANNY DRAKE left Cincinnati in September 1823, they headed for Kentucky. There Aleck, now twenty-five, prepared to take over theatrical management, which his father during the next year would cede to him. The elder Drake at over two hundred pounds only acted occasionally, in roles requiring minimal physical exertion, such as Duncan in *Macbeth* and Claudius in *Hamlet*. He increasingly retreated to his 150-acre farm on the Ohio River near Prospect, Kentucky.

Aleck's first stint at management came in late November in Frankfort, the annual stand during the legislative session. For two weeks he applied "his utmost exertions to please the public." Fanny of course carried leads, opposite James M. Scott, his "considerable merit" compared favorably to that of Kean and Cooper. His "Damon and Virginius surpasses [*sic*] any tragic acting we have ever had in Frankfort." Austin Cargill was "always respectable and pleasing," and Aleck entertained with comic songs, especially "The Hunters of Kentucky." Sam Sr. took the stage now and then, and was "always good."[1]

In early 1824 Aleck decided to bypass Lexington, which was undergoing a financial crisis and unable to support theatrical activity other than sporadic amateur performances. He took the company on to Louisville and opened a new season in his newly cleaned and repainted theater on January 17 with *The Soldier's Daughter* and *Nature and Philosophy*.

His company was led by Fanny, Alexander M. Wilson, Rosalie Pelby, and Scott. They carried most leads in classical tragedies (for example, *Bertram*, *Hamlet*), melodramas (such as *Castle Spectre*, *Timour the Tartar* (produced jointly with Pépin and Blanchard's Circus), comedies (for example, *School for Scandal, Poor Gentleman*) and an occasional pantomime (such as *The Deserter; or, The Power of Female Charms Over Men*).

Benefits began February 21 with one for Greek Independence which generated only $222. Scott's, on March 27, consisted of *Abaellino,* songs by Cargill and Mrs. Pelby, and *The Miller and His Men.* For Aleck's own benefit on April 24 he naturally chose comedies, *The Jew* and *Mock Doctor.* Continuing his father's ways, he appealed to "the justice and liberality of the lovers of the Drama" to pay off the accrued five-dollar-per-night tax owed to the Louisville trustees. Fanny was surprisingly not accorded a benefit. She and Aleck departed at season's end on May 12, she to open in New York at the Chatham Garden, and he to perform in occasional farces where he could. The rest of the company was left to fend for itself. For a few weeks the amateur Louisville Juvenile Thespian Society leased the theater, but soon closed (likely hit with the same tax).[2]

<hr />

In January 1824 James Caldwell achieved new heights of success in New Orleans. The risk he had taken by constructing his new American Theatre on Camp Street was about to pay off. Erected at a cost of $70,000, this first permanent English theater in New Orleans was a marvel of nineteenth-century architecture and engineering. Its imposing facade of five arches between Doric columns rested atop a flight of nine marble steps. Its brick construction was designed to deter destruction by fire. The gas illumination outside and in, comprised of 250 lights, was the first of its kind west of the Alleghenies, and only the third in the United States (after theaters in Philadelphia and Baltimore, and two years before any in New York). Its pit and boxes, accommodating eight hundred patrons on mahogany chairs with crimson upholstery, were carpeted to improve acoustics. The gallery seated another two hundred in less splendor. An interior decor of blue silk, rose damask ("calculated to set off the fair complexions of the ladies"), silver stars, and wreaths of flowers was commanded by a thirty-eight-foot-wide proscenium of gilded marble pillars. A staff of police enforced prohibitions on men wearing hats indoors, the smoking of "segars," and any behavior which disturbed "the general silence."[3]

Caldwell's highly capable stock company remained much the same as the previous year's, ensuring competence. At 7:00 p.m. on January 1, 1824, he strode onto the stage's apron and proclaimed his intention "To classic height exalt the rising age, and give to peerless, lasting fame the Stage." That night's performance consisted of the popular *Town and Country* and *Of Age Tomorrow*. Subsequent Mondays, Thursdays, and Saturdays saw a combination of established scripts (for example, *Rule a Wife, Rob Roy*) and new works (such as Noah's national drama *Marion* and Holcroft's comedy, *The Deserted Daughter*). Caldwell intended to anchor his productions with stars from the East. These began on January 16 with the Macbeth of William Pelby, followed by his Virginius, Hamlet, Antony in *Julius Caesar*, Damon, Petruchio, and the title role in Payne's *Brutus*, nearly all opposite the increasingly accomplished Jane Placide, still only twenty years old.[4]

After his stint as an actor/rider/tumbler for Pépin and Blanchard's circus in Lexington, Edwin Forrest, about to turn eighteen, appeared on Camp Street on February 4 to fulfill his obligation to Caldwell. Beginning that night, he undertook for eighteen dollars a week a series of leading and supporting roles such as Jaffier to Caldwell's Pierre in *Venice Preserved*, and Dorlin in Payne's melodrama *Adeline* opposite Placide in the title role. The most popular piece that spring was Pocock's *Zembuca*, which ran for six consecutive nights in April. Benefits began in mid-May, with Forrest enacting Ephraim Smooth in *Wild Oats*, then a few nights later Richard III. For his own benefit, Caldwell performed the title role in *Miller and His Men*, then concluded the season on June 8 with a benefit for the New Orleans Orphan Boys' Asylum. He then took the more talented half of the company, including Forrest and Placide, back to Virginia for the summer, leaving the other half under Ludlow's management to tour the South.[5]

Ludlow, twenty-nine, used the opportunity to initiate a five-year effort to establish theatre in the Deep South, in what would prove to be his truest test yet of managerial skill. In Nashville, he gathered as equal shareholders the small company who had not gone east with Caldwell. The going was rough. For a month they struggled to attract audiences to the Cherry Street Theatre with such lighthearted pieces as *Honey Moon, Poor Gentleman*, and *Highland Reel*. Attracting only small audiences, Ludlow took them further south, to Huntsville, Alabama, where he had unsuccessfully performed between 1818 and 1822. As a result of the fire of 1821, they performed in the large room of the Bell Tavern for five weeks using rudimentary costumes and props and several utilitarian scenic backdrops. But this engagement too proved unprofitable, causing Ludlow's first defections: Wilson, Gray, and William Forrest left to join Caldwell, leaving Ludlow considerably short of males. He believed, however, that their presence in Huntsville, performing for "a cultivated and highly respected class of persons," prompted civic leaders to initiate a subscription to build a permanent theater for his (but in reality, Caldwell's) later use.[6]

In early October Ludlow took his diminished company to Cahawba, the swampy, temporary state capital of Alabama, where they performed in a "miserable, forlorn-looking building" on the outskirts of town, "poorly-arranged" for what had been amateur theatrical performances, at times surrounded by shin-deep water. (Severe flooding the following year led to its abandonment as capital.) After box office receipts decreased from "tolerably good" to "miserable pittances," they left to try their luck in Mobile, which had seen no theatrical activity since Emanuel Judah's and other amateur troupes in 1822.[7]

Ludlow had arranged in June to have a permanent theater ready there by November 1, but upon arrival was distressed to find only the exterior brick walls erected and work only begun on the stage. He frantically solicited financial backing and contracted with carpenters and painters, leading to its completion in seven weeks. The 60-by-110-foot brick building, situated on the site of an old Spanish fort on the southeast corner of Royal and Theatre streets, seated (variously) six hundred to seven hundred patrons. They opened on Christmas Eve with Ludlow's favorite script, *Honey Moon*, and a farce, *The Liar*.

Temporizing with plays having predominantly female casts, many showcasing the "young, handsome and sprightly" Sarah Riddle, sixteen, Ludlow was forced out of his "line" to play such tragic characters as Virginius and Macbeth. Eventually, he added John H. Wells, George O. Champlin, Henry Young, and Edward Morrison (amateurs, likely). He drew enough patrons from Mobile's population of three thousand to justify remaining there until spring 1825, during which time he contracted for several lavish scenic drops, which ate up any profits. From Mobile he took his meager company to Tuscaloosa for the summer, performing in the ballroom of Hogan's Hotel through October.[8]

~~~~~~~~~~

The 1825 return to New Orleans of Caldwell and his company signals the end of that city's consideration as a theatrical frontier, establishing his permanent theatrical status there. This new season of his American Theatre on Camp Street was an acknowledged success from its opening on January 3 with *Soldier's Daughter* and *No Song, No Supper*. His company was the largest and most accomplished he had yet assembled, and Caldwell himself had matured into a versatile, dynamic actor. Sol Smith, even in later years when the two men fought, said, "I have never yet beheld his equal as a light comedian. [He played] the whole range of tragedy . . . as if he were running the chromatic scale of the gamut in music. No actor gave greater satisfaction to Southern audiences than he did. He was scrupulously guarded in giving the true text of Shakespeare when performing *his* characters."[9]

Favorable attendance allowed Caldwell to initiate short runs of successful shows, such as William Moncrieff's *Tom and Jerry* (with Caldwell, Wilson, and Russell in the leads), which ran January 16–21. As he had done with Junius Brutus Booth, Caldwell introduced visiting stars to his audiences at the American, beginning on March 2 with six-foot-plus British tragedian William Augustus Conway, thirty-six, who had immigrated to the United States two years earlier after receiving demoralizing reviews in his home country. New York reviews had been favorable. As Hamlet, "His whole soul seems absorbed by the intensity of his melancholy and sensibility." Now, in New Orleans, Conway played an eight-night engagement which included *Othello*, with Caldwell as Iago and Rosina Rowe as Desdemona, drawing an overflowing crowd.[10]

After Conway's departure, in keeping with Caldwell's experimentation with assigning leads to various company members, he entrusted the role of Iago to Edwin Forrest, presumably to his own Othello. Among several nights of *Pizarro* he rotated the key male roles of Rolla, Pizarro, and Alonzo among himself, Wilson, and Forrest, and the key female roles of Cora and Elvira among Jane Placide, her older, widowed sister, Caroline Placide Waring, and Mrs. Battersby. A May 22 production of *Richard III* featured Mr. and Mrs. Noke in the leads, despite Noke's normal assignment as orchestra leader.[11]

A noteworthy event that season was the April 10–15 visit to New Orleans of the Marquis de Lafayette, touring the United States to warmhearted hospitality and universal accolades for his contribution to American independence a half century before. On April 11 he attended first the American Theatre for Caldwell's 7:00 p.m. welcoming address and "the new historical play," *La Fayette; or, the Castle of Olmutz* (the site of Lafayette's imprisonment, 1794–97), then moved at 9:00 to the Théâtre d'Orléans to see *L'École des Vieillards*. On April 14 he returned to the Orleans for a Creole vaudeville, *Lafayette in New Orleans*, before heading north to other frontier cities.[12]

Shortly before the season ended on May 28, Caldwell provided Forrest with a choice role, that of Colonel Mordaunt in a week-long run of a Moncrieff melodrama, *Cataract of the Ganges*. Despite this encouragement, and Forrest's having been received as "the idol of the community," he fell out with Caldwell over an infatuation with Jane Placide, already Caldwell's paramour. Forrest demanded of Caldwell "the satisfaction of a gentleman" (that is, a duel), which elicited only laughter from Caldwell. Forrest denounced him as a scoundrel and coward and departed in high dudgeon into the frontier interior, to live for two months with a native chief, an association which yielded verisimilitude to his later portrayal of native characters.[13]

~~~~~~~~~~

Back from New York and nearly as determined as Caldwell to reestablish his theatrical hold on the frontier, Aleck Drake in early February 1825 reassembled his company in Louisville for its regular spring season. He determined this year to expand his circuit back into Lexington, Frankfort, and Cincinnati. His company consisted of fewer family members, although he and Fanny still formed its nucleus. As was often the case in the close-knit world of traveling theatrical troupes, Sam Jr., twenty-eight, had in April 1824 married Anna Palmer Fisher, fifteen, bringing her into the family business. But Sam Sr. no longer acted, and Julia Drake, who in March 1823 had married Cincinnati banker/poet/newspaper editor Thomas R. Fosdick, no longer acted, caring for their newborn son, William.

In Louisville the Drake company performed on Saturdays and Wednesdays, beginning on February 5 with *The Apostate*. Their repertoire for the next eight weeks remained much as it had for the past three years, with such familiar pieces as *Pizarro, Miller and His Men, Catharine and Petruchio, Lying Valet, Day After the Wedding,* and *Abaellino.* For those eight weeks, except for occasional recitations, Fanny did not act, due to her delivery of a daughter, Julia (named for her actress aunt), who herself would one day marry into a different theatrical family and deliver other future actors. On April 16 Fanny returned to the stage to costar with the itinerant Conway in *Hamlet.* For a week they performed together in *Gamester, Stranger,* and (for Conway's farewell benefit on April 23) *Jealous Wife* and *Wedding Day.* (This was Kentuckians' last chance to see Conway, as he would in 1828 commit suicide by leaping from his ship en route back to England.)

Hailed as a "hometaught [sic] favorite" who "from his earliest days has been a great support to our stage," Aleck closed the season on May 5 but reopened for two special performances. The first, a week later, honored the visiting Lafayette, who received a standing ovation. (When Lafayette moved on to Cincinnati, he was similarly honored and entertained by its amateurs, augmented by Sol Smith and his younger brother Sam, a noted singer, as they had done for Andrew Jackson in late March.) The second was a benefit for Aleck himself on May 18, which he desperately needed, having recently been robbed "of a very considerable sum of money."[14]

By early June, the Drake company was on its way to Lexington to try to revive professional theatrical activity there, replacing the amateur Lexington Thespian Society. The Drake company performed in the ballroom of Keen's Hall. Sparse newspaper notices only report that "the company is not very strong, but the performances are good," particularly those of Fanny, Aleck, Sam Jr., and Albert J. Marks, a "short, fat, round-faced, good-natured" comedian. After a closing benefit for Fanny on June 28 of *Douglas* and *Lock and Key,* Aleck spent July and August personally overseeing the ongoing renovation of Usher's neglected theater. His company performed for most of July at Greenville Springs, known for its medicinal waters, in Harrodsburg, Kentucky.[15]

On Monday, August 29, with Fanny as Miss Hardcastle in *She Stoops to Conquer*, Aleck proudly reopened Usher's Lexington Theatre. It featured a new pit and boxes, new drop curtain, and a thorough repainting and redecorating. He had also expanded his company, adding Joseph Page (up from Caldwell), Henry R. Crampton, and actors named Katen, Lewis, Mrs. Justis, Miss Neville, and Miss Andrews, who may have been acquired from the amateur troupe, as they do not continue with the Drakes after this engagement.

Unfortunately, after the novelty of opening night, business fell off, attributed to the poor economy, unseasonably hot, dry weather, and "lots of private parties among the fashionables." To gin up revenue, Drake brought Mr. and Mrs. John Carter up from Caldwell's company, billing them as stars "from the Baltimore and Philadelphia theatres." They took the leads in *Mountaineers* and *Of Age Tomorrow* on September 12 and *Woodman's Hut* and *Irishman in London* on September 19.[16]

But business failed to improve, leading Drake to plead for patronage. Box office fell so short that it imposed on him "the painful duty of stating the impossibility of proceeding with the season, unless the friends and lovers of the drama" came forward. He promised exciting novelties, new scenery, and an improved orchestra under the direction of Sam Jr. The *Kentucky Reporter* reminded its readers that "our town never before enjoyed [such] a well-regulated theatre, though it has seldom been so ill-supported." As the company performed *The Rendezvous* and "the celebrated out and out classic, comic, operatic, Didactic, Moralistic, Aristophanic, Localic, Terpsichoric, Panoramic Camera Obscura, &c, Extravaganza Burletta, of Fun, Frolic, Fashion and Flash in two acts called *Tom and Jerry*," attendance began to improve.[17]

But it did not last, even as the *Reporter* doubled down: "The drama ought to be encouraged as it affords both amusement and instruction and often restrains those vicious and low indulgencies which corrupt the taste and the habits of the gay and inexperienced." After a series of benefits, including Sam Jr.'s Macbeth, Aleck closed in Lexington on November 3 and took the company to Frankfort, hoping for better results.[18]

In their absence Usher's theater—along with its "dwelling house adjoining"—was sold at auction on November 8, following six years of litigation over debts owed to a raft of creditors. The new owners allowed Drake upon returning to Lexington to continue to perform in the theater, beginning November 19 with Fanny in the title role of *Evadne*, followed two nights later by her Florinda in *Apostate*. Her acting was hailed as the best "that has ever been witnessed by the playgoing people in this town" and her husband as "one of our best performers—one who spares no pains to make himself acceptable. . . . Whether the boxes be full or empty A. Drake exerts the same spirit."[19]

But poor box office continued, and he took the company back to Frankfort within two weeks, to coincide with the legislature's session. When it concluded, he brought them back to Lexington, opening on December 17 with *Evadne*. Within a week of Fanny's benefit on December 27 of *As You Like It* and *Day After the Wedding*, her husband closed the disappointing Lexington engagement, not to return for almost three years.[20]

~~~~~~~~~~

During the fall of 1825 Ludlow continued his quest to establish a southern theatrical circuit, albeit in a lesser orbit. After his summer in Tuscaloosa, he took his small company in October to Montgomery, Alabama, which had not enjoyed anything close to professional theatre since Judah's 1822 venture and a series of comic lectures and songs by widower John Vaughan (with two of his children, ages nine and six, in tow) in January 1824. Its population not yet fifteen hundred, Montgomery seemed a considerable risk to support such an effort, but Ludlow was game.

He secured performance space in the garret of a brick building at the corner of Commerce and Tallapoosa streets, the Montgomery Thespian Society monopolizing the ballroom of the Montgomery Hotel. This demoralizing space could only be reached by ascending a crude flight of exterior stairs and stooping through a low window. The rough wooden seats, all on a dead level, lacked any covering. Stage space was so limited that the actors were compelled to dress in their rooms downstairs and, wrapped in cloaks, enter the same window and thread their way through the audience to the stage. "If a change of dress was required during the progress of a play, it had to be done behind a temporary screen across one corner of the room."[21]

The company was small but competent. They performed from October 20 (*The Review*) through November 4 (*Town and Country*), including a few challenging scripts (*Bertram, Damon and Pythias,* and *Jane Shore*). After they left, Montgomery would see no professional theatre for three and a half years. Ludlow and his company then headed for Mobile.[22]

<hr />

With his position in New Orleans secure, Caldwell in the summer of 1825 turned his back on eastern cities such as Richmond and Charleston, which had brought him recognition and success in America. Instead, he renewed his efforts to establish a wide theatrical circuit: Nashville, Huntsville, Natchez, Cincinnati, and Lexington. This was the dawn of the "Caldwell era" beyond New Orleans.

He took his company in late June first to Nashville, which since Ludlow's departure had been entertained only by an amateur thespian society. There, Caldwell advertised his intent to overcome the difficulties and expenses required for a professional company to prevail. Performing on Mondays, Wednesdays, Fridays, and Saturdays, they provided essentially the same repertoire as in New Orleans, including *School for Scandal, Rendezvous, Laugh When You Can, The Liar, The Aethiop,* and *Tom and Jerry.* Caldwell usually took leads, including Hamlet, Gossamer in *Laugh When You Can,* and the title role in *Aethiop* opposite Jane Placide's Cephania. But despite new scenery and costumes, Caldwell was thwarted by low attendance, possibly due to "the unusual warmth of the season." He closed in Nashville on August 10, vowing to renew his efforts in fall, when the weather improved, leaving the city to the amateur thespians.[23]

He then hedged his bets by again splitting his company, keeping half in Nashville and sending the others to Huntsville under Wilson, who was also to oversee the construction of its theater. Caldwell opened with his half on October 24 in Nashville, taking the lead in *Honey Moon.* As Duke Aranza, this "great favorite . . . could not be better." Other roles were played by comedian W. C. Drummond, a "fine symmetrical" actor with "a good, full and flexible voice" who had been performing on the frontier for six years. He "produced an electrical effect upon the audience" with his "great muscular power" and "freedom and vigor of his movements."[24]

The rest of the Nashville troupe came in for similar accolades. Russell's "wonderful command over the muscles of his face" produced "an irresistible proclivity to laughter. He is, and deservedly, a great favorite." His wife succeeded with a voice "peculiarly adapted to the light, sprightly tones of gaiety and joy." Her Widow Cheerly was "absolutely inimitable. She enters perfectly in the joyous, thoughtless light-hearted hilarity of the Widow's character. . . . Her smile is absolutely bewitching." Mrs. Rowe shone in characters of "artless, unsuspecting, innocent simplicity [and] naiveté." Mrs. Higgins, as "a cross-grained, querulous old woman, possesses great excellence."[25]

Othello followed, along with *School of Reform* and *Young Widow*, before Caldwell left to join his Huntsville actors, trading places with Wilson. In Nashville, Wilson proved a poor draw—bordering on total apathy—in such roles as Virginius, Pierre in *Venice Preserved*, and Shylock in *Merchant of Venice*.

He had been popular in Huntsville, though, and Caldwell's appearance there afforded "Euripides" of the *Huntsville Democrat* the chance to pen a lengthy comparison of their Hamlets. Wilson's was "more immediately and carelessly transported into the moment." Caldwell's was founded on technique, with a keen awareness of the power and eloquence of his soliloquies and how to "make his points." He exhibited "a judgment and taste decidedly superior to Mr. Wilson," although "both have exceeded our most sanguine calculations." Both men were supported by Jane Placide's Ophelia, idolized for a talent among "the highest tribunal her profession can ever bring." Her face reflected "every change, shade and inflection of the mind which can *alone* stamp superior dignity on any performance."[26]

Caldwell was shrewd in his decision to expand into Huntsville. Although its 1825 the population was only 1,512, the town was expanding rapidly on the strength of its cotton industry and rampant land speculation. Building on Ludlow's groundwork there, including the impetus for the erection of a theater (to open in 1826), Caldwell applied superior financial and personnel resources to establish a beachhead, making Huntsville a part of his expanding circuit. Ludlow, 330 miles to the south in Mobile, was understandably resentful, "almost pathological in his conviction that Caldwell wanted to ruin him."[27]

Deriving revenue that fall from both Huntsville and Nashville, Caldwell compounded his earnings in early December by bringing his Huntsville actors back to Nashville to perform scripts which necessitated the combined company. They opened on December 5 with a lavish staging of Shakespeare's *King Henry IV*, with Caldwell as Hotspur and Jackson Gray as Falstaff. For three weeks they performed equally challenging works, including *Macbeth* (Caldwell, with Jane Placide as Lady Macbeth), *Aethiop* (Caldwell in the title role, with Jane as Cephania), the melodrama *Magpie and the Maid* (Jane as Annette for her benefit), and the historical drama *Frederick the Great* (Caldwell in the title role, opposite Jane and Mrs. Rowe). By the end of December they were on their way back to New Orleans for their regular winter season, eagerly awaited by its population, which now topped 35,000. Wilson, however, returned to Huntsville on Caldwell's behalf to oversee the completion of its theater.[28]

~~~~~~~~~~

Meanwhile, Aleck Drake in early 1826 was attempting to maintain his hold on Louisville. His company remained small (himself, Fanny, Sam and Anna Drake, Mr. and Mrs. Carter, Henderson, Katen, Page, and Miss Andrews), necessitating frequent doubling of roles. They opened on January 31 with *Tom and Jerry*, with once- or twice-a-week performances of familiar pieces, including *Douglas, Heir at Law, Apostate, Pizarro, Padlock*, and *Hunter of the Alps*. A benefit for Louisville Masons on February 4 yielded $140. On February 15 a Mrs. Johns, on her way from Montreal to join Caldwell in New Orleans, stopped by to cover leads for a few nights, likely freeing Fanny for childcare. Johns enacted Mrs. Haller in *Stranger*, Little Pickle in *Spoiled Child*, and the title role in *Jane Shore*.

Aleck took the first night of benefits for himself, on March 22, performing *Miller and His Men*, a comic song, and *The Lady and the Devil*. But the night's take was disappointing, so he scheduled another for himself at season's end. Fanny's on April 29 was attended by Prince Karl Bernhard of

Saxe-Weimar-Eisenach, thirty-two, who found the troupe disappointing despite a well-filled house. Except for her, he thought "the dramatic corps were very ordinary. . . . Most of the actors were dressed very badly, had not committed their parts, and played in a vulgar style. One actor was so intoxicated that he was hardly able to keep his legs." Aleck's closing benefit on May 10—*Forty Thieves,* followed by an olio of songs, dances, recitations— was again disappointing, possibly due to the city's smallpox epidemic. Discouraged but undeterred, he and his company left for Cincinnati.[29]

~~~~~~~~~~~

Still competing with Drake and Caldwell on the frontier, Ludlow had opened in Mobile on December 28, 1825, in the newly repainted Royal Street Theatre. Gradually, during the winter and early spring of 1826, he enlarged his company by adding vocalist John Still; Alexander Wilson (briefly, en route to Huntsville, who likely kept Caldwell well appraised of Ludlow's actions in Alabama); comedian Thomas Placide, Jane's brother, eighteen, discouraged by the limited opportunities afforded him by Caldwell and hired by Ludlow as a "walking gentleman" for ten dollars a week; Abram W. Jackson, twenty, whose bearded, dark features made him suitable for heavies, at the same rate; Mr. and Mrs. Albert J. Marks; and Samuel Emberton from Drake. Bringing the total complement to twenty-two were John Young and B. McKinney and men named Wilton, Pilley, and Ballow (probably amateurs, for utility roles). Ludlow also allowed Eliza Riddle, now fourteen, to graduate from occasional olio dances to small roles in farces, the beginning of a highly successful career on the stage.[30]

For four months they played a variety of dramas (for example, *Douglas, Thérèse, George Barnwell, Jane Shore,* and *Guy Mannering*), melodramas (such as *Broken Sword, Forest of Rosenwald,* and *Tale of Mystery*) and comedies (for example, *Lovers' Quarrels, The Poor Soldier,* and *Catharine and Petruchio*). Ludlow's grandiose vision even prompted him to employ this company in tragedy, including *Macbeth* on April 21.

At the close of the Mobile season in early May he sent his wife and children by sea to New York. Then, scouting the state of theatrical affairs on the frontier, he proceeded to Louisville, where he visited the elder Drake, and to Cincinnati, where he noted that the Columbia Street Theatre was "still standing, but unoccupied." He then headed to Philadelphia and New York to recruit professionals to compete more forcefully against Caldwell and Drake during the 1826–27 season on the frontier.[31]

~~~~~~~~~~

While Ludlow was in New York, Caldwell turned his focus again to his Huntsville theater. Completed in mid-January 1826 under Wilson, who would manage it in Caldwell's absence, the small building was initially used by amateur thespians for lighthearted fare. Caldwell needed Huntsville to be a success to offset the more than $6,000 he had lost on his New Orleans season, which had concluded on May 29. He nevertheless had retained sufficient funds to underwrite part of the Huntsville theater's construction, which is more than Ludlow had done in 1824 when plans for it were first broached. Still, Ludlow fumed for years that the civic leaders of Huntsville had promised *him* its use and blamed Wilson's duplicity for the loss of this opportunity.[32]

Caldwell publicized his Huntsville theater widely, assuring potential patrons "that every possible exertion will be made for the purpose of eliciting the best patronage," meaning riffraff would be kept away. On opening night, July 24, he delivered a properly pretentious dedicatory invocation: "O fostering Genius of the rising Stage / Display the treasures of thy classic page / Here let the tragic and the comic Muse / Mingle their crimson and their airy hues." Then followed inaugural productions of *Honey Moon* and *Of Age Tomorrow*.[33]

The productions Caldwell provided Huntsville reflected a tasteful balance of comedy (for example, *Belle's Stratagem*, *Spoiled Child*, *Tom and Jerry*), melodrama (such as *Devil's Bridge*) and tragedy (for example, *Macbeth*, *Stranger*, *Pizarro*). While all of his actors performed well, it was Jane Placide who shone the brightest. Her most evident asset, notably employed as Lady Macbeth and as Elvira in *Pizarro*, was "her complete identification with the character which she personates. . . . Every look, every motion, every gesture [is] correct and masterly, particularly anger, revenge, love and pity." Her speaking voice was "clear, forcible and distinct," and her singing voice, "sweet, melodious and flexible."[34]

But disappointingly small audiences turned out. One reviewer regretted "that this company, respectable and highly gifted as they are, and possessing every imaginable claim to public patronage, are too numerous for the limited support which our small village can extend." Even the vaunted Placide on the night of her benefit failed to draw "a larger share of that patronage to which she is so justly entitled." By the end of the short Huntsville season on September 2, Caldwell's own benefit (appropriately, *The Managers in Distress*), he had lost another $2,000. Yet, being a shareholder of the theater, he committed to an additional six years' lease before taking his troupe back to Nashville.[35]

There, he set up shop for a few nights in the old "barn" on Cherry Street until his new theatre was complete. Standing on the corner of Union and Summer Streets (the latter now Fifth Avenue), it eventually cost Caldwell, together with its lot, $20,000, only partially ($2,200) covered by the sale of $100 shares. Completed in eighty-nine days, it welcomed nearly six hundred people on its opening night, October 9, when Caldwell delivered the customary dedication, followed by *Soldier's Daughter* and *Turn Out*. The new building was deemed "an ornament to our town" and the company's performance unsurpassed. They played to good houses in Nashville until December 23, then headed back to New Orleans.[36]

~~~~~~~~~~

Aleck Drake spent the summer of 1826 in Cincinnati with his company in the Columbia Street Theatre, leased to him by Longworth and Symmes. The city had been left without professional theatre for two years. There, Julia Drake Fosdick rejoined the troupe, and Aleck added several other actors: Anne and John Greene and A. W. Jackson (these from Ludlow), Kelsey (from Caldwell), and a few of the more talented amateurs, including its president, Boyd Reily. (The use of amateurs required Aleck on at least one occasion to take over mid-performance for a neophyte paralyzed by stage fright.) However, they continued to face religious opposition. Sol Smith's brother Martin, editor of the city's *Independent Press,* reminded its citizens of the "ancient dignity" of theatre, which would be better supported "if it were not for the preachers and their sanctified followers."[37]

Still, attendance lagged. The group's centerpiece was still Fanny, who charmed all with her performance as Claudine in *Devil's Bridge* on July 15. The troupe was thrust into grief, however, when handsome, convivial Sam Jr. died at age twenty-nine on July 30. According to Ludlow, a dissolute lifestyle had been the cause: "He was the victim of his appetites, and they finally destroyed him."[38]

The company was bolstered in early October by the addition of Mr. and Mrs. Sol Smith and Mr. and Mrs. Lemuel Smith, and occasional forays from retirement of Sam Sr. To generate audience, Aleck spent more than was prudent on new scenery and costumes for a lavish production of *Forty Thieves* in early November. But box office still flagged, due according to Martin Smith's newspaper to the fact that "respectable persons" had to thread their way through "boys, negroes, wenches, lewd women and devils of all sorts, sizes and kinds" to gain admission.[39]

Facing complete failure, Aleck instituted a sharing system among the company, perceived as one-sided by some, including Sol Smith, as it was applicable when receipts fell, but upon their improvement the cast would receive salaries only. Openly disgruntled, Smith in December took his wife, his brother and his wife, the Greenes, and a handful of others barnstorming to various Kentucky towns (Frankfort, Paris, Maysville, and Nicolesville) through May 1827. Attendance varied sharply depending on the weather.

The depleted Drakes soldiered on in Cincinnati, grateful for the drawing power of Fanny, who throughout November and December 1826 carried leads such as Meg Merrilies, Lady Anne, Lady Randolph, Mrs. Haller, Elvira, and Rosalind in *As You Like It.* All too often, though, the unrefined audience failed to appreciate her efforts. During "the most intense scenes" of *Pizarro,* "a quartet of New Yorkers in the front row . . . distracted the audience by frequent laughs and vulgar criticisms." Some of the actors further hindered her during *As You Like It,* as they "substituted their own language for that of Shakespeare."[40]

In early February 1827 Aleck instituted benefits, and on February 24 drew to a close his dogged nine-month season with Fanny's benefit in *Wives as They Were*. One optimistic Cincinnati paper opined that "the encouragement given to Mr. Drake has been such as to determine this gentleman to fix himself permanently at Cincinnati, and it is more than probable that he will build a new Theatre here next season." But as they headed back to Louisville in early March, the Drake company was close to collapse.[41]

Ludlow was doing everything in his power to avoid a similar fate. In New York during the summer of 1826 he would find slim pickings, as most of the capable actors were already committed to managers who paid more than he could offer. It took him until August to corral sixteen new performers. Ten were acceptably experienced: Mr. and Mrs. E. R. Davis, Mr. and Mrs. George T. Rowe (she the former Miss Fenton) and his sister Caroline, William Anderson, J. E. Watson, Thomas Gough, Philip Le Brun, and Mrs. Mary J. Ball (a pretty, clever, flirtatious comedienne who would become a favorite on the frontier). The other six were rank novices: William A. Kidd, William Rutter, James Byrnes, twins Almira and Emeline Dunham (minors placed under Mrs. Ludlow's care), and Miss Mary Ann "Marian" Meek. Of these, the sprightly, Brooklyn-born Meek showed the most potential, and would later achieve a minor stardom. Only eighteen, she was already "quite a handsome-looking lady" with "a symmetrical form, a melodious voice, and a very pretty face of the blonde character" that would soon lead to her being considered by many one of the most beautiful women on the American stage.[42]

Returning with them to the frontier by stagecoach in mid-August, Ludlow stopped briefly in Pittsburgh, where he acquired two more novices, Horatio N. Barry and Charles Francis McClure. He barely met expenses, performing for a few nights (with *Honey Moon*, *Rendezvous*, *Iron Chest*, and *Day After the Wedding*) in the dilapidated theater on Third Street. A committee was soliciting subscriptions for a new theater, to be built on Fifth Street, but that effort would not reach fruition for another seven years.[43]

When Ludlow left Pittsburgh, Gough defected, continuing to perform there as a solo professional during the 1826–27 winter, occasionally joined by Frances Hartwig (the former Mrs. Samuel Tatnall), now touring as a star. Upon reaching New Orleans en route to Mobile in November, Ludlow received a grievous shock: his son Taylor had died while under the care of Louisianian William Harding, to whom the Ludlows had entrusted the boy in summer 1823 while touring. Now, Ludlow threw himself into work in Mobile.

Heading into 1827, he would compete mightily for supremacy on the frontier with Drake and Caldwell, each striving to establish a circuit which might consistently generate enough funding to keep the wolf from the door.

10

STRUGGLES & STRENGTHS

(1827–1828)

JAMES CALDWELL CONTINUED his plans to expand his theatrical circuit by focusing next on St. Louis, which still had no permanent theater. Fundraising for one had been abandoned in 1822. St. Louis was now an incorporated city with a population approaching five thousand, but had experienced no professional performances since the departure of Jones's castoffs in May 1821. As with most other cities on the frontier, an amateur thespian society had filled in, performing such standards as *Rivals, Rendezvous, Poor Gentleman, Soldier's Daughter,* and *Mountaineers* in a large converted brick salt house on Second Street, just north of Olive Street (like the other early St. Louis theaters, its site is now part of Gateway Arch Park). Because it lacked ventilation, it was known by performers and audience alike as the "hot house."[1]

Caldwell saw a clear opportunity, enhanced by a massive effort in 1827 by the federal government to improve travel on the Mississippi River by removing treacherous snags. In early May of that year he sent carpenters to St. Louis to renovate the uncomfortable "hot house," expanding it fifty feet to the rear to accommodate a true stage. He planned to lease it for seven years.

Soon after closing his New Orleans season on June 8, he brought his company by steamboat up to St. Louis. Visiting actor Joe Cowell somewhat hyperbolically considered them "the best by far on the continent." Caldwell would play nearly all leads, often opposite Placide. They opened on June 27, playing four nights a week. Caldwell had promised at the outset to provide St. Louisans "much better entertainment than they could expect." But public response was not favorable, attributable primarily to the theater's stifling atmosphere amid an unusually hot summer. One newspaper warned in late July that "if houses are not better attended . . . it will be long before we shall have another opportunity of enjoying the delectable amusement which the Drama affords. Will it not go abroad that there is no taste in St. Louis for theatrical representations?"[2]

For eight weeks, through August 23, Caldwell and his company served up a variety of scripts which they had perfected in New Orleans, including *Stranger, Spoiled Child, Town and Country, Hamlet* (Caldwell, to Placide's Ophelia), *Pizarro* (Placide's Elvira was "powerful" and "unrivaled"), *Macbeth, School for Scandal, The Review, Henry IV, Part I* (Gray as Falstaff and Caldwell as Hotspur), *Belle's Stratagem, Forty Thieves,* and *Rule a Wife.*[3]

The two biggest draws in New Orleans during the past season had been Lydia Kelly and Thomas Abthorpe Cooper, but both had declined to migrate with Caldwell's company to St. Louis. Instead, they tried to revitalize the fortunes of Aleck Drake. In Louisville, his company opened on March 10 at the newly named City Theatre, but after the first week the *Advertiser* reported, "We have visited the theatre every night since its opening, but were sorry to find the performances so thinly attended," an all-too-familiar lament across the frontier. Neither comedy (for example, *Wives as They Were, Paul Pry*) nor tragedy (such as *Othello, Douglas*) excited the public. Kelly, thirty-one, a beautiful, feisty British actress specializing in high comedy, arrived in early April. But even her best roles, such as Beatrice in *Much Ado About Nothing,* which had been a hit in New Orleans, met with only apathy in Louisville.[4]

Two weeks later Drake took his actors across to Cincinnati to support Kelly. There she was more enthusiastically received, "charming the admirers of dramatic merit with her vocal and histrionic powers" as Juliana in *Honey Moon.* She donated $80.25 of her benefit earnings to the Cincinnati Hospital. But after her departure, when Drake took his company back to Louisville to begin benefits, box office again sagged.[5]

Cooper had gone first to Mobile, opening for Ludlow on April 21 for ten nights at the Royal Street Theatre as Macbeth, Virginius, Damon, Richard III, Leon in *Rule a Wife,* Hamlet, Rolla, Beverly in *The Gamester,* and Petruchio. From there, he traveled by steamboat to Louisville, perhaps lured by the chance to reprise with Fanny Drake their *Othello* and *Macbeth* of 1822. Fanny, though, was only occasionally able to appear on stage, and that only in minor roles (for example, Emilia instead of Desdemona, played by Julia Fosdick). She would that fall deliver her fourth child, Samuel Alexander Drake III, named for his grandfather and late uncle.[6]

Cooper opened for Drake in Cincinnati with *Macbeth* on May 28, 1827, the first of five nights, but was only moderately successful. Still, he bruited about that he might erect a new theater in the city, and announced that he was going to New York and then Europe to recruit actors for the venture. This never reached fruition. Following Cooper was the starring engagement in early June of Cornelia Burke Jefferson (the recent wife of Joseph Jefferson II), and in July that of Emanuel Judah in such classical roles as Shylock and Richard III. Then, leaving instructions for alterations on the interior and exterior of the Columbia Street Theatre (including a twelve-foot extension in the rear, a safer entrance and exit, and a paved sidewalk in front), Drake took his company northeast.[7]

Their first stop was the as-yet-unincorporated market town of Cleveland, whose population was closing in on one thousand, but which had experienced no professional theatre since Blanchard's troupe in 1820. For a week in mid-July Drake's company performed such popular pieces as *Poor Gentleman, Poor Soldier, Paul Pry,* and *Catharine and Petruchio.* Audiences were good, the town having become "so dull that the citizens have found it necessary to employ a company of amusers to relieve them from the burden of ennui," and Drake took in nearly $300.[8]

In Pittsburgh in early September his featured star instead of Fanny was again Julia Fosdick, noted for her Mrs. Haller, for which Fanny had achieved renown. Julia was rapidly acquiring her own fame and following, evidenced by a published poem that fall which avowed that "no mortal form, no mortal feature" could engender such a rapture in any theatregoer who "gazed upon a being not of earth."[9]

But in the northern reaches of the frontier Drake's company faced continued religious opposition. Editorials in both towns excoriated the theatre. In Cleveland: "The fascinations of the stage have plunged many of the fairest youths of America deep in pollution [and] extremes of dissipation and debauchery." In Pittsburgh: "It is sincerely hoped that none of our citizens will be found so lost to a sense of moral obligation and regard to the good of society as to encourage, in future, the contaminating amusement of the drama." Drake's visit to Pittsburgh represented the last professional performances there for over five years.[10]

〜〜〜〜〜〜

In Mobile, Ludlow had closed after Cooper's departure, taking his company—largely still those he had recruited in the East, minus Mary Ball, who married and left the company—in late May via New Orleans to Nashville. There he acquired brothers Joseph and Solomon Page (the former a veteran of both Caldwell and Drake). After opening on Market Street on June 10, the small company performed three nights a week through August 25, struggling to attract good houses with a familiar repertoire long on comedy and farce: *Stranger, Busy Body, John Bull, School of Reform, Paul Pry, Foundling of the Forest, Cure for the Heart Ache, El Hyder* (an equestrian melodramatic spectacle by William Barrymore, with real horses), *Timour the Tartar, Poor Soldier,* and *Speed the Plough,* with a smattering of new pieces, rarely repeated.[11]

Ludlow knew he had a good thing in Mary Ann Meek, and he provided her with plum roles in almost every production. At first somewhat shy, she grew in confidence as reviewers increasingly praised her. Mrs. Ludlow, too, was gaining confidence. Previously, "she could scarce be heard." Now, "she displayed a correct judgment, a distinct articulation, and in many instances a pathos of voice particularly touching." Plaudits rolled in for Ludlow himself ("a diamond without a flaw"), J. E. Watson, Sarah Riddle, and the widowed Mrs. Vos. But the inexperience of a few showed all too plainly. William Kidd's cockiness—a trait which "it would do him no harm to get rid of"—rendered him inept in any line of business: "In tragedy he makes everybody laugh; and in low comedy, it appears as if he wished to be thought the most graceful and accomplished character in the play," but ended up looking like "the inmate of an insane hospital." A few mugged for cheap laughs, with one performing "a ridiculous caricature," as if he were at a fair where "freaks cut their ridiculous capers." Another was cautioned to "not introduce quite so many ill-timed and inapplicable jokes." A lethargic actor "looked for all the world as though he had taken a heavy dose of opium." The "agreeable" Almira Dunham "warbles like a Nightingale, but speaks so fast as frequently to become confused, and her utterance is thereby rendered indistinct." Her fetching figure in *Mogul's Tale* "was displayed to great advantage in her oriental costume, but her evident embarrassment rendered her too inanimate."[12]

As was too often the case, Ludlow's hopes were dashed by thin houses, and he took his troupe south to Huntsville, hoping to dislodge Caldwell's foothold there. "I occupied the theatre that had originally been intended for me, which was erected in 1825 and of which I had been deprived by the treachery of Alexander M. Wilson," he recorded. Caldwell, "finding it unprofitable," had closed on September 2, and Ludlow opened there two nights later. At first it was another losing operation, but box office improved slightly before he closed on October 18. When the theater was soon afterward sold at auction, Ludlow believed he had been saved from "a great misfortune" by not committing himself to a permanent presence in Huntsville.[13]

He continued his odyssey, on to Tuscaloosa, where they opened on October 31 in a hotel ballroom with *Honey Moon* and *No Song, No Supper*. They continued for four nights a week through December 8. The day before they closed, Mary Ann Meek married fellow actor Charles McClure, "a good-natured man." The couple, only nineteen, would continue to play juveniles but soon add youthful romantic leads.[14] By the time the Ludlow company returned to Mobile at year's end, they had traveled over a thousand miles in seven months, primarily by horse and wagon.

~~~~~~~~~~

Ludlow's future partner, Sol Smith, had by June 1827 returned to long-neglected Lexington. (The only theatre there since Drake's departure at the end of 1825 had been a visit in June 1826 by dogged itinerant monologist John Vaughan.) Local favorites, Scotsman Henry Crampton and his wife, Rose, had resurrected the old Usher theater and now welcomed the Smith troupe. "Small but very respectable in character and talent," they performed three weeks of such standards as *Mountaineers, Poor Soldier,* and *Honey Moon.* Their nadir came the night of June 27, when the theater was broken into and vandalized, with considerable damage. Their spirits recovered, however, three nights later, when U.S. secretary of state Henry Clay attended, greeted with sustained applause. The company moved on in July to play a week or so each—to consistently disappointing returns—in Harrodsburg Springs, Nicholasville, Versailles, Georgetown, and Shelbyville, from which Smith took his actors to Nashville to join Caldwell's company.[15]

Caldwell, planning his Nashville season to coincide with the session of the Tennessee legislature, had engaged Junius Brutus Booth to appear for four nights, beginning on November 28. Booth followed *Bertram* with *Othello* (as Iago), *Town and Country,* and *Iron Chest.* A celebrated attendee one night was Andrew Jackson. Booth being the *raison d'être* for this engagement, Caldwell returned to New Orleans, while Sol Smith took a few of the actors on another barnstorming tour of Tennessee and Kentucky towns, before rejoining Caldwell. One of those remote towns, Clarksville, Tennessee, provided a moment of hilarity. During a performance of *Stranger,* "one of our auditors became so interested in the last scene that he got up and addressed my brother [Lemuel, playing the titular Stranger], as follows: 'Come, Smith, look over what's past and take back your wife, for I'll be d—d if you'll get such another in a hurry!'"[16]

From Nashville, Booth headed north to Cincinnati. There, Aleck Drake, back from Pittsburgh, was struggling since opening on November 19 (postponed nearly two weeks due to his own illness). At first, he had counted on his postpartum wife, his sister Julia, and Mrs. Jefferson—now a regular member of the company—to draw audiences. Fanny continued "year after year to enlarge the circle of her admirers and elevate the character of the stage," and Julia charmed all with her "rustic innocence" and beauty. Sam Sr., still appearing sporadically, gave "appropriate dignity or humor" to his characters, and Aleck remained "the soul of feeling and of glee." Some of their choices, though (for example, Fanny's being ill-suited for the femme fatale Millwood in *George Barnwell*) were not well received. The rest of the company came in for criticism, along with boorish behavior among the audience, which discouraged women from attending.[17]

Such misbehavior was hardly limited to Cincinnati. When Mississippi legislators attended a performance in Nashville, an utter lack of decorum reigned. One actress "was frightened into hysterics by the tremendous whooping of a good-natured gentleman from the western district . . . who had never been in Drury Lane or Covent Garden." Too often, "men who in other situations act as gentlemen, when they enter the theatre seem to forget who they are, and laying aside all restraint, indulge in conduct that would disgrace a bacchanalian mob. If anything is said or done on stage that is calculated to elicit applause, . . . the whole house rings, and the whole neighborhood is disturbed with yells not unlike those of drunken Indians."[18]

Booth opened in Cincinnati on December 11 as Richard III and gave "almost unmingled satisfaction to a large and discriminating audience." On December 14, watching his Sir Edward Mortimer in *Iron Chest*, the audience sat "spellbound and electrified by [his] almost super-human powers." He followed these with Hamlet, closing with Othello opposite Fanny on December 17. But bad weather brought disappointingly small audiences, the engagement costing Drake several hundred dollars. One reviewer feared that the cost against the profit of performing in the West would discourage eastern stars like Booth from appearing in the coming years.[19]

Drake then took his company to Louisville for a few nights to support Booth, who afterward departed for New Orleans. Drake opted to forego his usual winter visit to Frankfort—apparently by now a losing proposition— and returned to Cincinnati, opening on January 21, 1828, with *Lady of the Lake*, featuring "really very beautiful" new scenery by Jefferson. Drake improved his company by hiring a promising newcomer, Edward Raymond, to play leads opposite Fanny. On January 28 Raymond played Rolla to her Elvira, "one of the finest specimens of the histrionic art that can be afforded to any American theatre." In her closing scene, as she reflects on Pizarro's "seducing her from her convent; the anguish of her mother, and the murder of her brother by her seducer, she exhibited a burst of passion and an acuteness of feeling that melted every individual present." Unfortunately, attendance was poor due to inclement weather.[20]

Although suffering from unspecified "delicate health," Fanny in late February supported the visiting Judah in *Virginius, Merchant of Venice*, and *King*

Lear. Judah, though, "failed to secure an enthusiastic reception." In mid-March, even a lavish "grand marine spectacle," *The Flying Dutchman,* fared no better. Closing another disappointing season, Aleck took the company to Louisville, hoping for success. For ten more unprofitable weeks there (March 29–June 4) they ran through a repertoire of generally lighthearted pieces before yielding the City Theatre stage to a troupe of French acrobats and returning to Cincinnati.[21]

There, from mid-June to mid-July they persevered. Some bills, such as *The Floating Beacon* on June 18, only drew "a very thin house" despite its being "an exquisite treat." In the leading role of Mariette, Fanny "exerted herself successfully to a very high pitch of her exquisite power, in scenes of pathos and distraction." Aleck counted on her to draw crowds, as the *Gazette* noted: "She is the chief support of the company." A brief starring visit by Edwin Forrest, now twenty-two, "from the Bowery Theatre, New York," including his *Brutus,* with Fanny as Tullia, seemed to help. But other productions generated only "respectable" houses.[22]

~~~~~~~~~~

Ludlow, too, was struggling, and gave up trying to compete with Caldwell in Nashville and Huntsville. He did manage to complete a "tolerably good" season in Mobile from January 18 through May 13, 1828. Two minor stars, William Anderson and John Still (as lead actor and vocalist, respectively), helped draw audiences, supported by Ludlow's moderately competent company. While not as experienced as Caldwell's, it had remained largely intact. Their repertoire included such standards as *Stranger, School of Reform, Guy Mannering, Othello, Paul Pry, Bertram, Wandering Boys, Town and Country, Mountaineers, Honey Moon,* and *Poor Soldier,* plus some new pieces, including *Exchange No Robbery* (for four nights) and *The Wife's Stratagem.* Faced with competition from J. Purdy Brown's visiting circus, Ludlow combined forces with Brown to stage *El Hyder* and "a celebrated comic, heroic, operatic, tragic, pantomime, burletta, spectacular extravaganza in two acts by Thomas Dibdin, Esq., called *Don Giovanni; or, A Spectre on Horseback*" (with Still in the lead role).[23]

But Ludlow yearned for greater respectability and acclaim. He decided to go to New York, to sign additional actors and stars and to gain eastern managerial experience. Sending his wife, the McClures, and Dunham to New York by sea, he traveled to New Orleans, then scouted potential new territory in Louisville, Cincinnati, Pittsburgh, Sandusky, Detroit, Buffalo, and Albany, before arriving in New York in early June. He had corresponded with, and now met with, Cooper about jointly managing its "diminishing" Chatham Theatre. Using the actors he had sent ahead, he opened there in September, but soon realized Cooper had duplicitously reneged on his end of responsibilities and would contribute minimal effort.[24]

Among the stars Ludlow engaged for the Chatham was Aleck Drake. Like Ludlow, Aleck and Fanny had gone to New York at the close of their summer 1828 season to acquire better actors to be able to compete more effectively against the Caldwell juggernaut. Aleck played low Irish comedy for Ludlow and Cooper in September, and Fanny starred off and on in serious dramas at the Park and Bowery theaters from mid-September to mid-November. Among her costars were major names: James Wallack, Thomas Hamblin, and Edwin Forrest.

In the Drakes' absence, their company in late August performed briefly in Lexington. They appear to have used the old Usher theater, which was again advertised for sale, with no evidence that it did sell. Relying on vestigial amateurs to fill out casts, they performed into the fall such standard comedies as *Wives as They Were*, *Magpie and Maid*, and *Lottery Ticket*, and a melodrama, *The Cataract of Ganges*.

~~~~~~~~~~

Caldwell in spring 1828 was not about to let either Drake or Ludlow encroach on his burgeoning empire. After closing his New Orleans season, he took his company by steamboat north to Natchez, arriving close to midnight on a dark, rainy night and tramping with them up the muddy bluff past the profanely boisterous denizens of Natchez-Under-the-Hill. Accompanying them on the steamboat and carrying nine-year-old Mary Ann Russell uphill was lawyer and poet William Henry Sparks, who recalled that "Caldwell alone was cheerful; Sol Smith joked and Russell swore."[25]

On April 30 Caldwell opened the new theater in Natchez with an inaugural address delivered by Rosina Rowe, followed by *Honey Moon* (leads by Caldwell and Mrs. Russell), songs by Mrs. Smith and Mrs. Russell, and *Of Age Tomorrow*. The theater had been in the works since January 1826 (its cornerstone not being laid until October 31 of that year). Completed at a cost of over $10,000, of which Caldwell owned forty shares, it stood on the south side of Main Street midway between today's Rankin and Pine streets. Built of brick, the fifty-by-ninety-foot edifice could accommodate over six hundred in its pit, two tiers of boxes, and a gallery, all warmed by two fireplaces and brightened by five large windows on either side. Lacking a greenroom or sufficient wing space, it contained dressing rooms excavated below the stage into earth which had contained a moldering graveyard. (Low comedian Sol Smith quipped that when he played First Gravedigger in *Hamlet* he had not far to look for a skull to represent Yorick and other bones to strew about.)[26]

Caldwell brought to Natchez the full strength of his New Orleans company minus Jane Placide, who had left for New York. For eight weeks, through May and June, they performed four nights a week. Rosina Rowe played most leads opposite Caldwell, for example, Ophelia to his Hamlet on May 10 (*Hamlet*'s first staging in Natchez), and Cora to his Rolla and Mrs. Russell's Elvira on May 24. The company's repertoire was a mix of classical tragedy (such as *Richard III*, *Virginius*, *Damon and Pythias*), melodrama (for example, *Timour the Tartar*) and a preponderance of comedy (*Comedy of Errors*, *She Stoops to Conquer*, *Poor Gentleman*, *Paul Pry*, *Catharine and Petruchio*). At least seventeen of the pieces presented that spring were new to Natchez, ensuring a relatively profitable season. Nearly everyone got a benefit, including little Mary Ann Russell, who danced and sang between acts. She had become a local favorite, "always greeted with unequivocal marks of favor. Her innocent smile, light step and airy form, with the exquisite grace displayed in every motion, almost transport us to the region of Fairyland."[27]

"Highly respectable" houses attended, although some citizens stayed away due to the late hour (sometimes well after 11:00) at which the evenings' bills concluded. At least one Natchez newspaper, the *Ariel*, remained consistently supportive, considering the performances uniformly excellent.

One fault, though, particularly rankled: "Performers should not introduce in their songs any expressions that do not properly belong to them, or recite anything at variance with the author's intentions, particularly such as are of improper or indelicate nature." Anyone who persisted "will be hissed off the stage."[28]

Caldwell worked hard to establish his Natchez theater as a safe, moral environment. In doing so, he earned commendation for his "industry and perseverance," for his efforts at security, and for his choice of scripts. "We are well aware that prejudices exist among many of our best citizens against theatrical performances," asserted the *Ariel*, but "where a theatre is instituted under proper regulations it affords not only amusement of a very rational description, but instruction of a most important and salutary kind." If people sought diversion, "it is certainly better to spend a few hours at night in a Theatre . . . than wasting time spending money and risking reputation in places of an improper and disorderly character." Realizing that "a well-regulated theatre" was necessary for "the eradication of dissolute principles," Caldwell strove to "put down all attempts at disorder or irregularity, particularly loud talking during the performance."[29]

He then headed for New York (perhaps lured by Placide), and the Russells left for Boston, where Richard had secured a position as acting manager of the Tremont Theatre. Under the management of treasurer James S. Rowe, Caldwell's company traveled to St. Louis. There, from July 19 to October 14, in the old Salt House Theatre on Second Street they performed four nights a week with a repertoire that included *Soldier's Daughter*, *Othello*, *Merchant of Venice*, *Forty Thieves*, and *Road to Ruin*.

But attendance was poor and critical response severe. "Hints to the Theatrical Company of St. Louis" were freely bestowed: Sol Smith tended to overdo his low comedy, injecting improvised humorous lines; he should stick to comic songs instead of love songs, and certainly eschew tragedy; Mrs. Ludlow was obviously inexperienced; some leads were deficient in their lines and volume; others should consult a dictionary; utility players ought to learn their lines and maintain appropriate facial expressions; Palmer and Cambridge were "beyond all hope": "Palmer should not be so comical in tragedy, nor Cambridge so tragical in comedy"; "Tragedies should be avoided during the warm weather"; and "the Theatre should not be open so often." As for technical elements, better stage technicians were warranted and should not be seen; more appropriate scenery and furnishings were needed—for example, the same scene should not be used to represent the Ducal palace of Venice and Desdemona's bedchamber ("Othello as commander general of the Venetian forces . . . ought to be able, out of his pay, to furnish his wife's bedchamber a little better," and "the Senate table ought to be a little more than two feet square," with a better tablecloth); and the orchestra should play more "national tunes and popular airs between the pieces."[30]

By this engagement's close, various explanations for its failure included the unseasonably hot weather and the actors themselves: we "have become sated with them," and "some new faces" would be welcome. Undeterred, Caldwell later that fall proposed building a new theater in St. Louis. He submitted to its civic leaders a prospectus for one to be erected immediately on the site of the existing theater, which would seat six hundred, with a front of fifty-three feet and extending one hundred feet to the rear. Its estimated cost of $15,000 would be raised through $100 shares, of which Caldwell himself promised to purchase seventy-five. However, it was never realized under Caldwell.[31]

~~~~~~~~~~

In fall 1828, the circuits of each manager were more or less solidified, yet each faced significant financial challenges. Caldwell's company was still the most impressive, but Drake and Ludlow were close on his heels, struggling in their own way.

Drake's Achilles Heel was an inconsistent supporting company. "The females of the company are all able to sustain their parts tolerably, some of them excellently." But as for the men, "The contrast is often both ludicrous and painful. Nothing can be more provoking than to witness some miserable pretender mouthing and ranting in Pizarro or Rolla, to Mrs. Drake or Mrs. Fosdick." Another weakness was Drake's outlay of funds for such extravagant productions as *Flying Dutchman,* whose lavish scenery distracted from the acting, a cost which could never be recouped. It would be better, thought one reviewer, for Drake to focus on more modest scripts performed by "a small company of good conduct." Another regretted the preponderance of outdated melodramas, "mere skimble skamble stuff, made up of songs without sentiment and of incidents . . . of show and parade" which left audiences "confounded by their noise and disgusted by their insipidity." Such were "derogatory to the dignity of the drama." More Shakespeare was urged, although tragedy generally remained out of the range of the company's abilities.[32]

When the Drake company opened in Cincinnati on October 25 with *Honey Moon,* several members of the company still required frequent prompting. Julia and Raymond carried leads, but visiting stars Fanny Drake, Junius Brutus Booth, Edwin Forrest, and a troupe of French dancers were expected by late November. Aleck Drake, severely ill with fever and increasingly discouraged, attempted to play leads, some outside his comic ability, such as Duke Aranza in *Honey Moon* and the title role in *Rob Roy,* but was panned for his ranting, which deserved to be "hissed off the stage." He publicly threatened to abandon Cincinnati entirely, but the *Gazette* implored him not to, adding, "If Mr. Drake's efforts as a manager are not sustained, we may as well abandon the Theatre altogether."[33]

On November 26 Fanny arrived to play Elvira in *Pizarro* opposite Raymond's Rolla. She drew raves for the manner in which she balanced Elvira's "indignation and virtuous sentiment," keeping the character from being objectionable. Aleck had excised from both scripts anything that was "vulgar, obscene or impure," but audiences remained sparse. On November 28 Fanny and Raymond's *Apostate* attracted only twenty persons, a fact bemoaned by the *Gazette,* which questioned whether Cincinnati deserved such talent: "There are few companies in any provincial towns that can boast more talent than this. . . . If the talents of this lady, who is one of our own citizens, will not command patronage here, she is not censurable for seeking it in other places, nor will her husband and father be censurable for following her example."[34]

After playing Meg Merrilies in *Guy Mannering,* the title role in *Evadne,* and Elvira again, Fanny departed for a star turn in New Orleans, to be supported through April 1829 by Caldwell's superior company, leaving her husband to fill a week before Booth's arrival. Again, Julia and Raymond stepped up, carrying leads in *William Tell, Poor Soldier,* and with Aleck for his benefit on December 6, *The Miser* and *The Lives of Robin Hood and Little John.* Booth's opening on December 13 with *Richard III* revitalized Drake's box office, to the point that he had to cut off the sale of tickets. *Iron Chest* (opposite Julia), *King Lear,* and *A New Way to Pay Old Debts* filled houses to their utmost capacity. But when Booth departed like Fanny for New Orleans, Aleck again confronted penury.

~~~~~~~~~~

Caldwell's company drifted south in fall 1828 from St. Louis. Six members (the four Smiths plus Cambridge and Wilkie) with much doubling of roles played four nights in late October in Port Gibson, Mississippi. Although the town had an active amateur thespian society, this visit remedied a near-decade-long absence of professional theatre. Now, performances of *Village Lawyer, Stranger, Mountaineers,* and *Honey Moon* drew full houses every night. Mrs. Lemuel Smith was thought superior, especially as Mrs. Haller. Sol Smith was criticized again for his "ill-timed and inappropriate" humor and inconsistent performance in *Mountaineers.* But in general, "the whole company performed well."[35]

In early November they traveled by horse and wagon to Natchez, joining most of the rest of the company. They opened November 14 with *Soldier's Daughter* and *Spectre Bridegroom,* and for a month played five nights a week, drawing much the same audience every night. The *Natchez Statesman and Gazette* recommended fewer performances, since both audience and actors "are nearly jaded out." Their repertoire, though, provided a wide variety of scripts, ranging from *School for Scandal* to *Pizarro* (Pearson as Rolla, Mrs. Molly Crooke—née Mason and then Entwistle—as Elvira, and Mrs. Lemuel Smith as Cora) and *Macbeth* (H. A. Williams and Crooke receiving star billing as the murderous couple).[36]

In this dynamic river town, a favorite was *The Gambler's Fate,* which ran for three nights. Crooke earned star status as Portia opposite Williams's Shylock on November 21, the two providing "as correct readings as any heard upon these boards." But overall, the engagement was not successful critically or financially. Wrote one haughty reviewer, except for a few leading actors, "we have never seen so much wretched playing," including a few unnamed actors who "made their appearance in a state of inebriation." In early December, Rowe took the company back to New Orleans, where they enjoyed one of Caldwell's most successful seasons.[37]

~~~~~~~~~

Noah Ludlow, back from closing his disappointing management of the Chatham theater in New York in mid-October, immediately began shoring up his southwestern circuit from his base in Mobile, at his Royal Street Theatre. The season began there in early December 1828 "with every prospect of being a pleasant and profitable one." His company, including several actors he had acquired in New York, consisted of thirty-four versatile performers (twenty-three men, nine women, two children), among them the inexperienced twenty-year-old future star Thomas D. Rice (for low comedy, two years before his impersonation of "Jim Crow"). Ludlow promised Mobilians such stars as Cooper, Forrest, and Louisa Lane.[38]

They opened on December 8 with *Speed the Plough* and *The Review*, then moved quickly into tragedy, with Frances Hartwig carrying leads—for example, Mrs. Haller, Elvira (with new hire Thomas Ansell as Rolla and Mary Ann McClure as Cora), Albina Mandeville in *The Will*, Imogine in *Bertram* (with Ansell in the title role), and Belvidera in *Venice Preserved*. (Ludlow soon realized that Ansell was totally inadequate, though, and relegated him to minor roles.) Hartwig proved herself equally adept in comedy— for example, Little Pickle in *Spoiled Child*, Mrs. Oakly in *The Jealous Wife*, and Priscilla Tomboy in *The Romp*, before she left to become an itinerant star. Nearly every night Rice or Ludlow's daughter, seven, entertained with comic songs and dances.

British-born George Holland, thirty-seven, arrived in early January 1829. A skilled actor, vocalist, and imitator, he had come to the United States in 1827 at Booth's invitation, and instantly became a popular success at the lowbrow Bowery Theatre in New York. It may have been Booth who encouraged him to venture into the frontier. Holland opened for Ludlow on January 7 with his ludicrous signature burletta, *Day After the Fair*, which involved his imitation of assorted animals, and for a week presented his "eccentric piece," *The Whims of a Comedian,* consisting of ventriloquism and similar skills, and such comic roles as Rob Tyke in *School of Reform.*

Through February 6 the company filled the gaps between stars with popular pieces like *Castle Spectre, Foundling of the Forest,* and *Town and Country* (these with another new hire, Charles Booth Parsons, in the lead) and several nights of a "Grand Historical Pantomime," *La Perouse.* McClure in *Family Jars* "threw everybody on the stage with her entirely into the shade," and Rice shone as Wormwood in Buckstone's *Lottery Ticket,* exhibiting early the imitative skills that would bring him international fame in three years.[39]

Cooper, fresh from performing for Caldwell in New Orleans, appeared for two weeks beginning February 9, providing Mobilians with his *Virginius,* followed by *Honey Moon, Gamester, Damon and Pythias, Julius Caesar, Macbeth,* and *Rule a Wife.* Ludlow then again joined forces with J. Purdy Brown, creating a hybrid Dramatic and Equestrian Company to perform such melodramas as *El Hyder* and *Timour the Tartar,* with Parsons in the title roles opposite McClure and Mrs. Ludlow. The experiment succeeded, and Ludlow and Brown planned an excursion into other towns on the frontier, until fate intervened.[40]

However, in the early morning hours of Sunday, March 1, Ludlow's theater burned to the ground, ten days past the date he had allowed its insurance to lapse. Frantic efforts by an army of citizens failed to arrest the flames before the building was totally destroyed. Ludlow, the "owner of more than one half of the building and scenery destroyed, besides being sole owner of a large amount of wardrobe, music and books, and other valuables that could not be soon, if ever, replaced," was devastated. A public meeting was called to offer aid, which eventually provided about $2,000, which Ludlow immediately applied to building a new theater on St. Francis Street, but it was the start of a disastrous period for him.[41]

11

ALECK, FANNY & TROLLOPE

(1829)

BY THE END OF THE 1820S, visiting stars from the East were flowing more readily into the frontier on the heels of Thomas Abthorpe Cooper, Junius Brutus Booth, Lydia Kelly, Céline Céleste, young Edwin Forrest, and the even younger Louisa Lane. The frontier was by now sending its own stars east, including Fanny Drake and T. D. Rice. It was evident, observed the *Cincinnati Gazette,* that the Ohio River "has become the great thoroughfare for all theatrical stars traveling from New York to New Orleans."[1]

In Cincinnati, Aleck Drake relied increasingly on stars to bring in audiences. On January 3, 1829, he introduced another he had acquired in New York. Accompanied by her husband Edward, celebrated vocalist Mary Ann Povey Knight, twenty-four, had immigrated to New York from England, where she had met with minor fame at Drury Lane. More skilled at ballads than opera, she was a comfortable fit on the frontier. In such vehicles as *Love in a Village* (as Rosetta to the Young Meadows of Aleck), *Fountainbleu* [*sic*], and *Maid or Wife,* she played to sold-out houses for a week in Cincinnati. She also provided a concert in a local assembly room for those holding moral objections to the theatre.

And those objections continued strong in Cincinnati. An editorial in January 1829 decried the "indelicacy" of Drake's stage. Some of his actors were accused of delivering salacious lines and bits of business which "succeed in raising a laugh at the expense of decency." How "can the stage be held up as a school for morals when . . . such language is used and such allusions made as would be totally inadmissible" in society? "Shall that which a father, a husband or a brother would at home think too gross for the eye or the ear of a female pass with impunity in the theatre?" Drake seemed simultaneously obstinate and oblivious to the charge of "offending against the moral sense of refinement of his audience. . . . It should not be a matter of surprise to the manager that his boxes are often destitute of females."[2]

When Mrs. Knight departed for New Orleans, Aleck again turned to his sister Julia and Edward Raymond to carry leads, taking major supporting roles himself. They were generally successful in such standards as *She Would Be a Soldier*, *The Curfew*, and *William Tell*. There were also failures. One was a new melodrama by a local playwright, entitled *The Rifle*, and another *The Gambler's Fate*, in which "the scenery was poor, the house uncomfortable, [and] the whole performance mirrored the abject poverty of the company." Seeking to bolster the Drake Circuit and adequately support the proliferating guest stars, Aleck and Samuel Drake Sr. (still minimally active) now split the company, Aleck taking half to Louisville and his father retaining the other half in Cincinnati.[3]

In mid-January 1829 Caldwell likewise divided his New Orleans company, sending half to Natchez to support Booth, nominally its manager. (However, as Sol Smith, and doubtless others, noticed, even at this early stage of his career Booth was often "indisposed," exhibiting "eccentricities" which "interfered somewhat with the interests of the theatre.") Caldwell questionably sent word to Natchez that he had "no motives of pecuniary profit" in sending Booth and his actors there, intending their appearance only "for the gratification of a people from whom I have received marks of favor, which I duly appreciate."[4]

They opened in Natchez on January 29 with Booth's *Richard III* and *Rendezvous*, and played four nights a week. The sole reviewer applauded Booth for surmounting a dearth of good scenery or costumes. Although his *Othello* was "a failure throughout," his *Stranger*, opposite the superb Mrs. Haller of Molly Crooke, more than made up for it: "It was no longer Booth that we gazed upon—it was the Stranger. . . . A deep and awful intensity of gloom pervaded his whole soul." However, Booth's engagement was marred by a supporting company shaky in their lines. If they had "any mercy upon Mr. Booth, they will either commit their parts to memory, else bring their books upon the stage and read them. That such powers as Mr. B's should be trammeled by the blunders of ignorance or laziness, is sacrilege." Numerous instances of mispronounced words were also cited. Perhaps Caldwell had kept the stronger part of his company back in New Orleans.[5]

Following Booth's *Hamlet* on February 9 and *Richard III* four nights later (after a two-day bout of "indisposition"), he returned to New Orleans, just as George Holland arrived. After opening on February 17 with *Day After the Fair*, for a week Holland kept Natcheans in stitches with such comedies and farces as *Sweethearts and Wives, Weathercock, Paul Pry,* and *The Secret*.

After two weeks of company benefits, the next star opened on March 11. Nine-year-old phenomenon Louisa Lane—who as Louisa Lane Drew would become the matriarch of a theatrical dynasty—had debuted in Liverpool at age five, in Philadelphia at seven (as Duke of York to Booth's Richard III), in Baltimore (as Albert to Edwin Forrest's William Tell), and New York (like Forrest, a Bowery success). Chaperoned as she traveled by her dear mother Eliza Lane and stepfather John Kinlock, in Natchez she enacted Dr. Pangloss in *Heir at Law* and six different characters in *Actress of All Work*. Such "protean" roles became a specialty of numerous actresses later in the century, notably Maggie Mitchell. Lane also portrayed Little Pickle in *Spoiled Child* and, in one remarkable evening, performed thirteen different roles among the farces *Old and Young, Miss in Her Teens,* and *Twelve Precisely*.

Reviewers raved. Her Pangloss was "sustained throughout with an ability that would have been highly creditable in the mature age of either sex." Praised for her face, walk, line readings, and stage business, perfect for each of her characters, she demonstrated "an extraordinary intellect and exalted virtues." "In a word, she is a prodigy." Sadly, however, "she has been compelled to play to thin houses." For her March 21 benefit, she performed the final two, most exciting, swordplay-filled acts of *Richard III*.[6]

On March 23, Edwin Forrest, at twenty-three now a major star in the East, opened as Damon in *Damon and Pythias,* with Molly Crooke as Hermion and her husband as Pythias. For a week Forrest was lionized as far more effective and powerful than Cooper as Hamlet, Lear, Rolla, and Payne's Brutus. "Our expectations, high as they were raised by the fame that had preceded him, were amply realized." In the final act of *Damon and*

Pythias, "A deep spell rested upon the audience. The shocks were electric. Terror—absolute terror was visible upon every countenance."[7]

Deftly shuffling his stars, Caldwell sent up from New Orleans Mary Ann Knight, who in early April provided a week of light romantic roles, including Rosetta in *Love in a Village*, Julia Mannering (not the unnerving Meg Merrilies) in *Guy Mannering*, and Marian Ramsay in *Turn Out*. She was followed by Mr. and Mrs. John Sloman, also up from New Orleans, he a low comedian-vocalist and she as tragic heroines. This competent, but not stellar, British couple had debuted in the United States, in Philadelphia, in 1827 and in New York a year later. Now, in Natchez, they cycled through such standards as *Isabella, Venice Preserved, Gamester,* and *Jane Shore* (with Mrs. Crooke's Alicia pronounced "one of the most respectable performances of the season"), bringing the spring 1829 season in Natchez to a close on May 2.[8]

However, as commendable as these stars were, sparse attendance was the rule all season, which ended up a financial failure. Many nights the house only yielded twenty to thirty dollars, even for stars. The *Southern Galaxy* attributed the failure to poor support from Caldwell's company, which was "beyond redemption," although Caldwell himself attributed the poor attendance to caustic reviews.[9]

As a postscript to the season, Natcheans on June 5 watched a single performance by a troupe of French dancers who had visited Cincinnati the previous fall. Led by Claude Labasse and his young wife, the former Francisque Hutin, they included a future star of the first magnitude, the teenaged Céline Céleste. The troupe had recently scandalized eastern audiences with their short, diaphanous skirts and exposed limbs, causing ladies to flee and men to ogle. Their reception in Cincinnati and Natchez was likely just as controversial.

<hr />

Meanwhile, Aleck Drake had taken his half of the Drake company to Louisville, where they opened on January 31, 1829, with *Virginius*, with Raymond in the title role and Julia Fosdick as Virginia. Sam Sr., perhaps not yet fully trusting his son's management, or simply enjoying performing the role, came along to enact the blundering Sir David Dunder in the afterpiece,

Ways and Means, before returning to Cincinnati. For two months, this reduced Drake company survived in Louisville without stars, with Raymond
and Julia carrying leads and Aleck entertaining with comic songs. Their
repertoire was balanced between light (for example, *Honey Moon, Paul Pry*)
and heavy (*Gambler's Fate, Damon and Pythias*).

George Holland broke the cycle for a week in late March; then it was
three more weeks of just the company, whose benefits presented more
of the same (for example, *Stranger, Devil's Bridge,* and *Highland Reel*). Between each evening's plays, Mrs. Rowe, Miss Rowe, Miss Petrie, and Harry
Crampton and his eight-year-old daughter, Charlotte Julia, entertained with
songs and dances. The protean Louisa Lane, fresh from performing with
the other half of the Drake company in Cincinnati, arrived for a few nights
on April 29. She overlapped with Fanny Drake in such serious pieces as *The
Apostate,* then left for a week each in Frankfort, Lexington, and St. Louis.

Mary Ann Knight appeared in Louisville for a week in early May and
then left with Aleck, Fanny, and most of the Louisville actors for Cincin-
nati. They reopened the refurbished Columbia Street Theatre on Monday,
May 25. It was considerably larger, with a fifty-foot square stage, commodi-
ous lobbies and gallery, refreshment rooms for ladies and gentlemen, and
$100 worth of new scenery. Knight began with *Brother and Sister* and *Turn
Out,* followed on May 26 by Forrest as Damon in *Damon and Pythias,* with
Fanny as Calanthe. Forrest performed through June 17, always opposite
Fanny, in *Pizarro, Virginius, Othello* (with Anderson as Iago), *Hamlet, Brutus,
Venice Preserved,* and *William Tell,* and then headed for Louisville.

In afterpieces, Aleck shone, and it was he and Fanny—early frontier theatrical royalty—who drew the most critical adulation, especially when they
appeared together, as in *Catharine and Petruchio.* Her Elvira was pronounced
"the finest specimen she has ever given on our boards." They also drew the
praise of the visiting, often-querulous British authoress Frances Trollope,
who attended performances of *Hamlet* and *Venice Preserved.* She considered
Fanny's line of business "the highest walk of tragedy, and his, the broadest
comedy, [but] I have known them to change characters for a whole evening together, and have wept with him and laughed with her." In comedy,
Aleck "was superior to any actor I ever saw. . . . Let him speak whose words

he would from Shakespeare to Colman, it was impossible not to feel that half the fun was his own." He had the power of "drawing tears by a sudden touch of natural feeling." Fanny's voice and talent were "decidedly first-rate. Deep and genuine feeling, correct judgment, and the most perfect good taste distinguish her play in every character. Her last act of Belvidera is superior in tragic effect to anything I ever saw on the stage [excepting] Mrs. [Sarah] Siddons." Forrest, though, failed to impress Trollope: "What he may become I will not pretend to prophecy." He "roared" and "not even Mrs. Drake's sweet Ophelia could keep me beyond the third act."[10]

Trollope thought the theater itself "small, and not very brilliant in decoration," and its audiences decidedly unimpressive: "It was painful to see these excellent performers playing to a miserable house, not a third full." Conversely, she knew of London managers who hired "paltry third-rate actors . . . who would immediately draw crowded houses and be overwhelmed with applause." In Cincinnati, "an annoyance infinitely greater" was "the bearing and attitudes" of the predominantly male audience, who attended in short sleeves, propped their feet up, and sat backward on the ledges of boxes with "the entire rear of the person presented to the audience." Worse, "the spitting was incessant, and the mixed smell of onions and whiskey was enough to make one feel even the Drakes' acting dearly bought. . . . The noises, too, were perpetual, and of the most unpleasant kind; the applause is expressed by cries and thumping with the feet instead of clapping, and when a patriotic fit seized them and 'Yankee Doodle' was called for, every man seemed to think his reputation as a citizen depended on the noise he made."[11]

When Forrest departed for Louisville on June 18, Fanny remained in Cincinnati to play leads opposite Cooper, at fifty-three making his last appearance on the frontier, through June 22. His repertoire was generally heavy, including *Bertram, Gamester, Rule a Wife, Venice Preserved,* and (improbably) *Catharine and Petruchio.* Fanny's benefit on June 24 was aided by the next stars, the French dance troupe, including Céleste, who for a week exhibited her embryonic acting talent in melodramas. By June 27 Fanny was in Louisville to appear opposite Forrest for a week in the same roles they had performed in Cincinnati. When he departed for Nashville, she boomeranged to Cincinnati, leaving her husband to close out in Louisville after a few nights of the French dancers and Louisa Lane. (During all this, the handful of actors left in Louisville provided occasional evenings of song and dance, memorably visited on June 24 by former secretary of state Henry Clay.) The Drake circuit was finally functioning as Aleck and his father intended.

~~~~~~~~~~

Throughout 1828 and 1829 other, smaller towns were still transitioning from amateur thespian societies to struggling professional troupes. In spring 1828 a ragtag company styling itself the Theatrical Corps of Pensacola had tried to make a go of it, the first professional company there since Vaughan's in 1822. The itinerant troupe consisted of John and Frances Hartwig, Samuel P. Jones, Lear, Myers, and Mrs. DeGrushe (a member of that 1822 Vaughan company now in her thirteenth season on the frontier).

From mid-April to late May 1828, they had performed such standards as *Douglas, Day After the Wedding,* and *Castle Spectre* before heading by ship to Philadelphia. In February 1829 the Hartwigs returned, adding George Saunders, thirteen-year-old Mary Vos (whose father had died in 1826), and Mr. and Mrs. T. D. Rice (on short-term loan from Ludlow). For six weeks, using amateurs to fill out casts, they presented such varied pieces as *Day After the Fair, Irish Tutor, Pizarro,* and *All the World's a Stage.* Mrs. Rice contributed songs while her husband performed protean comedy roles and a "comic dance" which may have been an early form of "Jim Crow." But the company apparently disbanded, and Pensacola remained bereft of theatre for nearly a decade.[12]

In February 1829 Sol Smith returned to Port Gibson, Mississippi, with a handful of actors (the four Smiths, plus actors named Murray and Tatem) cleaved from Caldwell's New Orleans company. According to Smith they were "warmly greeted by the inhabitants." The local paper regretted the need for the company's considerable doubling of roles, but understood that "the patronage of our small population though liberally extended, is entirely insufficient to the support of a more expensive company." Their next stop was Vicksburg, where they acquired frontier theatre veteran Abram W.

Jackson. Leasing for four weeks the small theater of the town's amateur thespian society, they met "with unvaried success," then returned to Port Gibson for another week or two "with but moderate success."[13]

From May 23 through June 3, augmented by the amateurs of yet another thespian society, they performed in Memphis, then only "a very small river town" incorporated in 1826. Their humble venue was "a room, fitted up for the occasion, in the house of Mr. Young, next to his large warehouse, then on the banks of the river." Their eight nights yielded a total of only $319, but inspired the construction two years later of Memphis's first theater, a frame building on the northwest corner of Jackson and Chickasaw streets. When Smith headed south by wagon, the amateur Memphis thespians continued intermittently on their own. Smith and company performed next in Somerville, Tennessee, earning $39, then Bolivar and Columbia (averaging $60 a night) and Pulaski, Tennessee, and Jackson, Mississippi, where twelve nights in a log theater generated $480.[14]

In Alabama, seven nights of performing in a hotel garret in Florence yielded $251, and in Tuscumbia six nights in late July brought in $150, with Huntsville averaging $50 a night. There, to counter religious objections, the troupe provided *Gambler's Fate*, only to have a rube in the audience interrupt their performance with attempts to take up a collection to aid the impoverished wife of the titular gambler. After Tuscumbia, Smith lost the services of his brother and sister-in-law, who departed for Cincinnati and then Pittsburgh.[15]

September 9 found the small company in the state capital, Tuscaloosa, where they finished out the year. There, continuing their efforts to placate religious objections, they staged *Don Juan in Hell; or, the Libertine Destroyed*, "with all the 'accessories' of snakes spitting flames, fiends with torches, red fire and blue blazes" to represent, stated the bills, "the INFERNAL REGIONS, into which the amorous Don was to be cast without benefit of clergy!" Unfortunately, the fiery special effects ignited the scenery, ending the performance. "The bigoted portion of the Tuscaloosans seized upon the circumstance," recalled Smith, "and held it up as a warning to all play-goers, [alleging] that no good could possibly come from encouraging profane stage-plays in a Christian community." Smith contrived a public explanation that the flames had all been a special effect, but in the end they left Tuscaloosa, having played "to houses which barely paid expenses." On some nights of this grueling sixteen-hundred-mile tour they had drawn only a few dozen townsfolk.[16]

<center>~~~~~~~~~~</center>

In the aftermath of the March 1, 1829, Mobile fire, in an effort to recoup his losses, Ludlow sent his company to Montgomery under the direction of stage manager Charles Booth Parsons, with Mrs. Ludlow as manager and treasurer. Some of his actors and musicians, however, went their own ways. Those who remained performed a practiced repertoire (for example, *Honey Moon, Day After the Wedding, Heir at Law, The Review*), but Ludlow realistically "did not expect to make any money" in Montgomery.[17]

They returned to a new theater in Mobile on St. Francis Street, which had been constructed under Ludlow's personal supervision in forty-two days. (Ironically, it, too, would burn by year's end.) After opening on May 2 with *The Dramatist* and (appropriately) *Fire and Water,* Ludlow provided benefits for nearly all members of the company, including his hardworking stage carpenters. J. Purdy Brown and his horses returned, and the joint company provided *El Hyder, Timour the Tartar,* and *Valentine and Orson,* these now starring Frances Hartwig (over from Pensacola, whose previous husband, Samuel Tatnall, had trained her as an equestrienne).

Brown then stated his intention to take his circus performers—performing under their own tent amphitheater—through Mississippi, Tennessee, Missouri, and Kentucky, meeting Ludlow in Louisville, where Ludlow was to erect a temporary venue to seat about five hundred spectators. With the aid of his stage carpenter named McConkey, Ludlow did so on a vacant lot on Jefferson Street, nearly adjacent to the theater where the tail end of Drake's company was performing. Easily converted from a stage to a circus arena—with removable seats in the pit—it was put up "in the cheapest possible way" in two weeks. An adjoining livery stable was to be used for Brown's horses.[18]

With no word yet from Brown, Ludlow temporized in late June by presenting familiar dramatic pieces, including *Honey Moon, Rendezvous,* and

She Would Be a Soldier. After about a week he received startling news from Brown: the equestrian troupe would meet Ludlow not in Louisville, but in Cincinnati on July 4. Ludlow frantically truncated his Louisville stay and took his actors to Cincinnati. There, the only available venue—the Drakes occupying the Columbia Street Theatre—was the old Globe, once again renamed, as the Amphi Theatre [*sic*], with a circus ring replacing the pit seats. Recalled Ludlow, "It was a dirty, dingy place, into which I was really ashamed to invite people."[19]

Nevertheless, the joint Dramatic and Equestrian Company was up and running by July 8, doing moderate business. But as Ludlow acknowledged, by the end of the second week, "the ring performances began to stale and the dramatic ones lacked novelty." Brown then shocked him again by announcing his departure, with his horses, for figuratively greener pastures. Ludlow, resentful and feeling betrayed—although the two men had only a gentleman's agreement and no signed contract—vowed to keep going with his own company. This only lasted another week, with box office sagging even further. He then closed the theater and retrofitted it, enlarging the stage, adding seats where the ring had been, and adding a gallery (for fifteen cents admission). But, he concluded, "the legitimate drama appeared to possess but little attraction for the Cincinnatians."[20]

Had he continued, he would have been competing against a formidable array of talent at the Columbia Street Theatre. There, not only had Fanny Drake returned from Louisville, but stars continued to visit through July into mid-August, including Louisa Lane and the Slomans (each performing the same repertoire they had toured with all season). However, Drake, too, was suffering financially from a mandated closure the first week of August due to a licensing dispute, and on August 15 he ended the season. It was becoming increasingly evident that actor Joe Cowell, who visited in fall 1829, was correct: "Cincinnati bore the name of a very *bad* theatrical town."[21]

~~~~~~~~~~

In Nashville, Caldwell too was suffering that summer, but by his own making. Announcing the same stars (Forrest, the Slomans), he once again upped ticket prices. Forrest in his usual roles—Othello, Hamlet, Lear, William Tell, and Brutus—earned rave reviews. "The expectations of those who had never seen him before were fully realized and generally surpassed." He was no longer "a raw, inexperienced youth," but was now "probably . . . unsurpassed as a tragedian by any actor in the world." However, Caldwell's decision to raise ticket prices from $1.00 to $1.50 was "met with marked dissatisfaction," and Forrest played to nearly empty houses. Another factor may have been the ubiquitous religious opposition. "Frequent attendance upon the theatre," shrilled one Nashville moralist, "especially by youth and the laboring class of society, is calculated to destroy every good habit." Any idea of theatre being a force for edification was "chimerical. I would just as soon expect a brothel to be converted into a school of chastity, a gambling house into a school of honesty, or a tippling shop into a school of temperance." In August, leaving his company to support any stars who came by that fall, Caldwell left for New York, where he opened in September opposite Lydia Kelly and the Slomans.[22]

~~~~~~~~~~~~

In Cincinnati, the retrofitting on his theater done, Ludlow reopened for three nights a week in late August with more lowbrow offerings. Along with the usual comedies and farces (for example, *Town and Country, Tom and Jerry, Of Age Tomorrow*), came a series of melodramatic spectacles. The most lavish was the nautical drama *Paul Jones*, featuring a fully rigged, operational ship, moving on a perilous theatrical "sea" and Ludlow in the leading role of Tom Coffin. Among others were *Cherry and Fair Star, Bride of Abydos, Floating Beacon*, and *Aethiope*.

In late September, Ludlow engaged vocalist James Howard, twenty, to carry leads in *Guy Mannering, Rob Roy*, and *Devil's Bridge*. Little availed, despite encouraging reviews. Despite "admirable" and "judicious" performances and weather that was "uncommonly cool and pleasant," a "beggarly account of empty boxes" resulted. It appeared that "the taste of our citizens leads them to prefer pieces abounding in show and buffoonery, thunder, lightning, and brilliant scenery, to those which are calculated to interest the feelings, to improve the mind, and to make a lasting impression on the mind." By early October, with Drake about to reopen the Columbia Street

Theatre, Ludlow decamped for Louisville with his company. But he felt keenly the defections of Parsons, Rice, and McConkey to Aleck Drake.[23]

Opening in Cincinnati on October 13, Drake decidedly had an edge, between his wife, the other stars he had booked, and all new scenery and machinery. He provided a few nights of *Pizarro*, with Fanny as Elvira, before the arrival of their first star, Thomas S. Hamblin. Having immigrated from England four years before, Hamblin at age twenty-nine was striving to carve out a reputation in classical tragic heroes. Standing well over six feet tall, with a ruggedly handsome face and sturdy build, his only drawbacks were asthma, which at times incapacitated him onstage, a tendency toward stiff posturing (an increasingly outdated style), and a growing infamy as an adulterous libertine.

He had acted with Fanny in New York the previous fall, including a memorable *King John* on November 11, 1828, he in the title role, with Fanny as Constance and Forrest as Faulconbridge. Consequently, now in Cincinnati they required little rehearsal as they launched on October 19 into a familiar series: *Virginius, Hamlet, William Tell, Brutus,* and *Macbeth.* Fanny appeared at her best, playing Ophelia with "a great deal of tenderness and simplicity. Her delicate bewilderings, and the glimmering sense in the deranged scene, afforded one of the finest pictures we have ever seen on the stage." The nearly all-male audience—ladies staying away either from Hamblin's reputation or the severe overcrowding in the theater—was enthusiastic, as were reviews.[24]

When Hamblin left—for Nashville, to play opposite Jane Placide, supported by the rest of Caldwell's company—attendance in Cincinnati dropped off. Fanny continued to carry a wide range of leads, including Paul in *Wandering Boys*, Lady Teazle in *School for Scandal* (opposite Aleck as Sir Peter), and the title role in *Thérèse* (with new scenery, machinery, and fireworks developed by Rice). Dyspeptic actor Joe Cowell attended a performance of *School for Scandal* at Aleck's invitation and left with a mixed assessment of Fanny. She was "a very fine-looking woman and plenty of her." However, her western twang offended his ears, sounding "uncouth and very unLady-Teazle-like." Still, "she got great applause; everybody seemed very much pleased with her, and she seemed very much pleased with herself."[25]

Cowell agreed to perform for a few nights for half the box office take, but was less than impressed with his first rehearsal, held in a rundown, cluttered greenroom, with a demoralized cast huddled around the fire. "When a manager ceases to pay," Cowell concluded, "he soon ceases to have any authority. The rehearsals, therefore, did not deserve the name. The distribution of the characters the performers settled among themselves." As *Paul Pry*, as Crack in *Turnpike Gate*, and as Abel Day in *Honest Thieves*, Cowell drew moderately well, but not enough to help Drake, who by that time "was so far in debt that he could not leave the state until he was relieved by the insolvent law." To help the Drakes, Cowell and his nine-year-old son Sam, assisted by orchestra leader Joseph Tosso (a Paris-trained violinist), agreed in early December to perform a special "grand olio" evening of scenes and songs, hosted by the still-visiting Trollope in the ballroom of her hotel for the cream of Cincinnati society.[26]

After Cowell's departure, Fanny again took up the weight of leading roles, including Mariette in *Floating Beacon*, Colin in *Nature and Philosophy*, and Marian Ramsey in *Turn Out*. Her strength of character further exerted itself on the night of December 11, when fire broke out on Main Street. With no fire engines available, citizens formed a bucket brigade from the river. In doing so, reported the *Liberty Hall and Cincinnati Gazette*, "the ladies were conspicuous for the promptness, energy and success with which they acted. Among them we observed Mrs. A. Drake, of the Cincinnati theatre, who with an eloquence and force of character peculiar to herself, exhorted and rebuked those who stood idly looking on, until, for shame, they were compelled to follow her example, and that of the ladies, in putting their hands to work." Before the fire was extinguished, twenty-nine buildings were destroyed, but the theater was spared.[27]

Cowell had gone to Louisville, where Ludlow had returned in late October to his slapdash temporary structure erected in summer, which he now dubbed the Theatre-Melo-Dramatic. Announcing he would provide escapist entertainment four nights a week, he opened November 11 with *Honey Moon*, he as Duke Aranza and his wife as Juliana. For two weeks the company provided similar fare, including *The Review, Catharine and Petruchio, Guy Mannering, Poor Soldier,* and *Rob Roy.*

Hamblin opened there on November 27 in *Virginius,* greeted by "a numerous and highly delighted audience." "Never was the character of Virginius ... more accurately conceived or more glowingly and impressively developed." Ludlow, though, paid dearly for Hamblin's presence, agreeing to his "exorbitant" demand for half of the gross receipts for six nights, plus a benefit on the seventh. Still, "this truly eminent performer" drew crowds. Realizing the powerful chemistry between Hamblin and Mary Ann McClure, Ludlow billed them as equal stars in *Iron Chest, Merchant of Venice,* and *Hamlet.* In fact, Hamblin spoke so warmly of "the promising talents of Mrs. McClure" that he took her with him when he left for New Orleans. (There, however, she was sidelined by Caldwell in favor of Placide, but Hamblin later hired, and grew personally closer to, both her and Almira Dunham when he took over New York's Bowery Theatre.)[28]

When Cowell arrived in Louisville on December 9 for a brief engagement in his same Cincinnati roles, he was repulsed by his surroundings. As "wretched" as Cincinnati was, at least it held a real theater, with a fairly talented acting company. Ludlow's "theater" was a "cattle shed or stable" with a temporary stage. "The yard adjoining, with the board fence heightened and covered with some old canvas, supported by scaffold poles to form the roof, and rough seats on an ascent to the back, and capable of holding about two hundred persons, constituted the audience part of the establishment, the lowest benches nearest the stage being dignified by the name of boxes, and the upper, nearest the ceiling, the pit." As for Ludlow's "strolling company, ... nothing I had ever seen in the way of theatricals could be likened to this deplorable party." Among their "unexperienced talent ... there was not one redeeming point." Yet, Cowell played to crowded houses and saw fit to praise Ludlow's "strict financial correctness and skill."[29]

Next up was a visit by actor-vocalist John Still in such melodramas as *Zembuca, El Hyder,* and *Don Giovanni*—on horseback, perhaps animals left behind by Brown—and reruns of *Paul Jones.* Ludlow opened 1830 with company benefits, interspersed with new works. Prominent among them was W. T. Moncrieff's travel burletta, *Paris and London,* with a twenty-five-hundred-square-foot moving panoramic background, which had been a hit in New York two years before (and presumably purchased by Ludlow when he was there).[30]

He hoped for increased revenue from guest stars Edward Raymond (who also had performed for him at the Chatham) and French dance sisters Mademoiselles Céleste and Constance. These ladies "quite surprised the Louisville people." Their dancing "was rather repulsive to the staid ladies who had not been in the habit of seeing females kick up their heels quite so high." Ludlow closed out this "very miserable" season on March 22 and took his company back to Cincinnati.[31] His fortunes uncertain, he would face even greater challenges in the new decade.

12

NEW HORIZONS
(1830–1840)

AS THE 1830S OPENED, with frontier veteran Andrew Jackson completing his first year as U.S. president, regular theatrical seasons with permanent theaters and routine visits by eastern stars were established in more frontier towns. But in all locations, any theatrical foothold remained somewhat tenuous, with new challenges always looming.

At the Columbia Street Theatre in Cincinnati, the Drake company met the new year with a mixture of success and tragedy. Clara Fisher, at eighteen already a star in the East, had appeared through the holidays in classical comedic leads—for example, Lady Teazle and Widow Cheerly. A child prodigy in London, this "plump, fresh, lively, English girl" at sixteen had conquered New York, where "her youth, her vivacity, and her genuine talent placed her very high in public estimation." Fisher, along with the serious roles of Fanny Drake and the comic antics and songs of Rice, yielded good reviews but weak houses throughout the month of January.[1]

On January 28 Aleck Drake gave his last performance, a comic song following Fanny's tragic turn in *Virginius*. His sudden death on February 10 was attributable, observed one Cincinnatian, to overwork: "His disease was no doubt hastened by his constant labor in painting the stage during the cold days in the beginning of February." Eulogies were eloquent: "Mr. Drake's comic powers were of the highest order; and from having received his theatric education principally in the west, he may fairly be pronounced an original. He had no models before him, from [whom] he might have derived advantages and ideas." He showed "some of the best qualities of the heart; he was benevolent and charitable [and] was ever ready to forego his own comfort and profit. His whole life has been devoted to the amusement of the public, and had he been a worldly man he might have died in affluence." "As a citizen and gentleman, a neighbor and friend, a husband and parent, he discharged his duties with cheerfulness and fidelity. As a comedian, he stood unrivaled in the West."[2]

Drake descendant George D. Ford recalled family lore that "at the report of his death, the legislatures of Ohio and Kentucky adjourned for the day, and people cried in the streets of Cincinnati," although contemporary newspapers do not record this. For a combined memorial and benefit on February 24 for Fanny, who was left in dire financial straits, having received no salary for months, Mrs. Trollope contributed a monody. "Apollo Addressing the Muse" included the words, "Alas poor Aleck! Wilt thou then no more / In thy own matchless mellow drolling / Set e'en the dullest mortals in a roar / Might make the Gods envy their reveling."[3]

Aleck's death brought his father back into management. Sam Sr.'s formula for success was strict audience decorum, and he published rules: there would be no loud talk, no boisterous conduct, no wearing of hats, no cracking of nuts, no throwing of "nutshells, apples, etc.," from the upper tiers, no indiscriminate reserving of large numbers of seats, and, remarkably, no smoking, "a practice at once dangerous and offensive." (Regrettably, such behavior was hard to quell. A few years later, William Charles Macready's performance in Cincinnati was interrupted by half of a sheep carcass thrown onto the stage from the gallery.)[4]

But within a year, when the Columbia Street Theatre burned, the elder Drake would yield Cincinnati to Ludlow and Caldwell. For now, he ceded management in Louisville to stage manager Charles Booth Parsons.

Parsons's company reopened at Louisville's City Theatre on March 26 with *Foundling of the Forest* and *Lottery Ticket*. For a week they performed a familiar repertoire, including *Thérèse* (Julia Fosdick) and *Day After the Fair*, until the arrival of Edward Raymond in his usual tragedies. Fanny, her mourning over, reappeared on April 2 starring opposite him in the title role in *Evadne*, followed by other tragic leads. Raymond remained until the close of the season, performing intermittently, often opposite Fanny, who performed almost every night. Another benefit for her and the children occurred on April 12, and Trollope's monody was repeated between

The Stranger and *Catharine and Petruchio* (Fanny and Parsons in the leads in both).[5]

Mid-April brought a week of dancers Monsieur Benoni and his seven-year-old daughter Virginia, along with Monsieur Feltman, "the highly accomplished grotesque comic performer," and his wife, a "universally approved female dancer." Along with their performances, such pieces as *Evadne, Douglas,* and *The Review,* continued. Lane appeared for a week in early May with her usual repertoire. Rice applied his mechanical skills to a production of *Pizarro,* creating a "grand revolving sun" and his comedic skills in debuting his colorful "Jim Crow" routine on May 21 between a new melodrama, *The Kentucky Rifle,* and the farce, *Who's the Dupe?* As its popularity grew, he had to perform some version of it nearly every night. In early June actress-vocalist Elizabeth Feron and ropewalker John Cline performed for a week.[6]

End-of-season benefits included Parsons's on June 10, as Othello with Raymond as Iago. Two nights later a "Benefit of Jim Crow" also included *William Tell* (Parsons, with Fanny in breeches as Albert), followed five nights later by a benefit for the Louisville Orphan Asylum. Parsons closed the season on June 19 with another benefit for Fanny, she as *The Irish Widow* and delivering a comic song, plus *Innkeeper's Daughter.*[7]

Parsons would return with many of these same actors—notably including Fanny and Rice—in mid-September to Louisville's City Theatre and provide professional entertainment with such visiting stars as Raymond and Cowell. Their repertoire included such standard pieces as *Town and Country, Damon and Pythias, William Tell, Virginius* (starring Raymond, on his way to Nashville), *Honey Moon,* and *Apostate.* Before their close at the end of the year, the company had provided theatregoers with many "an instructive evening's entertainment, . . . far different from a brawling place of inebriety or that of lounging away their evening in indolence or indulging in gloomy retrospection or the mind's inanity."[8]

<hr />

Before Louisville, Feron and Cline had been performing widely in the South. Sol Smith, managing a contingent of Caldwell's New Orleans company at the time, engaged Feron for Montgomery, Alabama, for two nights during his brief commitment there, January 25 through February 6, earning good business. Smith cleverly rewrote some of the dialogue in various comedies and farces to account for the convenient presence of a piano in certain scenes, to allow Feron to launch into song. Her share of the two weeks' box office of $883 was $101.[9]

From Montgomery, Smith took his company to Selma for nine nights, taking in an average of $70 a night. Bypassing Mobile, which still lacked a decent theater, they opened in Natchez on March 10. There, they were to perform four nights a week for five weeks in their standard repertoire, including *Honey Moon, Town and Country, Castle Spectre, Hunter of the Alps,* and *Gambler's Fate*, with the usual farces. The Benonis and Feltman, en route to Louisville, were booked for a brief appearance in late March.

But the first week's receipts fell $150 short of expenses, cutting deeply into the $1,100 Smith had brought to Natchez (and at that rate would almost entirely deplete it). So, he tried splitting his company, sending half under Williams to Port Gibson, nearly fifty miles away, to perform three nights a week for five weeks. Williams, though, encountered equally dire financial results and wrote to Smith for support, meaning his acting. Consequently, for a month Smith rode horseback between the two towns, performing on alternate days in each. By mid-April, "My profits at Port Gibson equaled my losses at Natchez." Sending his actors back to Caldwell, he left Natchez with $1,200 and headed north.[10]

With his wife, brother Lemuel, and Abram and Emeline Jackson, he played three nights in Vicksburg (clearing $175) and arrived in Cincinnati in late May. There, he found that Ludlow had opened with his company at the Columbia Street Theatre on April 24. Ludlow's first visiting star had been Lane, followed by the Benonis and Feltman, who danced "with a style of dressing that [is] perfectly decorous and modest." They were followed by Molly Crooke (née Entwistle) in *Soldier's Daughter, Luke the Laborer, Honey Moon,* and *Rob Roy*.

Now, Sol and Martha Smith joined Ludlow—it is unclear what happened to the rest of Smith's actors—playing leads in melodramas (for example, *Broken Sword*) and comedies (*Hypocrite, No Song No Supper*) for a week in late May. The press was immediately supportive. Smith "has a claim on the sympathy of the lovers of the drama, on account of his recent misfortunes—having twice suffered by fire within a year past." (His temporary St. Francis Street Theatre in Mobile had also just burned.) Cline, too, appeared for a week and filled houses. A highlight of the season, as it had been in Louisville, was *Paris and London*.[11]

In mid-June, Caldwell, too, arrived in Cincinnati to assess his chances for expanding his circuit there, and agreed to guest star for two nights. When Ludlow closed the season on July 17 and dismissed his company, Caldwell hired several. Ludlow went with Cline to Pittsburgh, which still lacked a theater. The only venue available there, which Lane had used in mid-April, was the Concert Hall of dancing master J. C. Bond on Penn Street. Ludlow operated there to "fluctuating business" in August, then relinquished Pittsburgh to H. H. Fuller, a Buffalo manager who organized "a very respectable stock-company." Under Fuller's management "considerable changes and improvements were effected in scenery, decorations, etc.," but he soon left all of it to the Pittsburgh amateur thespians.[12]

Ludlow erroneously asserts in his memoirs that Caldwell asked him in Cincinnati to manage a contingent of his company that fall in St. Louis, Natchez, and Nashville, an arrangement which he happily accepted, having "found there was no way of making a living by acting in the towns I had recently been working in." However, that venture was managed by Jackson Gray and James S. Rowe, Caldwell's treasurer in New Orleans, and it was not until 1831 that Ludlow would manage a tour for Caldwell—not the first time Ludlow muddles his chronology.[13]

~~~~~~~~~~

St. Louis, not quite ready for theatrical permanence, was entertained sporadically in early 1830 by its amateur thespians, but now Gray and Rowe provided Caldwell's professionals. They opened there on June 12 with *She Stoops to Conquer* and *The Hotel*. Two nights later Jane Placide made her first appearance of the season, as Orilla in *Adrian and Orilla* opposite young (twenty) Joseph M. Field's Adrian, followed by Mrs. Rowe's Little Pickle. Field exhibited "a good general appearance, . . . a good deal of spirit, some taste, and a pretty correct conception of his part," and Placide was "chaste and powerful," clearly the best in the company. Gray, though, acted Orilla's father without "a proper conception of the character."[14]

For another ten weeks Placide carried leads in comedies (for example, *Wives as They Were*) and tragedies (*Gambler's Fate, Thérèse*). When Caldwell himself appeared in early July, Placide played opposite him (Mrs. Haller to his Stranger and Beatrice to his Benedick in *Much Ado About Nothing*). When Caldwell left for New Orleans en route to an engagement at the Park Theatre in New York, Parsons made a brief star appearance in late July, playing opposite Placide. Major female roles not taken by Placide were played by Mary Ann McClure or Rosina Seymour Rowe.

But amid all this multicity theatrical musical chairs, neither Placide nor Caldwell nor Parsons increased revenue, and the season was ultimately a disappointment. One reviewer attributed Caldwell's eventual decision not to pursue plans to erect a theater in St. Louis to that summer's poor attendance. It persisted throughout most of August despite varied offerings, including *Devil's Bridge* (Mrs. Rowe as Bellino in breeches opposite Placide as Countess Rosalva), *Foundling of the Forest, Lady of the Lake, Cure for the Heartache, Roland for an Oliver, Day After the Wedding, William Tell, Lover's Vows, Rob Roy*, and *The Romp*. By August 24, Gray and Rowe opted to close and head for Nashville, leaving St. Louis again to its thespians.[15]

Nashville, incorporated in 1806 with a population in 1830 of 5,566, seemed more promising than St. Louis. From September 13 to November 23 in Caldwell's 1826 theater, Gray and Rowe added a raft of new, mostly forgettable plays: *Alonzo the Brave and the Fair Imogine, Black-Eyed Susan, Brian Borohime, The Eighth of January, The Green-Eyed Monster, Husbands and Wives, Jonathan Postfree, Father and Daughter, The Libertine, The May Queen, The Veteran and His Progeny, She Would and She Would Not*, and *Maid or Wife*.

Raymond and McClure carried most leads until the arrival on November 8 of guest-star actor-vocalists Mr. and Mrs. William Pearman. Caldwell himself returned from New York on November 19 to perform for the benefit night of Mrs. Rowe, praised both for her merits as an actress and for "the favorable estimation in which she is held in private." The lavish closing night provided an opera, *The Barber of Seville* (with the Pearmans as Count

Almaviva and Rosina, plus Caldwell and Holland), *The Secret* (Holland and Mrs. Rowe), and *The Liar* (Caldwell).[16]

~~~~~~~~~~~

In Cincinnati, after Aleck Drake's death, his father occasionally emerged from retirement and half-heartedly managed the remnants of their company. But except for brief engagements in fall 1830 and spring 1831 at the Columbia Street Theatre, he ceded dominance in Cincinnati to Caldwell, focusing instead on Louisville. By fall 1831 Caldwell was making good his intention to build a theater in Cincinnati, despite its reputation as a poor theatrical town. It had by 1830 reached a population of 24,831, a more-than-adequate pool of potential audiences to allow Caldwell, despite lingering religious opposition, to compete against the Columbia Street Theatre.

With the opening of his new Cincinnati Theatre on July 4, 1832, he finalized his control of theatrical activity there. Said to have cost $40,000, the 70-by-120-foot brick edifice stood on Third Street between Sycamore Street and Broadway and seated (variously) 1,300 to 1,500 people (or up to 2,000 when crammed) and was lit throughout by Caldwell's signature gas lighting. On that first night, following the usual dedicatory prize-winning oration, the bill featured Caldwell as Frank Heartall in *Soldier's Daughter*, and *No Song, No Supper*. The casts were formed of Caldwell's New Orleans company, with the notable addition of Mr. and Mrs. Richard Russell, back from what had been a disenchanting experience in management in Boston and New York. Two nights later Placide made her first appearance, playing opposite Caldwell in *Stranger* and *Honey Moon*. With such luminaries as Edwin Forrest and Junius Brutus Booth making star appearances during the 1832–33 season, there was no question that Cincinnati was no longer on the theatrical frontier. When the venerable Columbia Street Theatre burned in 1834, any competition was removed.[17]

~~~~~~~~~~~

For three years, 1830 to 1833, the elder Drake tried to hold on in Louisville, incorporated in 1828 with a population of nearly ten thousand. In early 1830 he rebuilt the rundown theater on Jefferson Street, christening it the City

Theatre, dedicated to blending "rational amusement with instruction, that mankind might know how to estimate honor and virtue." Relatively small at fifty-two by one-hundred feet, it seated a modest seven hundred. Drake opened it on March 26, 1830, less than two months after Aleck's death, with star turns by Parsons and Rice in *Foundling of the Forest* and *Lottery Ticket*, respectively. Rice achieved stratospheric fame in this theater since that May 21 performance, as "Sambo (the Negro Boy)" in *The Kentucky Rifle*, in which character he had introduced his "Jim Crow" routine, repeated several times that week and thousands of times internationally thereafter. (But faithful to Drake, Rice remained with the company until September.) In fall 1830, Drake turned over management in Louisville to Parsons and except for rare stage appearances remained on his Prospect, Kentucky, farm, where he died on October 17, 1854.[18]

For the 1830–31 season, Parsons booked such stars as Clara Fisher, Charles Kean, James M. Scott, and Joe Cowell, but by July 1831 Caldwell again encroached. At the outset of 1831 he had tapped Ludlow as tour manager for part of his New Orleans company, sending them first to Natchez, then St. Louis, and now to Louisville, where they opened on July 26 for twelve nights, apparently with Drake's acquiescence. Mainstays of the company were the Ludlows, McClures, and Smiths, but the Smiths became increasingly alienated from Ludlow and departed from Louisville with some of the other actors, to barnstorm across the South. In early September, Caldwell himself appeared, but was not well received when he attempted tragedy. In *Hamlet* and *Gamester*, he ranked "by no means so high as we were led to believe."[19]

Otherwise, Parsons held the Louisville company together for three more years, with Rice making frequent visits. Caldwell, too, brought actors each year on their way to Cincinnati. His biggest star, in early 1834, was Junius Brutus Booth in his first appearance on the frontier for five years, which involved some of his most unhinged behavior, including being jailed for drunkenness.

~~~~~~~~~~

When the Ludlow-managed Caldwell troupe performed in Natchez for two months in late winter 1831, they drew their audiences from a population of over three thousand, but their efforts were hindered by religious opposition, egged on by *Mississippi Gazette* editor Andrew Marschalk, who refused to run theatrical notices and derided all actors as a "wretched melee of paltry trash composed of vapid and high-sounding appellations!" Nevertheless, they set up in Caldwell's 1828 Main Street theater, and delighted patrons with stars from the East. The first was Clara Fisher, now nearly twenty, in late February. Caldwell persevered in Natchez as he did in other cities, and within a few years was bringing in such stars as Mrs. Mary Duff, comedian James H. Hackett, child prodigy Master (Joseph) Burke, and the acrobatic Ravel Family.[20]

~~~~~~~~~~

From 1830 to 1835, St. Louis, as its population grew from just under five thousand to over eighty-three hundred, Caldwell again saw opportunity. During that time, in his remodeled Salt House Theatre—first managed by Gray and Rowe and then by Ludlow—many of the same stars, including Rice, appeared, along with such names as Fanny Drake (belatedly making her St. Louis debut on April 25, 1831) and the brilliant but "dissipated" tragedian Augustus A. Addams in 1833. A new shining light in 1833 was tragedienne Miss Mary Vos, now eighteen, the daughter of the late St. Louis theatrical pioneer John H. Vos.

These stars were supported by New Orleans actors, with McClure and Placide dominant, and Caldwell making occasional appearances. These seasons had their ups and downs, the latter sometimes brought about by bouts of cholera. Ludlow recorded that their spring 1831 engagement brought in "very fair business," but Smith deemed it an "utter failure" (this just before their estrangement). By 1835, there were far more ups than downs, as theatre was finally, firmly entrenched in St. Louis.[21]

~~~~~~~~~~

Since the serial theater fires in Mobile, no one had staged productions there until January 25, 1832, when Smith, down from Huntsville and Tuscaloosa, opened in a makeshift theater over a billiard parlor. The city's population of little more than three thousand drew its considerable wealth from cotton, making it an attractive theatrical proposition. Smith had brought a small company that included his wife and brother Lemuel, and they supported second- and third-tier stars, including Henry J. Finn and Raymond. Smith managed to turn a slight profit before merging with Purdy Brown's equestrian troupe to perform in a new playhouse on St. Emmanuel Street.[22]

When Brown died in June 1834, Ludlow moved in, still smarting from being euchred by Caldwell in Huntsville. For several years both Ludlow and Smith had jockeyed for position in Montgomery, Alabama, and now both sought to establish a permanent presence there and in Mobile, united against Caldwell. Hence, despite their differences they began in a roundabout, tentative manner to sound each other out about a partnership to manage theaters, primarily in St. Louis and Mobile but in other southern and western towns as well. This was effected in 1835.[23]

∿∿∿∿∿∿∿∿

Since Smith's efforts in 1829, with its population by 1830 still under seven hundred, Memphis endured only an occasional performance by barnstorming actors until March 1837. Then, a modest frame building on Market Street was converted into a theater by two actors from Nashville, J. Warrell and Thomas M. Groves. Their small company, in which Mrs. Groves played female leads, performed a light repertoire, with occasional works by Shakespeare, for two months, three or four nights a week, and then returned to Nashville. In spring 1839, frontier theatre veteran Austin Cargill with James Delmon Grace, a former member of Sol Smith's troupe, arrived in Memphis with another small company which performed in the same Market Street facility. But they, too, soon departed, and it was not until the early 1840s that stars, including Addams and Yankee comedian Dan Marble, appeared, and not until 1842 that another theater opened, albeit in a converted stable, and 1846 before a legitimate theater was constructed.

∿∿∿∿∿∿∿∿

A year before Ludlow and Smith formed their partnership, another duo formed theirs. In 1834, two tragedians, Edwin Dean, thirty, the second husband of frontier actress Julia Drake Fosdick, and David D. McKinney, twenty-six, an alcoholic, hotheaded Bowery Theatre actor, threw in their lot together for a new, triangular theatrical circuit consisting of Buffalo, Cleveland, and Detroit, with occasional forays to Columbus (much of their travel presumably on Lake Erie). Dean had initially partnered with Parsons, but switched a year later to McKinney, in Buffalo.[24]

The Dean and McKinney company, organized in summer 1834, was relatively competent. It consisted, beside the managers, of the new Mrs. Edwin Dean (Julia having died in 1832), Henry Trowbridge, his sister-in-law Martha M. Trowbridge, Marble, low comedian and frontier veteran William Forrest and his wife and son, and actors named Waters (whose "Zip Coon" imitated Rice's Jim Crow), Marsh, Potter, Buel, and Mr. and Mrs. Barstow (she playing soubrettes).[25]

They headed first, in late July 1834, to Detroit, in Michigan Territory, where they leased the City Theatre from David C. McKinstrey. The brick building on State Street had originally been a Methodist chapel, and seated about four hundred. The only theatrical performances in Detroit since 1816 had been those of its soldier-amateurs, except for brief appearances by two itinerant troupes. The first had been H. H. Fuller's comedians in summer 1827, who for $35 were granted a license to perform. The other was a month-long appearance in spring 1834 by "Eberle, Powell & Co.," who performed in a makeshift structure on the northeast corner of Jefferson and Woodward avenues and left no evidence of their membership or bills. Neither of these troupes returned to Detroit.[26]

Dean and McKinney opened in the City Theatre on July 31 with *Pizarro*, with McKinney as Rolla, Martha Trowbridge as Elvira, and Mrs. Forrest as Cora, and *Animal Magnetism*. The *Democratic Free Press* urged attendance for its "salutary effect upon the intellectual and moral state of society" and "its tendency to prevent the intrusion of vice." The company was pronounced "without exception the best that has ever visited," and attracted sizable audiences.[27]

In mid-September, as an outbreak of cholera threatened Detroit, Dean and McKinney took their leave, publicly thanking its citizens for their "kindness and liberality." They went next to Cleveland, which had seen only occasional performances since Blanchard's troupe in 1820, including

Drake's brief visit in 1827. Now, from September 25 through October 18, 1834, Dean and McKinney performed in Italian Hall, which seated 450 on backless benches, on the third floor of the brick Erie Building. Their repertoire included *Soldier's Daughter*, *Othello* (McKinney in the title role, with Dean as Iago), *Richard III* (Dean's favorite role), *Rendezvous*, *Floating Beacon*, *Thérèse*, and *Damon and Pythias*. They would return, as part of their circuit, for four years.[28]

Their next stop was their home base, Buffalo, where they opened on October 21 with *Soldier's Daughter*. Buffalo, incorporated in 1832 with a population in 1834 of nearly fifteen thousand, had since 1821 seen only occasional itinerant performers in various converted spaces, one being on the east side of Main Street below Lafayette Square. The most promising had been a troupe in 1824 managed by John G. Gilbert and Henry and Martha Trowbridge. The two managers played comic old men, with Martha carrying female leads. They had also made stops in Cleveland—bringing that city its first Shakespeare—and Columbus, Ohio, but their partnership soon ended, and Mrs. Trowbridge signed on with Dean and McKinney.

In Buffalo, an Albany manager, William Duffy, had erected a modest wood-frame theater on the corner of South Division and Washington streets in 1834, which he named the Buffalo Theatre. But within two years he was eclipsed by Dean and McKinney and the building converted to a church. Now, Dean and McKinney performed on the upper floor of a store on Seneca Street, promising Buffalonians their "assiduous attention to the comfort and amusement of the audience."[29]

A new theater was under construction in Buffalo by Benjamin Rathburn, but until it was completed, Dean and McKinney returned to Detroit and Cleveland for spring and early summer 1835. The brightest addition to their company that spring was Mary Ann McClure, whom McKinney knew from the Bowery Theatre and who now supplanted Martha Trowbridge. McClure's performances were hailed as "unequalled," demonstrating "genius, study and perseverance," predicting her rank as "first on the American stage." She and McKinney had brought from the Bowery scripts, mostly melodramas, that had been hits there, including *The Last Days of Pompeii*, with McKinney as Arbaces and McClure as the blind Nydia.[30]

Leaving Cleveland, they headed in mid-July back to Buffalo, to their new home, the Eagle Theatre. The seventy-by-one-hundred-foot brick-and-stone edifice featured all the latest stage equipment and a four-tiered semicircular house with copious private boxes (available for $100 to $150 per season), all illuminated by Buffalo's first gas lighting. Dean and McKinney opened on July 20, 1835, with a more-than-six-hour extravaganza that included a variety of olio acts, *Hunchback* and *Taming of the Shrew*, the leads in both (as would usually be the case) being McKinney and McClure. Among Dean and McKinney's early stars that season were Rice and Marble.

Summer 1835 took them back to Detroit to compete against a brief appearance of Duffy's much smaller troupe. Between visits by Dean and McKinney to Detroit over the next few years, major stars such as Charlotte Cushman would perform there, and another temporary theatre would be built, this one on Gratiot Street. (It would not be until 1849 that a permanent theater would be erected, the Metropolitan on Jefferson Avenue.)

From mid-October through mid-November 1835, Dean and McKinney performed in Cleveland, then moved on to Columbus (for the meeting of the state legislature, as had been the case in Frankfort, Kentucky, two decades before). The first performances in Columbus had occurred in 1827 and 1828 in converted rooms in the Old Market House on West State Street by what may have been the Drake company, remembered by one theatregoer as wretched: "The poor creatures had mouthed [the play] so horribly that the audience soon tired of it and . . . the actors were hissed off the stage." Two years later Gilbert and Trowbridge's troupe had performed in Young's Coffee House. In July 1830 Louisa Lane had stopped by to perform as she toured.[31]

As had been so often the case in other Ohio towns, though, religious opposition pronounced any theatrical performances as "worldly, wicked, and associated with undesirable practices." To accommodate them, Dean and McKinney stated their willingness to changes any offensive passages in scripts, but "would not stand by and let those who admittedly knew nothing about the theater create a false impression and ruin the means of livelihood for a large group of people."[32]

With Martha Trowbridge reciting the obligatory inaugural address, Dean and McKinney opened on December 21, 1835, in the first building in Columbus specifically erected as a theater, the Columbus Theatre on the west side of High Street between Broad and Gay streets. At 50 by 120 feet, with three tiers of boxes, it could be converted to an arena to accommodate equestrian performances, and optimistically seated fifteen hundred at a time when Columbus's population stood at four thousand. Its heating system was flawed from the start, however, and the "poor actors shivered until their teeth chattered and their breath was visible two feet from their nostrils." Still, conditions must have improved, for Dean and McKinney returned to Columbus for all four years of their partnership, always during the legislative season, but they never reaped much profit there.[33]

They were more successful in Cleveland, opening a new theater there in spring 1836 on the corner of Superior Street and Union Lane, paying seventy-five dollars for a one-year license to perform. They opened on May 31 with *Hamlet*, the first of many years and many stars to grace the Cleveland stage.

Another frontier city, just below the Dean and McKinney circuit, saw its first theatre in the 1830s. Chicago had been scouted by William Blanchard in the early 1820s, but he had found it "a mere trading post for skins" where "it was useless to try to perform." In 1833, when a few itinerant novelty artists (for example, ventriloquists) arrived to perform in taverns, it was still "one chaos of mud, rubbish, and confusion." The first theatrical performance occurred in 1837 in the converted dining room of the United States Hotel (until 1836 the Sauganash Hotel), on the southeast corner of Lake and Market streets, accommodating about two hundred from a population of forty-two hundred. Actor-managers Harry Isherwood and Alexander MacKenzie brought a small troupe—eight men and three women, an offshoot of the Dean and McKinney company—there in October 1837 (seven months after Chicago's incorporation). Isherwood thought the hotel "a queer-looking place" which "stood at some distance out on the prairie, solitary and alone."[34]

During 1836 and 1837 MacKenzie had managed theaters for Dean and McKinney in Cleveland, Columbus, and Detroit. Now, in Chicago, he and

Isherwood applied for and received for $125 a six-month performance license from the Chicago Common Council. They remained there through early January 1838, staging at least thirty-four plays, including such standard pieces as *Hunchback* and *Stranger*. Leads were carried by Isherwood, Henry Leicester, and the recently widowed Mary Ann (Mrs. David) Ingersoll.[35]

Isherwood and MacKenzie in 1838 brought to Chicago—from New York via Albany, Buffalo, and Lakes Erie, Huron, and Michigan—an improved company that included nine-year-old Joseph Jefferson III, destined to be one of the greatest comedians of the century. Acquiring permission to perform—for a lower fee of $100—Isherwood and MacKenzie set out to convert the third floor of the Rialto auction house on the corner of Dearborn and South Water streets into a theater. This Chicago Theatre, accommodating up to four hundred, opened on May 10, 1838, with *The Stranger*. Young Jefferson considered it a "beautiful" place, with a greenroom that was "a perfect gem." (From Chicago these actors traveled to Springfield, the capital of Illinois, where according to Jefferson they obtained the help of lawyer Abraham Lincoln in circumventing performance licensing fees.)[36]

Only in February 1847 would Chicago would see its first building specifically erected as a theater, a frame building on Randolph Street near Dearborn, built at a cost of $4,000. It would flourish for many years under the management of John Blake Rice, with visits by prominent stars.

~~~~~~~~~~

Pittsburgh meanwhile had remained without a permanent theater, regular season, company or stars, despite its incorporation in 1818 and an 1830 population of 12,568. This was finally rectified when the New Pittsburgh Theatre opened on September 2, 1833, at 306–310 Fifth Street under the management of Francis Courtney Wemyss. This handsome two-story building, 57 by 130 feet, housed two tiers in a rose and gold interior, lit by eighteen chandeliers. Wemyss proudly booked some of the biggest stars from New York and Philadelphia, among them Rice, Fisher, Addams, and Forrest.

These stars were supported by a highly capable company, including the recently widowed Sophia Turner and her two young daughters, Ellen and Julia (in old women, child, and breeches roles, respectively);

John Sefton and Wemyss himself in low comedy roles; and Mr. and Mrs. Charles L. Green, she as leading lady. Some of Wemyss's highest box office grosses occurred in that first month during the concurrent engagements of Forrest and Addams (for example, as Damon and Pythias, Virginius and Icilius, Othello and Iago, Rolla and Pizarro, and Macbeth and Macduff, respectively).[37]

Wemyss continued to successfully manage the Pittsburgh Theatre until 1841, yielding it then to William Dinneford. Significantly, it was from Pittsburgh during the early 1830s that an unusual, innovative iteration of frontier theatre would emerge: the showboat.

13

SHOWBOATS

LIKE SAMUEL DRAKE'S FORAY into the frontier in 1815, William Chapman's in the spring of 1831 was a family affair. Both men, journeying in late middle age down the Ohio River from Pittsburgh, sought a theatrical success denied to them and their kin in the major cities of the East. But whereas the river was for Drake merely the means to his end of new audiences in new towns, for Chapman it would provide the theatrical venue itself.

He was descended from an acting family. His grandfather, Thomas Chapman (ca. 1683–1746), had been an actor at Lincoln's Inn Fields, Covent Garden, and Drury Lane theatres from at least 1723, celebrated for his tragic and comedic roles. These included the narrator in the original production of John Gay's *Beggar's Opera* in 1728, the year he married an actress/dancer likely named Hannah. Their two sons both died young: one was killed in the American colonies in Braddock's Defeat in 1755, and the other was lost at sea after fathering America's showboat progenitor in Barnstable, England, in 1760.[1]

As a teenager, William began studies at Oxford (his descendant George Ford suggests it was for the ministry) but at eighteen dropped out to tour the provinces as an actor. During that time, notes Durang, he "tamed his rampant style to the judicious and chaste of sound and action." Debuting at Drury Lane in 1782, he played there and at Haymarket through at least 1792, primarily in supporting comic roles. In 1804 he secured a position at Covent Garden. There, over many years, he earned a creditable reputation for playing sentimental old men, and returned in summers to the Haymarket. He also toured for a time with John Richardson's Traveling Theatre, founded in 1798.[2]

In 1806 he married Penelope Britt, a celebrated Irish actress at Covent Garden. She had been to America and performed at the John Street Theatre post-Revolution, then returned to the Dublin stage and in 1805 to Covent Garden. She bore William four sons: twins Samuel (variously) V./H. (1799–1830) and William B. Jr. (1799–1857), Bernard (dates unknown) and George (1803–1876); and two daughters, Therese Sarah (?–1871) and Elizabeth (dates unknown). They also raised as their own William Jr.'s illegitimate daughter, Caroline (1818–1876). (According to Ford, William Jr. left home at eighteen with "a taste for the rakish, a trait that was a source of grievance to his parents." He also implies young William, having comprised the virtue of Caroline's mother, had to stealthily flee England out of fear for his life.)[3]

Of the Chapman children, William B. Jr. (henceforth "W.B.") entered the acting profession first, playing Fleance in 1810 to his father's Macbeth, with the renowned Sarah Siddons as Lady Macbeth and Charles Kemble as Macduff, at Covent Garden. This theatrical family remained in London, with both parents acting at Covent Garden, until the early 1820s. By 1826, worsening economic conditions mandated their looking to the New World for employment. As Junius Brutus Booth wrote from London to his father, already in America, in February of that year, "The distress is so excessive . . . that men look upon each other doubtful if they shall defend their own or steal their neighbor's property. Famine stares all England in the face. As for theatricals, they are not thought of, much less patronized. The emigration to America will be very numerous, as it is hardly possible for the middling classes to keep body and soul together."[4]

The two eldest Chapman sons, W.B. and Samuel, made the journey first, arriving in New York in early 1827 along with W.B.'s recent bride, the former Phoebe Taylor, reputedly a gifted organist (who may or may not have known the truth about little Caroline). Samuel had married in 1822 and fathered a son, Harry, whom he brought to America, and who would also one day become an actor (there is no evidence that Harry's mother came with them). They were followed that summer by their parents, brother George, sister Sarah, and little Caroline (Bernard and Elizabeth remaining in England). For the next four years this acting family played Albany, Troy, Trenton, Wilmington, Philadelphia, and, eventually, New York.[5]

W.B. was the first to secure employment in New York City, debuting on September 13, 1827, as Billy Lackaday in *Sweethearts and Wives,* and Crack in *Turnpike Gate* at the Bowery Theatre, which had only opened the previous October. Having brought "a high name from the London Theatres," he was immediately granted leading roles in comedies and farces, extolled as "the best low comedian who makes us laugh loudest and longest, without buffoonery and grimace," an unusual commendation for a Bowery actor. "His comic singing is more effective than that of any other comedian on our stage," and he quickly became a great favorite. He acted there and at the Chatham Street Theatre intermittently for two years (but not during the brief Ludlow-Cooper management of the latter). Samuel debuted on October 21, 1827, at the Chestnut Street Theatre in Philadelphia, carving out a different line of business, that of leading tragic roles (such as Pierre in *Venice Preserved* and Romeo).[6]

Their father debuted in New York, also at the Bowery, on October 2, 1828, as Iago to the Othello of Edwin Forrest. (It is tempting to imagine Forrest relating stories of his travels on the frontier, likely the first William Sr. would have heard of that possibility.) He soon established himself as a respectable portrayer of "heavies" and, being well into his sixties, old men (for example, Pescara for W.B.'s benefit of *Apostate,* and Old Dornton in *Road to Ruin,* with his son as Silky). Eleven-year-old Caroline pitched in, acting as "Miss Greenwood" on June 12, 1829, in the role of Phoebe in *Paul Pry* for her father's benefit at James Hackett's newly rechristened American Opera House, Chatham Street. Sarah acted, too, but rarely.

In fall 1829 William Sr. switched to the far more respectable Park Theatre, still playing old men (for example, Jarvis in *Gamester,* supporting visiting star James Caldwell, who also might have spoken enthusiastically of the frontier). When Forrest appeared, Chapman played Gloucester to his Lear, and was the original Sir Arthur Vaughan to Forrest's famed Metamora. Throughout, recalls Durang, "Mr. Chapman [Sr.] was extremely gentlemanly and respectable in his personal aspect and suavity of manners, but was eccentric and brusquely impetuous in temper at times." He wore spectacles always, which he once forgetfully kept on as he rushed tardily onstage as the Ghost to Hamblin's Hamlet, causing the audience to collapse in laughter.[7]

Samuel in May 1829 had taken over the management of Philadelphia's Walnut Street Theatre in partnership with John Greene (another frontier veteran). Drawing actors from the recently failed Chestnut Street and Arch Street theatres, Samuel and Greene paid their actors poorly, offering them shares of negligible profits. That summer Samuel married again (it being unclear whether or when Harry's mother died), into a formidable theatrical dynasty: Philadelphia actress Elizabeth Jefferson, nineteen, with two years of acting experience behind her, was the daughter of Joseph Jefferson II and the aunt of young Joseph Jefferson III. Elizabeth Chapman soon "became one of the most approved favorites of the theatre, and led the tragedy and comedy heroines with éclat." Among her notable early performances was as Alice in one of the earliest *Rip Van Winkles,* performed on October 30, 1829. The title role in that production, which would become her nephew's most famous role, was enacted by her new husband's brother.[8]

W.B. had come down to Philadelphia that fall not only to act but, according to Ford, as a silent partner in management. He was "a sterling low comedian," remembered Durang, "dryly sparkling with legitimate comic expression," as well as "a most excellent comic singer. . . . His forte, however, was in the eccentric characters. . . . He was a short man, about five feet five inches, very stout built, had a very dark complexion, and a sharp little black eye." Rare for a low comedian of his era, he adhered closely to a playwright's text and eschewed mugging for cheap laughs.[9]

The 1829–30 Walnut Street season looked promising, with commitments from such stars as Booth, Hamblin, Clara Fisher, and ropedancer John Cline. Samuel even introduced Harry, now seven, to the stage. But by January 1830 Samuel and Greene were nearly out of funds. Seeking a cause of their persistent losses, they squared off against their treasurer and co-lessee, a man named Edmonds, who after extensive recrimination and litigation, was exonerated. On January 22 they abruptly closed the theater and Greene withdrew from management. Samuel, arrested for his debts, was jailed for twenty-four hours until bailed out by friends. On February 20 he and W.B. announced a spring season.

But trouble continued to plague them. A lavish production of *Faustus* cut deeply into their limited funds. During a new production of *Gasper-*

oni; or, The Roman Bandit, guest star Matilda Flynn was nearly killed in an onstage fall. And in mid-May, Samuel fell ill, also from a fall, and had to be carried home from the theater. He had written a new piece, *The Mail Robbers,* based on a real, contemporary event, and had ridden his horse to the location in which it occurred, to sketch the scene for the play's realistic scenery. His horse had thrown him, injuring his shoulder, which was further abraded by costume armor he wore the next night, which was unseasonably warm, exacerbated by the stage lights. The resultant blood poisoning led to his collapse and his death on May 15 at age thirty-one. Manager F. C. Wemyss, who had been instrumental in bringing the Chapmans to America, eulogized him as "a man of varied talent, of much literary knowledge, and an [*sic*] universal favorite." His epitaph was respectful: "To Their Favorite Comedian / By the Citizens of Philadelphia / His Friends Adored Him / Even his enemies loved him."[10]

His widow and brother kept the Walnut Street Theatre operating through the summer of 1830. A benefit for her on May 26 raised $500 (nearly $15,000 today), but by fall she left the Chapmans to rejoin her Jefferson clan and eventually achieve minor stardom in New York. William Sr. and W.B. persevered, opening a fall 1830 season. George, acting as "Mr. Greenwood," joined them on stage, as did Caroline, still as "Miss Greenwood." Now twelve, she played Portia in *Merchant of Venice* "with much judgment, and read the part well, without committing the sin of overemphasizing Portia's speech on mercy. [Her] grace and soul were inherent." But failure haunted them and by mid-December all but W.B. abandoned Philadelphia and headed west, by stagecoach, to Pittsburgh. (W.B. stayed through March 1831, acting at the Arch Street, Walnut Street, and Chestnut Street theaters, then for a few weeks in New York at the Bowery Theatre in September, before joining the rest of his family on the river.)[11]

In Pittsburgh, this clannish family grew even closer, having forsaken an East Coast theatrical establishment in which "no single theatre was willing to give the whole family employment." It was said that they communicated through a secret verbal and sign language. In early June 1831 they settled into the Red Lion Hotel on St. Clair Street, near the Allegheny River. Its proprietor, Captain Cyrus Brown, allowed them to offset part of the cost of their keep by performing some nights in the hotel dining room. Brown was also a sometime shipbuilder, a not uncommon vocation in this industrial city whose population had nearly doubled in the previous decade.[12]

Seeking a more enduring venue, the Chapmans found that the only surviving theater had been converted into a machine shop. From somewhere—conversations with men like Forrest and Caldwell, the ubiquity of Pittsburgh's shipbuilding operations, or his own native ingenuity—William Chapman Sr. derived the idea for a floating theater that might bring entertainment to river communities down the Ohio and Mississippi rivers.[13]

This he contracted with Brown to build. But Chapman's showboat, far from the iconic gleaming, white, twin-stacked steamboat of Broadway and movie lore, was a humble flatboat, a square-ark broadhorn, launched into the Allegheny River in July 1831. Ludlow saw it tied up at Cincinnati and described it as "a large flat-boat with a rude kind of house built upon it, having a ridge-roof, above which projected a staff with a flag attached, upon which was plainly visible the word 'Theatre'." Built of oak and white pine, it was (by various descriptions) eighty to one hundred feet long and sixteen to thirty feet wide, with access via a wide doorway at its bow. A double row of low clerestory windows admitted daylight, and its interior at night was lit by "a circle of tallow-dripping candles fixed to a barrel hoop suspended from the roof." Inside, "hard board seats stretched from one side of the boat to the other, while at the far end was a little stage with muslin curtain and tallow candles for foot lights." Here was "music, madness, moonshine, philosophy, poetry, and performances—comedy, tragedy and farce—and all going by water. . . . The stage was a little platform raised from the bottom of the boat, and the accommodations of the patrons . . . resembled somewhat the pit of a country playhouse. Boxes there were none." The orchestra consisted of "a fife, a triangle, and a bass drum, on which was discoursed most eloquent music."[14]

Variously called "Chapman's Ark" or "Chapman's Floating Theatre," it was "very rudely built. The staves that supported the roof were pinned into the upright joists with large oak pins, and when a steamer would pass, the heavy swells would cause the pins to creak in a horrid and discordant manner." Inside, though, observed one Cincinnatian, it was "very neatly and tastily fitted up. . . . The seats are well arranged, and in all respects better calculated for the ease and comfort of the audience than in the Cincinnati Theatre during the past season."[15]

Actor Tyrone Power praised its "scenery, dresses, and decorations, all prepared for representation. At each village or large plantation, he [Chapman] hoists banner and blows trumpet and few who love a play suffer his ark to pass the door, since they know it is to return no more until the next year; for, however easy may prove the downward course of the drama's temple, to retrograde upwards [upriver] is quite beyond its power. Sometimes a large steamer from Louisville, with a thousand souls on board, will command a play whilst taking in fuel, when the profits must be famous. The *corps dramatique* is, I believe, composed of members of his own family, which is numerous, and, despite of alligators and yellow fever, likely to increase and flourish. When the Mississippi theatre reaches New Orleans, it is abandoned and sold for firewood; the manager and troop [*sic*] returning in a steamer to build a new one, with such improvements as increased experience may have suggested."[16]

Propelled solely by the current, with long poles used to keep it in the deepest channels away from the shore and avoid snags and "sawyers" (submerged trees, most removed by the massive government effort of 1827), the Floating Theatre required its pilot—in Chapman's case a hired river man—to be cognizant of all information in the latest edition of Zadok Cramer's *Navigator*. To go up smaller tributaries, such as the Green and Arkansas rivers, "It was pole and warp and tow and row, and row and tow, and pole and warp." The perennial threat posed by river pirates required keen-eyed lookouts and defensive weaponry.[17]

Accounts of the first year of Chapman's operation, 1831–32, enumerate the Floating Theatre's inhabitants as eleven, consisting of nine Chapmans, one other actor, and the hired boatman. The nine Chapmans were William Sr., his wife and mother, George, Sarah, Caroline and Harry, plus—after September 1831, having finally given up in Philadelphia—W.B. and Phoebe. In 1834 George, by now specializing in villains, enlarged the company by marrying on board the Floating Theatre widow Mary Ross Parks, who brought two children of her own: Alonzo and Belle.[18]

The Chapmans were not, as sometimes portrayed, "a jolly family lazily floating down the Mississippi, doing an occasional show, and spending more time fishing than working." They worked hard for long hours. Each morning, well before daybreak (to avoid morning winds), they progressed twenty to thirty miles downriver, averaging "about five miles an hour, wind and current favorable." At the next town they tied up, and company members posted bills (created by Phoebe) and blew a trumpet to announce the evening's bill. Although admission was nominally priced at fifty cents for adults and twenty-five cents for children, bartered items such as produce, eggs, bacon, and chickens were accepted. (One actor's benefit night left him with "a barrel of bear's grease, two bear skins, two legs of venison, a bag of pecans, a bunch of squirrels, seven turkeys, a fox skin, a dirk knife, a keg of lard, a dozen chickens, *and seventeen dollars!*")[19]

Everyone was greeted at the door by William Sr., and performances began at sundown. The repertoire favored serious drama, primarily Shakespeare and such standards as *Stranger*—their most-produced piece—leavened by nightly farces, a favorite of which was *Catharine and Petruchio*. (The transient nature of the Floating Theatre and the concomitant lack of newspaper notices renders attempts to identify specific bills nearly impossible.) William Sr. "doubled more parts than any other actor on record, was captain, first engineer, pilot, landlord, head cook and bottle washer. The actors were likewise required to double a good deal, [for example] doubling Mercutio with the part of deck hand."[20]

Occasionally, hooligans undid the mooring lines while performances were in progress. The most clearly described incident occurred during a performance of *Hamlet*: "The philosophic Dane strutted and fretted his brief hour upon a leaky flat boat on the tide waters of the Mississippi, before a very select audience (of some twenty-five individuals). They pronounced it beautiful, and [cheered] any especial outbreak and tear of passion." The performance proceeded smoothly until act 4, when the stage manager, from the wings, exhorted the audience to shift to one side, to minimize a leak on the other, so as to avoid Ophelia having to "bail out her own untimely resting place!" After the deaths of Claudius, Gertrude, Laertes and Hamlet, "the blanket [curtain] fell amidst the shouts of applause."

However, upon attempting to disembark, the audience discovered the boat adrift. "During the play some mischievous wag had cast off the fastening that held the boat to her moorings and now, actors, audience, theatre and all, were on their winding way to the Gulf of Mexico!, having already drifted down the current nine miles." The audience, with "great difficulty and swearing," trudged "through interminable swamp and across muddy creeks. . . . Half the party lost their shoes and all their tempers," arriving home near sunrise as "squalid, tired, bespattered and hungry wretches."[21]

Another problem was staying current with local ordinances. One afternoon the Chapmans were stopped by a Virginia sheriff (at that time Virginia bordered the Ohio River) for performing without a license. Fortunately, though, "the pillar of the commonwealth loved whiskey," and William Sr. invited him into the cabin, where the sheriff partook heartily until "as he got on deck he toppled overboard" and Chapman cast off.[22]

That first season, among their stops were towns in which embryonic theatre had already been established, including Memphis (except for Sol Smith, its first professional theatre), Port Gibson, Vicksburg, and Natchez. The effort was so successful that, as soon as Chapman had completed the meandering eighteen-hundred-mile journey to New Orleans and sold the flatboat for firewood, he and his family boarded a steamship for New York, to acquire more scripts, scenery, and actors.

One of those hired for the 1832–33 season (mid-season, in Louisville) was seventeen-year-old aspiring actor/scenic artist John Banvard, who recorded a few upgrades on that season's vessel: "box seats were built along the sides of the boat extending over the water. Wooden guards were built behind these boxes to prevent water from splashing over the spectators." (These, however, having been assembled in the fall while green, warped and leaked profusely as they aged.) It was in part due to Banvard's scenic artistry that Chapman was able this second season to stage more elaborate melodramas, such as (appropriately) *The Floating Beacon*. Chapman, though, failed to pay Banvard, who left in New Orleans.[23]

Nevertheless, the Floating Theatre's second season proved equally profitable for its manager, sufficient to buy "five horses and a wagon, with enough left over to build a larger, more permanent boat for next season," their third. Returning east by land this time, family lore has it that they were held up by highwaymen and forced to perform a play under duress. When it appeared they would still be robbed, it was only Caroline's pleas not to take their small chest, which she tearfully avowed contained the body of her dead child, that the Chapmans were allowed to leave, saving its actual contents: the profits of their just-completed season, in gold.[24]

By 1836 Chapman had acquired enough profit to purchase a small steamboat, thus enabling them to travel against the current, expanding their territory by ascending "such tributaries as the Wabash, the Green, the Tennessee, the sluggish Yazoo, and even tiny Bayou Sara." Its stage was larger—twenty by six feet—and its seating capacity increased, accommodated now in chairs instead of hard backless benches. Chapman ordered new scenery and enlarged the company from eleven to twenty-one: thirteen performers (five actresses and eight actors), and eight boatmen.[25]

Staying longer in each town, the Chapmans began to collect their first reviews. In Natchitoches, Louisiana, on the Red River, in February 1837, it was reported that "Caroline Chapman sustains her characters with great beauty and simplicity, neither doing too much nor too little, . . . Sarah Chapman performs with much energy and effect," and Harry Chapman "for his age [now fourteen] is a prodigy. His singing is very good. . . . All perform so well as to give general satisfaction."[26]

This was a more polished operation, approaching our modern perception of showboats: "The bills are posted weeks in advance. On the appointed day the floating theatre comes in sight, flags flying, band playing, or a steam-organ filling the whole region with its obstreperous harmonies. The huge floating monster steams round, with its head up stream, moors to the bank and throws out its gangways. A crowd of idlers, black and white, gathers on the shore to stare at it, and get glimpses of the actors and actresses. . . . The hour of performance arrives at last. [Spectators] fill the boxes and parquette [and] gallery. Orchestra strikes up, curtain rises, tragic sensations, screaming farces, roars of laughter, rounds of applause, and under all the great current of the Mississippi sweeping onward to the Gulf."[27]

In addition to new audiences, the 1836–37 season brought additional complications. Chapman had been visiting Natchez since 1834, but this season was different. Tying up at Natchez-Under-the-Hill, he sought to avoid having to perform for its notoriously rowdy populace. Consequently, he arranged to rent the more upscale Main Street Theatre in Natchez proper. Steaming upriver, he had stopped for one night at Fort Adams, Mississippi, and sent an advance man ahead to Natchez to rent the theater. But complications arose over who had the right to lease the building out, and the agent signed a lease for sixty dollars per week with the wrong man. Upon arrival and about to perform for their first night, Chapman was arrested by the correct owner-stockholder. Kept overnight, Chapman forfeited his plans and withdrew, at a cost of $348, which included $200 legal fees and $108 for "jail fees." He and his company—now five actresses and nine actors—performed instead aboard his showboat, remaining in Natchez for nearly three weeks, but he rarely afterward returned to Natchez.[28]

Chapman was by now also attracting stars. In May and June 1837 British-born Charles Kemble Mason, the nephew of John Philip Kemble, performed tragic leads on the Floating Theatre, drawing full houses on the Red and Mississippi rivers. In spring 1838 second-tier Bowery stars William and Anna Hield and Louisa Johnson performed for a spell.

For three more seasons Chapman continued with his steamboat to ply the rivers of the frontier, each summer returning to Cincinnati, where the boat had been built. The 1838–39 season was his last, however, as he died at its close near Manchester, Ohio, eulogized for his "excellent character" and "quick study and retentive memory." Even on short notice, "he would study and play a part from scene to scene without the aid of the prompter." "Known at all the principal landings on the principal rivers of the South," he "always sustained a good reputation."[29]

Penelope took over management of the Floating Theatre, renaming it Chapman's Floating Palace, and carried out seven more seasons, rebuilding it once. In 1847 she sold it to Sol Smith, by then a prosperous manager in partnership with Noah Ludlow across the frontier. In showboating, however, Smith proved far less lucky. On the second day of his first voyage down the Ohio River in his new showboat, thoroughly restocked and redecorated, he collided with a much larger steamboat, which cleaved his in two. He barely escaped with his life and never returned to showboating.

But Chapman's legacy was broad. On the Erie Canal in 1836 Henry Butler had fitted up a canalboat as a floating theater-cum-oddities museum, setting out each spring from Troy, New York. "During the 1840s and 1850s," reports showboat historian Philip Graham, "dozens of small showboats swarmed over the river systems of the Middle West, bringing entertainment to hundreds of river landings." But rather than "legitimate drama and professional acting," these boats featured minstrelsy, diverting lectures, and traveling medicine shows.[30]

In 1845 in New York City, Hamblin crony Tom Flynn set afloat the Temple of the Muses, "two stories high, built on an old steamboat called the *Virginia of Baltimore*." "With galleries, boxes, pit, scenes and machinery, as well as commodious cabins for dressing rooms [and] a printing press [to generate] the bills of the play," it also contained "a large stage, well-painted interior and scenery," and a "saloon which will hold more than Palmo's Opera House," all "brilliantly lighted with gas." Docked first at the foot of Spring Street and then Canal Street, Flynn opened it on April 2, 1845, with plans to tour the Hudson River. It was, however, an almost immediate failure, quickly becoming "a nuisance, and finally was sold by the sheriff for firewood." A similar venture in October 1845 met a similar fate.[31]

Perhaps the grandest showboat effort was Gilbert R. Spalding and Charles J. Rogers's two-story, two-hundred-by-sixty-foot "Floating Circus Palace," built for $42,000 and launched on the Ohio River in Cincinnati for the 1851–52 season. Housing a regulation-sized circus ring, a museum allegedly containing 100,000 curiosities, dressing rooms, offices, and a three-tiered seating arrangement that could accommodate, by various accounts, 2,500 to 3,400 persons, it traveled the frontier rivers (albeit using a steam towboat, without propulsion of its own) at least through 1856. The Civil War put a temporary end to showboating, but some resumed afterward, a few continuing operations into the early twentieth century. These latter efforts included French's New Sensation, launched in 1878, and the Wonderland, built in 1906 and managed by N. F. Thom.[32]

The surviving Chapman family, still vital, still talented, and still highly motivated, turned their attention after the demise of their paterfamilias's dream to the newest frontier: the Far West.

14

~~~~~~

EARLY CALIFORNIA

(1847–1850)

BY THE TIME THE REMAINING Chapmans, now comprising two generations, reached California, English-language theatrical activity had existed
there for four years. The Seventh Regiment of the New York Volunteers,
mustered on Broadway in summer 1846, had sailed in September on the
Thomas H. Perkins, arriving in San Francisco on March 6, 1847, to subdue
its population (of less than five hundred) as part of the Mexican-American
War. These soldiers included some with a theatrical bent who en route had
performed *The Golden Farmer, Raising the Wind,* and *Bombastes Furioso* as
part of Christmas and New Year's celebrations. Theirs was one of only a
handful of ships that year to land in San Francisco, renamed from Yerba
Buena only five weeks before. Soon after disembarking, the regiment split,
sending companies to Sonoma, Santa Barbara, and Monterey, where the
newest frontier of theatre was opened.[1]

Until being disbanded in September 1848 at war's end, these amateur
soldier-thespians performed their shipboard repertoire on land in various
converted buildings. In Sonoma this took place in "a neat, squat, adobe
hall" built in Mission style, belonging to General M. G. Vallejo, and intended for use as a storehouse. Due to crop failures, it lay unused and
Vallejo offered it to the soldiers, who converted it into a playhouse. "A
platform was erected at one end of the structure, and on either side of it,
boxes. Slanting upward and away from the stage at a gentle angle, rows
of rough benches were placed on stalwart supports," seating at most two
hundred. Scenery was minimal, and the act curtain was an Indian blanket.
A multiethnic audience attended the opening bill of *Golden Farmer*, selected
because "one of the members of the company had a copy of the text in

book form." Its three female parts were played by "beardless youths." An early newspaper notice apprised Sonomans of the "amateur Thespian club" which "performs weekly to crowded audiences. We understand good taste is displayed in the management, selection of plays, scenery, decorations, costume, &c." They performed on Saturday evenings, and their acting was "as *bueno* as could be expected." Their productions in 1849 included *Lady of Lyons* and an abridged *Othello*.[2]

In Santa Barbara, a detachment of soldiers in August 1847 performed minstrel shows, *The Lady of Lyons, Richard III,* and farces. In Monterey, "a plain, low, narrow, not very long, quite unimpressive, white building, partly of plastered adobe, partly of wood, at the corner of Scott and Pacific Streets," which had recently been constructed by retired sailor Jack Swann as a sailors' boarding house, served as a crude theater. There, the soldiers' repertoire into 1848 included *Putnam, Golden Farmer,* and *Damon and Pythias.* Replacement soldier amateurs continued their efforts into February 1850, staging among others excerpts from Shakespeare's *Henry IV,* under the direction of engineer-humorist Lt. George Horatio Derby, at the Union Theatre. Theirs remained the standard of excellence in California, out-classing Sonoma and Santa Barbera, until the advent of theatrical activity in Sacramento and San Francisco.[3]

Soldiers posted to Los Angeles in spring 1848 performed there in quarters adapted for theatrics at a cost of over $5,000. It seated three hundred, with more-than-adequate scenery, opening on July 4. Their bills included *The Marble Statue, Bombastes Furioso,* and the ineluctable *Golden Farmer.* In January 1849, replacement soldiers continued the tradition. And, as had been the case a half century before in Kentucky, their ranks were augmented by professionals, two of whom would come to figure prominently in California theatre: John "Jack" Harris and C. E. (Charles Edward, "Ned") Bingham. They initiated a new Los Angeles season in February 1849 with *Castle Spectre, Thérèse, Pizarro,* and excerpts from *Hamlet.*[4]

But no one yet had erected a building expressly intended as a theater. A group of civic-minded young men in San Francisco aimed to rectify that in early May 1848, going so far as to draw up bylaws and solicit subscriptions. They acknowledged that their efforts might be "rather objectionable to the tastes of some," but hoped it would gradually bring about "what is so much to be desired—a better state of society."[5]

But no sooner had the subscriptions started to roll in than the bottom fell out of their plans. Gold Fever struck. Although the first discovery had been made at Sutter's Mill on February 13, word did not reach San Francisco until mid-May, and the famed Gold Rush did not get underway until December, after word of the discovery had reached the East and President Polk made it official by displaying samples. That winter it exploded.

At first, San Francisco emptied as everyone headed for the goldfields. But by early 1849, as historian H. W. Brands describes, "as the Pacific fleet of argonauts from Latin America and Australia started to arrive, the town began to fill up again." Then, "the incessant rush lent a peculiar disorder to the place. Nothing appeared permanent; most of the buildings were actually tents: canvas tossed over a few boards and tied down against the winds that arose off the Pacific each afternoon and blew sand and dust everywhere. . . . The few trees that had graced the virgin peninsula had nearly all vanished, cut for lumber or firewood." Haphazard wooden construction made fire a constant, widespread threat, yet when it rained, a sea of mud made unpaved streets impassable, and flooding often occurred. Still, by the end of the year 1849, San Francisco's population would swell from two thousand to twenty-five thousand.[6]

Amid this chaos the first efforts to establish a theater emerged. In August 1849 W. A. Buffum publicized his intention "to erect a large and commodious Theatre in San Francisco," to be "a respectable and popular place of resort and amusement for families and strangers," featuring a "talented operatic and ballet company." He began selling subscriptions for "a series of Operas, Ballets, Vaudevilles, Dramas, and Pantomimes, on a scale of splendor worthy the great metropolis of the Pacific." Plans for the new building were available for public inspection. By late September, Buffum had engaged a manager for his new enterprise, thirty-five-year-old comedian A. W. (Augustus William) Fenno, who had acted for Caldwell in 1828 and in the intervening decades in New York and Boston. Fenno sent word seeking actors from Australia, but also left for the East "for the purpose of procuring a large and efficient theatrical company." Buffum hired builders H. Adler and M. Chapelle to construct his new American Theatre on Portsmouth Square, fifty feet wide and eighty-four feet deep, specifically using "California wood," to be completed by January 1, 1850. A joint stock company was formed for its administration.[7]

For unknown reasons, none of this ever came to fruition. Fenno apparently never returned, and by January 1851 was again acting in New York. When the Australian actors arrived, they kept going northeast, to Sacramento, with "a floating population of about five thousand people." There, nearer to the goldfields, they would face "more in the shape of vice and iniquity than ever they saw before." Still, an actual theater had been completed there, the first in California specifically built for that purpose. As architecturally primitive as the tents of San Francisco, the Eagle Theatre on Front Street between I and J had been constructed by Zadok Hubbard and Gates Brown at Gold Rush–inflated prices (especially for lumber) of $30,000 in little more than two months, from late July to early September 1849. Adjoining the Round Tent Saloon, through which admission could be gained, the theater consisted of a wooden frame with blue canvas stretched over it, topped with a sheet-metal roof and only the bare ground for a floor. Only thirty by sixty-five feet, it could hold between four hundred and seven hundred people (depending on how tightly they were packed) on rough benches under three candlelight chandeliers, with a "dress circle" accessible only via stepladder. Its stage facilities consisted of a sixteen-foot-deep stage lit by oil lamps, with large shipping crates for dressing rooms. Admission rates were $2, $3, and $5, payable in gold dust ($12 to the ounce) weighed on the treasurer's scale.[8]

The first performance in the Eagle Theatre came on September 25, a minstrel troupe from Stockton, for that one night. Its formal opening on October 18 offered a double bill: *The Bandit Chief; or, the Forest Spectre*, and *Love in Humble Life*. Assembled by manager Charles (variously) B./P. Price, who also acted, the company consisted of leading man J. B. (John Bowman) Atwater, who had crossed the American Plains, destitute and partly barefoot; Mr. and Mrs. Henry Ray, from Australia and New Zealand, she being the sole female member and "a Dancer and Vocalist of superior talents"; Henry F. "Hank" Daly; J. H. (John Herbert) McCabe; Tench Fairchild, a comedian and comic singer; and two soldier-amateurs, veterans of the Mexican-American War, named Jack Harris, who played "heavies," and Lt. A. W. Wright. The scenery, displaying only three locations (woods, a street, and an all-purpose interior) "has been beautifully decorated by Mr. LEWIS a scenic artist of acknowledged reputation." For three performances a week, the Rays received $275, with the others' salaries ranging from $20 to $60 per night. The collective orchestra received $60 a night, the treasurer $50 per week, and the doorkeeper $28 per week, "on account of the extra risks he ran." (There was "not unfrequently a fight. Revolvers and knives would make their appearance freely.") Total nightly expenses ran to $600.[9]

Among the opening-night audience were vocalist-monologist Stephen C. Massett and poet and literary critic Bayard Taylor, who recorded their impressions: "It had been raining hard and blowing a gale of wind the whole day, and the strength and durability of the building had been sorely tried. However, as the hour drew near for the opening of the doors, a crowd of anxious miners thronged the entrance, and despite the winds and torrents of rain, the place was immediately filled." The structure itself "would have been taken for an ordinary drinking house but for the sign 'Eagle Theatre,' which was nailed to the top of the canvas frame. Passing through the bar-room we arrive at the entrance. The spectators are dressed in heavy overcoats and felt hats with boots reaching to the knees. The sides of the theatre are canvas, which when wet, effectually prevents ventilation and renders the atmosphere hot and stifling. The drop-curtain, which is down at present, exhibits a glaring landscape with dark brown trees in the foreground, and lilac-covered mountains against a yellow sky. The overture commences; the orchestra is composed of only five members, under the direction of an Italian [V. Bona, from New York's Park Theatre] and performs with tolerable correctness." (The five were a fiddle, a violin, a flageolet [a woodwind in the flute family], a big drum, and a triangle.) "The bell rings; the curtain rolls up; and we look upon a forest scene."[10]

The acting failed to impress Massett and Taylor: "The interest of the play is carried to an awful height by the appearance of two spectres, clad in mutilated tent-covers, and holding spermaceti candles in their hands. Mrs. Ray rushes in and throws herself into an attitude in the middle of the stage; why she does it, no one can tell. This movement, which she repeats several times in the course of the first three acts, has no connection with the tragedy; it is evidently introduced for the purpose of showing the audience that there is, actually, a female performer. The miners, to whom the sight of a woman is not a frequent occurrence, are delighted with these passages and applaud vehemently." Massett replicated her atrocious manner of speaking: "I would rather . . . rap his cold fangs areound [*sic*] me, than surrender meself to the cold himbraces of a 'artless willain!" The Young Norval of *Douglas* (presumably one of the amateurs), was "a gentleman who had been unfortunate at the diggings, and had only recently found out the proper channel in which to display his genius." He required the escalating intervention of the prompter, well-seasoned with curses.[11]

The full house included "quite a number of fine looking, well-costumed ladies, the sight of whom was somewhat revivifying." The sole newspaper reviewer sidestepped any details of the performance's "many imperfections, which we have no doubt will be corrected after a few representations." Within a week, as good attendance continued, the company showed improvement and "the owners realized a very handsome profit." The actors, though, struggled with "little wardrobe and few books." The company purchased a copy of *Box and Cox* "for an ounce of gold dust." Of course, "every play produced had to be so altered as to require one lady only."[12]

There were other, more immediate problems. Despite the Eagle's fronting on a levee, flooding of the Sacramento River sometimes covered the seats nearest the stage, and rowdy miners in the audience knocked each other backward into the water for a guffaw. Despite the initial full houses, Hubbard and Brown could not meet creditors' notes and the theater was sold in early November to a local judge. Atwater, newly named manager in early November, closed for a week of retooling. Reopening with *Douglas*, he drew criticism for its heaviness. "Petite comedies, burlesques and farces, at any rate something light, could be better produced and meet with more general satisfaction. Another actress to assist Mrs. Ray would be an advantage."[13]

Atwater adjusted, offering such pieces as *Honey Moon, William Tell, Stranger, Floating Beacon, Charles II*, farces *Young Widow* and *Box and Cox*, and a pantomime, *The Shoemaker in Trouble*. But attendance was disappointing, and the winter of 1849–50 proved to be one of unusually heavy rainfall. One night just before Christmas, a violent Southeaster blew in mid-performance. When the curtain rose, the theater was "high and dry—but before the first piece was over, the water commenced to make its appearance through the cracks of the floor [a recent improvement over the bare ground], and by the time the second piece got fairly under way, so deep had the water become, that the 'groundlings' were forced to stand on the benches." Eventually, half the town was submerged to the level of the few second stories.[14]

Another set of new owners reopened the Eagle a week later, on Christmas Eve, with *Beacon of Death* and *The Wife*, but these were still too heavy. Pleaded the *Placer Times*, "A low comedian is sadly needed at this house, as a theatre without fun is almost as bad as a circus without a clown." Flooding attacked again on January 4, 1850, and the Eagle closed. Its latest owners—named McDowell, Fowler, and Warbass—dragged what remained of it about two hundred feet east to a new site on Second Street, replacing its canvas walls with wood. It would reopen in March under a new name. Atwater and his actors decamped to San Francisco.[15]

There, on January 16, 1850, they provided that city's first theatrical activity, *The Wife* and *Charles II*, played on a makeshift stage on the second floor of Washington Hall on Washington Street between Kearny and Dupont, over Foley's Saloon, abutting the rear of the office of the *Alta California*.

That newspaper's reviewer left a performance frustrated: "The manager cannot hope to give satisfaction, unless he can manage to seat his audience, and present to the back seats as well as the front a view of the stage. The lights were improperly placed, and insufficient in number to produce effect." A week's time brought second thoughts: "The actors deserve to be encouraged, their social position elevated and regarded with a more lenient eye." But despite a week of doing "very fair business," Atwater closed up shop on January 24, his treasurer having gambled away all of their funds at cards (a not infrequent Gold Rush–era occurrence). The same reviewer decided that the real cause for failure was the ineptitude of the actors: "The company could expect but little else. None of them were professional people, or at all events, had fretted but a very brief hour upon the stage, and certainly not in the same line of business which they were here compelled to assume." Another significant flaw: "having only one female, compelling many pieces to be 'cut' unmercifully."[16]

The actors dispersed, Mr. and Mrs. Ray departing for the Sandwich Islands (now Hawaii). Atwater signed on with San Francisco circus impresario Joseph A. Rowe, thirty, who had erected a tent on the block bounded by Kearny, Clay, Montgomery, and Sacramento streets in late October. (The first minstrel show in San Francisco, the Philadelphia Minstrels, had performed a week earlier at Bella Union Hall on Washington Street above Kearny.) Carpenters engaged by Rowe spent the last two weeks of January converting his circus ring into a functioning theater, adding "a large and commodious stage, building 'wings,' 'flats' and 'tormentors.'" Scenic artists, too, were hard at work.[17]

Rowe's efforts were augmented by the timely arrival of nine new performers, most from the Victoria Theatre in Sydney, Australia. They were leading actors Mr. and Mrs. Nesbit McCron, Mr. and Mrs. John Hambleton (he a versatile low comedian and his beautiful wife playing soubrettes), and Mr. and Mrs. Batters (variously Batturs, he playing heavies and she a vocalist), plus Thomas S. Campbell (previously a merchant captain), George Mitchell, and Mr. Carleton, "a celebrated Eastern amateur."[18]

Rowe's Olympic Amphitheatre opened on February 4, 1850, with a welcoming address by Mrs. Hambleton, followed by *Othello*—arguably the first professional Shakespeare in California, just ahead of Derby's *Henry IV* in Monterey—and an Edward Stirling farce, *Bachelor's Buttons*. Hambleton played Iago to the Othello of Carleton. Later performances included *Richard III*, with Hambleton in the title role and his wife as Lady Anne. As historian Helene Koon has pointed out, the miners who comprised Rowe's audience did appreciate Shakespeare. Not all fit the persistent popular image of unsophisticated, uneducated roughnecks. Many, coming from the East, had likely seen dramatic productions, even if amateur, and valued such productions as "sustenance for the spirit." Eking out a bare existence in an indescribably challenging environment, "plays, especially Shakespeare, offered a special kind of escape from the rigors of prospecting."[19]

But equestrian-infused melodramas gradually came to predominate, and despite an admission price of two to five dollars, full houses greeted Rowe's company. Atwater ("a young gentleman of considerable talent") increasingly earned commendation, especially in such melodramas as *The Bandit Chief.* Mrs. Hambleton was "a deserving candidate for popular favor."[20]

Within days of Rowe's opening, a modicum of competition presented itself in the form of the small but elegant, brick and stucco Theatre Nationale on Washington Street between Montgomery and Kearny. Owner Henri Gunter and manager Edouard Delamarre offered an assortment of "light French Vaudevilles, Pantomimes, and musical pieces." Its "English Director" was one of the company, New York veteran James Evrard (variously Everard), who would soon make his own mark in California. Among many other buildings, the Nationale would burn three months later.

A greater problem for Rowe in February was the illness which struck several of his actors, notably McCron. Attendance began to fall off. Then, Rowe booked a star who would come to be a towering figure on the California stage. Sarah Kirby, thirty-six, brought experience from Boston, New York, and London. The widow of actor J. Hudson Kirby, famed for his over-the-top melodramatic death scenes, she debuted at the Olympic on February 21 as Pauline in *The Lady of Lyons*, opposite Atwater's Claude Melnotte. Keeping Kirby's name for theatrical purposes, she had married J. B. Wingard, who had brought her to California in early January. As ambitious as she was talented, Kirby began planning with Wingard and Atwater to manage their own theater in Sacramento, where Atwater went in March to secure a company of actors, some of whom would follow him from Rowe's.[21]

At the Olympic, where she repeated Pauline, Kirby was well received, praised for her "tall graceful figure and handsome face. Her voice is clear and musical. . . . Her conception of the character is good and she played it in a very pleasing, lady-like manner." She "will unquestionably prove a favorite." For a week, alternating nights with Rowe's equestrians, she played leads opposite a recovered McCron, until his "indisposition" returned. On March 2, a "most unpleasant" incident occurred: "Mr. McCron in the character of Richard [III] forgot what is due to the dignity of the character, to the profession in which he is engaged, and to the public, and presented himself before the audience in an improper condition [that is, inebriated]. A difficulty occurred between him and Mrs. Kirby [playing Lady Anne], an appeal to the audience was had and the dreadful question of nationality [McCron being English] raised. Of course, the audience sided with the lady. Mr. McCron was hissed, sought in vain to stem the disapprobation and was removed from the stage by the management." When McCron attempted to deliver a public apology, Hambleton "appeared and stated that neither he or his wife would ever again present themselves upon that stage if Mr. McCron was again permitted to appear, as he had not only insulted the public but heaped indignities upon the company." An enmity quickly developed as well between Mrs. McCron and Mrs. Kirby.[22]

Kirby, deemed a "very estimable lady, a graceful equestrian and a great favorite with the public," took her benefit on March 9 as *The Wife.* Within a week, though, Rowe took his own benefit and ceased performances, due to "the continuous rainy weather," the "very heavy outlay for the production of theatrical entertainments," and the ongoing "disaffection and a want of harmony in the company." In late April he sold the Olympic to circus clown William H. Foley (who used it for bullfights until it burned on June 14), and headed like Kirby and Atwater for Sacramento.[23]

A short-lived replacement for Rowe's Olympic in San Francisco, the Phoenix Theatre on Pacific Street opened on March 23 under Hambleton's management. Forming the California Farce Company, devoted to light entertainment, were Hambleton and his wife, actor and scenic artist T. S. Campbell, Gilbert, Wilson, Phillips, and Australians Miss Sophie (Sophia Anderson) Edwin and Miss H. Edwin (relationship unknown). The opening bill consisted of two farces, *Seeing the Elephant* (a phrase satirizing the gullible easterners seeking their fortune in California gold), *The Fox and the Wolf,* and an olio of songs and dances, all for two dollars. A later highlight was Mrs. Hambleton's portrayal of eight different characters in the protean farce *Winning a Husband,* a title that ironically would have dire repercussions before a year was out. On March 24 the Phoenix Exchange opened on Portsmouth Square, featuring tableaux and scandalously draped "model artist exhibitions." But both of these entities were lost to fire on May 4, 1850.

~~~~~~~~~~~~

In Sacramento in spring 1850, two theaters were under construction. The first, erected by A. P. Petit and James Queen, rose on the north side of M Street, near Front Street, fifty feet across, one hundred feet deep, and thirty feet high, originally designated the National Theatre. The other, built on Second Street between I and J streets by McDowell, Fowler, and Warbass from the ruins of the old Eagle, was the Tehama, appropriately named for an indigenous phrase meaning "high water."

The Tehama won the race to completion. Its two-tiered house (pointedly eliminating the depravity which a third-tier might invite, "so that ladies and families can go to the Tehama without having their sensibilities shocked by the vulgar and brutal of both sexes") seated up to a thousand, and its stage measured thirty-six feet deep. It was to be managed by J. B. Atwater and Sarah Kirby.[24]

They had assembled a small company: Olympic veterans Mr. and Mrs. Hambleton, Mr. and Mrs. McCron (he sometimes billed as "Mr. Nesbit"), Hank Daly and Tench Fairchild from the old Eagle, Sophie Edwin, recruited from the Phoenix, Mrs. Lynes, and orchestra leader/violinist Signior Bona, also from the Eagle.

An over-capacity house at ticket prices from two to four dollars crammed in to enjoy the first night, March 25, 1850, which consisted of Kirby and Atwater again as Pauline and Claude in *Lady of Lyons,* its first performance in Sacramento, a comic song by Fairchild and the farce *The Dumb Belle.* Critical response was expansive, with Kirby and Atwater earning special commendation. "All the characters were very credibly sustained," and "the whole company were 'up' in their parts, which was quite a refreshing circumstance."[25]

For six nights a week, decent-sized crowds patronized their offerings, which were alternatingly light (for example, *Family Jars, Rent Day*) and heavy (*The Wife, Othello*—McCron in the title role to Atwater's Iago—and *Stranger*). On April 22 the company was augmented with Los Angeles veteran Ned Bingham, W. S. Fury, and actors named Alexander, Campbell, and Wilson. Hence, larger-cast productions were provided: *Don Caesar de Bazan, Lady of the Lake, Iron Chest, Apostate,* and *Richard III* (Hambleton). A benefit for Masons and Odd Fellows' Hospital on May 7 raised $1,129. Kirby, Atwater, and the Hambletons carried leads through the close of the season on May 31 following a series of highly successful benefits. The Tehama had acquired "a most invaluable prestige of popularity and success." Mrs. Kirby seemed to always "hit upon the happy medium between too much and too little passion, which is always true to nature."[26]

Some in their audiences, however, failed to appreciate their efforts: "We would suggest to the hombres who frequent what is vulgarly called the pit of the Tehama, that they behave themselves a little better. One would think that some of them knew better the business of the stage than those on it, so particular are they to raise a yell when the slightest mistake occurs."[27]

But a rival loomed. This was the edifice erected by Petit and Queen, originally the National, renamed before its opening the Pacific Theatre. James Evrard had promised to bring a company from the East for it, specifically some from the famed Billy Mitchell's Olympic Theatre in New York, where he had performed, including its centerpiece Miss Mary ("Our Mary") Taylor. But Evrard failed to appear with them. Nevertheless, the theater rose to completion by late April 1850 at a cost of over $40,000 ($1.4 million today), featuring lavish boxes, saloons, and lounges, and a thirty-six-by-forty-one-foot stage. Like the Tehama, it would accommodate up to one thousand patrons. Notably, "five or six doors are to be put in the front end, so that in case of fire, they could all be thrown open at once, rendering egress very easy."[28]

On April 25 a Grand Dress ball was held to celebrate the theater's completion, with twenty-five-dollar tickets quickly snapped up by "over 100 gentlemen and about 40 ladies," and "brilliancy and beauty reigned throughout." Evrard having failed to provide a company, the newly arrived Joseph Rowe jumped in to fill the breach. He converted the stage to a circus ring "nearly as large as [that of] the Olympic Amphitheatre in San Francisco." His equestrian troupe opened on May 2 to raucous applause from a full house, which continued for weeks. Rowe, "the undaunted manager, appears at last to have struck the true vein." He began arranging the construction of his own amphitheater in Sacramento on Front Street between K and L streets, which was ready for his equestrian troupe by July 4.[29]

Mrs. Kirby must have been alarmed by the competition in Sacramento, for she reopened for a summer season on June 18 with a new comanager, C. R. (Charles Robert) Thorne, from New York's Chatham Theatre. They advertised for actors: "No amateurs need apply." They hired low comedian William Barry, Tench Fairchild, George Kour, and Hank Daly, and stole two of Rowe's stars, husband and wife Ernesto and Fanny (née Manten) Rossi, he a singer-actor-magician and she a versatile dancer. Kirby enacted Lady Randolph in *Douglas* for her benefit on July 11, with tickets available from her residence next door to the theater. Summer productions included *Damon and Pythias, Pizarro* (with Thorne as Rolla; his wife, Maria Ann, as Elvira; and Kirby as Cora), *Perfection,* and *Day After the Wedding,* closing on August 8.[30]

Kirby spent the hiatus in San Francisco, where she bruited it about that she intended building a new, more sumptuous theater in Sacramento adjoining the existing Tehama. With this in mind, she enlisted Atwater to go east "to procure professional artists, a wardrobe and a complete stage library, with which he will return in three months."[31]

In San Francisco, D. G. "Doc" "Yankee" Robinson, the "liveliest, most irrepressible, most ubiquitous of all the comedians and all-around men of the theatre" (also a playwright) had teamed with James Evrard (the no-show of National/Pacific repute). They had spent spring 1850 constructing a theater on the north side of California Street between Kearney and Montgomery streets in spring 1850. But thwarted by a massive fire on May 4, they had barely gotten underway when another fire struck, on June 14, reducing it to ashes (another fire would occur on September 17).[32]

By July, Robinson and Evrard's Dramatic Museum was rebuilt, fifty feet long by twenty feet wide, with a capacity of four hundred and appropriate boxes, gallery, and saloon. The "cozy little theatre" opened on July 4 with *Seeing the Elephant,* performed by a company comprised predominately of amateurs, with Robinson playing leads. George Tirrell created scenic backdrops, and tickets cost one to two dollars. Robinson and Evrard advertised for additional performers, one of which Sarah Kirby firmly declined to be. Although the company was deemed "even better than it was thought possible to secure in San Francisco," with a repertoire of farces and comic songs, the box office did not generate funds sufficient to place bills in newspapers until mid-November. By December they had closed, and Robinson and Evrard migrated to Sacramento.[33]

〰〰〰〰〰〰

From San Francisco, Kirby had headed to Stockton, California, to perform and to recruit actors, with an eye to possibly managing there. In March 1850, Ned Bingham had teamed with W. S. Fury to convert the second and third floors of the assembly room of Stockton House into the Corinthian Theatre, staffing it primarily with soldier amateurs, plus a Mrs. Jones. Their success with occasional performances of scripts like *Box and Cox, Bombastes Furioso,* and *The Wife,* had drawn Kirby. She opened on August 17 for a week opposite Bingham, starting with her set piece, *Lady of Lyons.* Journalistic carping about sight lines, inappropriate costumes, and inconsistent performances, however, may have given her pause about managing in Stockton. By early September the Corinthian had closed, and was thereafter used only for lectures and large meetings.[34]

Kirby instead returned to Sacramento in early September, intent on reopening the Tehama as a rival to the Pacific, to which Thorne had migrated, taking a one-year lease. To its larger, better facility he brought a mostly new company, consisting of himself, his wife, Maria Ann; her sister and brother-in-law, Mr. and Mrs. (Louis and Emilie/ly) Mestayer; Mr. and Mrs. William Dinneford; Henry Coad (from New Orleans); Henry Jackson; A. W. Wright; James H. Vinson; J. C. Harrington; James Cook; and tragedian James Stark.

The Canadian-born Stark, thirty, would come to play a significant role in Kirby's life. He had studied in England under famed actor William Macready and now brought four years of experience in supporting roles in London and New York. Regarded by contemporaries as "an admirable actor, [whose] some few characters were exceptionally fine," including Beverly in *Gamester* and Richelieu, he was also "a man of kind and generous feelings." Some compared him favorably to the young Edwin Booth, who would visit California in two years; compared to Stark's brilliance, it was said, Booth "paled an ineffectual fire."[35]

Thorne's company opened on August 12 with "the whole interior of the house painted and decorated at enormous expense" and new scenery and machinery, in *Damon and Pythias*. Their repertoire balanced serious drama (for example, *Maid of Croissey, The Avenger*) and farce (such as *Eton Boy, Nature and Philosophy*), with comic songs by Fairchild. But attendance was poor from the outset, exacerbated by a week-long "Squatter's Riot" quelled only by the local militia, which forced the temporary closure of the Pacific. By August 30, despite good reviews, the troupe had disbanded, Thorne had gone east to recruit new actors, and the Pacific was sold at auction. Some of the actors, in an ever-evolving fluidity resembling that of the early frontier, went over to Kirby at the Tehama, including, fortuitously, Stark.

Another Sacramento venue started promisingly in August and staggered along intermittently through the winter. This was Lee's Theatre Hall (also known as Lee's Exchange Theatre) on J Street, under the management of the itinerant John Hambleton, who in the meantime had attempted (ultimately unsuccessfully) to start a theater in Coloma, California. His bills in Sacramento featured a Spanish ballet troupe, several melodramas and farces, some vaudeville, and a dancer from New Orleans, the highly touted Mademoiselle Juliet. Stark even put in a few guest appearances.

~~~~~~~~~~

On September 9, 1850, the very day that California achieved statehood, Sarah Kirby reopened the Tehama Theatre in Sacramento, using some of the actors from Thorne's Pacific, including Stark, who soon became her comanager. Two weeks later, Kirby's husband, J. B. Wingard, purchased the theater and the lot it stood on. From now on, as part of their operating costs, they would be paying a licensure tax, passed by the state legislature three weeks before, of "not less than twenty dollars, nor more than two hundred and fifty dollars for one year."[36]

As usual, the opening bill was *Lady of Lyons*, with Kirby and Stark in the leads (their first performance together), as was the case in almost every production for the next month. Most were tragedies or serious dramas: *Virginius, Thérèse, Iron Chest, Venice Preserved, Stranger, Hamlet, Mountaineers, Damon and Pythias*, and *Brutus*. Large houses and reviewers responded enthusiastically. In *The Rent Day*, as Rachel Heywood, Kirby "excelled herself. She took the house by storm." There were dramatic passages in which Stark was "truly sublime. . . . The more he is heard, the better he is appreciated." A special benefit of *Hamlet* on September 27 raised over $1,000 "for flour and other necessaries of life" for outbound overland emigrants, "to save their lives and give them both hope and strength to continue their long and desolate journey."[37]

This was by now "as good a company as the generality of the theatres in the States can boast." Their October 7 production of *Macbeth* saw the return of the Hambletons, he as Hecate to the usual leads of Stark and Kirby, and she in the ensuing farce. Hambleton generally played major supporting roles (for example, Horatio). Kirby, although only twenty-seven, began to yield some younger roles (such as Ophelia, taking Gertrude for herself) to Mestayer, and awarded Lady Anne (opposite Stark's oft-repeated Richard III) to Mrs. Hambleton, enacting the more matronly Queen Elizabeth herself. Breeches roles (for example, Albert to the William Tell of Stark), also went to the fetching Mrs. Hambleton. Of course, fitting leads (such as Portia in *Merchant of Venice*), she kept.[38]

Talent flocked to the Tehama. When Mestayer left in mid-October, Sophie Edwin signed on, the same week that George Mitchell (from the failed Exchange) and Irish comedian-vocalist E. B. Zabriskie joined. The Kirby-Stark company began running larger ads, a sign of their ever-improving fortunes. But these were reversed at the end of October when a cholera epidemic struck Sacramento, and on November 2 they closed the Tehama until further notice. With journalistic plaudits ringing in their ears—Stark "has won for himself golden opinions among the denizens of Sacramento city," and Kirby had been "the favorite of Sacramento, . . . nightly greeted by her admirers, her friends here, with a spontaneous, a flattering welcome"—they headed for San Francisco.[39]

15

GOLD RUSH THEATRE

(1850–1853)

IN SAN FRANCISCO, part of a bi-city managerial round robin, Kirby and Stark in November 1850 leased the new Jenny Lind Theatre. It had been constructed by Thomas Maguire, a "shrewd, somewhat illiterate Irishman who could not read the plays he produced, and seldom bothered to sit through their performance." This handsome, swaggering former hack driver, saloonkeeper, and Tammany Hall leg man in New York had come to California in 1849 like so many others to seek his fortune. Establishing himself as the saloonkeeper in, and part owner of, the Parker House on Portsmouth Square, he rebuilt it after a fire that Christmas Eve. He did so yet again—the second of his *six* losses to fire—after the Great Fire of September 17, 1850, adding the Jenny Lind on its second and third floors. Able to seat nearly eight hundred, surrounded by frescoed walls and ceiling, it was "the neatest and most commodious affair in the city." Opened on October 30 with variety acts, Maguire switched to legitimate drama upon meeting Kirby and Stark.[1]

Beginning with *Damon and Pythias* on November 4, they provided San Francisco with its first regular professional theatrical season. Subsequent offerings, primarily comprising their old Tehama repertoire with themselves in the leads, were *Othello* (during which Stark suffered a "severe wound" in the Moor's death scene), *Virginius, The Wife, Hamlet, Merchant of Venice, Richelieu, Pizarro,* and *Venice Preserved.* Reviewers exalted Kirby and Stark as they had in Sacramento: "His acting is true to nature and to the text, his conception of character is echo to the poet's thought, and his very soul for the time seems to be the idea of the author"; "Mrs. Kirby's characters are studied, chaste, correct, and the highest praise is due her." Comedies drew noticeably smaller houses.[2]

November 16 brought personal tragedy, however. Late that afternoon, Kirby's husband and Tehama owner J. B. Wingard was galloping his horse down Stockton Street when a low rope stretched across the street knocked him to the ground. He died early the next morning, his wife and Stark by his side. The company donned mourning badges for thirty days, and the Jenny Lind remained closed for a week. During that week carpenters under Maguire's direction worked day and night to deepen the stage to forty feet, raise the floor of the parquette, enlarge the pit, add a saloon and a dress circle of boxes, and hang a new act curtain.

The renovations were doubtless aimed at meeting new competition presented by the opening nearby of the Adelphi Theatre on Clay Street on November 9. Manager D. F. Wilson and stage manager William Barry guided its company which included a few Tehama veterans, including Ned Bingham, Emilie Mestayer, and Tench Fairchild (who soon defected to Kirby and Stark). Wilson and Mestayer carried most leads in a repertoire of serious drama that closely mirrored that of the Jenny Lind, sometimes presenting an identical bill within a day or two of Kirby and Stark's.

The two theaters drew similarly large audiences, with the Jenny Lind gaining the edge in full houses on the strength of Kirby and Stark's acting, for most of December. Wilson tried bringing in guest stars, beginning on December 9 with actress-vocalist Mme. Caroline Duprez, with the December 11 appearance of Nesbit McCron as Othello, with Wilson as Iago and Duprez as Desdemona. Still, one reviewer was "pleased that the managers no longer require her to sing, because her voice is evidently unsuited to the stage." By Christmas, Wilson had turned over management to Bingham, who emphasized comedies and farces, causing Duprez, too, to defect to the Jenny Lind. By February 1851 the Adelphi was home to Italian opera, and on May 4 it burned to the ground.[3]

At the Jenny Lind, Kirby and Stark granted Duprez a few leading roles—eliciting mediocre reviews—while they remained the true stars. But A. W. Wright, the Hambletons, and a comedian named Downey were close behind in the public's favor. Most nights the company earned "the most vigorous and earnest applause," and a few times "were greeted with a house crammed to its utmost capacity."[4]

But trouble was brewing backstage. On January 12, 1851, the Hambletons gave their last performance together, ironically *The Happy Man* by Samuel Lover, and "were called to the footlights by a delighted audience after the fall of the curtain." On the afternoon of January 14 Mrs. Hambleton committed suicide in her boardinghouse by drinking potassium cyanide. For some time, she had confided in Kirby that her husband was abusive, showing her the marks on her neck where the excessively jealous Hambleton had attempted to strangle her. She also revealed that she had "conceived an ardent attachment to a member of the company, Mr. [Henry] Coad, who returned it with equal ardor," and had asked her husband for a divorce.[5]

Hambleton threatened to kill Coad, an action actually attempted a few days later by Downey, for which he was hauled before the local magistrate and released on a peace bond. Coad tried to kill himself in the same manner as Mrs. Hambleton, but was discovered in time. In the days following, Hambleton published a long denial of any abusive behavior in their supposedly idyllic marriage, accusing Coad of seduction and Kirby of covering up his wife's secretive affair. Kirby subsequently published a lengthy refutation of Hambleton's denial. Ted Hutchinson and W. H. Crowell submitted affidavits verifying they had seen evidence of Hambleton's abuse.[6]

Kirby ultimately emerged the cleanest. The Jenny Lind reopened on the evening of January 16 to a supportive press: "When the deserving have been traduced, and an attempt made to ruin them in public estimation, it is the duty of the public to sustain them by its encouragement." Kirby faced down a raucous crowd egged on by fans of Hambleton and won them over with a compelling speech. For two weeks, now including Sunday evening performances, all appeared normal, with full houses and glowing reviews for *Hamlet, New Way to Pay Old Debts, William Tell,* and *King Lear.* Stark took all leading roles, earning "a fame which only awaits a broader field and more ample opportunities to become national and worldwide." A lavish production of *Forty Thieves* (with T. S. Campbell as Ali Baba) ran for nearly a week.[7]

However, another problem simmered. The departure of E. B. Zabriskie, who claimed unjust treatment by the management, along with that of Hambleton and Downey, forced Kirby and Stark to assign male roles to females. Duprez rebelled, considering a breeches role below her dignity. She clashed harshly with Kirby, at one point physically attacking her, but was thwarted by police intervention. Just before curtain time on February 2, Duprez attempted suicide by taking poison. She lived, but remained "hysterically mad" for weeks. (In addition to Mrs. Hambleton, a Sacramento actress at Lee's Theatre Hall, Mrs. Hubbel, had attempted suicide on January 17. After Duprez's attempt, one journalist opined, "It seems as though our actresses had all run suicide-crazy.")[8]

Kirby and Stark persevered, recruiting new actors and instituting new casting, offering a "new Othello" with Wright in the title role opposite the Iago of amateur John Able, who despite tolerable reviews was not retained. Throughout February they offered a far greater percentage of lighthearted entertainment, in which Mr. and Mrs. Bingham, Barry, and two replacements for Duprez, Miss Montague and Anna Burrell, shone. (Burrell "really surprised us by the versatility of talent which she displayed.")[9]

In mid-February, their finances secure, Kirby and Stark took a handful of their actors and, leaving stage manager Campbell in charge, returned to post-cholera Sacramento. There they committed several thousand dollars to repairs of the Tehama. Then it was on to Stockton, where a new theater had been constructed over the town's most successful saloon, El Placer on the corner of Centre and Levee streets. Stockton had had only desultory theatrical activity since Fury's Corinthian efforts. In October, Kirby had sent over a few actors to test the waters, including the Binghams, Emilie Mestayer, Hank Daly, Fairchild, and Coad, and their success encouraged her now.

She and Stark opened at the new El Placer on February 12 with *Damon and Pythias* and *Spectre Bridegroom*, deemed "a very indifferent bill for an opening night. They may do a good business for a couple of weeks, but their success is problematical, times being so hard that persons can scarcely afford to patronize theatrical representations sufficiently to remunerate the managers." In fact, despite being "the handsomest in the city," the saloon downstairs had just closed, due to a heavy tax on foreign miners (ostensibly implemented to discourage Mexican gamblers).[10]

Upstairs, Kirby and Stark were a decided hit. In *Hamlet*, "Mrs. Kirby, as the Queen, shone pre-eminently; possessing the graceful accessory of personal beauty, her admirable acting showed to greater advantage." Of Stark, "We verily believe, the boys would expend their last shilling, so great a favorite has he become."[11]

Encouraged, they returned with their actors to San Francisco in time to perform *Lady of Lyons* at the Jenny Lind on February 27. A new hire as Claude Melnotte, a Mr. Johns/Johnnes—likely an amateur—was a failure: "His reading was anything but truthful, his misquotations not a few, his delivery a declamation more suited to a camp meeting than a theatre, [delivered] in that peculiar sing-song mannerism of voice which violates the ears' sense of music, wearying and fatiguing the listener." He was let go.[12]

In March, crowded houses greeted the company's repertoire of Shakespeare (for example, *King Lear, Merchant of Venice, Macbeth*) and other serious dramas (such as *Richelieu, Stranger, Virginius*). Kirby and Stark trusted several company members with leads, including Mrs. S. A. Mansfield, who took the lead opposite Bingham on his benefit night of *Don Caesar de Bazan*, and Anna Burrell, who enacted Ophelia opposite Stark. A new actress from New Orleans, Mrs. Madden, portrayed Kate O'Brien in *Perfection* to good notices.

On March 16 Kirby and Stark took most of the company to Sacramento, to the Tehama, which she now owned, being Wingard's widow. Their rationale was that "the Jenny Lind Theatre was so limited in capacity that its attractive nights could not pay the loss sustained by thin houses on other occasions, and that this had forced [them] to leave the city until a more commodious theatre shall be ready."[13]

Bingham took over the lease of the Jenny Lind, adding McCron and the apparently recovered Duprez to his largely amateur company to play leads in such familiar pieces as *William Tell, Othello, Lady of Lyons*, and *Iron Chest*, and two melodramas, *Timour the Tartar* and *Lady of the Lake*. A new comedy, Morris Barnett's *The Serious Family*, which had run for over 120 nights in New York the previous season (with frontier offspring Caroline Chapman in the cast), proved popular. However, lacking the cachet of Kirby and Stark and beset by heavy spring rains, Bingham drew only "respectable" houses from his opening on March 17. He closed in mid-April, after which the Jenny Lind was used only for occasional music and vaudeville acts. The last straw had been Robinson and Evrard's reopening of their Dramatic Museum on California Street on April 9, which "has knocked the breath out of the Jenny Lind, which is about 'caving.'"[14]

~~~~~~~~~~

While Robinson and Evrard (he and his wife playing leads) had been in Sacramento in February, they had rented the Tehama with a small company, including the Mestayers and Fairchild, criticized as inferior. When Kirby arrived, she evicted Robinson and Evrard but found the renovations she had ordered were incomplete. It was not until March 18 that the Kirby-Stark company, with Campbell still as stage manager, could open, their large audience enjoying *Honey Moon*. The joint managers delivered appropriate remarks of gratitude for their warm reception.

Through March and April, facing no competition, they drew good houses— "nightly thronged to overflowing"—for their usual repertoire of serious drama, playing nearly all leads themselves. Occasionally they imparted a lead or two to Coad, Burrell (for example, Ophelia), or Mrs. Mansfield and, if comedic, to Barry or Downey. Their chief vocalist, Miss Montague, "who has an exceedingly sweet voice" was "quite pretty, and gets frequent encores." On April 21 they brought on Nesbit McCron to carry such leads as Richard III and William Tell while Stark returned to San Francisco to make arrangements for managing the new Jenny Lind Theatre.[15]

By the time he returned to Sacramento on May 1, competition had materialized in the form of the Pacific Theatre, reopened the month before under new owners. Beginning April 4, amateur James Rodgerson and his Melo-Dramatic Company had leased it for light entertainment. His chief attractions were professional ringers: Rowe veterans Mr. and Mrs. Batters, the peripatetic Madame Duprez (apparently resigned to playing breeches roles), the ubiquitous Fairchild, and a minstrel act, the Sable Harmonists. Despite a low admission of only fifty cents to a dollar, after a large opening-night crowd, attendance ebbed, and a series of misfortunes struck. Rigging lines were fouled and/or cut by unknown persons, "the stage manager was utterly incompetent to perform the duties devolving upon him," and several fights broke out among their audiences.[16]

By May 3, Rodgerson was gone (Duprez remained) and Batters took over, his "efficient management" aiming to operate the theater "on a good basis, and not as they were before, where all was disorder." That lasted a week. Then, the energetic Robinson alone—Evrard had publicly dissolved their partnership—brought in his Dramatic Museum Company from San Francisco. They opened on May 8 with *Charles II, Spoiled Child* (Mrs. Mestayer as Little Pickle), and dances by Miss Josephine. A featured attraction was announced: "the beautiful Miss [Ada] Stetson of [very briefly] New York is about to appear as Pauline in *The Lady of Lyons*."[17]

In San Francisco, another massive fire (again on May 4) destroyed Robinson's Dramatic Museum, as well as the new Jenny Lind which Kirby and Stark were to manage. This was the fifth time in four years that Robinson lost his investment, including twice within the past eleven months. Kirby and Stark offered a benefit for him and his company at the Tehama, which raised $1,000. Unfortunately, they chose Sunday, May 11, for the event, drawing the ire of the religious community for performing on the Sabbath. Stark apologized, asserting that he had "done so because he thought it more likely to do good in the way of diverting men from greater evils, and because he had been urged to do so by many personal friends." Another benefit, on June 5 for Sacramento fire companies, raised $822. This altruism elevated him "to a high point in the esteem of nine-tenths of our community."[18]

Always seeking new audiences, Robinson then took his company upriver to Marysville, the main depot of the northern mining region. There, they performed comedies and melodramas from May 20 to June 6 to crowded houses in "a pretty, new theatre" on the corner of Second and High streets. From Marysville, he took his company nearly forty miles east to Nevada (later Nevada City), California.[19]

At the Tehama in Sacramento that spring, Kirby, Stark, and McCron continued to carry most leads, except for the occasional appearance by a guest star. The first was Miss Harriett Carpenter ("a lady of superior talents and education") on May 12 as Pauline, followed by Calanthe in *Damon and Pythias*, Desdemona (to the Othello of McCron, Iago of Stark, and Emilia of Kirby), Virginia (to Stark's Virginius), and Juliet to Stark's Romeo (with McCron as Mercutio). On May 20 Mr. and (the recent) Mrs. Evrard arrived to star in such dramas as *Perfection* and *Gamester* and an all-star *Hamlet* on May 26 (with Stark in the title role, Evrard as Horatio, his wife as Ophelia, Kirby as Gertrude, and McCron as the Ghost). A decided hit with Sacramento miners was *Mose in Sacramento; or, Life in California,* which transplanted the cocksure but chivalrous New York fireman to the West. It opened on May 27 for several nights. Irish comedian Timothy A. Lubey (variously "Luby" and "Lubbey"), visited for two weeks of ethnic comedies and farces in early June. "The generous and unselfish manner" in which Kirby and Stark yielded the spotlight to guest stars was deemed "worthy of all praise and commendation, and must be appreciated by a high-minded community."[20]

Still, their rough-hewn audiences sometimes got out of hand. The performance of *Virginius* was marred by boorish misbehavior: "Barring the perverted taste of some of the auditory, who laughed at the grave, solemn, and pathetic, and wept at the ludicrous, the evening's entertainment was most pleasant and gratifying. We haven't got quite used to such methods of appreciating the drama yet, but from the frequent examples set us, we shall expect very soon to be able to weep when we should laugh, and laugh when we should weep."[21]

Kirby and Stark decided to broaden their efforts in Sacramento, sending Campbell over to the Pacific Theatre (with some post-Robinson remodeling), with half of the Tehama company: Campbell, Kirby, McCron, Mansfield, Burrell, and Montague, with Carpenter for star power. They opened there on May 14 with *Gustavus the Third,* H. M. Milner's 1833 historical drama, followed by a grand masquerade ball. Unfortunately, the latter "was thinly attended by the fair sex, and but few of the gentlemen appeared in costume." Kirby and Stark wasted no effort hyping their twin theaters: "Crowds of curious citizens collected on the corner of J and 2nd Streets last evening to listen to the rival criers in their efforts to induce the theatrical community to visit the Tehama or the Pacific." A highlight at the Pacific was the transferred *Romeo and Juliet* from the Tehama, a benefit for Carpenter which earned her $1,226. As needed by a given script, Kirby and Stark freely moved actors between the two venues, a practice long established in the East.[22]

But within two weeks, despite reportedly full houses, they yielded the Pacific to C. R. Thorne's American Company and closed the Tehama, saying they intended to raze it. Thorne had arrived by steamer on May 23, bringing a number of actors and actresses from the East, including a surname familiar on the frontier: the post-showboat Chapmans. Combined with Kirby-Stark holdovers Coad, Fairchild, Carpenter, and Madden, Thorne's formidable company—arguably the strongest yet assembled in California—included comedian C. A. King; Irish comedian-vocalist James Seymour; David C. Anderson; T. C. Green; Ted Hutchinson; George and Mary Ross Parks Chapman, her son (and George's stepson) Alonzo Chapman, their daughter Mary Chapman; and Miss Clara Rivers. (Perhaps the most talented Chapman, Caroline, was enjoying success in New York.)

They opened on May 28, 1851, with *Don Caesar de Bazan* and *The Review*, plus olio songs and dances. Reviews were supportive: "the whole company bid fair to be favorites," especially the Chapmans, who were "old favorites and acquaintances well known to many of our citizens, and 'none name them but to praise.'" Significantly, "On no former occasion have we seen so many of the fair ladies of Sacramento within the walls of the theatre."[23]

Their summer season offered a judicious mix of comedies, farces, and serious drama, with Thorne and the Chapmans in the leads. Mrs. Chapman was an immediate hit in roles both serious and comic, notably her five protean roles (in the footsteps of Louisa Lane) in *Actress of All Work.* Anderson's old men similarly drew praise. The dances of Mary Chapman and Clara Rivers quickly became popular interludes, meriting almost daily mention in reviews, even providing the names for two new sailing yachts.

On June 6, Thorne added Mrs. Evrard, although her husband had designs on a Sacramento theater of his own. Within days of his arrival, he had met with an architect and developed plans for "an immense and beautiful brick theatre on the corner of K and Second Streets," adjoining the Orleans Hotel. The three-story brick Greek-style building was to be seventy-three by eighty-five feet. Stockholders were solicited (450 shares at $100 each) and a lot purchased for $8,000. Under the direction of Volney Spalding, construction was to commence around July 1 and be completed within ninety days, one of sixty buildings underway that month in Sacramento. Supposedly, Edwin Forrest had already promised to appear "as soon as he can be released from the suit now pending at law" (his exceptionally contentious divorce proceedings).[24]

Two theatrical weddings occurred in Sacramento that month. Carpenter married Fairchild (although he would live less than a year), and Kirby and Stark wed on June 14. They immediately took their newly christened California Pioneer Company to Marysville, close on Robinson's heels. Opening with *Othello* on June 16 for six nights of serious drama, they earned enthusiastic reviews, now billed as Mr. and Mrs. Stark. Stark announced his intention to travel to New York and Europe to hire actors for both Sacramento and his planned management of the new Jenny Lind in San Francisco. He sought qualified actresses "capable of playing first or second parts, which, with a single exception, is not the case at present. At times it has been almost impossible to obtain any capable of a higher destiny than a walking gentlewoman, and some staggering even at that. It has changed somewhat for the better, but the want is still very great."[25]

But Stark canceled his travel pans when on June 22 yet another fire swept through San Francisco, destroying Maguire's new three-thousand-seat Jenny Lind Theatre which Kirby and Stark were to manage, nine days after its completion. This cost Maguire, with other buildings, $100,000. He wasted no time renewing his efforts to rebuild. Consumed in the same conflagration was the small Adelphi, but it, too, would be rebuilt, opening on August 1 on Dupont Street with French vaudeville, with a capacity of less than six hundred.

~~~~~~~~~~

In Sacramento, Kirby and Stark again turned their attention to the Tehama, which had not been razed, booking a variety of guest performers, including danseuse Senorita Sophia Abalos and prima donna Senora Abalos. Bringing their Pioneer Company back from Marysville, they also produced melodramas, such as *The Carpenter of Rouen,* with all new scenery and costumes. But on August 14 the Tehama succumbed to that recurrent scourge of the frontier, fire, which destroyed it completely (the result of hot ashes disposed of too near its frame exterior). Mr. and Mrs. George Chapman, who had been borrowed from Thorne to appear as guest stars, helped evacuate fire victims, and she wrote a column about the fire for the *Alta California.* The Tehama, which had brought Sacramentans their first Shakespeare among so many other memorable performances, was not rebuilt, and the company disbanded.

~~~~~~~~~~

Thorne in summer 1851 announced plans to expand in Sacramento by renovating the old Lee's Exchange in conjunction with Volney Spalding and contractor A. P. Petit. They expected the work to be completed within sixty days, the building to house seventeen hundred patrons.

In the meantime Thorne produced a full summer season at the Pacific, including his own jam-packed benefit on June 12. After a brief hiatus, he reopened the Pacific on June 23 with a popular new melodrama, *Ernest Maltravers,* adapted by Louisa Medina from a novel by Bulwer-Lytton. With Thorne and Mrs. Chapman in the leads, it drew full houses and was repeated several times over the next two weeks. The pair proved similarly popular in such established fare as *William Tell, Honey Moon,* and *Jack Sheppard* (Mrs. Chapman in breeches in the title role).

In mid-July, however, Thorne abruptly turned over management to James Seymour and George Chapman and left for New York, ostensibly to recruit guest stars. Chapman took over Thorne's roles, and his wife drew plaudits for her protean roles in *The French Spy*, its first performance on the frontier.

~~~~~~~~~~~

On July 20, 1851, the steamship *Tennessee* brought to San Francisco the first established star from the East, Junius "June" Brutus Booth Jr., twenty-nine, namesake of the tragedian who had formed the vanguard of stars into the frontier in 1822. With Junius Jr. was his common-law wife, Harriet Mace, sixteen, with whom he had fled Boston to avoid imprisonment for adultery from a complaint filed by his legal wife, Clementina. He and Harriet were said to be "the handsomest couple in San Francisco." Booth, recalled a colleague, was "a model of manly beauty, very fond of athletic exercises, an admirable fencer, and sparred with skill and power; and, in addition to all this, he was of a genial, pleasant temperament, a plain-spoken, upright man." Tom Maguire had engaged him for his new Jenny Lind Theatre, but its destruction by that fire on June 22 forced a change of plans. Hence, Booth and Mace, along with comedian Fred M. Kent, Mrs. E. W. (Mary) Woodward and Miss Kate Grey, who had accompanied them on the *Tennessee* from the isthmus of Panama, headed upriver to Sacramento.[26]

There, they may have acted at the Starks' Tehama, but its lack of newspaper notices, and the curious denial of admission to reviewers there, leaves this moot. They did open at Seymour and Chapman's Pacific Theatre on August 21, with Booth in the title role of *The Stranger*, with Woodward as Mrs. Haller and Mace as Charlotte. The next night's *Pizarro* featured Booth as Rolla and Woodward as Elvira, and on August 26 it was *Othello* with Booth as Iago, Bingham as Othello, and Mrs. Chapman as Desdemona. They earned rave reviews. Booth was repeatedly compared favorably to his father, and "nothing could be more inspiring to Mr. Seymour." But the Pacific's season and drawing power were ending. After benefits for Booth (as Richard III) and Woodward (as Bianca to Booth's Fazio), Seymour and Chapman shuttered it, dispersing the company. Henceforth it would be used only for concerts.[27]

Along with the Chapmans, Booth promptly transferred his talent to Sacramento's new American Theatre (Spalding and Petit's remodeled Lee's

Exchange), where he became stage manager. He formed a strong, versatile company that opened on September 9, 1851, with a dedicatory address by Mrs. Chapman, followed by *All That Glitters Is Not Gold,* a dance by the perennially popular Misses Chapman and Rivers, *Turning the Tables,* and *The Mummy.* When the combined weight of the audience caused the dress circle to settle a bit mid-performance, though, more than a few patrons left.[28]

The cachet of the American was enhanced on September 20 by the return to Sacramento of C. R. Thorne. Thorne brought Frank S. Chanfrau, one of the first major eastern stars to appear in California, renowned for his impersonation of swaggering "Bowery B'hoy" Mose the Fireman, along with Chanfrau's costar, Miss Albertine [Manchester], who enacted Mose's "best g'hal," Lize. They opened on September 22 to a packed house, which became the norm for several weeks. But by mid-November, this new theater too would fall on hard times, sending Chanfrau and Albertine to San Francisco.[29]

Booth had already migrated there, freed up by Thorne's return. He finally took his place, as he had originally intended when he traveled to California, as manager and leading tragedian of Maguire's elegant rebuilt (third) Jenny Lind Theatre. It opened October 4. Standing three stories high, 75 feet across and 137 feet deep on Kearny Street facing Portsmouth Square, its brick construction and facade of yellow Australian sandstone promised protection from fire. Its opulent interior, seating two thousand, and its mammoth stage—"large enough to drill a regiment on," Maguire boasted—were unmatched in California and rivaled many theaters in the East.[30]

Booth was ably supported by theatrical veterans. These included stage manager James Evrard; Mary Woodward; Harriett Carpenter; Hank Daly, A. W. Wright; Wesley Venua, who brought fourteen years of New York experience; singer-actress Miss Montague; and of course by "the pretty Mrs. Booth," who was "destined to win and wear laurels as fresh . . . as her beauty is unfaded." A typical evening, October 19, presented *Pizarro,* with Booth as Rolla, Woodward as Elvira, and Carpenter as Cora, a bill which merited several reprises that fall. Comedies featured Fred Kent and visiting star T. A. Lubey.[31]

In late October, Chanfrau and Albertine signed on as well, drawing good houses. Evrard's wife, too, joined in November, as did Emilie Mestayer. Albertine's Dot in *Cricket on the Hearth*, opposite Woodward's Bertha and Booth's John Peerybingle, a role he had originated in New York five years before, was "rendered with such effect as to draw moisture from nearly every eye in the house." In its afterpiece, *The Toodles*, Chanfrau "took the house completely by storm." He and Albertine introduced Mose and Lize, in *New York as It Is*, to a crammed-full house on November 5. It ran for a week, replaced by *Mose in California* (a different version from the Tehama's, this one written specifically for Chanfrau by William Chapman in New York in 1849). Booth and Woodward's *Macbeth* on November 28 drew critical raves.[32]

The primary competition for the Jenny Lind in San Francisco that fall was Doc Robinson's American Theatre (not to be confused with its namesake in Sacramento) on the northeast corner of Sansome and Halleck streets. Equally elegant, with red plush seats and curtains and a capacity of more than two thousand, it was "as commodious as it is beautiful." Led by Mr. and Mrs. Stark, the Chapman family (George, Mary, Alonzo and Mary), Anna Burrell, James H. Vinson, comedian William Barry, and ingenue Sophie Edwin, its company was nearly as talented as that of the Jenny Lind. However, it had been erected so quickly (in only twenty-five days) that by the end of the October 20 opening night bill of Mrs. Stark's welcome address, Anna Cora Mowatt's play *Armand*, Chapman-Rivers dances, and the afterpiece of *A Day in Paris*, the theater had sunk two inches into its foundational sand and mud from the weight of its full house.[33]

Mrs. Chapman's three roles in *French Spy* and her breeches *Jack Sheppard* were immediate hits, as were Stark's tragedies, including *Hamlet* (with new singer-actress Emily Coad as Ophelia), *Iron Chest, Stranger, Damon and Pythias, Romeo and Juliet* (opposite Mrs. Chapman), and *Othello* (Chapman in the title role, with Stark as Iago and Burrell as Desdemona). Nearly every review celebrated the Chapman-Rivers dances.

In mid-November 1851 the Chapman family left to tour smaller California mining towns, where they found primitive theatrical conditions (typically, "hard wooden benches, muslin-lined walls, one inadequate heating stove, tallow candles for footlights, and a cramped stage with a cambric curtain"), but plentiful gold dust in payment. Their places were taken by Sacramento émigrés Mr. and Mrs. Thorne, their daughter Emily, Louis Mestayer, and J. A. Smith. With Emily dancing and playing ingenues, they finished out the year with such standard pieces as *Don Caesar de Bazan, Honey Moon, Mountaineers,* and *Richard III*.[34]

In early December the Starks defected from the American to the Jenny Lind, creating "the most splendid combination of theatrical talent ever formed in this state." They brought their Othello and Desdemona (to Booth's Iago), King Lear and Cordelia, and Virginius and Virginia. However, to Stark's Hamlet, Mace enacted Ophelia. When Mr. and Mrs. John Proctor, established stars from the East, arrived for a week in late December playing similar tragic roles, the reputation of the Jenny Lind was further solidified.[35]

<hr />

By 1852, theatrical conditions in California had improved markedly. Audiences could count on seeing tragedy and comedy decently acted, with a smattering of new scripts from New York. Marquee names from eastern theaters were appearing with some regularity. Regular, almost daily, reviews of performances occurred. Managers were staying above water, literally and figuratively. The theatrical frontier in the new Golden State was coming to a close.[36]

By the end of January, June Booth still held the stage of the Jenny Lind under Thorne's management, the George Chapman family was back from the mining towns and performing at the American Theatre in San Francisco, and the Starks were drawing good notices and good houses at the American in Sacramento following a week at the Jenny Lind. (In June 1852, George would purchase and manage Sacramento's moribund Pacific Theatre, but it would succumb to fire on November 2.)

Boorish behavior did persist, however, as evidenced one night during Stark's *Richelieu*: "Most revolting to every sense of decency, and every conception of intelligence, was the stupid, miserable, half-bred laughing among one or two individuals in the upper tier in the midst of the most impressive and solemn scenes."[37]

February saw the arrival in San Francisco by steamboat (from New York via the isthmus of Panama) of the next batch of stars: newlyweds Lewis Baker and Alexina Fisher Baker, William B. "Uncle Billy" Chapman, Caroline Chapman, and Mr. and Mrs. (William B. and Therese Chapman) Hamilton. The Bakers were the first to appear onstage, opening on February 14 at the Jenny Lind. The child of frontier actors Palmer and Agnes Fisher, Alexina Baker at thirty was among the brightest stars so far to migrate to California. She had debuted in New York at age eight, played juvenile versions of Richard III and Shylock, and by her early teens, due to her physical and emotional maturity, could enact demanding women's roles. She specialized in such traditional heroines as Julia in *Hunchback,* Pauline in *Lady of Lyons,* Bianca in *Fazio,* Portia in *Merchant of Venice,* and Rosalind in *As You Like It.* Reviewers gushed: "She can scarcely be said to act at all. Her intonations, action and looks are all natural; there is no straining for effect, no playing to the audience, . . . but apparently absorbed in the part she appeared almost to forget that there was a crowd listening to her." Her husband, a relative of Frank Chanfrau (who likely facilitated their California engagement) was a moderately good actor who ably supported her. For the rest of the year, at one California theater or another, they acted nearly every night, acquiring a minor fortune.[38]

Two weeks after the Bakers' California debut, William and Caroline Chapman, supported by the Hamiltons and Proctors, opened in Sacramento at the American Theatre, now owned by Maguire. Caroline, thirty-three, was now the most renowned performer in the family, having acted since age eleven, primarily in comedies. In New York she had established a reputation as "the most vivacious soubrette known to our stage," praised for her "versatility, almost unprecedented." This slender, graceful singer and comedienne was "not only entirely unsurpassed, but nearly unrivaled." Although plain-featured, her "lustrous dark eyes could convey at a glance more meaning, either of mirth or sadness, than any [other eyes] on the New York stage." As one colleague recalled, "Lacking feminine beauty, this lady was beautiful in soul and brilliant in talent." In California, in comedies like

Husband at Sight, Heir at Law, and *The Review,* she brought down the house and soon became known as "Our Caroline." Her father and the Hamiltons joined her onstage almost every night.[39]

In March considerable managerial changes and theater-hopping by stars ensued, doubtless creating confusion for theatregoers. On March 8 Robinson abruptly closed the Sacramento American, sending William Chapman to the San Francisco American and Caroline to the Jenny Lind. For three weeks Robinson posted daily notices asserting that his theater was undergoing repairs and would reopen in one week. He also ceded management of his San Francisco American on March 16 to James Stark. The Bakers, reportedly disappointed by declining attendance at Maguire's increasingly debt-burdened Jenny Lind, migrated to the small Adelphi Theatre (formerly known as the French Theatre) on March 1. Four nights later they moved again, to Stark's American, then on March 22 to Robinson's tardily reopened American in Sacramento. By mid-March both Chapmans, plus the Hamiltons and Proctors, were performing at the Jenny Lind. (During that brief appearance at the Adelphi, Lewis Baker saw a viable opportunity and took over its management, which would over the next two seasons prove extremely lucrative (bringing the Bakers a profit of $30,000).[40]

When the Chapmans left the Jenny Lind on April 11, the Bakers moved in, but by mid-May all were reunited on its stage. This only lasted until June 14, a benefit for Strangers' Hospital, announced as "the last performance at this establishment." For $200,000, Maguire eventually sold the Jenny Lind to the city of San Francisco, to be converted into a new city hall.[41]

~~~~~~~~~~

June Booth had remained stage manager of the San Francisco American, occasionally playing leads opposite the Chapmans, Bakers, Starks, Thornes, or whoever rotated in, together drawing consistently strong reviews. But in mid-March 1852 Booth decided to return east with Harriet to convince his famous father (and less-renowned younger brother, Edwin) to come out to California, to reap their fair share of the plentiful profits to be gleaned from nouveau riche miners. As San Francisco newspaper editor Frank Soulé wrote, in 1852–53 "there was still the old reckless energy. The old love of pleasure, the fast making and fast spending of money, the old hard labor and wild delights, jobberies and political corruption, thefts, robberies and violent assaults, murder, duels and suicides, gambling, drinking and general extravagance and dissipation." It was a place of "brave wickedness and splendid folly." In short, Junius Sr.'s preferred environment.[42]

But his health was declining, and he initially resisted his son's proposal, knowing what an arduous journey it entailed. Ultimately, he relented, "more for the novelty of the trip than a desire to perform there." Junius Sr., Jr., Harriet, and Edwin departed New York on June 21, landing at Colón, Panama, then crossed the isthmus by mule train, sleeping in shifts with cocked pistols, justifiably fearing marauders. Finally boarding another steamship to San Francisco, they arrived on July 28, greeted at the dock by a throng of theatrical professionals and a brass band furnished by Maguire.[43]

Their first stop was Maguire's last gasp with the Jenny Lind, where Caroline and William Chapman had been holding forth. Their comedies and farces yielded way to the senior Booth, who opened July 30 as Mortimer in *Iron Chest*. Unquestionably the greatest star yet to appear in California, he was "greeted with long, prolonged, vociferous and hearty applause. . . . To attempt criticism on the acting of such a man would be a tactless task, and entirely uncalled for." Supported by Edwin, the elder Booth moved through his usual repertoire for two weeks, including *New Way to Pay Old Debts, Mountaineers, Stranger, Macbeth, Hamlet, Othello, Merchant of Venice,* and *Richard III*, before traveling upriver to Sacramento to the American. He played there from August 19 through September 6, to generally enthusiastic audiences and reviews. (On November 2 the American like the Pacific would burn, part of a massive fire that destroyed seven-eighths of the city, but the American would be rebuilt the following spring.)[44]

From there Booth returned by river steamer to San Francisco, to Baker's Adelphi, for four nights, the penultimate engagement of his monumental career. Leaving Edwin behind, allegedly to hone his craft, he then traveled via Panama to his final engagement in New Orleans, where he was robbed, losing all of his California profits. On his way back to his home in Bel Air, Maryland, he died on a steamboat approaching Louisville on November 30. News of his death reached Edwin, just turned nineteen, amid a blizzard in the Sierra Nevada, where he was performing at various mining towns, his path at times intersecting that of the George Chapman family. Returning to California, Edwin launched into a prolonged period of alcohol-fueled grief, during which he would come into his own on California stages, on his way to becoming arguably the finest American tragedian of the century.

In the years following this vibrant era of frontier California, other stars would grace the stages of San Francisco and Sacramento, including Lotta Crabtree; Catherine Sinclair (Forrest's turbulently-divorced wife), who managed her own theater, the Metropolitan, in San Francisco; Matilda Heron; Laura Keene (a subsequent manager of the Metropolitan); and James Murdoch. The culmination of the "Golden Era" of California theatre would be the opening in January 1869 of the majestic California Theatre by comanagers John McCullough and Lawrence Barrett. It matched anything in the East.

16

THE REMAINING FRONTIER

ONCE THEATRE HAD BEEN established in California, the remaining frontier constricted over the next four decades, facilitated by proliferating railroad lines. For those towns yet unblessed with a theater, one figure—the Johnny Appleseed of theaters—rushed to alleviate their situation. Fellow actor Walter Leman recalled this "most remarkable character": "The ubiquitous, the ever-persuasive, the always-promising John S. Potter [1809–1869], who built more theatres and opened more theatres, and closed more theatres—I think he closed twice as many as he ever opened—than any man in the Union or out of it." Potter could "play any part in the drama at ten minutes' notice, in a black coat and wig, and would get the curtain up and down again, shift all the scenes, attend to the properties during the performance, and within five minutes or less after the fall of the curtain would have the receipts from the box office in his pocket and be out of sight of his ambitious actors, who waited around in vain for salary." Yet Potter "always operated on the edge of solvency."[1]

As early as 1835 he offered a theatrical season in long-neglected Lexington, Kentucky, in the "large room" of Masonic Hall. The following year he opened a season in Grand Gulf, Mississippi; in 1837 one in Natchitoches, Louisiana; and in 1838 yet another, in Little Rock, Arkansas. In early 1839 he built a large theater (seating twelve hundred) in Jackson, Mississippi, previously served only by a temporary one set up by Austin Cargill in December 1836 in Mansion House on South State Street. Also in 1839, Potter opened a theater in Dubuque, Iowa Territory, which he followed in 1841 by converting a stable on Main Street in Memphis, Tennessee, and a year later by opening one in Nashville. After five years in Richmond, Virginia, he returned to the frontier in January 1850 to open a new theater in Vicksburg,

Mississippi, then headed to California, only to find others had successfully preceded him.

In other states and territories, theatre emerged sporadically. The newly organized Republic of Texas was to have enjoyed its first theatre in 1837, eight years before Texas statehood. But the intended troupe, that of G. L. Lyons, perished when their schooner sank in a gale en route. The first professional theatrical performance in Texas took place in Houston on June 11, 1838, by managers actor Henri Corri of the St. Charles Theatre in New Orleans, and John Carlos, a local merchant. A full house enjoyed *Hunchback* with Corri as Clifford and Mrs. Emma Barker as Julia, followed by the "New National Texian Anthem," and the farce *Dumb Belle*. That fall, the president of the republic and former amateur actor Sam Houston attended a performance of *Perfection* and *Dumb Belle*. In January 1839 Carlos opened a competing theater and the two managers fell out, with Corri taking his troupe to Galveston.[2]

During the late 1830s the embryonic lead-mining town of Milwaukee, Wisconsin Territory, had to content itself with touring professionals, the most stellar being tragedian James Murdoch, who appeared in *Hamlet* in April 1839. The first professional companies came nearly a decade later, in late 1847, when Chicago impresario John B. Rice expanded his circuit northward, sending part of his company to perform in Military Hall. In the 1850s a vibrant German theatre emerged in Milwaukee.

Settlement in Iowa had spread west from the Mississippi River during the 1830s, with its population of over twenty-three thousand justifying the establishment of the Iowa Territory in 1838, with statehood granted eight years later. As with so many other frontier towns, Dubuque residents formed an amateur thespian society in 1837, and enjoyed performances on showboats (Chapman's chiefly among them) along the river. Comedies and melodramas predominated. By 1860, touring companies arrived to perform Shakespeare in the Julien Theatre.[3]

As had been the case in the early years of California, the first theatrical performances in Oregon Territory were those of a crew of sailors, in this case from a Hudson's Bay Company ship, the *Modeste*, anchored off Fort Vancouver. In May 1846 they presented *Love in a Village*, *Mock Doctor*, *The*

Mayor of Garratt, Three Weeks After Marriage, and *The Deuce Is in Him* before casting off. Then, for over a decade, only a handful of itinerant players came through Portland, notably the George Chapman family, up from California, in 1857, performing in the Portland Theatre on Front Street.[4]

When Mormon pioneers founded Salt Lake City, Utah, in 1847, they brought with them a tolerance for, and love of, theatre. In their short residence in Nauvoo, Illinois, they had staged plays, including a production of *Pizarro* in which Brigham Young played a high priest. By 1850 in Salt Lake City, they had organized an active amateur troupe, the Deseret Dramatic Association. In March 1862 they opened the large Salt Lake Theatre, built at a cost of $100,000, and various stars from the East made it a stop on their touring circuits.[5]

Prior to 1860, Nevada saw only scattered itinerant actors and minstrel troupes, performing in mining camps. That year the first theater in the then–Utah Territory (four years before Nevada statehood) was built in Washoe Valley. Its first actors were Philip M. Westwood's company from Salt Lake City. On September 29, 1860, the Howard Theatre in Virginia City opened with *Toodles* and Benjamin Webster's *The Swiss Swains,* drawing an overflowing house for its seven hundred seats. Also that fall, Carson City opened its first theater, John Q. A. Moore and Charley Parker's three-hundred-seat Saloon Theatre. California theatrical veteran James Stark brought a new level of professionalism when he brought his touring troupe to Nevada mining towns in fall 1861. On July 2, 1863, Julia Dean Hayne—daughter of frontier veteran Julia Drake Fosdick Dean—delivered the opening-night dedicatory oration in Tom Maguire's new Virginia City Opera House on D Street, followed by Bulwer-Lytton's *Money.* Three years later, Mark Twain would lecture from its stage.[6]

Theatre came to Colorado Territory for much the same reason it had to California: to entertain miners. The discovery of gold in 1858 and 1859 in an area that would encompass Denver drew thousands of argonauts, and California veteran Charles R. Thorne arrived in the latter year. October 1859 saw the erection of two theaters in Denver: Apollo Hall on Larimer Street and Reed's Theater in Cibola Hall on Ferry Street. Another opened in August 1860, built by John S. (Jack) Langrishe (regarded as the "father of Colorado theatre") and George McArthur. The culmination of frontier theatrical development in Colorado came on November 20, 1879, with the opening of the lavish Tabor Opera House in Leadville, financed by larger-than-life politician Horace A. W. Tabor.

Seattle, in Washington Territory, hosted itinerant actors up from Oregon as early as 1859, who performed in Plummer's Hall on the corner of Main and Commercial streets. One of the earliest, and most memorable, was that of Edith Mitchell, who gave a dramatic reading of Shakespeare to a "small but appreciative audience" who "manifested their satisfaction by frequent applause." A second venue, the Lyceum Theatre, opened in Olympia, Washington, in 1860.[7]

Theatre moved in from the East along with settlers into Kansas Territory as early as November 1856, just over four years before it was granted statehood. Among the first recorded performers were Monsieur Gabay's itinerant company, performing in Melodeon Hall in Leavenworth, the territory's first metropolis. In March 23, 1858, the Union Theatre opened there on the corner of Delaware and Third streets, converted from a large hall. In April 1858 it was joined by Scott's Theatre in Melodeon Hall and in late November 1858 by Stockton Hall on the corner of Delaware and Fourth streets. The ubiquitous Thorne and his family performed in Scott's and in the Union Theatre in spring 1858, including *The Wife, Richard III,* and *Othello.* When the National Theatre opened in Leavenworth in November 1858, Thorne took over its management.[8]

The first recorded theatre performance in Nebraska Territory occurred on May 28, 1857, in Omaha, in Armstrong and Clarke's storeroom. A small itinerant troupe consisting of men named Wright and Scott, and Mr. and Mrs. Powell, performed *The Merry Cobbler* and *Box and Cox* to a small audience due to unfavorable weather. The first actual theater was the Omaha Academy of Music, erected by the indefatigable John S. Potter in January 1867, two months before Nebraska statehood, following his management of the tour of Julia Dean Hayne to various western cities. Potter's first guest star in Omaha was third-tier star actress Melissa Breslau, who toured with her manager husband, J. M. Breslau, in such pieces as *Evadne* and *The Dumb Belle.*

West Virginia, formed as a new state in June 1863 during the Civil War, had seen theatrical performances while still a part of Virginia. But the new state came into its own on July 21 of that year, when actors from Baltimore's Front Street Theatre and the Pittsburgh Theatre combined to perform *The Venetian* and *A Ghost in Spite of Himself* in Wheeling's Washington Hall, followed three nights later with *Charles II* and *Black Eyed Susan.*

Three other states saw their first theatre during the Civil War. Minneapolis, Minnesota, gained its first theater, Harrison's Hall, in 1864, six years after statehood. That year, and for several years afterward, a small company managed by A. MacFarland, performed there and in the Pence Opera House, where they opened on June 21, 1867, with *Hunchback.* The first and second theaters in Boise, Idaho Territory, were both Potter efforts in 1864: the Idaho and the Forrest. These were followed, the same year, by the Jenny Lind and the Temple. Opening night at Potter's Idaho Theatre on August 11, 1864, featured guest star G. B. Waldron in *Lady of Lyons* and *Lottery Ticket.* Later star Hayne drew large, enthusiastic crowds. Barnstorming minstrels and actors arrived in Montana Territory during 1864 to perform in the Theatre Building in Post Office Block, Virginia City—derided by one visitor as "the shabbiest town I ever saw"—for audiences primarily of gold miners. On the intensely cold night of December 10 of that year the New Montana Theatre opened in Virginia City under manager DeWitt Waugh with *Faint Heart Never Won Fair Lady* and *Spectre Bridegroom,* followed by thrice-weekly performances.[9]

Dakota Territory was the last to acquire theatrical performances. The Bella Union, a saloon and theater, opened in 1876 on Main Street in Deadwood, Tom Miller, proprietor. By April 1877 it was joined by the Grand Variety Theatre, also on Main Street, Deadwood, with Al Swearingen, proprietor.

For much of the second half of the nineteenth century, frontier towns across America began sporting "opera houses," ostensibly an improvement on a mere theater. No town "could call itself civilized unless it could advertise programs in its very own opera house." Many were even grandiosely dubbed the Grand Opera House. No actual operas were performed, but it allowed civic leaders to foster the illusion that what transpired within those walls "was somehow more reputable and less damaging to its citizens than anything which was presented in a building called a theatre."[10]

Then, as noted in 1890 by the superintendent of the U.S. Census and reinforced in 1893 by Frederick Jackson Turner, the American frontier could be considered closed. It had taken most of the intervening century for theatre to be established throughout.[11]

NOTES

Introduction

1. Mark Twain, *Adventures of Huckleberry Finn* (New York: Oxford University Press, 2008), 119, 125.

2. Gary Scharnhorst, *The Life of Mark Twain: The Early Years, 1835–1871*, vol. 1: *Mark Twain and His Circle* (Columbia: University of Missouri Press, 2018), 64, 76–77, 81, 87, 102, 314. For "Nonesuch" specifics, see James H. Dormon Jr., *Theater in the Ante Bellum South 1815–1861* (Chapel Hill: University of North Carolina Press, 1967), 113.

3. The term "theater" is used in this book to denote a physical building; the term "theatre" refers to the art form, and is also used when part of the proper name of a nineteenth-century theater.

4. Frederick Jackson Turner, *The Significance of the Frontier in American History* (Madison: State Historical Society of Wisconsin, 1894), 2.

5. Based on U.S. Census data, Eslinger (ix–x, 58) estimates that "at least 100,000 adults, plus innumerable children, undertook this journey by 1800. . . . Indeed, within twenty years of initial settlement, a greater proportion of the national population had crossed the Appalachians (7.8 percent by 1800) than had followed the prospect of gold in California and land beyond the Rockies (2.6 percent by 1870)." By 1800, "roughly 7 percent of the national population lived west of the Alleghenies." Ellen Eslinger, *Running Mad for Kentucky: Frontier Travel Accounts* (Lexington: University Press of Kentucky, 2004).

6. See Douglas McDermott, "The Development of Theatre on the American Frontier, 1750–1890," *Theatre Survey* 19, no. 1 (May 1978) 63–78, for an elaboration on these early phases, although McDermott defines a first-phase company as comprising eight to ten players. His three phases are roughly congruent with those stated here. For the purposes of this study, "Frontier Theatre" is defined as English-language theatre. For a consideration of Spanish, French, and Native American performance, see chapters 1 and 2 in Felicia Hardison Londré and Daniel Watermeier, *The History of North American Theater* (New York: Continuum, 1998); and chapters 10–12 of Lilyan Zara Goff, "The Development of the Theatre on the American Frontier to 1850" (MA thesis, University of Southern California, 1940).

7. Noah Ludlow, *Dramatic Life as I Found It* (1880; rpt. New York: Benjamin Blom, Inc.,

1966), 172; Elizabeth A. Perkins, *Border Life: Experience and Memory in the Revolutionary Ohio Valley* (Chapel Hill: University of North Carolina Press, 1998), 46.

8. Charles Theodore Greve, *Centennial History of Cincinnati and Representative Citizens* (Chicago: Biographical Publishing Co., 1904), vol. 1: 465. Longworth was the grandfather of the future Speaker of the U.S. House of Representatives and husband of Alice Roosevelt, Nicholas Longworth III.

9. Alfred Lambourne, *A Play-house; Being a Sketch in Three Short Letters* (n.p., 1870), 16–17.

10. Ben Graf Henneke, "The Playgoer in America (1752–1952)," PhD diss., University of Illinois, 1956), 114–63; Richard Butsch, *The Making of American Audiences* (Cambridge, UK: Cambridge University Press, 2000), 33–50.

11. Perkins, 86–87.

12. Mabel Tyree Crum, "The History of the Lexington Theatre from the Beginning to 1860," PhD diss., University of Kentucky, 1956, 125–26. For a thorough consideration of religious opposition, see Claudia Durst Johnson, *Church and Stage* (Jefferson, NC: McFarland & Co., 2008).

13. S. C. Aiken, "The Theatre—a Dangerous Profession," *Daily Selma* (AL) *Reporter*, June 2, 1838.

14. Crum, 123–25.

15. Samuel Beckett, *Worstword Ho!* www.goethe.de/ins/us/en/sta/los/bib/feh/21891928 .html.

16. Digital History, "Closing the American Frontier," www.digitalhistory.uh.edu/disp _textbook.cfm?smtid=2&psid=3154.

1. Avant Amateurs (1790–1810)

1. *Kentucky Gazette*, Apr. 26, 1790. The first settlements in Kentucky were Harrodsburg and Boonesborough, both in 1775.

2. George W. Ranck, *History of Lexington* (Cincinnati: R. Clarke & Co., 1872), 203–4.

3. *Pittsburgh Gazette*, April 17, 1790.

4. John Home, *Douglas*, in *The British Drama*, vol. 1 (Philadelphia: Thomas Davis, 1850), 7.

5. René J. Le Gardeur Jr., *The First New Orleans Theatre 1792–1803* (New Orleans: Leeward Books, 1963), 6–11, 44–47; Juliane Braun, *Creole Drama: Theatre and Society in Antebellum New Orleans* (Charlottesville: University of Virginia Press, 2019), 21.

6. Le Gardeur, 2, 6, 10–11, 44–47; Braun, 21–24; Ned Sublette, *The World That Made New Orleans* (Chicago: Lawrence Hill Books, 2008), 242. In December 1803, the French governor of the Louisiana Territory, Pierre-Clément de Laussat, mandated its permanent closure as being unsafe (see Le Gardeur, 38–40).

7. Lafon's new actors included Messrs. L. S. Fontaine, Joseph Destinval, and Louis-François Clairville, and Mmes. Clairville and Delaure.

8. Le Gardeur, 28–33; Sublette, 245.

9. Le Gardeur, 40–41. Le Gardeur goes to painstaking lengths to debunk the incorrect but frequently restated impression that the first actors came to New Orleans under Tabary as early as 1791, whereas Tabary did not arrive until 1805.

10. West T. Hill Jr., *The Theatre of Early Kentucky* (Lexington: University Press of Kentucky, 1971), 19–20; Helen Langworthy, "The Theatre in the Frontier Cities of Lexington, Kentucky and Cincinnati, Ohio," PhD diss., University of Iowa, 1952, 24–28. Nearly all of these titles contained a subtitle, set off by a semi-colon, but these varied widely, subject to the whims of the producing theatre, and are not included in this study.

11. Langworthy, 24–28; *The Western Spy* (Cincinnati), Sept. 30, Oct. 10, 17 and 19, 1801. See also Robert Ralston Jones, *Fort Washington at Cincinnati, Ohio* (Cincinnati: Society of Colonial Wars in the State of Ohio, 1902), 55: "Towards the latter part of the fort's existence there were theatrical performances [also] in the old 'yellow house' of the Artificer's Yard [site of the fort's mechanical operations] which stood on the river brink in front of the fort." There is evidence that the soldiers at Fort Washington performed their own plays in their mess hall.

12. Ophia D. Smith, "The Early Theater of Cincinnati," *Bulletin of the Historical and Philosophical Society of Ohio* 13, no. 4 (October 1955): 235–36.

13. John Witherspoon. *The Works of John Witherspoon* (Edinburgh: J. Ogle, 1815), vol. 6: 59; Lynne Conner, *Pittsburgh in Stages* (Pittsburgh: University of Pittsburgh Press, 2007), 17; Peter Hay, *Theatrical Anecdotes* (New York: Oxford University Press, 1987), 294.

14. Crum, 599–600; Federal Writers' Project, *The WPA Guide to Louisiana* (San Antonio: Trinity University Press, 2013); Ranck, 300; *Kentucky Gazette*, April 15, 1810.

15. *Pittsburgh Gazette*, January 20, 1803; Fortescue Cuming, *Cuming's Tour to the Western Country (1807–1809)* (Cleveland: A. H. Clark, 1904), 82–83. Exhaustive efforts to discover Bromley and Arnold's first names proved unsuccessful; they appear in no other annals of theatre, and newspaper accounts only cite their conjoined surnames. Their performances included *Poor Soldier, John Bull, The Apprentice, The Jealous Husband*, and Moore's cautionary 1753 *The Gamester*. Conner (224n25) suggests other professionals may have preceded Bromley and Arnold.

16. *Pittsburgh Gazette*, January 7, 21, and 26, 1803; (Pittsburgh) *Tree of Liberty*, February 19, 1803; *Pittsburgh Post-Gazette*, April 16, 1922.

17. The Rannies' repertoire included *The Provoked Husband, Doctor and Patient, King Lilliput, A New Way to Pay Old Debts, The Unfortunate Gentleman, Ducks and Green Pease*, and a two-act pantomime, *Don Juan*. For a thorough treatment of Rannie's career, see: Charles Bruce Davis, "Ventriloquism: Identity and the Multiple Voice," PhD diss., University of Washington, 1997; and Charles Joseph Pecor, "The Magician on the American Stage, 1752–1874," PhD diss., University of Georgia, 1976.

18. Joseph Miller Free, "The Theatre of Southwestern Mississippi to 1840," PhD diss., University of Iowa, 1941, 18–30; Patrick Morgan Harrison, "Theatre in the Southern Mississippi River Frontier, 1806–1840," MA thesis, Stephen F. Austin University, 1991, 10, 18–23. For details of the formation of the Natchez Theatrical Association, see William B. Hamilton,

"The Theater in the Old Southwest: The First Decade at Natchez," *American Literature* 12, no. 4 (January 1941): 471–72. Among the early Natchez performances were *The Orphan, Poor Soldier, John Bull, The Belle's Stratagem, Heir at Law, Fortune's Frolic, A Cure for the Heartache, The Road to Ruin, Raising the Wind, Secrets Worth Knowing, The School of Reform, The Weathercock, The Jew, House to Be Sold,* and *Wild Oats.*

19. Nelle Smither, *A History of the English Theatre in New Orleans* (New York: Benjamin Blom, 1967), 8–9.

20. Grace Gay letter of 1927, quoted in Langworthy, 306; Ludlow, 90. Luke Usher was born February 3, 1757, to Noble Luke Usher and Anne Bloomfield Usher of Birr, Ireland. He married his first wife, Martha (Mathilda) Pilkington in 1785. While Ludlow's memory, especially regarding dates, is erratic and must be verified by other contemporary sources, his anecdotes and descriptions of fellow performers are generally accurate. There is confusion among secondary sources over whether Noble Luke Usher was Luke Usher's son or nephew, but Noble Luke's granddaughter, Grace H. Gay, the daughter of Agnes Pye Usher, asserts it was nephew.

21. Perkins, 163.

22. *Kentucky Gazette,* October 11, 1808; *Lexington Kentucky Recorder,* October 31, 1809; Hill, 25–26.

23. William Dunlap, *A History of the American Theatre from Its Origins to 1832* (1832; rpt., ed. Tice L. Miller, Urbana: University of Illinois Press, 2005), 350, quoting "the western journals." The first edition of Dunlap's translation includes no apostrophe in the title (*Lovers Vows*), but context suggests the plural possessive. Ludlow in 1880 (81) asserts that James Douglass "was, I believe," the son of David Douglass of the famed Hallam-Douglass troupe. Some theatre historians, for example, Arthur Hornblow and James H. Dormon Jr., perpetuated Ludlow's assertion. However, contemporary sources such as Dunlap and Durang identify only two Douglas-Hallam sons, Lewis and Adam, and extensive genealogical research provides no filial connection. Noble Luke Usher knew James Douglass in Canada and may have recommended him to his uncle for Lexington. The senior Usher may have made Beck's acquaintance in Philadelphia in the early years of the century.

24. For further information on such adaptations of Shakespeare, see Cedric Gale, "Shakespeare on the American Stage in the Eighteenth Century," PhD diss., New York University, 1945, and Charles H. Shattuck, *Shakespeare on the American Stage: From the Hallams to Edwin Booth* (Washington, DC: Folger Shakespeare Library, 1976).

25. Hill, 23–24; Henry McMurtrie, *Sketches of Louisville and Its Environs* (Louisville, KY: S. Penn Jr., 1819), 126; Ben Casseday, *The History of Louisville: From Its Earliest Settlement till the Year 1852* (Louisville: Hull and Brother, 1852), 117; J. Stoddard Johnston, *Memorial History of Louisville: From Its First Settlement to the Year 1896* (Chicago: American Biographical Publishing Co., 1895), vol. 1: 73.

26. Sara Sprott Morrow, "A Brief History of Theatre in Nashville, 1807–1970," *Tennessee Historical Quarterly* 30 (Summer 1971): 178. By the time the Duffs established themselves in Boston and New York in the early 1820s, she far outshone him as he succumbed to bouts

of gout and rheumatism (Joseph N. Ireland, *Records of the New York Stage from 1750 to 1860* [1866; rpt. New York: Burt Franklin, 1968], vol. 1: 297).

27. The small, initial Théâtre d'Orléans burned in September 1816.

28. These amateurs' comedies and comic operas were those of Charles Simon Favart, André Gretry, Nicolas Delayrac, Louis-Benoît Picard, Nicolas-Médard Audinot, François-Adrien Boïeldieu, and Dumaniant (Antoine-Jean Bourlin).

2. Itinerants (1810–1814)

1. John Bernard, *Retrospections of the Stage* (London: H. Colburn and R. Bentley, 1830), 96.

2. Charles Durang, *History of the Philadelphia Stage Between the Years 1749 and 1855* (1868; rpt. Ann Arbor: University Microfilms International, 1980), vol. 1: 18 and vol. 3: 280. Sophia Turner may justifiably be considered the first star actress of the frontier. See Mary M. Turner, *Forgotten Leading Ladies of the American Theatre* (Jefferson, NC: McFarland & Co., 1990), 38–51.

3. It is also worth considering that Douglass heard the drumbeats of imminent war with England, leading him to bring this company out of Canada. Conner (9) believes that his troupe performed in a "small makeshift theater beneath the auditorium of the original Masonic Hall on Wood Street."

4. *Kentucky Gazette*, December 18, 1810.

5. *Kentucky Gazette*, January 1 and 8, 1811.

6. *Kentucky Gazette*, February 19 and 26, 1811.

7. *Kentucky Gazette*, February 19 and 26, 1811. Among the company's other scripts that spring were Thomas Southerne's *Isabella*, *Spoiled Child*, Inchbald's translation of a Dumaniant farce *The Midnight Hour*, John Allingham's farce *Fortune's Frolic*, the pantomime *Harlequin's Vagaries*, *Village Lawyer*, Tobin's musical play *The Curfew*, Hoare's musical farce *The Prize; or, 2, 5, 3, 8*, Thomas Morton's *Secrets Worth Knowing*, Garrick's *Catharine and Petruchio*, Thomas Holcroft's *Tale of Mystery*, Royall Tyler's farce *The Farm House*, Colman's *Love Laughs at Locksmiths*, Friedrich Schiller's *The Robbers* and *Abaellino*, John Browne's melodramatic spectacle *Barbarossa, the Tyrant of Algiers*, and a pantomime, *Love and Magic*, Henry Fielding's translation from Molière *The Mock Doctor*, *Soldier's Daughter*, Isaac Jackman's farce *All the World's a Stage*, *Adelmorn*, Charles Kemble's farce *Budget of Blunders*, William Whitehead's *The Roman Father*, and Dibdin's farce *The Jew and the Doctor*.

8. Richard C. Wade, *The Urban Frontier* (Chicago: University of Chicago Press, 1959), 57–58; Langworthy, 191; Walter Havighurst, *River to the West: Three Centuries of the Ohio* (New York: G. P. Putnam's Sons, 1970), 116.

9. The troupe's scripts included *Animal Magnetism*, *The Wags of Windsor*, *Douglas* (with Sophia as Lady Randolph), *The Romp*, *The Farm House*, *The Prize*, *Secrets Worth Knowing*, Garrick's adaptation of Thomas Southerne's *Isabella* (with Sophia in the title role), *Spoiled Child* (Sophia's specialty), *Birth-Day*, *Weathercock*, and *Padlock*.

10. William Wood, *Personal Recollections of the Stage* (Philadelphia: Henry Carey Baird, 1855), 11; John Melish, *Travels in the United States* (Philadelphia: Thomas & George Palmer, 1812), 186. Huntingdon's surname is in some accounts rendered "Huntington," but most credible sources, including Wemyss and Odell, record it as "Huntingdon."

11. Grace Gay, letter in Langworthy, 306; *Lexington Reporter*, September 28, 1811.

12. Reese D. James, *Old Drury of Philadelphia* (New York: Greenwood Press, 1968), 4.

13. Grace Gay, letter to C. R. Staples, April 22, 1928, in Langworthy, 65–66. The L'Estranges had been brought to America in 1796 by Thomas Wignell for his Chestnut Theatre, where Harriet immediately debuted at age twelve. Harriet's first husband, a Philadelphia naval officer named Thomas Snowden, had deserted her shortly before drowning off the shore of Delaware.

14. *Quebec Mercury*, May 30, 1808; John Lambert, *Travels Through Lower Canada, and the United States of North America, in the Years 1806, 1807, and 1808* (London: Richard Phillips, 1810), 303; Grace Gay, letter in Langworthy, 304. In Montreal and Quebec, Noble Luke enacted Othello—arguably Montreal's first—and Harriet played Lady Randolph in *Douglas* and Volante in *The Honey Moon*.

15. *Kentucky Gazette*, November 26, 1811.

16. *Lexington Reporter*, December 3, 1811. See also *Kentucky Gazette*, December 24, 1811, for Usher's further rationale.

17. John James Audubon, *The Life of John James Audubon, the Naturalist* (New York: G. P. Putnam's Sons, 1868), 53.

18. *Kentucky Gazette*, February 18, 1812.

19. Ludlow, 70.

20. Francis C. Wemyss, *Chronology of the American Stage* (New York: J. J. Reid, 1852), 147; Wood, 113; *Pittsburgh Weekly Gazette*, January 18, 1903; *Kentucky Gazette*, November 24, 1812.

21. *Niles' Register* 3 (September 1812–March 1813): 397, en.wikipedia.org/wiki/Weekly_Register). Orlando Brown, "The Governors of Kentucky," *Register of the Kentucky Historical Society* 49 (April 1951): 96. Hill (84) suggests that the younger Ushers may not have acted in Kentucky during the 1812–13 season, citing Wemyss's *Chronology* (12) crediting them with the opening of the first theater in Norfolk, Virginia, in 1812. This is substantiated by Noble Luke and Harriet's granddaughter Grace Gay in a letter copied in Langworthy (307). Neither of their names appear in bills in Kentucky that season. Dunlap, however (371), notes the existence of a theater in Norfolk as early as 1804–5, and Hugh F. Rankin, *Theater in Colonial America* (Chapel Hill: University of North Carolina Press, 1965), establishes a theater there in the eighteenth century.

22. See *Western Courier*, March 22, 1813, notice of a benefit for Thornton of *Pizarro* and *Raising the Wind*, cited by Hill (90) as "the only notice of the 1813 Louisville engagement."

23. *Le Moniteur*, July 2, 1811; Roger P. McCutcheon, "The First English Plays in New Orleans," *American Literature* 11, no. 2 (May 1939): 188.

24. *Louisiana State Gazette*, July 31, 1811; McCutcheon, 188.

25. Conner, 10–11.

26. *Pittsburgh Weekly Gazette,* September 10, 1813. After this engagement, Kennedy left for Montreal, and Webster apparently abandoned acting.

27. Other plays of their repertoire included *Tale of Mystery, Ways and Means, Hunter of the Alps, Highland Reel, The Apprentice, Lovers' Vows, Love-à-la-Mode, Douglas, Raising the Wind, The Man of Fortitude, Love Laughs at Locksmiths, To Marry or Not to Marry, Irishman in London,* and *The Jew and the Doctor.*

28. *Monthly Mirror,* March 1806, 189.

3. Ushers and Turners (1814–1816)

1. Hill, 95; Harriet Usher was interred in the Louisville town (that is, unconsecrated) burying ground.

2. *Albany Register* and *Theatrical Censor and Critical Miscellany* cited in Muriel Arline Kellerhouse, "The Green Street Theatre, Albany, New York under the Management of John Bernard, 1813–1816," PhD diss., Indiana University, 1973,112. Ludlow (5) asserts that Usher would have preferred to open in Albany with *Macbeth.*

3. After Noble Luke's death, son James Campbell Usher was raised by General and Mrs. Arthur Lloyd near Ottawa. Agnes Pye Usher was adopted by Diana Lewis. Upon Diana Lewis's death on August 8, 1822, her estate went to Agnes, "providing the child's grandfather, Luke Usher of Lexington, is kept from control." However, an impoverished Agnes was the beneficiary of two Kentucky General Assembly relief acts (November 17, 1823, and January 14, 1824). Agnes's daughter maintained (Grace Gay letter in Longworthy, 310) that Agnes "carried a deep wound" from this neglect until her death at age twenty-five in 1834 in Lexington.

4. For specific dates and bills of amateur performances in Natchez, see Harrison.

5. Langworthy, 200–207. Some later sources place the Shellbark Theatre on the east side of Sycamore near Third, but Ophia Smith, "The Cincinnati Theater (1817–1830)," *Bulletin of the Historical and Philosophical Society of Ohio* 14, no. 4 (October 1956): 254, citing the (Cincinnati) *Western Spy* of October 2, 1819 and *Cincinnati Inquisitor* of October 5, 1819, places the later Columbia Street Theatre on the same site as "the old Shellbark Theatre on Columbia [later Second] Street, between Main and Sycamore." This is substantiated by Greve 1: 468.

6. *Missouri Gazette,* December 31, 1814, and February 4, 1815; William G. B. Carson, *The Theatre on the Frontier: The Early Years of the St. Louis Stage* (New York: Benjamin Blom, 1965), 5–17. As Carson notes, plays were performed in the Spanish colonies as early as 1598, and a handful of novelty performers appeared as early as 1812.

7. Smither, 11. For specific bills in New Orleans, see Smither, 11–15, and 195–97. For text of the proscriptive edict, see *Louisiana State Gazette,* June 19, 1816.

8. Dunlap, 205; Ludlow, 100; *Pittsburgh Weekly Gazette,* November 8, 1814. Collins brought minimal New York experience, having briefly performed at the Park Theatre in 1809.

9. Hill, 104; Ophia Smith, "The Early Theater of Cincinnati," 243. Caulfield died in Cin-

cinnati in April 1815 after a brief illness. Persistent efforts to determine Lucas's first name proved unsuccessful. Wemyss's *Chronology of the American Stage*, Brown's *History of the American Stage*, and Ludlow's memoir identify him only as "Mr. Lucas," as do all contemporary newspaper notices.

10. *Lear* was suppressed in England until the death in 1820 of "mad King George," due to perceived parallels. Although Edmund Kean in 1823 restored Shakespeare's tragic ending, Tate's version predominated in America.

11. *Pittsburgh Weekly Gazette*, March 11, 1815. Ludlow asserts that Emma Turner was "about twelve" in 1818. Conner (14) posits various causes for the Turner company's failure to return to Pittsburgh, including public wariness of theatre and the inadequacy of the venue, but none are conclusive.

12. James Rees, *The Life of Edwin Forrest* (Philadelphia: T. B. Peterson & Bros., 1874), 66; Rees in *Dramatic Mirror*, December 11, 1841. A rare remaining amateur performance in Lexington came on January 16, 1815, with Colman's *Who Wants a Guinea?* and a Samuel Beazley farce, *The Boarding House*.

13. The Cincinnati Thespian Society in fall 1815 presented *Speed the Plough*, *Fortune's Frolic*, *The Sleep Walker*, and *Weathercock*.

14. Later sources depended on Ludlow's unreliable chronology all too often. He provides a vague gap in his narrative from early June (11–12) to late July (12–13), during which he is unable to cite the order of towns the Drake company visits but says "there was little matter of interest connected with them." It is possible that the Drake company did not open in Pittsburgh until September (not mid-August, as Ludlow asserts, 55–65), at which time Ludlow could have rejoined them. Ludlow repeatedly minimized Turner's achievements to aggrandize his own accomplishments. Ralph Leslie Rusk (*The Literature of the Middle Western Frontier* [New York: Columbia University Press, 1925], vol. 1: 368n66) believes it is unlikely for this Lexington actor to be Noah Ludlow, but there is no other known Ludlow acting in the West at that time.

15. Rev. Charles Frederic Goss, *Cincinnati, the Queen City, 1788–1912* Chicago: S. J. Clarke Publishing Co., 1912), 107; Greve 1: 469.

16. Rusk 1: 369; *Louisville Courier*, June 15, 1815; Hill, 106–7. Ludlow (5) implies that Usher Sr. initiated the agreement with Drake.

17. While nineteenth-century orthography was certainly not definitive, Odell and Durham spell these actors' married surname with one *t*, but contemporary papers, William Winter, Francis C. Wemyss, T. Allston Brown, Reese D. James, and Ludlow use two.

18. *Kentucky Gazette*, July 31 and August 7, 1815.

19. Ludlow, 73.

20. *Kentucky Gazette*, October 9 and 16, 1815; Hill, 101. The suit dragged on until 1818. A central issue was whether Usher had rented all three circuit theaters to Turner, or just the one in Lexington, for $200 a year plus profits. See Hill, 107.

21. Durang, *History of the Philadelphia Stage* 1: 85. Drake himself never claimed primacy.

22. Durang, *History of the Philadelphia Stage* 2: 163.

23. Durang, *History of the Philadelphia Stage* 3: 49. Some sources, including Ford, refer to Aleck as Alex (perhaps due to newspapers' abbreviating and punctuating his name as "Alex."), but the preponderance of contemporary sources refer to him as Aleck.

24. Durang, *History of the Philadelphia Stage* 3: 49; Ludlow, 29, 33, 364–65; E.M.S., "Early Amusements in Cincinnati," *Cincinnati Commercial*, April 25, 1873.

25. Ludlow, 43. It remains unknown if this Mrs. Lewis was Diana Lewis who adopted Agnes Pye Usher, but that is strongly possible, as no company or bill lists her after 1820, and Diana died in 1822. If it was she, it also remains unknown what arrangements she made for Agnes upon her departure from Albany.

26. Ludlow, 7.

27. Durang, *History of the Philadelphia Stage* 3: 49.

28. Sol Smith (*Theatrical Management in the West and South for Thirty Years* [1868; rpt. New York: Benjamin Blom, 1968], 13) claims that Denny's first role was Amelia Wildenheim in *Lovers' Vows*, but Ludlow was a contemporary eyewitness.

29. Ludlow, 13–16.

30. Ludlow, 58.

31. Ludlow, 55. For a thorough account of Denny's career, see James Walton Swain, "Mrs. Alexander Drake: A Biographical Study," PhD diss., Tulane University, 1970.

32. Ludlow (64–67) provides a vivid account of this *Pizarro*.

33. (Lexington) *Western Monitor*, December 6, 1816.

34. John Mason Peck, *Forty Years of Pioneer Life: Memoir of John Mason Peck, D.D.* (Philadelphia: American Baptist Publication Society, 1864), 146.

35. Ludlow, 88; *Western Courier*, February 7, 1816.

36. *Western Courier*, March 16 and 27, 1816; Casseday, 117. See Hill, 121–23, for specific titles and actors receiving praise.

37. Hill, 123; *Western Courier*, April 10, 1816; John J. Weisert, "Beginnings of the Kentucky Theatre Circuit," *Filson Club Historical Quarterly* 34 (July 1960): 282.

38. Timothy Flint, *Recollections of the Last Ten Years in the Valley of the Mississippi* (1826; rpt. Carbondale: Southern Illinois University Press, 1968), 50–53; Ludlow, 89–90.

39. *Lexington Gazette*, April 29, 1816. It is unknown whether Mrs. Collins accompanied her husband to Lexington.

4. Turner v. Drake (1816–1818)

1. *Liberty Hall and Cincinnati Gazette*, January 8, 1816.

2. In June 1816 the Turners may have briefly returned to Pittsburgh, for its amateur thespians then featured a "Miss Turner" (Emma) as an interlude dancer for several nights. Carson (3) suggests that soldiers in Detroit may have performed as early as 1798, but the source of that information "is uncertain."

3. *Kentucky Gazette,* July 8, 1816.

4. (Lexington) *Western Monitor,* December 6, 1816.

5. (Pittsburgh) *Commonwealth,* November 12, 1816; Durang, *History of the Philadelphia Stage* 5: 230. The Savages left Turner for Drake in Louisville in March 1817, but were unable to make a mark there either and left at the end of that season. By 1818 they had forsaken acting entirely.

6. Ophia Smith, *Early Theater,* 247–49; *Liberty Hall and Cincinnati Gazette,* January 20, 1817.

7. *Liberty Hall and Cincinnati Gazette,* March 31, 1817.

8. Ophia Smith, *Early Theater,* 250; *Maysville Eagle,* June 27, 1817; John Palmer, *Journal of Travels in the United States of North America in 1817* (London: Sherwood, Neely, and Jones, 1818), 67.

9. Ludlow, 118; *Liberty Hall and Cincinnati Gazette,* July 14, 1817. The Cummins' name was variously spelled Cummings, generally derived from Ludlow's spelling, but contemporary playbills consistently omit the "g."

10. Durang, *History of the Philadelphia Stage* 1: 109, 2: 171–72; Charles Durang, *The Theatrical Rambles of Mr. and Mrs. John Greene,* ed. William L. Slout (San Bernardino, CA: Borgo Press, 2007), 27; Ireland 1: 266.

11. *Pittsburgh Gazette,* May 27 and June 17, 1817. Philadelphia manager William Wood qtd. in Durang, *Theatrical Rambles,* 34. Lewis brutalized his much younger wife from their marriage in 1815 until he abandoned her in Charleston in 1817 when she learned that he still had a wife and family in England. Divorcing Lewis, she happily married actor John Greene in 1818 and performed with him on the frontier.

12. Durang, *History of the Philadelphia Stage* 1: 109, 2: 171–72; *Pittsburgh Gazette,* August 5, 1817.

13. *Pittsburgh Gazette,* January 14, 1817.

14. Henry Bradshaw Fearon, *Sketches of America* (London: Longman, Hurst, Rees, Orme and Brown, 1818), 211–13.

15. *Pittsburgh Gazette,* August 12 and September 16 and 19, 1817.

16. *Pittsburgh Gazette,* December 5, 1817; Durang, *Theatrical Rambles,* 36; Durang, *History of the Philadelphia Stage* 1: 109. Entwistle's next scheme, managing in small Pennsylvania towns, led to his being jailed for debts in Lancaster and eventually to his suicide in New Orleans in 1821. Molly attained some measure of success in New York in the 1820s and, upon marrying Robert Crooke, in New Orleans in the late 1820s before her death there in 1835.

17. Ludlow, 105.

18. Ludlow, 113.

19. Ludlow, 115. Drake had published a notice as early as January 1817 (*Liberty Hall and Cincinnati Gazette,* January 20, 1817) that he intended bringing a troupe to Cincinnati, but held out for the erection of a new theater and the elimination of theatre taxes (See Rusk 1: 373).

20. *Kentucky Gazette,* August 23, 1817.

21. *Kentucky Gazette,* November 15, 1817.

22. Crum, 604–6.

23. McMurtrie, 126.

24. *National Banner and Nashville Whig,* October 20, 1817.

25. Durang, *History of the Philadelphia Stage* 2: 163. The reason for Fanny Denny's departure for the East may have been a pregnancy, as she by some accounts delivered a son, Alexander Edwin, in Covington, Kentucky, in May or June 1818. His birthdate was later said to be in late 1822, but his younger brother, Richard, was born July 4, 1822.

26. Ludlow, 43.

27. Ludlow, 118.

28. Ludlow, 138.

29. *Louisiana State Gazette,* March 20, 1818; Ludlow, 143–45.

30. *Louisiana State Gazette,* April 20 and 25, 1818; Ludlow 150.

31. Other than Ludlow's statement (66), little is known about "West India Jones" except a notice in the *Mississippi Republican,* May 21, 1818, regarding the Natchez debut the following night of Mr. Jones "late of the Theatre Kingston [Jamaica]" and a mention in Errol Hill's *The Jamaican Stage, 1655–1900* (Amherst: University of Massachusetts Press, 1992), 133: "In April 1829 the locally recruited English Company took up a five-month residency in the Kingston theatre under the management of Mr. [No first name] Jones." This could not be William Jones who acted with Drake and then partnered with Joshua Collins, as that Jones was in cities other than Natchez while West India Jones was there.

32. *Mississippi Republican,* May 28, 1818; Ludlow, 166.

33. See Ludlow, 167–70.

34. Carson (26–27) makes a cogent case for the troupe's Mr. Henry being newspaperman Isaac N. Henry.

35. *Missouri Gazette and Public Advertiser,* February 20, 1818.

5. Drake Ascendant (1819)

1. Durang, *History of the Philadelphia Stage* 5: 230. Ludlow (189) waspishly describes Palmer Fisher as having "a heavy, dull face, perfectly void of any expression." Some sources spell Mrs. Mongin's name as "Mongen," but genealogical records show Victor F. Mongin, and contemporary playbills list Mrs. Mongin.

2. *Kentucky Gazette,* October 16, 1818.

3. *Mississippi State Gazette,* November 13, 1818.

4. *Mississippi State Gazette,* November 21, 1818.

5. *Mississippi Republican,* December 11, 1818.

6. Weisert, "The First Decade at Sam Drake's Louisville Theatre," *Filson Club Historical Quarterly* 39 (October 1965): 288–89; Marilyn Casto, *Actors, Audiences, and Historic Theaters of Kentucky* (Lexington: University Press of Kentucky, 2000), 37–38; McMurtrie, 126; Federal Writers' Project of the Works Progress Administration for the State of Kentucky, *Kentucky: A Guide to the Bluegrass State* (New York: Hastings House, 1954), 112.

7. John Thompson Gray, *A Kentucky Chronicle* (New York: Neale Publ. Co., 1906), 120; *Louisville Public Advertiser*, March 6, 10, 13, and 20, April 10, and May 5, 1819; *Kentucky Gazette*, May 15,1819. For play titles and dates see John J. Weisert, *The Curtain Rose; a Checklist of Performances at Samuel Drake's City Theatre and Other Theatres at Louisville from the Beginning to 1843* (Louisville, KY, 1958).

8. Gray, 119. For specific bills and casting see Hill, 153–55, Weisert, "First Decade," 287–91, and playbills in the Filson Historical Society, Louisville, KY. Weisert ("First Decade," 289) believes the Jones of this company is Richard Jones, but bills list both Mr. and Mrs. Jones, and Richard Jones had just lost his wife. Other chronology suggests this was William and Julia Jones, especially in the lines of business each played.

9. Playbill from *Nashville Whig and Tennessee Advertiser*, December 5, 1818, in Oral Sumner Coad and Edwin Mims Jr., *The American Stage* (New York: Yale University Press, 1929), 133; Ludlow, 172–74. Ludlow recalls (315) seeing William Jones debut at the Park Theatre in New York in 1811. The amateurs who remained in Nashville continued to perform on their own, as evidenced by an ad in the *National Banner and Nashville Whig*, January 16, 1819, of the three-act comedy *The Rival Officers* and a two-act farce, *The Shipwreck*.

10. Sophia Turner's fame had spread to the East: by January 1819 the schooner *Sophia Turner* was plying the waters off Charleston and Savannah. There is no evidence from bills that William Turner and their children were present in Natchez, but they did follow Sophia to New Orleans.

11. *Louisiana Gazette*, March 13, 1819. For bills, see Smither, 199–200.

12. *Louisiana Gazette*, April 28, 1819.

13. *St. Louis Enquirer*, February 2, 1820; Carson, 33–34.

14. Harris Gaylord Warren, "Vignettes of Culture in Old Claiborne," *Journal of Mississippi History* 20 (July 1958): 125, 139–40; *Port Gibson Correspondent*, May 15, 1819. The *Correspondent* announces that Jones was "fitting up the old Theatre in a neat and comfortable manner," but there is no historical record of any theater, unless it was temporarily fitted up in the courthouse, as had been done in other towns. The Mississippi Department of Archives and History (email to author October 9, 2020) reported they "could not find any reference to a theater in Port Gibson in 1819."

15. *Pittsburgh Gazette*, November 13, 1818.

16. *Kentucky Gazette*, May 7, 1819.

17. Visitor John Stillman Wright, qtd. in R. Douglas Hurt, *The Ohio Frontier* (Bloomington: Indiana University Press, 1998), 369; *Liberty Hall and Cincinnati Gazette*, May 14, 1819; Langworthy, 126–27; Greve 1: 637. For more on the Drake effort, see Ophia Smith, "Early Theater," 253.

18. Langworthy, 126–27; (Cincinnati) *Western Spy*, October 2, 1819; *Cincinnati Inquisitor*, October 5, 1819; *Liberty Hall and Cincinnati Gazette*, October 25, 1819, and October 18, 1825.

19. No billing is extant for Mrs. Collins since their performing with the Turners in Pittsburgh in 1815.

20. (Cincinnati) *Western Spy*, June 19, 1819; *Cincinnati Inquisitor*, June 22, July 5 and 13, 1819; *Cincinnati Gazette*, June 25, 1819.

21. *Kentucky Gazette*, September 10, 1819.

22. Richard Lee Mason, *Narrative of Richard Lee Mason in the Pioneer West, 1819* (New York: C. F. Heartman, 1915), 31–32.

23. Durang, *History of the Philadelphia Stage* 1: 85.

24. The Clarksville theater is referred to in the *Clarksville Gazette* of September 16, 1820, as "the late theatre," and so may have burned.

25. Ludlow, 178–80.

26. *Nashville Gazette*, November 27, 1819.

27. Ludlow (180) credits newspaper editor Isaac Henry with the idea of starting a professional company in St. Louis, but adds that Vos "wrote, urging me to come on by all means."

28. *St. Louis Enquirer*, March 4, 1820; Durang, *History of the Philadelphia Stage* 3: 280.

6. Enter Caldwell (1820)

1. Durang, *History of the Philadelphia Stage* 2: 118–20.

2. Caldwell statement in Rees, *Dramatic Authors of America*, 54.

3. *Orleans Gazette and Commercial Advertiser*, January 6, 1820.

4. Bartow (first name unknown) had briefly performed classical tragic leads in Philadelphia and New York from 1816 to 1819, but left no mark.

5. *Louisiana Gazette*, February 2, 1820. For complete list of bills, see Smither, 201–2.

6. *Louisiana Gazette*, January 14, 1820.

7. *Orleans Gazette and Commercial Advertiser*, January 14, 1820.

8. *Louisiana Gazette*, February 2 and 14, 1820; Rees, *Dramatic Authors of America*, 54–55. Some estimates of Caldwell's profit range as high as $6,540; see Weldon B. Durham, *American Theatre Companies 1749–1887* (New York: Greenwood Press, 1986), 30.

9. *Mobile Gazette and Commercial Advertiser*, February 2, 1820; Mary Morgan Duggar, "The Mobile Theatre, 1822–1860," MA thesis, University of Alabama, 1941, 5; Benjamin Buford Williams, *A Literary History of Alabama: The Nineteenth Century* (Madison, NJ: Fairleigh Dickinson University Press, 1979), 138. Their repertoire included *Point of Honor*, *Fortune's Frolic*, *Revenge*, *Love à-La-Mode*, *Sylvester Daggerwood*, and *How to Die for Love*.

10. Free, 102.

11. Free, 104.

12. *Mississippi Republican*, February 22, 1820.

13. *Mississippi Republican*, March 28, 1820; Free, 105–10. After that, William Turner operated a printing and glazier's shop in partnership with his son Frederick in Philadelphia and died there in 1831. In the mid-1840s Sophia retired from the stage to Frankford, Pennsylvania, teaching elocution in her home. She then lived with Frederick until his death in 1848, and died at the home of his widow in Philadelphia in 1853. Both Turner daughters enjoyed brief

careers on the stage. As Free points out (109), Carr may have been Britisher Benjamin Carr, who debuted in New York at the John Street Theatre in 1794 or George Carr, a "singing actor" who performed in New York at various times between 1826 and 1830.

14. For a complete chronology of productions, casts and benefits, see Free, 483–88.

15. *Mississippi Republican,* January 11 and 25, 1820.

16. *Mississippi Free Trader,* April 25, 1820; *Mississippi Republican,* May 9, 1820.

17. Ludlow, 180.

18. Ludlow's chronology regarding traveling to St. Louis in the winter of 1819–20 is extremely muddled, as is his list of personnel, but Carson (37–41) straightens these out.

19. *St. Louis Enquirer,* Mar. 4 and 8, 1820.

20. Ludlow, 186; *St. Louis Enquirer,* March 11, 1820.

21. Letter from Savannah mayor T. U. P. Charlton dated November 7, 1820, thanking Drake in the *Kentucky Reporter,* December 18, 1820. Ludlow (190) explains that "there were three Lewises in Mr. Drake's [1820] company, but in no way related to each other. Mrs. Lewis was the same lady spoken of in the early chapters of this book." (This refers to the journey from Albany. Her husband, the former stage carpenter, disappears from all narratives.) Ludlow (188, 191) includes Fanny Denny in Drake's company, but she was already performing in the East.

22. *St. Louis Enquirer,* March 25 and April 8, 1820; Ludlow, 187–90.

23. *St. Louis Enquirer,* March 25 and 29 and December 6, 1820; Ludlow, 190.

24. *St. Louis Enquirer,* April 12, 15, and 22, 1820.

25. *St. Louis Enquirer,* April 19, 1820; Ludlow, 193.

26. Ludlow, 192.

27. Ophia D. Smith, "Cincinnati Theater," 256. The Green in this troupe was not John Greene, who was touring with his wife—the former Mrs. Henry Lewis—in 1820 with Blanchard's Equestrian-Acting Company in Canada.

28. *Liberty Hall and Cincinnati Gazette,* October 25, 1819, and October 18, 1825; (Cincinnati) *Western Spy,* March 16, 1820; *Cincinnati Literary Cadet,* March 16, 1820; *Cincinnati Inquisitor,* March 21, 1820. For financial details of the theater's construction, see Langworthy, 126–27 and 178–80 and Rusk 1: 403.

29. E.M.S., "Early Amusements in Cincinnati."

30. Ophia D. Smith, "Cincinnati Theater," 257–58.

31. Ophia D. Smith, "Cincinnati Theater," 255–57; *Liberty Hall and Cincinnati Gazette,* October 25, 1819; (Cincinnati) *Western Spy,* March 16 and 25, 1820; *Cincinnati Inquisitor,* March 28, July 11, 1820; E.M.S., "Early Amusements in Cincinnati."

32. Ophia D. Smith, "Cincinnati Theater"; Sol Smith, 22.

33. Sol Smith's account of this (22–23) is entertaining and more detailed.

34. *Louisville Public Advertiser,* August 23, 1820. See also Weisert, *Curtain,* 7, and "First Decade," 292.

35. *Lexington Public Advertiser,* April 22, May 17, June 24 and 28, 1820. In November 1825

Usher's theater was sold at auction to cover his debts. He died December 23, 1829, "aged about sixty-five years" (*Lexington Reporter*, December 24, 1829), having lost all material evidence of the theatrical legacy he had established.

36. *Lexington Public Advertiser*, July 22, 1820.

37. *National Banner and Nashville Whig*, August 16 and 22 and September 12, 1820; Mary C. Henderson, "Frontier Theatres and Stagecraft," in Don B. Wilmeth and Christopher Bigsby, eds., *The Cambridge History of American Theatre* (New York: Cambridge University Press, 1998), vol. 1: 404.

38. *Nashville Gazette*, September 16, 1820.

39. (Huntsville) *Alabama Republican*, November 3, 1820.

40. Free, 489. Fosdick may be the Thomas Fosdick who later wed Julia Drake. As an actor, notes Ireland (vol. 1: 230), Allen "was nobody, or, at most, not worth speaking of" and was extremely hard of hearing, which noticeably hindered his performances.

41. *Mississippi Republican*, December 19 and 26, 1820.

7. The First Frontier Stars (1821–1822)

1. *St. Louis Enquirer*, December 2, 1820; *St. Louis Gazette*, January 10 and February 3, 1821. For a full list of productions during this season, see Carson, 67–68.

2. *Liberty Hall and Cincinnati Gazette*, January 24–April 18, 1821. In 1810, Lexington had a population of 4,326 and Cincinnati, 2,540; by 1820 this was reversed, Lexington having grown only to 5,279, while Cincinnati soared to 9,642. E.M.S., "Early Amusements in Cincinnati," asserts that the Drakes opened the Columbia Street Theatre in September 1820, and "played but a month." However, no extant contemporary evidence corroborates this.

3. *Liberty Hall and Cincinnati Gazette*, January 24–April 18, 1821. Rees, *Dramatic Authors of America*, 49; Ophia D. Smith, "Cincinnati Theater," 259.

4. *Louisiana Gazette*, February 20, 1821. For a full list of productions during this season, see Smither, 203–4.

5. *Louisiana Gazette*, February 20, 1821, and March 12, 1821. While in New Orleans, Caldwell missed the birth of his first child, William Shakespeare Caldwell, born February 11 in Fredericksburg, Virginia.

6. *Louisiana Gazette*, March 26, 1821.

7. *Louisiana Gazette*, March 26, 1821.

8. Rees, *Dramatic Authors of America*, 53–55.

9. *Nashville Clarion*, June 27, 1821; *Nashville Gazette*, June 30, 1821.

10. *Nashville Clarion*, July 4, 1821.

11. *Nashville Gazette*, July 7, 1821.

12. Allen obituary, *New York Atlas*, November 6, 1853. George Clinton Densmore Odell (*Annals of the New York Stage* [New York: Columbia University Press, 1927–49], vols. 3: 233 and 5: 141) describes Allen as a "manager, king, prince, common beggar, propertyman, painter,

prompter, tailor" who became "permanently sunk from actor to costumer [to Edwin Forrest]." Allen was called "Dummy Allen" due to being partially deaf and suffering from an adenoidal condition with caused him to noticeably mispronounce *m*'s and *n*'s as *b*'s and *d*'s. For more on Allen, see William G. Dodd, "Theatrical Entertainment in Early Florida," *Florida Historical Quarterly* 25 (October 1946): 121–74, and Fletcher.

13. After Allen's departure, managers Cazenave and Hanna had little luck. Mrs. Price died August 20, 1821, near Baton Rouge.

14. *Baton Rouge Gazette,* November 24, 1821; Fletcher, 51.

15. *Kentucky Gazette,* October 15, 1821; Ireland 1: 362.

16. *Cincinnati Gazette,* August 8, October 10 and 27, 1821; Langworthy, 91; Ophia D. Smith, "Cincinnati Theater," 259.

17. *Cincinnati Gazette,* October 27, 1821; Durang, *History of the Philadelphia Stage* 2: 163; Swain, 57.

18. Ophia D. Smith, "Cincinnati Theater," 259.

19. Several of Fanny Drake's obituaries backdated her marriage to 1816 to legitimize the birth of her sons Alexander Edwin and Richard.

20. For more on Belinda Groshon's life, see *Cincinnati Enquirer,* March 13, 1949.

21. *Cincinnati Gazette,* February 13, 1822; *Cincinnati Advertiser,* February 12, 1822; *Liberty Hall and Cincinnati Gazette,* February 13, 1822.

22. *Louisiana Gazette,* November 11, 1821; notice dated December 21, 1821, in *Natchez Gazette,* January 5, 1822.

23. *Louisiana Gazette,* January 15, 1822; Shattuck, 49–50.

24. Paul Smith Hostetler, "James H. Caldwell: Theatre Manager," PhD diss., Louisiana State University, 1964, 55–56; Smither, 34, citing *Louisiana Gazette,* May 31, 1822.

25. *Louisville Public Advertiser,* January 9, 1822. Wilson would achieve greater recognition at the Bowery Theatre following these western appearances.

26. *Louisville Public Advertiser,* January 9, 1822. Alexander Palmer Fisher died in 1827.

27. *Louisville Public Advertiser,* January 19, February 6, 16, 23, and 27, 1822.

28. *Louisville Public Advertiser,* March 27, 1822.

29. *Kentucky Gazette,* April 4, 1822.

30. *Lexington Reporter,* May 6, 1822.

31. The Pavilion Theater had been founded along with the Globe Inn and Vauxhall Gardens by sea captain Archibald Woodruff.

32. *Cincinnati Independent Press,* September 12, 1822; *Dramatic Mirror,* December 11, 1841.

33. *Liberty Hall and Cincinnati Gazette,* May 15 and 18, 1822; *Cincinnati Gazette,* May 15, 1822.

34. *Liberty Hall and Cincinnati Gazette,* May 25, 1822.

35. Greve 1: 639, quoting "the newspaper."

36. Ludlow, 237–43; *National Banner and Nashville Whig,* March 6, 1822.

37. Eliza Vaughan died August 13, 1822, age twenty-two, leaving John with three small children.

38. Clinton W. Bradford, "The Non-Professional Theater in Louisiana," PhD diss., Louisiana State University, 1952, 46–62; Williams, 138; Coad and Mims, 144. For names of Judah's Montgomery company, see Henry W. Adams, *The Montgomery Theatre, 1822–1835* (Tuscaloosa: University of Alabama, 1955), 42.

8. Collins and Jones (1822–1823)

1. William Rounseville Alger, *Life of Edwin Forrest* (1877; rpt. New York: Arno Press, 1977), 99; Arthur W. Bloom, *Edwin Forrest: A Biography and Performance History* (Jefferson, NC: McFarland & Co., 2019), 12; Durang, *History of the Philadelphia Stage* 5: 231.

2. Coad and Mims, 138.

3. Alger, 100–101.

4. Dwyer was, according to Ireland (vol. 1: 268), "frequently careless and inattentive to his duties, lacked study, and his conception of character [lacked] discrimination."

5. Rees, *Dramatic Authors of America*, 50–51; Alger, 102; Bloom, 13, 158.

6. *Kentucky Gazette*, February 13, 1823 (review dated January 30); *Lexington Reporter*, February 17 and September 20, 1823.

7. *Lexington Reporter*, February 17, 1823; *Columbia* (University) *Daily Spectator*, February 28, 1929.

8. Greve 1: 39; Ophia D. Smith, "Cincinnati Theater," 262; Sol Smith, 26–27.

9. Alger, 111–12; A. G. W. Carter, "Reminiscences of the Theaters of Cincinnati," *Cincinnati Commercial*, January 1 and March 5, 1882; Ophia D. Smith, "Cincinnati Theater," 263; *Cincinnati Enquirer*, March 26, 1823; *Cincinnati Independent Press*, March 27, 1823; *Cincinnati Advertiser*, March 29, 1823.

10. Ophia D. Smith, "Cincinnati Theater," 263; Greve 1: 39; Carter, to indicate the Globe's decline, cites a bill from February 27, 1824, featuring a thirteen-year-old tumbler-contortionist. Lucas died in 1824 while traveling with Sol Smith's company.

11. Johnston 1: 64; *Argus of Western America*, September 26, 1822.

12. *Cincinnati Advertiser*, June 7 and July 2, 1823. Carter, January 1, 1882. Carter relates the Othello anecdote as one Forrest told him in 1866, which he may have misremembered from his Othello of November 4, 1823, which Bloom (160) accounts his first. No extant newspaper notices show Forrest performing Othello that summer. However, Ophia D. Smith, "Cincinnati Theater," cites the specific casting of Cargill and Riddle as if working from a contemporary bill or review, no longer available.

13. *Cincinnati Advertiser*, June 4 and 7, 1823.

14. *Cincinnati Advertiser*, June 4 and 7, July 12, 1823.

15. Ophia Smith, "Cincinnati Theater," 264–65; Bloom, 159.

16. Ophia Smith, "Cincinnati Theater," 264–65; Bloom, 159. *Liberty Hall and Cincinnati Gazette*, October 24, 1823; *Cincinnati Independent Press*, October 30, 1823; *Dramatic Mirror*, December 11, 1841.

17. The company consisted of Caldwell, Mr. and Mrs. Richard Russell (he also as stage manager), Mr. and Mrs. (Mary, formerly Mrs. Seymour) Bloxton and her adopted daughter Miss Rosina Seymour, Mr. and Mrs. Ludlow, Mr. and Mrs. Baker, Mr. and Mrs. John Higgins (he also as prompter), Mr. and Mrs. Joseph Hutton, Mr. and Mrs. Noke (he as orchestra leader), William Forrest (Edwin's elder brother), Edwin "Ned" Caldwell (the manager's brother), Jackson Gray, William H. Benton, William McCafferty, James Scholes, Moses T. Scott, H. A. Williams, Arthur F. Keene, Lewis, Hays, Harp, Petrie, Taylor, Garner (a noted vocalist), treasurer James S. Rowe; Mrs. Dames, and Placide. Mary Bloxton, who had made her American debut at the John Street Theatre in New York in 1796, was, according to Ireland (vol. 1: 141) "an illiterate woman, but she was called a great beauty, and her strong, powerful voice found many admirers, although it lacked sweetness and cultivation." Her specialty was chambermaids and rustic characters. According to Ludlow (235), the Bloxtons' marriage was rancorous, as he was half her age and allegedly lusted after Rosina until Rosina's marriage to Rowe. Williams had failed to make his mark in New York, proving "altogether unequal to the rank of first light comedian" (Ireland 1: 327).

18. *Louisiana State Gazette,* January 17 and February 10, 1823; Durang, *History of the Philadelphia Stage* 3: 256.

19. For thorough details of bills, see Smither, 35–38 and 205–8. *For Freedom Ho!* was apparently Caldwell's adaptation of Pocock's 1813 *For England Ho!*

20. *Louisiana State Gazette,* January 14, 17, 27, and March 3, 1823.

21. For a thorough examination of French-speaking theatre in New Orleans, see Braun. Gray remained with Caldwell for fifteen seasons, playing old men.

22. Free, 136–37.

23. Dwyer's roles included Gossamer in *Laugh When You Can,* Belcour in *West Indian,* Vapid in *The Dramatist,* Rover in *Wild Oats,* Tangent in *The Way to Get Married,* Charles Surface in *School for Scandal,* and Young Wilding in *The Liar.*

24. *Mississippi Free Trader,* May 14 and 15, 1823.

25. Hostetler, 62.

26. *Louisiana State Gazette,* May 12, 1823.

27. *Louisiana State Gazette,* May 12, 1823.

28. The actors Caldwell sent up to Natchez were Mr. and Mrs. Russell, Mr. and Mrs. Higgins, Mr. and Mrs. Rowe, Mr. and Mrs. Noke, Jackson Gray, Scholes, William Forrest, and Jane Placide.

29. *National Banner and Nashville Whig,* August 18 and September 1, 1823.

30. *Lexington Reporter,* June 16, 1823; *Kentucky Gazette,* June 19, 1823.

31. Sol Smith, 27; Bloom, 15, 160.

32. *Kentucky Gazette,* December 25, 1823; *Lexington Reporter,* December 27, 1823.

33. *Cincinnati Gazette,* January 16, 1824. The company now consisted of Davis, Henderson, Rowe, Eberle, Joey Williams, Sturdevant, Sweeney, Mr. and Mrs. Sol Smith, Sol's brother Lemuel Smith, Mrs. and Miss Riddle, and Miss Fenton.

34. The City / Globe Theatre then slid into obscurity.

35. Sol Smith, 29. Joey Williams, who did not join Smith in going east, would soon afterward meet a gruesome end, devoured by wolves while traveling on foot through northern Florida.

36. Ludlow, 214; E.M.S., "Early Amusements in Cincinnati."

37. Caldwell letter in *Dramatic Mirror*, December 18, 1841.

9. The Caldwell Era (1824–1826)

1. *Frankfort Argus*, November 26, 1823; (Frankfort) *Commentator*, December 6, 1823.

2. Weisert, "First Decade," 299. For a complete listing of Drake's and the thespians' 1824 productions in Louisville, see Weisert, *Curtain*, 11–12.

3. *Louisiana Advertiser*, December 18, 1828 and February 6, 1829.

4. Smither, 41. Caldwell's 1824 company included his brother Ned, Mr. and Mrs. Richard Russell (he as stage manager and prompter), Mr. and Mrs. Noah Ludlow, Mr. and Mrs. John Higgins, Mr. and Mrs. William Noke (he as orchestra leader), Mr. and Mrs. James S. Rowe (he as treasurer, she the former Rosina Seymour), William Forrest, Jackson Gray, William McCafferty, James Scholes, Joseph Page, Moses Scott, John Dalton, George Frethy, Samuel P. Jones, Garner, plus Mrs. Baker, Mrs. Bloxton, Mrs. Victor Mongin and Jane Placide. John Varden was stage machinist, S. Symons the gas engineer, and Antonio Mondelli the scenic artist.

5. For a complete listing of Caldwell's 1824 productions in New Orleans, see Smither, 208–12.

6. Ludlow, 256–57. Ludlow's company included his wife, Mr. and Mrs. Mongin (he as treasurer), Mr. and Mrs. Noke, Gray, Frethy, William Forrest, Samuel P. Jones, Ned Caldwell, William Riddle, and Mary L. Riddle and her daughter Sarah (another daughter, Eliza, twelve, would soon be acting as well), plus Alexander Wilson from Drake.

7. Ludlow, 258; Dormon, 115n53.

8. Ludlow, 263–67.

9. Sol Smith, 48, 173. Caldwell's 1825 company comprised Edwin and William Forrest, Wilson, Mr. and Mrs. Russell, their daughter Mary Ann (age six), Mr. and Mrs. Higgins, Mr. and Mrs. John Greene (married in 1818, she the former, abused wife of Henry Y. Lewis), Mr. and Mrs. John Carter, Mr. and Mrs. Parker, McCafferty, Garner, Page, Gray, Moses T. Scott, John Moore, Lemuel Smith, Kelsey, Murray, Barnett, Mary Bloxton, Mrs. Rowe, Mrs. Battersby, Jane Placide, and Jane's older, widowed sister, Caroline Placide Waring.

10. Odell 3: 99; *New York American*, January 14, 1824.

11. *Louisiana Courier*, March 3, 1825; Durang, *Theatrical Rambles*, 109. For a complete listing of Caldwell's 1825 productions in New Orleans, see Smither 212–13.

12. J. Bennett Nolan, *Lafayette in America, Day by Day* (Baltimore: Johns Hopkins Press, 1934), 282–83.

13. *New Orleans Mercantile Advertiser*, May 2, 1825; Bloom, 17–18; Hostetler, 90–91.

14. *Louisville Public Advertiser,* May 14, 1825; *Louisville Morning Post and Commercial Advertiser,* May 17, 1825.

15. *Kentucky Reporter,* June 6, 1825; Ludlow, 270.

16. *Kentucky Reporter,* September 12, 1825.

17. *Kentucky Reporter,* September 19 and October 10, 1825.

18. *Kentucky Reporter,* November 7, 1825.

19. For details of this litigation, see Crum, 283–84. *Kentucky Reporter,* November 21, 1825; *Cincinnati Daily Gazette,* November 22, 1825. Luke Usher, having served as member of Lexington Board of Trustees and steward of Transylvania University, would die on December 23, 1829, as bereft of assets as when he started in Baltimore thirty years before.

20. Pépin's Circus, which followed Drake in Lexington, likewise resorted to pleading for support, the manager stating in the *Kentucky Reporter* of November 24, "This is the first time in my life that I have appealed to the generosity of the public, but when my consort with four children pierce my heart with their cries of want it cannot be deemed derogatory in letting the world know it, when it is my only wish to do all in my power to render assistance to them as a husband and father."

21. Adams, 14–16; Ludlow, 303. Ludlow erroneously dates this first Montgomery engagement, in this crude facility, as occurring in December 1827, but contemporary newspaper notices corroborate its occurrence two years earlier.

22. Ludlow's company consisted of himself, his wife, and their daughter, six; John and Anne Greene (up from New Orleans post-Caldwell) to carry leads (she in tragedy and he in Irish comedy); the dependable Mr. and Mrs. Mongin and Samuel P. Jones (still playing villains) for major supporting roles; plus Thomas Ballow, Ned Caldwell, George O. Champlin, Samuel Emberton (old men), George Frethy (low comedy), John H. Wells and his young daughter (for olio dances), and Mrs. John Vos and her daughter Mary. According to Durang (*Theatrical Rambles,* 124n3), Philadelphian Jones was "an imposing and noble-looking man with a commanding and impressive countenance" who demonstrated an uncanny ability to memorize, "capable of committing an entire newspaper at first reading."

23. *National Banner and Nashville Whig,* June 25 and August 13, 1825.

24. *National Banner and Nashville Whig,* October 31 and November 21, 1825; *Nashville Republican,* October 29, 1825. Caldwell kept Mr. and Mrs. Russell, Lowry, Kelsey, De Grove, Thomas Placide (brother of Caroline, Jane and Eliza), Mrs. Rowe, Mrs. Higgins, and Mrs. Frances Hartwig.

25. *Nashville Republican,* October 29, 1825.

26. *Huntsville Democrat,* November 18, 1825. McCafferty, Moore, and William Forrest played key supporting roles in Huntsville for Wilson and now for Caldwell in *Honey Moon, Stranger, Damon and Pythias, Othello, Merchant of Venice, Macbeth,* and *Of Age Tomorrow.*

27. Dormon, 87.

28. For personnel and bills of the 1826 and later seasons in New Orleans, no longer considered "frontier" in this study, see Smither.

29. Karl Bernhard, *Travels in North America* (Philadelphia: Carey, Lea & Carey, 1828), vol. 2: 133.

30. Ludlow, 268–72. Although Ludlow is often mistaken on dates, these names are borne out in bills.

31. Ludlow, 274.

32. *Louisiana Public Advertiser*, May 29, 1826; Hostetler, 105–6.

33. *Southern Advocate*, July 21, 1826; (Frankfort) *Commentator*, August 26, 1826.

34. *Huntsville Democrat*, August 4 and September 1, 1826.

35. *Huntsville Democrat*, August 4 and September 1, 1826.

36. Hostetler, 107–8; *National Banner and Nashville Whig*, October 11, 1826.

37. Ophia D. Smith, "Cincinnati Theater," 270.

38. Ludlow 33, 364.

39. Ophia D. Smith 271, "Cincinnati Theater," quoting *Cincinnati Independent Press*.

40. Ophia D. Smith 272, "Cincinnati Theater," quoting *Cincinnati Independent Press*.

41. *Cincinnati Chronicle and Literary Gazette*, March 3, 1827.

42. Durang, *History of the Philadelphia Stage* 3: 71 and 5: 240; Ludlow, 397.

43. Heading the list of subscribers to the new theater was Congressman James S. Stevenson, previously affiliated with the Pennsylvania Population Company, who pledged over $500, but who upon completion of the subscription drive refused to turn over the purchased property to the shareholders until forced to do so by the courts.

10. Struggles and Strengths (1827–1828)

1. Actor John Vaughan, with his son, ten, and daughter, seven, had returned to St. Louis from time to time to deliver a moral lecture at its courthouse.

2. *Missouri Republican*, June 21, 1827; *Missouri Observer and Advertiser*, July 25, 1827; Joe Cowell, *Thirty Years Passed Among the Players in England and America* (New York: Harper & Brothers, 1844), 85. Caldwell's company now consisted, in addition to himself, of Mr. and Mrs. and Miss Russell, Mr. and Mrs. Higgins, Mr. and Mrs. Jackson, Gray, Kelsey, Duffy, Still, McCafferty, Moore, Lowry, Murray, Samuel P. Jones, Emberton, Mulhollon, Lear, Sandford, Palmer, Jane Placide, Miss Carpenter, Mrs. Rowe, Mrs. Bloxton, Mrs. Johns, Mrs. Hartwig, and ballet master and principal dancer Monsieur Tatin.

3. *Missouri Republican* and *Missouri Observer and Advertiser*, June 27–August 23, 1827.

4. *Louisiana Public Advertiser*, March 17, 1827.

5. *Cincinnati Chronicle and Literary Gazette*, April 21, June 30, and September 1, 1827.

6. Ludlow (287) recalls opening this Mobile season on December 28, 1826.

7. For Cooper's plans see *Kentucky Gazette*, June 8, 1827, and *Cincinnati Chronicle and Literary Gazette*, November 15, 1827.

8. (Cleveland) *Western Intelligencer*, July 27, 1827.

9. Ophia D. Smith, "Cincinnati Theater," 272, quoting *Liberty Hall and Cincinnati Gazette*, October 1, 1827.

10. (Cleveland) *Western Intelligencer,* July 27, 1827, and March 5, 1828, rpt. from *Pittsburgh Spectator.*

11. *National Banner and Nashville Whig,* June 16–August 25, 1827. The new pieces included *The Mogul's Tale, Modern Collegians, The Forest Rose* (with Ludlow as Jonathan and his wife as Sally), *Exchange No Robbery, The Disagreeable Surprise, Two Galley Slaves, Swedish Patriotism, The Cataract of the Ganges, The Bride of Abydos,* and *Actor of All Work* (with A. J. Marks in the protean characters initially created by Louisa Lane).

12. *National Banner and Nashville Whig,* June 16–August 25, 1827.

13. *National Banner and Nashville Whig,* June 16–August 25, 1827; Ludlow, 292–96.

14. Durang, *History of the Philadelphia Stage* 5: 240.

15. *Kentucky Reporter,* June 29 and July 4, 1827.

16. Sol Smith, 49.

17. *Cincinnati Chronicle and Literary Gazette,* December 8, 1827.

18. *Kentucky Reporter,* November 28, 1827, quoting recent *Mississippi Statesman.*

19. *Kentucky Reporter,* December 15, 1827; *Cincinnati Republican,* January 25, 1828.

20. *Cincinnati Republican,* January 22 and 25, 1828; *Daily Cincinnati Gazette,* January 29, 1828.

21. Langworthy, 100.

22. Swain, 90–91; *Daily Cincinnati Gazette,* July 2, 1728.

23. Adams, 45; Ludlow, 303–4; *Mobile Commercial Register,* January 17–May 13, 1828. The company consisted of Ludlow and his wife (leads and soubrettes) and daughter (who at age six could perform olio songs), John and Anne Greene (she carrying leads), Charles and Mary Ann McClure (playing juvenile leads), George and Louisa Rowe (he as prompter, she playing old women), Watson, A. J. Marks, Horatio N. Barry, Samuel P. Jones, Ned Caldwell, William A. Kidd, William L. Riddle, Edward S. Duncan, Thomas Talbot, Miss Almira Dunham, Mrs. Vos, Miss Mary Vos, and orchestra leader Henry Heidman.

24. Odell 3: 415; Ludlow, 311–27.

25. William Henry Sparks, *The Memories of Fifty Years* (Philadelphia: Claxton, Remsen & Haffelfinger, 1872), 446–47.

26. (Natchez) *Ariel,* February 13 and October 27, 1826; Free, 174–79; Hostetler, 119–20; Sol Smith, 52.

27. (Natchez) *Ariel,* May 31, 1828. Caldwell's Natchez company included Mr. and Mrs. Russell with their children Mary Ann and Richard Jr., Mr. and Mrs. Higgins, Mr. and Mrs. (James S. and Rosina) Rowe, Mr. and Mrs. (Sol and Martha) Smith, Mr. and Mrs. Lemuel Smith, Mr. and Mrs. Crampton (he specializing in Scottish and Irish characters) and their two daughters (ages seven and twelve), Gray, Anderson, McCafferty (as scenic artist and second low comedian), H. N. Cambridge, Still, Palmer, Porter, Haskett, Lear, Wilkie, and Mrs. Bloxton (who died in Natchez on June 8). Horatio Barry joined in mid-June, up from Mobile.

28. (Natchez) *Ariel,* May 3 and 17 and June 7 and 21, 1828.

29. (Natchez) *Ariel,* May 3 and 17 and June 7 and 21, 1828.

30. *St. Louis Republican,* August 5 and 26, September 3, 1828.

31. *St. Louis Republican,* August 5, September 16, October 7, 1828.

32. *Liberty Hall and Cincinnati Gazette,* October 16, 1828; *Cincinnati Republican,* October 10, 1828.

33. Ophia D. Smith, "Cincinnati Theater," 275; *Liberty Hall and Cincinnati Gazette,* November 27, December 6, 1828.

34. Ophia D. Smith, "Cincinnati Theater," 275; *Liberty Hall and Cincinnati Gazette,* November 15 and 28 and December 1, 1828.

35. *Port Gibson Correspondent,* November 1, 1828.

36. Sol Smith, 56. The company now consisted of Mr. and Mrs. Kenny/ey, Mr. and Mrs. H. Williams (he as first low comedian until the return of Russell), Robert and Molly Crooke, Barry, George Hernizen, McCafferty, Henry G. Pearson (for male leads), Fred Henderson, Augustus William Fenno (age fourteen), Mrs. Higgins, and vocalist Dr. Carr (the replacement for Still, derided by Sol Smith as having "a thundering voice, and what he lacked in musical skill he more than made up in impudence and assurance). Durang (*History of the Philadelphia Stage* 2: 172) relates that all three of Mrs. Mason/Entwistle/Crooke's husbands "maltreated [her] or made her domestic relations uncomfortable," and she returned to the stage to play "the comedy old ladies" and "the matrons of heavy tragedy." She finally "found a friendly asylum under the roof of James H. Caldwell" in New Orleans until she passed away in 1835 in her fifty-fifth year.

37. *Natchez Statesman and Gazette,* December 4, 1828; (Natchez) *Southern Galaxy,* November 27, 1828.

38. Ludlow, 329. The company consisted of Ludlow and his wife and daughter, Mr. and Mrs. William Baldwin (he as prompter), Mr. and Mrs. John (Sarah) Carter and child, Mr. and Mrs. McClure (she to continue playing leads), Mr. and Mrs. Edstrom (he as ticket seller), Mr. and Mrs. Hartwig, Mr. and Mrs. Honey, Charles Booth Parsons (who would function as stage manager), Thomas Ansell (hired for leads in tragedy), Cambridge, Watson, J. W. Childs, Edward S. Duncan, Rice, Caldwell castoff Still, William C. Drummond (previously a dancer), Daniel Reed, William Anderson, Barry, Thomas Pierson, novice Hamilton Hosack, Alexander Egbert, Prior, Mrs. John H. Vos and her daughter Mary Vos, and the strikingly beautiful Miss Almira Dunham, plus orchestra leader J. C. Lefolle.

39. Ludlow, 332.

40. Ludlow, 337–38. For a thorough consideration of *El Hyder,* see Douglas S. Harvey, *The Theatre of Empire* (New York: Routledge, 2010), 148–49.

41. Ludlow, 333–34; *Mobile Commercial Register,* March 2, 1829; *Ohio State Journal and Columbus Gazette,* April 9, 1829.

11. Aleck, Fanny, and Trollope (1829)

1. *Liberty Hall and Cincinnati Gazette,* January 8, 1829.

2. *Cincinnati Chronicle,* January 3, 1829.

3. *Cincinnati Chronicle*, January 3, 1829; Ophia D. Smith, "Cincinnati Theater," 276.

4. Sol Smith, 56; (Natchez) *Southern Galaxy*, January 22, 1829.

5. (Natchez) *Southern Galaxy*, February 2, 1829.

6. (Natchez) *Southern Galaxy*, March 12 and 19, 1829.

7. (Natchez) *Southern Galaxy*, March 26, 1829.

8. (Natchez) *Southern Galaxy*, April 30, 1829.

9. (Natchez) *Southern Galaxy*, April 16 and May 7, 1829.

10. *Daily Cincinnati Gazette*, June 10, 1829; Mrs. [Frances] Trollope, *Domestic Manners of the Americans* (London: Whittaker, Treacher & Co., 1832), 114–17.

11. Trollope, 114–17.

12. *Pensacola Gazette*, April 18, 25, 28, May 9, 30, 1828, February 3, 17, March 10, 20, 1829; Jack L. Bilbo, "Economy and Culture: The Boom-and-Bust Theatres of Pensacola, Florida, 1821–1917," PhD diss., Texas Tech University, 1982, 15–17.

13. Sol Smith, 57; *Port Gibson Correspondent*, February 14, 1829. Smith is generally more forthright about the degree of success in a given town than Ludlow.

14. Sol Smith, 57–58; Charles Clifford Ritter, "The Theatre in Memphis, Tennessee, from its Beginnings to 1859," PhD diss., University of Iowa, 1956, 11–16.

15. Sol Smith, 59–60; *Huntsville Democrat*, August 14, 1829; Dormon, 108–9.

16. Sol Smith, 60–61. Their repertoire consisted of *Honey Moon, Young Widow, 'Tis All a Farce, Day After the Wedding, Poor Soldier, Stranger, Fortune's Frolic, Soldier's Daughter, Lover's Quarrels, Warlock of the Glen, Mountaineers, Family Jars, Turn Out, The Sultan, Gambler's Fate, No Song No Supper*, and *Magpie and Maid*. Mrs. Sol Smith's songs were especially well received.

17. Ludlow, 335–36; Adams, 18–20 and 45. Ludlow's remaining actors were Mr. and Mrs. William Baldwin, Mr. and Mrs. Francis McClure, Mr. and Mrs. John Carter, J. W. Childs, Alexander Egbert, Edward S. Duncan, Thomas Ansell, Thomas Pierson, J. E. Watson, T. D. Rice (back from Pensacola), H. N. Cambridge, Mr. and Mrs. Edstrom, Mr. and Mrs. Honey, Mrs. Vos, and Misses Mary Vos, and Almira Dunham.

18. Ludlow, 339.

19. Ludlow, 340–41.

20. Ludlow, 341–43.

21. Cowell, 90.

22. *National Banner and Nashville Whig*, July 18 and August 15, 1829.

23. *Liberty Hall and Cincinnati Gazette*, September 10, 1829; Ludlow, 347. The company was now comprised only of the Ludlows, Mr. and Mrs. A. W. Jackson (she the former Emeline Dunham), Mr. and Mrs. McClure, Barry, Duncan, McCafferty, Cambridge, Egbert, Watson, Scott, Miss Almira Dunham, Miss Eliza Petrie, and neophyte newcomers William Kidd (from Caldwell), H. Wolford, and Miss Caroline Rowe.

24. *Liberty Hall and Cincinnati Gazette*, October 22–23, 1829; Langworthy, 197. For a thorough treatment of Hamblin's talent and character, see Thomas A. Bogar, *Thomas Hamblin and the Bowery Theatre* (New York: Palgrave Macmillan, 2018).

25. Cowell, 86–87.

26. Cowell, 86–87; *Cincinnati Chronicle and Literary Gazette*, December 5, 1829; Swain, 114; Ophia D. Smith, "Cincinnati Theater," 278–81.

27. *Liberty Hall and Cincinnati Gazette*, December 17, 1829.

28. *Louisville Public Advertiser*, November 28, 1829; *Louisville Courier-Journal*, January 8, 1922; Ludlow, 354; Bogar, 50–51.

29. Cowell, 90.

30. Weisert, *Curtain*, 24–27.

31. Ludlow, 362, 369.

12. New Horizons (1830–1840)

1. E.M.S., "Early Amusements in Cincinnati"; Odell 3: 300.

2. *Liberty Hall and Cincinnati Gazette*, February 15 and 20, 1830; *Louisville Public Advertiser*, February 26, 1830.

3. George D. Ford, *These Were Actors: The Story of the Chapmans and the Drakes* (New York: Library Publishers, 1955), 181; *Daily Cincinnati Gazette*, February 24, 1830; Ophia D. Smith, "Cincinnati Theater," 281–82.

4. "The Rules and Regulations of the Cincinnati Theatre, May 1, 1830," handbill printed by Whetstone and Burton, Ohio State Historical Society Library, Cincinnati, quoted in Langworthy, 132–33; Peter George Buckley, "To the Opera House: Culture and Society in New York City, 1820–1860," PhD diss., State University of New York at Stony Brook, 1984, 55.

5. Parsons's company included among others (some from Ludlow): himself, Oxley, Howard, Muzzy, Henderson, McCafferty, Pearson, Mr. and Mrs. Rowe, Miss Rowe, Mrs. Carter, Miss Petrie, Julia Fosdick, and T. D. Rice (already billed as being "from the New York theatres," having stopped off to perform briefly in Lexington in mid-March). Although Julia still acted as Mrs. Fosdick, her husband had died in August 1829.

6. Weisert, *Curtain*, 29–31.

7. Fanny would remarry, unhappily, to the "very intemperate" Kentucky state legislator and poet George Washington Cutter. Within a few years they would separate and divorce; he died in 1865 and she on September 1, 1875 (Greve 1: 37).

8. *Louisville Public Advertiser*, September 13, 1830.

9. For examples of Smith's arrangements of dialogue, see Sol Smith, 63. His company consisted of himself and his wife, Mr. and Mrs. Crooke, Anderson, Campion, Cole, Kidd, Marks, Myers, Perry, Williams, Mrs. Graham, Mrs. Honey, Mrs. Petrie, Mrs. Vos, and shortly Lemuel Smith.

10. Sol Smith, 63–64.

11. *Cincinnati Chronicle of Morals and Art and General Literature*, April 17, 1830; *Cincinnati Republican*, April 27, 1830.

12. *Cincinnati Republican*, May 7, 1830; *Pittsburgh Weekly Gazette*, April 13 and 16, 1830;

John E. Parke, *Recollections of Seventy Years and Historical Gleanings of Allegheny, Pennsylvania* (Boston: Rand, Avery & Co., 1886), 105; Rusk 1: 391; Conner, 15.

13. Ludlow, 368.

14. *St. Louis Beacon,* June 17, 1830.

15. *St. Louis Beacon,* July 8 and 15, 1830.

16. *National Banner and Nashville Whig,* November 18, 1830.

17. Hostetler, 177; Rusk 1: 404; Langworthy, 184. Caldwell's new theater, too, would be destroyed by fire, on October 25, 1836.

18. *Louisville Public Advertiser,* December 20, 1832.

19. *Louisville Focus,* September 13, 1831.

20. *Mississippi Gazette,* June 22, 1833.

21. Ludlow, 379; Sol Smith, 72.

22. Tragically, Lemuel Smith was murdered in Milledgeville, Georgia, in December 1832 at age twenty-seven. Raymond shortly after that committed suicide in a bout of delirium tremens, throwing himself off a wharf in Boston.

23. For a balanced account of the formation of this partnership, see Dormon, 121–23. The partnership continued into the 1840s, flourishing primarily in St. Louis, Mobile, and New Orleans, achieving a preeminence which allowed them to recruit actors, book stars, and amass lucrative box office totals unmatched by minor managers. The partnership lasted until 1853, ending in a quarrel which left the two men not speaking for the rest of their lives. Ludlow treats Smith far more harshly in his memoirs than the reverse; Smith largely eschews mentioning Ludlow except obliquely.

24. Dean had married Drake in April 1830, eight months after the death of her husband, Thomas Fosdick. The Deans' daughter, Julia Dean, born in July 1830, became a celebrated tragedienne. Julia Drake Fosdick Dean died at age thirty-two in November 1832. Edwin Dean toured for years with his daughter, playing such roles as Master Walter to her Julia in *Hunchback,* until his death in 1876. (*The Detroit Free Press* on October 12, 1846, reported Dean's abortive suicide attempt, stabbing himself in a Boston store.) One who knew McKinney asserted that he "was everybody's friend but his own, being too much given to social indulgences." (Samuel Manning Welch, *Home History: Recollections of Buffalo During the Decade from 1830 to 1840* [Buffalo, NY: P. Paul & Bro., 1891], 365). McKinney had for parts of three seasons created problems, including a near-riot, for Bowery manager Thomas S. Hamblin (Bogar, 118–20).

25. The Potter in this company may have been John Sharp Potter (1809–1869), who built theaters across the frontier over the next three decades.

26. Rusk 1: 391–93 and 409–10; Friend Palmer, *Early Days in Detroit* (Detroit: Hunt & June, 1906), 980–83.

27. *Detroit Democratic Free Press,* July 30 and August 6, 1834.

28. *Detroit Democratic Free Press,* October 1, 1834; Gerhard W. Gaiser, "The History of the Cleveland Theatre from the Beginnings to 1854," PhD diss., University of Iowa, 1953, 42–49.

29. *Buffalo Patriot and Commercial Advertiser,* May 27, 1834. Duffy was stabbed to death by one of his actors in February 1836. When Martha Trowbridge's husband, Edward, died, his widow remarried, first to comedian Joshua Silsbee, then when he died in 1855, to William Adams Chapman (not to be confused with William B. "Uncle Billy" Chapman; see also "This is JOSH SILSBEE," rjbuffalo.com/silsbee.html).

30. *Detroit Democratic Free Press,* May 27, 1835. McClure did achieve stardom in New York and elsewhere, touring widely for another decade.

31. Lucile Clifton, "The Early Theater in Columbus, Ohio, 1820–1840," *Ohio History Journal* 3 (July 1953): 234–37; Marcia A. Siena, "The History of the Great Southern Theater, Columbus, Ohio," MA thesis, Ohio State University, 1957, 3.

32. Clifton, 234–36.

33. Clifton, 237–38.

34. Durang, *Theatrical Rambles,* 79; Arthur W. Bloom, "Tavern Theatre in Early Chicago," *Journal of the Illinois State Historical Society* 74 (1981): 217–25.

35. Mrs. Ingersoll was the daughter of Joseph Jefferson I. David Ingersoll had just died in Nashville of alcoholism.

36. Joseph Jefferson III, *The Autobiography of Joseph Jefferson* (New York: Century Co., 1890), 22–23; Arthur W. Bloom, "The Jefferson Company, 1839–1845," *Theatre Survey* 27, nos. 1–2 (November 1986): 89–153. It remains controversial whether the Lincoln story actually occurred. A thorough analysis may be found in Benjamin McArthur's "Joseph Jefferson's Lincoln: Vindication of an Autobiographical Legend," *Journal of the Illinois State Historical Society* 93, no. 2 (Summer 2000): 155–66.

37. Sophia Turner retired from the stage in 1834 along with her daughters, both of whom died tragically young (Ellen in 1836 and Julia in 1848).

13. Showboats

1. Much of the Chapman family background devolves from George Ford's *These Were Actors,* which is partially fictionalized but derived from family lore, his mother being Blanche Chapman Ford, the daughter of Harry Chapman. Ford writes (vii): "All the Chapmans I have known claimed Thomas Chapman to be their paternal ancestor." See also "Thomas Chapman" in Philip H. Highfill Jr., Kalman A. Burnim, and Edward A. Langhans, *A Biographical Dictionary of Actors, Actresses, Musicians, Dancers, Managers & Other Stage Personnel in London, 1660–1800* (Carbondale: Southern Illinois University Press, 1975), vol. 3: 158–62.

2. Ford, 167–68; Durang, *History of the Philadelphia Stage* 3: 39; *Theatre Dictionary* of 1805, quoted in Highfill, Burnim, and Langhans, 164.

3. Ford, 84. The primary source for Penelope Britt's early life is again Ford; nothing in Odell vol. 1 supports this, or cites any Penelope Britt. As (variously) Ter/Therese/a, Sarah later acted under the name Sarah Chapman; she is identified here as that. William B. will be differentiated from his father using his initials.

4. Asia Booth Clarke, *Booth Memorials: Passages, Incidents, and Anecdotes in the Life of Junius Brutus Booth (the Elder)* (New York: Carleton, 1866), 85.

5. Ford (104) implies that Penelope Britt did not live to return to America, but later sources indicate her presence on her husband's showboats and her succeeding him in managing them.

6. *Albion (New York)*, September 15, 1827; Durang, *History of the Philadelphia Stage* 3: 39.

7. Durang, *History of the Philadelphia Stage* 3: 39.

8. Durang, *History of the Philadelphia Stage* 3: 37; Andrew Davis, *America's Longest Run: A History of the Walnut Street Theatre* (State College: Penn State University Press, 2010), 62. The manager of the Arch Street Theatre that spring had been frontier veteran Aaron J. Phillips. It may have been Elizabeth Chapman who encouraged Isherwood and MacKenzie to bring her nephew to Chicago in 1838 (see chapter 12, above).

9. Durang, *History of the Philadelphia Stage* 3: 39.

10. Davis, 64; Rees, *Dramatic Authors of America,* 38; Ford, 113.

11. Durang, *History of the Philadelphia Stage* 3: 34.

12. Franklin Graham, *Histrionic Montreal* (Montreal: J. Lovell, 1902), 12.

13. Another source of the seed for Chapman's idea may have been John Greene, who Durang in his *Theatrical Rambles* asserts developed the first, primitive, showboat on the Ohio River well before Chapman, but no proof of this exists, and Durang provides no citation. Many others have depended on Ludlow, who asserts a similar claim, but Ludlow's 1817 flatboat was merely used to transport actors down the river, not to perform on.

14. Ludlow, 568–69; Ford, 116–19; Havighurst, 265; Arthur Hornblow, *A History of the Theatre in America* (1919; rpt. New York: Benjamin Blom, Inc., 1965), vol. 1: 348–49; *Nashville Tennessean,* June 30, 1835.

15. Chapman scenic artist John Banvard in John Hanners, *"It Was Play or Starve": Acting in the Nineteenth-Century American Popular Theatre.* (Bowling Green, OH: Bowling Green State University Press, 1993), 12–13; Charleston (SC) *Daily Courier,* May 14, 1836, quoting "a Cincinnati paper of 29th ult." (April 29, 1936); Philip Graham, *Showboats: The History of an American Institution* (Austin: University of Texas Press, 1976), 17–18.

16. "[Tyrone] Power's Impressions of America," *Preston (England) Chronicle and Lancashire Advertiser,* February 13, 1836.

17. Wayne H. Claeren, "Pittsburgh and the First Showboat: A New Angle on the Chapmans," *Historical Society Notes and Documents* (Pittsburgh: Historical Society of Western Pennsylvania), vol. 59 (April 1979): 234–37.

18. Mary (1813–1880) bore twenty children, and survived all but three.

19. Claeren, 232; Havighurst, 265; Jonathan Falconbridge Kelly, *Dan Marble* (New York: Dewitt & Davenport, 1851), 108.

20. Kelly 104–5; Graham 14–17. Graham (15) notes, however, that the Chapmans' itinerary may be partially traced from items in the Johnson Memorial Collection in the Louisiana State University Archives.

21. *Nashville Tennessean,* June 30, 1835. Other persistently repeated anecdotes describe a late entrance onstage caused by landing a mammoth catfish, but that is likely apocryphal, and adamantly rebutted by Claeren.

22. Kelly, 105–6.

23. Ford, 123; John Hanners, "The Adventures of an Artist: John Banvard (1815–1891) and His Mississippi Panorama," PhD diss., Michigan State University, 1979, 22–23. Banvard, augmented by a handful of disaffected musicians, then emulated Chapman by launching his own vessel to display "living statues" and his panoramas of riverine scenery and life.

24. Ford, 126–31.

25. Graham, 18–20; Claeren, 237; Havighurst, 266.

26. *New Orleans Times-Picayune,* February 18, 1837, quoting the "just started" *Natchitoches Herald.*

27. Thomas Low Nichols, *Forty Years of American Life* (London: J. Maxwell and Co., 1864), 394–95.

28. Graham, 18–20; *Mississippi Free Trader,* July 13 and August 1, 1837.

29. *New Orleans Times-Picayune,* August 15, 1839; *London Observer,* October 6, 1839.

30. Graham, 21–29.

31. *New York Evening Post,* February 12, 1845; *Baltimore Daily Commercial,* March 10, 1845; *New York Daily Herald,* April 1 and 3, 1845; Graham, 25–26; Kelly, 104.

32. Graham, 21–29; Patrick S. Gilvary, "The Floating Theatre: An Analysis of the Major Factors of Showboat Theatre in the United States," PhD diss., Ohio State University, 1975, 55, 93–94. Numerous accounts provide the name as "Spaulding," but Joseph S. Schick in "Early Showboat and Circus in the Upper Valley," *Mid-America: A Historical Review* 32, no. 4 (October 1950): 215n14, definitively establishes the spelling as "Spalding," based on early legal documents. For a thorough treatment of this venture, see P. Leavitt and J. Moy, "Spalding and Rogers' Floating Palace, 1852–1859," *Theatre Survey* 25, no. 1 (1984): 15–27.

14. Early California (1847–1850)

1. Sgt. Joseph Evans, "Around the Horn with Colonel Stevenson's Regiment in 1846," *Society of California Pioneers Quarterly* 7: 247.

2. William Albert Curtis, "The First Theater in California," *Out West* 28 (June 1908): 479–81; George R. MacMinn, *The Theater of the Golden Age in California* (Caldwell, ID: Caxton Printers, Ltd., 1941), 22; *Californian* (San Francisco), April 19, 1848.

3. MacMinn, 23–25. Monterey also enjoyed Spanish-language theatre; see *Californian,* October 6, 1847, dateline Monterey September 29, 1847.

4. MacMinn, 26.

5. *Californian,* May 10 and September 30, 1848.

6. H. W. Brands, *The Age of Gold* (New York: Doubleday, 2002), 203.

7. *Weekly Alta California,* August 31, September 6, 20, and 27, 1849.

8. Charles Vernard Hume, "The Sacramento Theatre, 1849–1885," PhD diss., Stanford University, 1955, 36–41; Alonzo Delano, *Life on the Plains and at the Diggins* [*sic*] (Buffalo: Miller, Orton and Mulligan, 1854), 97; unpublished letter of C. F. Kirkland in Meade Minnigerode, *The Fabulous Forties* (New York: G. P. Putnam's Sons, 1929), 340.

9. *Weekly Alta California,* September 27 and October 11, 1849. John H. McCabe, "Historical Essay on the Drama in California," *First Annual of the Territorial Pioneers of California* (San Francisco: W. M. Hinton & Co., 1877), 73. It is possible that scenic artist Lewis may have been James O. Lewis, previously of the frontier theatre.

10. Stephen C. Massett, *Drifting About* (New York: Carleton, 1861), 135–36; Bayard Taylor, *Eldorado; or, Adventures in the Path of Empire* (New York: G. P. Putnam, 1850), 29–31, 276–77.

11. Massett, 135–36; Taylor, 29–31, 276–77.

12. Massett, 135–36; Taylor, 29–31, 276–77; McCabe, 73; *Placer Times,* October 20 and 27, 1849.

13. *Placer Times,* November 17, 1849.

14. MacMinn, 32–33; Massett, 138.

15. *Placer Times,* December 29, 1849.

16. *Daily Alta California,* January 18, 24, and 25, 1850. Washington Hall, used intermittently after that for minstrel performances, burned down in May 1850.

17. *Daily Alta California,* January 24 and 29, 1850.

18. McCabe, 76.

19. Helen Wickham Koon, *How Shakespeare Won the West: Players and Performances in America's Gold Rush, 1849–1865* (Jefferson, NC: McFarland & Co., 1989), 4.

20. *Daily Alta California,* February 15 and 17, 1850.

21. *Daily Alta California,* January 24, 1850. Kirby's husband was variously reported as "Wingerd," "Wingered," and "Wingate," but the preponderance of historical documents suggests "Wingard."

22. *Daily Alta California,* February 24 and 25, March 4 and 6, 1850.

23. *Daily Alta California,* March 8, 12, and 18, 1850.

24. *Placer Times,* March 30, 1850.

25. *Placer Times,* March 30, 1850.

26. *Placer Times,* May 22, 1850; *Sacramento Transcript,* April 3, 1850.

27. *Daily Alta California,* August 11, 1850.

28. *Placer Times,* March 23, 1850.

29. *Sacramento Transcript,* April 10, 1850; *Placer Times,* April 26 and May 24, 1850; *Sacramento Transcript,* May 4, 1850; MacMinn, 34; Hume, 60.

30. *Daily Alta California,* June 21, 1850; *Sacramento Transcript,* June 25, 1850.

31. *Daily Alta California,* August 3, 1850.

32. MacMinn, 41.

33. *Daily Alta California,* July 4, 1850.

34. See lengthy review in *Marysville Daily Herald,* August 30, 1850, dateline Stockton, August 24.

35. *Sacramento Transcript*, August 10, 1850; Walter M. Leman, *Memories of an Old Actor* (San Francisco: A. Roman Co., 1886), 247–48; Ernest Harold in Washington, DC, *National Republican*, January 31, 1876.

36. *Marysville Daily Herald*, August 20, 1850.

37. *Sacramento Transcript*, September 21, 27, and 30, October 16–17, 1850.

38. *Sacramento Transcript*, October 16, 1850.

39. *Sacramento Transcript*, November 5, 1850. Within a month nearly five hundred Sacramentans died of cholera.

15. Gold Rush Theatre (1850–1853)

1. MacMinn, 43; David Dempsey and Raymond P. Baldwin, *The Triumphs and Trials of Lotta Crabtree* (New York: William Morrow, 1968), 101; *Daily Picayune*, November 4, 1850. For a thorough treatment of Maguire's career, see Lois Foster Rodecape, "Tom Maguire, Napoleon of the Stage," *California Historical Society Quarterly* 20 (December 1941): 289–314, and 21 (March 1942): 39–74. Kirby and Stark's company consisted of themselves, treasurer W. H. Crowell, Mr. and Mrs. John Hambleton, C. Smith, George Mitchell, Sophie Edwin, E. B. Zabriskie, Michael Dellon, T. S. Campbell, H. Carey, Hardy H. Oates, Francis B. Harrington, James L. Byers, J. L. Morton, Henry Tibbes, Theodore (Ted) Hutchinson, John H. McCabe, and Oswald Harrison.

2. Edmond M. Gagey, *The San Francisco Stage* (New York: Columbia University Press, 1950), 23; *Daily Alta California*, November 6, 1850.

3. MacMinn, 79.

4. *Daily Alta California*, January 6 and 13, 1851.

5. *Daily Alta California*, January 13–17, 1851; *Sacramento Transcript*, January 17, 1851.

6. For a detailed account of the Hambleton suicide saga, see MacMinn, 68–83, and Jane Kathleen Curry, *Nineteenth-Century American Women Theatre Managers* (Westport, CT: Greenwood Press, 1994), 38–39.

7. *Sacramento Transcript*, January 17, 1851; *Daily Alta California*, January 25, 1851.

8. *Sacramento Transcript*, February 3, 1851.

9. *Daily Alta California*, February 22, 1851.

10. *Daily Alta California*, January 26 and February 12, 1851.

11. *Sacramento Transcript*, January 18 and February 28, 1851, quoting the *Stockton Times*.

12. *Daily Alta California*, February 28, 1851.

13. *Daily Alta California*, March 17, 1851.

14. *Sacramento Daily Union*, April 16, 1851, dateline San Francisco April 13.

15. *Sacramento Transcript*, March 20, 1851; *Marysville Daily Herald*, April 17, 1851; *Sacramento Daily Union*, April 28, 1851.

16. *Sacramento Transcript*, April 25, 1851.

17. *Sacramento Transcript*, May 3 and 10, 1851; *Marysville Daily Herald*, May 10, 1851. Aug-

mented by a few defectors from the Tehama, the Dramatic Museum Company consisted of Robinson, C. "Nat" Hayward, James Vinson, Harry Edwards, Fairchild, Stewart, Willard, Shattuck, Mrs. Madden, Mrs. Mestayer, Miss Josephine, and Miss Clarence (playing juveniles).

18. *Sacramento Daily Union*, May 15, 1851.

19. Leman, 250.

20. *Sacramento Daily Union*, May 29 and October 2, 1851.

21. *Sacramento Daily Union*, May 17, 1851.

22. *Sacramento Daily Union*, May 15–16, 1851.

23. *Sacramento Transcript*, May 29, 1851; *Sacramento Daily Union*, May 29, 1851.

24. *Sacramento Daily Union*, June 7, 17, and 19 and July 8, 1851.

25. *Daily Alta California*, April 6, 1851.

26. Leman, 273; Stanley Kimmel, *The Mad Booths of Maryland* (New York: Dover Publications, 1969), 82.

27. *Sacramento Daily Union*, August 22, 1851. For clarification of their possible appearance at the Tehama, see Susan Carol Holmes, *"Junius Brutus Booth, Jr.: A Pioneer Actor-Manager of the California Stage,"* M.A. thesis, San Jose State College, 1971. The *Sacramento Daily Union*, July 7, 1851, reports, "The performances at the Tehama we are unable to speak of, as our Reporter, contrary to the usual etiquette, was denied admission."

28. Booth's company consisted of himself, Harriet, all three Chapmans, Bingham, Seymour, C. A. King, T. C. Green, W. T. Pritchard, J. T. Hammond, J. H. Wynkop, William Arlington, W. B. Stevenson, W. B. Rice, L. C. March, Fred Kent, Ted Hutchinson, C. J. Houpt, Kate Grey, Mrs. Woodward, and Clara Rivers.

29. For further elucidation of Mose and Lize, see Bogar, 186.

30. Dempsey and Baldwin, 102.

31. *Daily Alta California*, October 24, 1851.

32. *Daily Alta California*, November 2, 1851.

33. *Daily Alta California*, October 20, 1851.

34. Paula Mitchell Marks, *Precious Dust: The American Gold Rush Era: 1848–1900* (New York: William Morrow and Co., 1994), 207.

35. *Sacramento Daily Union*, December 1, 1851.

36. For a more detailed description of theatrical conditions in California by this time, see Gagey, 13–17.

37. *Sacramento Daily Union*, January 28, 1852.

38. *Daily Alta California*, February 15, 1852.

39. Ireland 2: 461; Works Progress Administration, *The Starks, The Bakers, The Chapmans / San Francisco Theatre Research* (San Francisco: WPA, 1938), 84–85; Leman, 258.

40. Interview with Alexina Fisher Baker in George O. Seilhamer, *An Interviewer's Album: Comprising a Series of Chats with Eminent Players and Playwrights* (New York: Alvin Perry & Co., 1881), 77.

41. *Daily Alta California*, June 12, 1852.

42. Frank Soulé, John H. Gihon, and James Nisbet, *The Annals of San Francisco* (New York: D. Appleton & Co., 1855), 500–501. Kirby and Stark then toured Australia. In 1868 Kirby divorced the increasingly alcoholic Stark, after which she married a Dr. Gray of New York, who soon died, leaving her a healthy inheritance, whereupon she married Charles R. Thorne, outlived him, and died in San Francisco on December 8, 1898.

43. Clarke, 48. See also Stephen M. Archer, *Junius Brutus Booth, Theatrical Prometheus* (Carbondale: Southern Illinois University Press, 1992), 215.

44. *Daily Alta California*, July 31, 1852.

16. The Remaining Frontier

1. Leman, 240–42. See also Wilmeth and Bigsby, eds., *Cambridge History of American Theatre* 1: 197–200.

2. Joseph Gallegly, *Footlights on the Border: The Galveston and Houston Stage Before 1900* (The Hague, Netherlands: Mouton & Co, 1962), 21–26, 47.

3. "Early [Iowa] Performing Arts History," www.iowapbs.org/iowapathways/mypath/2571/early-performing-arts-history.

4. Alice Henson Ernst, "Stage Annals of Early Oregon from 1846 to 1875," *Oregon Historical Quarterly* 42, no. 2 (June 1941): 151.

5. Ann W. Engar, "Theater in Utah," www.uen.org/utah_history_encyclopedia/t/THEATER_IN_UTAH.shtml.

6. Margaret G. Watson, *Silver Theatre: Amusements of the Mining Frontier in Early Nevada 1850 to 1864* (Glendale, CA: Arthur H. Clark Co., 1964), 33–77, 134.

7. *Washington Gazette*, April 26, 1864.

8. See James C. Malin, "Theatre in Kansas, 1858–1868," www.kshs.org/p/theatre-in-kansas-1858-1868-1/13135.

9. Esther Porter, "A Compilation of Materials for a Study of the Early Theatres of Montana (1864–1880)," MA thesis, University of Montana, 1938, 5, 23; *Montana Post*, December 10 and 17, 1864.

10. George D. Glenn and Richard L. Poole, *The Opera Houses of Iowa* (Ames: Iowa State University Press, 1993), 3–4.

11. Digital History, "Closing the American Frontier," www.digitalhistory.uh.edu/disp_textbook.cfm?smtid=2&psid=3154.

BIBLIOGRAPHY

Abernethy, Thomas Perkins. *The Formative Period in Alabama, 1815–1828*. Montgomery: Brown Printing Co., 1922.

Adams, Henry W. *The Montgomery Theatre, 1822–1835*. Tuscaloosa: University of Alabama, 1955.

Alger, William Rounseville. *Life of Edwin Forrest*. 1877. Rpt. New York: Arno Press, 1977.

Baldwin, Leland D. *Pittsburgh: The Story of a City 1750–1865*. Pittsburgh: University of Pittsburgh Press, 1937.

Bancroft, Hubert Howe. *History of California*. San Francisco: History Co., 1884–90.

Barnes, Michael John. "Trends in Texas Theatre History." PhD diss., University of Texas at Austin, 1993.

Berkin, Nicole. "Economies of Touring in American Theatre Culture, 1835–1861." PhD diss., City University of New York, 2015.

Bernard, John, Brander Matthews, Laurence Hutton, and William Bayle Bernard. *Retrospections of America, 1797–1811*. New York: Harper & Brothers, 1887.

Bernheim, Alfred L. *The Business of the Theatre*. New York: Actors' Equity Association, 1932.

Bloom, Arthur W. *Edwin Forrest: A Biography and Performance History*. Jefferson, NC: McFarland & Co., 2019.

Bogar, Thomas A. *Thomas Hamblin and the Bowery Theatre*. New York: Palgrave Macmillan, 2018.

Boucher, John Newton. *A Century and a Half of Pittsburg [sic] and Her People*. New York: Lewis Publishing Co., 1908.

Braun, Juliane. *Creole Drama: Theatre and Society in Antebellum New Orleans*. Charlottesville: University of Virginia Press, 2019.

Carson, William G. B. *The Theatre on the Frontier: The Early Years of the St. Louis Stage*. New York: Benjamin Blom, 1965.

Carter, A. G. W. "Reminiscences of the Theaters of Cincinnati." *Cincinnati Commercial*, January 1 and March 5, 1882.

Casseday, Ben. *The History of Louisville: From Its Earliest Settlement till the Year 1852.* Louisville: Hull and Brother, 1852.

Claeren, Wayne H. "Pittsburgh and the First Showboat: A New Angle on the Chapmans." *Historical Society Notes and Documents* (Pittsburgh: Historical Society of Western Pennsylvania), vol. 59 (April 1979): 231–39.

Clapp, William W., Jr. *A Record of the Boston Stage.* Boston: J. Munroe and Co., 1853.

Clark, Thomas D. *A History of Kentucky.* Ashland, KY: Jesse Stuart Foundation, 1992.

Clarke, Asia Booth. *Booth Memorials: Passages, Incidents, and Anecdotes in the Life of Junius Brutus Booth (the Elder).* New York: Carleton, 1866.

Clifton, Lucile. "The Early Theater in Columbus, Ohio, 1820–1840." *Ohio History Journal* 3 (July 1953): 234–46.

Coad, Oral Sumner, and Edwin Mims Jr. *The American Stage.* New York: Yale University Press, 1929.

Conner, Lynne. *Pittsburgh in Stages.* Pittsburgh: University of Pittsburgh Press, 2007.

Cowell, Joe. *Thirty Years Passed Among the Players in England and America.* New York: Harper & Brothers, 1844.

Crum, Mabel Tyree. "The History of the Lexington Theatre from the Beginning to 1860." PhD diss., University of Kentucky, 1956.

Cuming, Fortescue. *Cuming's Tour to the Western Country (1807–1809).* Cleveland: A. H. Clark, 1904.

Davis, Andrew. *America's Longest Run: A History of the Walnut Street Theatre.* State College: Penn State University Press, 2010.

Dempsey, David, and Raymond P. Baldwin. *The Triumphs and Trials of Lotta Crabtree.* New York: William Morrow, 1968.

Dormon, James H., Jr. *Theater in the Ante Bellum South, 1815–1861.* Chapel Hill: University of North Carolina Press, 1967.

Dunlap, William. *A History of the American Theatre from Its Origins to 1832.* 1832. Rpt., ed. Tice L. Miller. Urbana: University of Illinois Press, 2005.

Durang, Charles. Arranged and Illustrated by Thompson Westcott. *History of the Philadelphia Stage Between the Years 1749 and 1855.* 1868. Rpt. Ann Arbor: University Microfilms International, 1980.

———. *The Theatrical Rambles of Mr. and Mrs. John Greene,* ed. William L. Slout. San Bernardino, CA: Borgo Press, 2007.

Durham, Weldon B. *American Theatre Companies 1749–1887.* New York: Greenwood Press, 1986.

E.M.S. "Early Amusements in Cincinnati." *Cincinnati Commercial,* April 25, 1873.

Eslinger, Ellen. *Running Mad for Kentucky: Frontier Travel Accounts.* Lexington: University Press of Kentucky, 2004.

Federal Writers' Project. "The Theater," *The WPA Guide to Louisiana*. San Antonio: Trinity University Press, 2013.

Fletcher, Winona Lee. "Andrew Jackson Allen, 'Internal and External Costumer' to the Early Nineteenth Century American Theatre." PhD diss., Indiana University, 1968.

Flint, Timothy. *Recollections of the Last Ten Years in the Valley of the Mississippi*. 1826. Rpt. Carbondale: Southern Illinois University Press, 1968.

Ford, George D. *These Were Actors: The Story of the Chapmans and the Drakes*. New York: Library Publishers, 1955.

Free, Joseph Miller. "The Theatre of Southwestern Mississippi to 1840." PhD diss., University of Iowa, 1941.

Gagey, Edmond M. *The San Francisco Stage*. New York: Columbia University Press, 1950.

Gale, Cedric. "Shakespeare on the American Stage in the Eighteenth Century." PhD diss., New York University, 1945.

Gates, William Bryan. "The Theatre in Natchez," *Journal of Mississippi History* 3 (April 1941): 71–125.

Gilvary, Patrick S. "The Floating Theatre: An Analysis of the Major Factors of Showboat Theatre in the United States." PhD diss., Ohio State University, 1975.

Goss, Rev. Charles Frederic. *Cincinnati, the Queen City, 1788–1912*. Chicago: S. J. Clarke Publishing Co., 1912.

Graham, Franklin. *Histrionic Montreal*. Montreal: J. Lovell, 1902.

Graham, Philip. *Showboats: The History of an American Institution*. Austin: University of Texas Press, 1976.

Greve, Charles Theodore. *Centennial History of Cincinnati and Representative Citizens*. Chicago: Biographical Publishing Co., 1904.

Hamilton, William B. "The Theater in the Old Southwest: The First Decade at Natchez." *American Literature* 12, no. 4 (January 1941): 471–85.

Harrison, Patrick Morgan. "Theatre in the Southern Mississippi River Frontier, 1806–1840." MA thesis, Stephen F. Austin University, 1991.

Havighurst, Walter. *River to the West: Three Centuries of the Ohio*. New York: G. P. Putnam's Sons, 1970.

Henderson, Mary C. "Frontier Theatres and Stagecraft." *In* Wilmeth and Bigsby, eds., *Cambridge History of American Theatre* 1: 399–423.

Highfill, Philip H., Jr., Kalman A. Burnim, and Edward A. Langhans. *A Biographical Dictionary of Actors, Actresses, Musicians, Dancers, Managers & Other Stage Personnel in London, 1660–1800*. Carbondale: Southern Illinois University Press, 1975.

Hill, West T., Jr. *The Theatre of Early Kentucky*. Lexington: University Press of Kentucky, 1971.

Hornblow, Arthur. *A History of the Theatre in America*. 1919. Rpt. New York: Benjamin Blom, Inc., 1965.

Hostetler, Paul Smith. "James H. Caldwell: Theatre Manager." PhD diss., Louisiana State University, 1964.

Hume, Charles Vernard. "The Sacramento Theatre, 1849–1885." PhD diss., Stanford University, 1955.

Ireland, Joseph N. *Records of the New York Stage from 1750 to 1860*. 1866. Rpt. New York: Burt Franklin, 1968.

Johnson, Claudia Durst. *Church and Stage*. Jefferson, NC: McFarland & Co., 2008.

Johnston, J. Stoddard. *Memorial History of Louisville: From Its First Settlement to the Year 1896*. Chicago: American Biographical Publishing Co., 1895.

Jones, Robert Ralston. *Fort Washington at Cincinnati, Ohio*. Cincinnati: Society of Colonial Wars in the State of Ohio, 1902.

Jordan, Harold Trice. "Thomas Cooper: A Biographical Chronology." PhD diss. Tulane University, 1968.

Kelly, Jonathan Falconbridge. *Dan Marble*. New York: Dewitt & Davenport, 1851.

Langworthy, Helen. "The Theatre in the Frontier Cities of Lexington, Kentucky and Cincinnati, Ohio." PhD diss., University of Iowa, 1952.

Le Gardeur, René J., Jr. *The First New Orleans Theatre 1792–1803*. New Orleans: Leeward Books, 1963.

Leman, Walter M. *Memories of an Old Actor*. San Francisco: A. Roman Co., 1886.

Leonard, Lewis Alexander, ed. *Greater Cincinnati and Its People; a History*. New York: Lewis Historical Publishing Co., 1927.

Ludlow, Noah. *Dramatic Life as I Found It*. 1880. Rpt. New York: Benjamin Blom, Inc., 1966.

MacMinn, George R. *The Theater of the Golden Age in California*. Caldwell, ID: Caxton Printers, Ltd., 1941.

Massett, Stephen C. *Drifting About*. New York: Carleton, 1861.

McCabe, John H. "Historical Essay on the Drama in California." *First Annual of the Territorial Pioneers of California*. San Francisco: W. M. Hinton & Co., 1877, 72–78.

McCutcheon, Roger P. "The First English Plays in New Orleans." *American Literature* 11, no. 2 (May 1939): 183–99.

McDermott, Douglas. "The Development of Theatre on the American Frontier, 1750–1890," *Theatre Survey* 19, no. 1 (May 1978): 63–78.

———. "Touring Patterns in California's Theatrical Frontier 1849–1859." *Theatre Survey* 1, no. 1 (May 1974): 18–28.

McMurtrie, Henry. *Sketches of Louisville and Its Environs.* Louisville, KY: S. Penn Jr., 1819.

Morrow, Sara Sprott. "A Brief History of Theatre in Nashville, 1807–1970." *Tennessee Historical Quarterly* 30 (Summer 1971): 178–89.

Odell, George Clinton Densmore. *Annals of the New York Stage.* 15 vols. New York: Columbia University Press, 1927–49.

Perkins, Elizabeth A. *Border Life: Experience and Memory in the Revolutionary Ohio Valley.* Chapel Hill: University of North Carolina Press, 1998.

Phelps, Henry P. *Players of a Century: A Record of the Albany Stage, Including Notices of Prominent Actors who Have Appeared in America.* Albany: J. McDonough, 1880.

Pratt, Helen Throop. "Souvenirs of an Interesting Family," *California Historical Society Quarterly* 7, no. 3 (September 1928): 282–85.

Ranck, George W. *History of Lexington.* Cincinnati: R. Clarke & Co., 1872.

Rees, James. *The Dramatic Authors of America.* Philadelphia: G. B. Zieber & Co., 1845.

———. *The Life of Edwin Forrest.* Philadelphia: T. B. Peterson & Bros., 1874.

Rose, William Ganson. *Cleveland: The Making of a City.* Cleveland: World Publ. Co., 1950.

Rusk, Ralph Leslie. *The Literature of the Middle Western Frontier.* New York: Columbia University Press, 1925.

Shattuck, Charles H. *Shakespeare on the American Stage: From the Hallams to Edwin Booth.* Washington, DC: Folger Shakespeare Library, 1976.

Sherman, Robert L. *Chicago Stage: Its Records and Achievements.* Chicago: Robert L. Sherman: 1957.

Smith, Ophia D., "The Cincinnati Theater (1817–1830)." *Bulletin of the Historical and Philosophical Society of Ohio* 14, no. 4 (October 1956): 250–82.

———. "The Early Theater of Cincinnati." *Bulletin of the Historical and Philosophical Society of Ohio* 13, no. 4 (October 1955): 231–53.

Smith, Sol. *Theatrical Management in the West and South for Thirty Years.* 1868. Rpt. New York: Benjamin Blom, 1968.

Smither, Nelle. *A History of the English Theatre in New Orleans.* New York: Benjamin Blom, 1967.

Spears, Raymond S. "Mississippi Boat Theatres." *Harper's Weekly,* September 4, 1909, 13–15.

Sublette, Ned. *The World That Made New Orleans.* Chicago: Lawrence Hill Books, 2008.

Swain, James Walton. "Mrs. Alexander Drake: A Biographical Study." PhD diss., Tulane University, 1970.

Tallman, Jennifer. "Shakespearean R/Evolutions: A Cultural History of Shakespeare in Early America 1750–1826." PhD diss., University of Wisconsin–Madison, 2004.

Territorial Pioneers of California, San Francisco. *First Annual of the Territorial Pioneers of California*. San Francisco: W. M. Hinton & Co., 1877.

Trollope, Mrs. [Frances]. *Domestic Manners of the Americans*. London: Whittaker, Treacher & Co., 1832.

Turner, Frederick Jackson, and State Historical Society of Wisconsin. *The Significance of the Frontier in American History*. Madison: State Historical Society of Wisconsin, 1894.

Turner, Mary M. *Forgotten Leading Ladies of the American Theatre*. Jefferson, NC: McFarland & Co., 1990.

Vitz, Robert C. *The Queen and the Arts: Cultural Life in Nineteenth-Century Cincinnati*. Kent, OH: Kent State University Press, 1989.

Wade, Richard C. *The Urban Frontier*. Chicago: University of Chicago Press, 1959.

Warren, Robin Ogier. "Acting Feminine on the South's Antebellum and Civil War Stages." PhD diss., University of Georgia, 2005.

Watermeier, Daniel J. *American Tragedian: The Life of Edwin Booth*. Columbia: University of Missouri Press, 2015.

Weisert, John J. "Beginnings of the Kentucky Theatre Circuit." *Filson Club Historical Quarterly* 34 (July 1960): 264–85.

———. *The Curtain Rose; a Checklist of Performances at Samuel Drake's City Theatre and Other Theatres at Louisville from the Beginning to 1843*. Louisville, KY, 1958.

———. "The First Decade at Sam Drake's Louisville Theatre." *Filson Club Historical Quarterly* 39 (October 1965): 287–310.

———. "Golden Days at Drake's City Theatre," *Filson Club Historical Quarterly* 43 (July 1969): 255–70.

Wemyss, Francis Courtney. *Theatrical Biography; or the Life of an Actor and Manager*. Glasgow: R. Griffin, 1848.

Williams, Benjamin Buford, *A Literary History of Alabama: The Nineteenth Century*, Madison, NJ: Fairleigh Dickinson University Press, 1979.

Wilmeth, Don B., and Christopher Bigsby, eds. *The Cambridge History of American Theatre*. New York: Cambridge University Press, 1998.

Wilson, Erasmus, ed. *Standard History of Pittsburg [sic], Pennsylvania*. Chicago: H. R. Cornell and Co., 1898.

INDEX